THE EUROPEAN UNION DECIDES

European legislation affects countless aspects of daily life in modern Europe, but just how does the European Union make such significant legislative decisions? How important are the formal decision-making procedures in defining decision outcomes, and how important is the bargaining that takes place among the actors involved? Using a combination of detailed evidence and theoretical rigour, this volume addresses these questions and others that are central to understanding how the EU works in practice. It focuses on the practice of day-to-day decision-making in Brussels and the interactions that take place among the member states in the Council, and among the Commission, the Council and the European Parliament. A unique data set of actual Commission proposals is examined, against which the authors develop, apply and test a range of explanatory models of decision-making, exemplifying how to study decision-making in other political systems using advanced theoretical tools and an appropriate research design.

ROBERT THOMSON is a Lecturer in Political Science at Trinity College Dublin.

FRANS N. STOKMAN is Professor of Social Science Research Methodology at the Interuniversity Center for Social Science Theory and Methodology (ICS), University of Groningen, The Netherlands.

CHRISTOPHER H. ACHEN is Roger Williams Straus Professor of Social Sciences at the Department of Politics, Princeton University.

THOMAS KÖNIG is Professor of Political Science at the German University of Administrative Sciences Speyer.

POLITICAL ECONOMY OF INSTITUTIONS AND DECISIONS

Series editors

Randall Calvert, Washington University, St. Louis
Thrainn Eggertsson, Max Planck Institute, Germany, and University of Iceland

Founding editors

James E. Alt, Harvard University
Douglass C. North, Washington University, St. Louis

Other books in the series

Alberto Alesina and Howard Rosenthal, *Partisan Politics, Divided Government, and the Economy*

Lee J. Alston, Thrainn Eggertsson and Douglass C. North, eds., *Empirical Studies in Institutional Change*

Lee J. Alston and Joseph P. Ferrie, *Southern Paternalism and the American Welfare State: Economics, Politics, and Institutions in the South, 1865–1965*

James E. Alt and Kenneth A. Shepsle, eds., *Perspectives on Positive Political Economy*

Josephine T. Andrews, *When Majorities Fail: The Russian Parliament, 1990–1993*

Jeffrey S. Banks and Eric Allen Hanushek, eds., *Modern Political Economy: Old Topics, New Directions*

Yoram Barzel, *Economic Analysis of Property Rights, 2nd Edition*

Yoram Barzel, *A Theory of the State: Economic Rights, Legal Rights, and the Scope of the State*

Robert H. Bates, *Beyond the Miracle of the Market: The Political Economy of Agrarian Development in Kenya, 2nd Edition*

Charles M. Cameron, *Veto Bargaining: Presidents and the Politics of Negative Power*

Kelly H. Chang, *Appointing Central Bankers: The Politics of Monetary Policy in the United States and the European Monetary Union*

Peter F. Cowhey and Mathew McCubbins, eds., *Structure and Policy in Japan and the United States: An Institutionalist Approach*

Gary W. Cox, *The Efficient Secret: The Cabinet and the Development of Political Parties in Victorian England*

Gary W. Cox, *Making Votes Count: Strategic Coordination in the World's Electoral Systems*

Gary W. Cox and Jonathan N. Katz, *Elbridge Gerry's Salamander: The Electoral Consequences of the Reapportionment Revolution*

Continued on page following index

THE EUROPEAN UNION DECIDES

Edited by

ROBERT THOMSON, FRANS N. STOKMAN,
CHRISTOPHER H. ACHEN AND
THOMAS KÖNIG

CAMBRIDGE UNIVERSITY PRESS
Cambridge, New York, Melbourne, Madrid, Cape Town, Singapore, São Paulo

Cambridge University Press
The Edinburgh Building, Cambridge CB2 2RU, UK

Published in the United States of America by Cambridge University Press, New York

www.cambridge.org
Information on this title: www.cambridge.org/9780521679947

First published 2006

Printed in the United Kingdom at the University Press, Cambridge

A catalogue record for this book is available from the British Library

ISBN-13 978-0-521-86189-2 hardback
ISBN-10 0-521-86189-6 hardback
ISBN-13 978-0-521-67994-7 paperback
ISBN-10 0-521-67994-X paperback

Contents

Figures

Tables

Notes on contributors

CHRISTOPHER H. ACHEN is Professor of Politics at Princeton University. His research interest is political methodology, particularly its application to empirical democratic theory, American politics, and international relations. He is the author of two books, *Interpreting and Using Regression* and *The Statistical Analysis of Quasi-Experiments*, and co-author of a third, *Cross-Level Inference*. He was the first president of the Political Methodology Section of the American Political Science Association, and is a member of the American Academy of Arts and Sciences. He has received fellowships from the Center for Advanced Study in the Behavioral Sciences, the National Science Foundation, and Princeton's Center for the Study of Democratic Politics. He is also the recipient of an award from the University of Michigan for lifetime achievement in training graduate students.

JAVIER ARREGUI is a Lecturer at the Department of Political Science at the University of Pompeu Fabra Barcelona, Spain. His research interests include decision-making in the European Union, bargaining models, policy implementation and Spanish politics. At the time of this study, he was a PhD candidate at the University of Groningen, the Netherlands.

STEFANIE BAILER is a Lecturer in Comparative Politics at the University of Zurich, Switzerland. Her research interests include decision-making in the European Union and in western and eastern European politics, European Union politics, and civil society development. During the time of the research for this book she completed her PhD at the University of Konstanz, Germany, and worked at the Rijksuniversiteit Groningen, the Netherlands, as well as at the University of Michigan, Ann Arbor.

Notes on contributors

VINCENT BOEKHOORN is a doctoral candidate at the Radboud University Nijmegen, the Netherlands.

MADELEINE O. HOSLI is Associate Professor in International Relations at Leiden University, the Netherlands. She studied political science and economics at the universities of Zurich and of St. Gallen (Switzerland) and has taught at the European Institute of Public Administration (EIPA) in Maastricht, the Graduate Institute of International Studies (Geneva), the University of Michigan, Ann Arbor and the Vrije Universiteit Amsterdam. Her main research interests are in international political economy, institutions and European integration.

THOMAS KÖNIG is Professor in Political Science at the German University for Administrative Sciences Speyer. His main research is on the effects of political institutions on decision-making, legislative analysis and game theory, in particular with applications to the European Union and Germany. He is directing the DOSEI research team on European constitution building and a project on Unitarisation by Europeanisation.

ANTTI PAJALA currently works as a post-doctoral researcher at the Department of Political Science at the University of Turku, Finland. He received his PhD in 2003. His research interests are mainly empirical, including a priori oriented measurement of voting power in national parliaments and the institutions of the European Union. Another field of interest is Finnish parliamentary voting cohesion and voting similarity in plenary sessions. He has published scholarly articles in both international and Finnish journals.

SVEN-OLIVER PROKSCH is a PhD student in the Department of Political Science at the University of California, Los Angeles. At the time of this study he was a student at the University of Konstanz, Germany. His current research interests include legislative politics in the European Union and comparative constitutional politics.

GERALD SCHNEIDER is Professor of Political Science at the Department of Politics and Management of the University of Konstanz, Germany, and Executive Editor of *European Union Politics*. He has authored or co-authored more than 100 scholarly articles on EU politics, decision-making, the causes and consequences of armed conflict, and the management of violent disputes. His current research focuses on political polarisation, decision-making under stress, and the effects of political events within the EU on financial markets.

TORSTEN J. SELCK is Reader at the University of Nottingham. At the time of this study he was a doctoral candidate at Leiden University. His research interests include models of decision-making and political change, European integration and European Union politics, and research methods for political economy. Publications include articles for *Constitutional Political Economy*, *European Union Politics*, the *Journal of Common Market Studies*, the *Journal of European Public Policy*, and the *Journal of Theoretical Politics*.

BERNARD STEUNENBERG is Professor of Public Administration at Leiden University, the Netherlands, and Fellow of the Netherlands Institute of Government. His current research interests are the analysis of legislative decision-making in the European Union, the implementation of EU directives in member states, and the analysis of institutional change.

FRANS N. STOKMAN is Professor of Methods and Techniques of Social Scientific Research at the Department of Sociology, University of Groningen. His research lies mainly in the areas of collective decision-making and social networks. The International Network of Social Network Analysis awarded him the Georg Simmel Award in 2004. He is the author of many publications in international journals and in the university presses of Cambridge, Yale and Oxford (see http://web.inter.nl.net/users/stokman). In 1995 and 2001 he was a Fellow at the Netherlands Institute for Advanced Study (NIAS) in the Humanities and Social Sciences. In the year 1987–88 he was the Dutch Visiting Professor at the Center for Political Research, Institute for Social Research, University of Michigan, USA. Between 1993 and 2002 he was Scientific Director of the research school of the Interuniversity Center for Social Theory and Methodology (ICS). He is a board member of diverse Dutch and German non-profit organisations, including the research school (School of Management, SOM) of the faculties of Business Studies and Economics at the University of Groningen.

ROBERT THOMSON is a Lecturer at the Department of Political Science, Trinity College Dublin. His research interests include decision-making in the European Union, democratic performance, policy implementation, and applied policy analysis. He holds a PhD from the University of

Groningen in the Netherlands, where he wrote a thesis on the fulfilment of election pledges in coalition governments. During most of the present study, he was a post-doctoral researcher at the University of Groningen.

ADRIAN M. A. VAN DEEMEN is Associate Professor at the Nijmegen School of Management, Radboud University of Nijmegen, the Netherlands.

MIKA WIDGRÉN is Professor at the Turku School of Economics and Business Administration, Finland. His research interests include European integration and regionalism, Finland's trade with Eastern Europe, EU decision-making, institutional design, political economy, and applied game theory.

Preface

This book examines legislative decision-making in the European Union. The analyses reported here use some of the most powerful conceptual tools available to social scientists for this task: a range of competing explanations, formalised as models, of decision-making in the European Union. Some of the explanations are grounded in previous research on legislative choice and focus on the impact of formal decision-making procedures on policy outcomes. Others draw inspiration from research on various types of informal bargaining through which actors exert influence. Most of these explanatory models have not yet been tested in the context of EU decision-making. Some have been tested on very limited data sets and in small pilot studies, while others have been developed during the course of this project.

This is not only, or even primarily, a theoretical exercise. The analyses are performed on a large data set, compiled specifically for this study, containing information on 162 controversial issues raised by recent legislative proposals in the European Union. In the following chapters, the explanatory models are presented and illustrated by applying them to examples from this broad selection of controversial issues. They are then applied to all cases in the data set. After comparing the results of these applications, we formulate insights into the processes through which controversies are resolved and decision outcomes are reached in the legislative arena of the European Union. None of the explanatory models has been tested on as large a data set as the one we have collected in this project. Never have such a variety of political decision-making models been tested against each other in a contest to evaluate their relative performance.

The idea for this project grew out of a European Consortium for Political Research (ECPR) sponsored research workshop in Bergen,

Norway, in September 1997, organised by Madeleine Hosli and Adrian Van Deemen, and assisted by Christopher Achen, to which some of the current members of the research group were also invited. At that time, discussions were taking place in the literature on European decision-making between researchers using spatial theories of voting and those employing other approaches. A few years earlier, in 1994, the volume *European Community Decision Making: Models, Applications and Comparisons*, edited by Bruce Bueno de Mesquita and Frans Stokman, had been published. In that exemplary study, two alternative explanatory models from a class of bargaining models were applied to Council decision-making on sixteen controversial issues. The results indicated that a more concerted effort along these lines would provide valuable insights, and might even help distinguish among competing approaches to explaining EU decision-making.

The present study expands the scope of that previous work considerably: first, by broadening the range of explanations considered to include recently developed models of legislative choice and a greater variety of bargaining models; and second, by investing in the collection of a much larger data set, including information on the European Commission and the European Parliament. After the research workshop in Bergen, which had the primary aim of drawing up a full research proposal, the research group was formed and enlarged to its current fifteen members. The group 'Decision Making in the European Union' (DEU) was then officially recognised by the ECPR, and our research began in earnest at the end of 1999. In addition to this book, there is an accompanying special issue of the journal *European Union Politics* (Stokman and Thomson (eds.) 2004), which contains other results of the present study.

During the course of this project, we have run up large debts of gratitude to many organisations and individuals. This is an incomplete list of the many who have helped us along the way. We received financial support from the Dutch Science Foundation (NWO), the German National Science Foundation (DFG) and the Finnish Yrjö Jahnsson Foundation. The Netherlands Institute for Advanced Studies in the Humanities and Social Sciences (NIAS) also provided facilities for meetings.

Between the Spring of 2000 and early 2002, more than 150 in-depth interviews were held with experts on the decision-making situations we selected for study. These individuals were mainly civil servants in the European Commission, the permanent representations of each of the fifteen member states in Brussels and the European Parliament. We also interviewed experts from interest groups in Brussels. These individuals provided detailed information on the cases we selected for study. We thank these individuals not by name, but by their institutional affiliations, to respect the discretion we promised them. Decision-making in the Council of Ministers, which has traditionally been shrouded in secrecy, is becoming more open. Jacob Visscher and his staff at the Council's Transparency Unit opened up Council decision-making to us as much as possible.

Colleagues who have reviewed various versions of one or more of the following chapters, and who have advised us during the course of the project include the following: Thomas Braeuninger, Bruce Bueno de Mesquita, Christophe Crombez, Antoaneta Dimitrova, Samuel Eldersveld, Adrienne Héritier, Mel Hinich, Simon Hug, David Knoke, Jan-Erik Lane, Annick Laruelle, Mikko Mattila, James Morrow, Hannu Nurmi, Robert Pahre, Paul Pennings, the late Roy Pierce, and René Torenvlied. Their input has sharpened our thinking on the project as a whole and on the significance of its results. In the final stages of the project we received valuable encouragement and support from Randall Calvert, John Haslam and others at Cambridge University Press.

1

Explaining legislative decision-making in the European Union

ROBERT THOMSON AND MADELEINE O. HOSLI

1.1 INTRODUCTION

This book examines how legislation is made in the European Union (EU). Taking decisions in the European Union requires overcoming controversy and disagreement. European decision-makers' ability to resolve controversy has been tested by three developments. First, the number of member states increased from six to 25, with the prospect of further enlargement in the near future. Second, changes to the formal decision-making procedures increased the institutional power of the European Parliament. Third, the European Union expanded its involvement in policy areas from its focus on the internal market and freedom of movement across borders to include economic and monetary union, environmental policy, competition, and social policy among others.

There are numerous recent and high-profile examples of the challenges European decision-makers face in reaching political agreements amid controversy. One such example concerned the question of whether Germany should be given an official warning under the Stability Pact for its excessive budget deficit. Germany was not allowed to vote on the proposal to give such a warning, since the warning was directed against itself. Nonetheless, with the help of the Italian Presidency, it managed to turn unanimous support for the proposed warning into a vote against the proposal. The European Commission opposed this decision, and successfully overturned it in the European Court of Justice. This outcome, and the way it was achieved, challenged the view that important decisions

We thank Christpher H. Achen, Randall Calvert, Adrienne Héritier, Jan-Erik Lane, Thomas König, Frans Stokman, and the members of the Decision-making in the European Union (DEU) research group for helpful comments on an earlier version of this chapter.

need the support of all member states, even when this is not formally required.

Even more severe political problems arose in connection with the ratification of the European constitutional treaty and the 2007–2013 budget negotiations. The French and Dutch referenda on the constitutional treaty revealed a large gap between European decision-makers and public opinion in at least some of the member states. Whatever may have motivated the no-voters, the rejection of the constitutional treaty was widely interpreted as a sign that large parts of the population viewed EU decision-making as too complex, that they opposed increasing European involvement in national affairs, and that EU enlargement was undesirable. The impact of the referenda was also felt during the negotiations on the 2007-13 budget. The controversies centred around the British rebate system and the large net payments of some member states, in particular those of the largest net contributors, the Netherlands and Sweden. The British Prime Minister Blair refused to discuss any change to the British rebate, which had been negotiated by Prime Minister Thatcher in 1984, without a fundamental revision of the European agricultural support system. In response, the French President Chirac refused to reopen negotiations on agriculture because of an earlier agreement on the agricultural system, which limited those expenditures until 2013. To complicate matters further, the Dutch Prime Minister Balkenende demanded a sizeable reduction in the net payments of the Netherlands. It is generally believed that the no-vote in the Dutch referendum contributed to the firm position taken by the Dutch negotiators. In the final stage of the negotiations, the representatives of the new member states offered to lower the budget for structural funds as a way out of this impasse. However, even this did not enable the old member states to bridge their differences and agreement failed due to negative votes of the UK, the Netherlands, Spain, Sweden and Finland.

Although such high-profile controversies and grand declarations by government leaders after European summit meetings are noticed most widely, these are only part of politics in the EU. The enactment of general visions for Europe in seemingly everyday policy decisions is just as important, because it is these decisions that affect citizens' lives. The large body of EU legislation is important because it affects just about every area of political, economic, social and cultural life in Europe. Legislation adopted at the European level often requires or induces related policy decisions by national and regional governments. EU legislation contains provisions on a wide range of everyday policy questions, from how many hours can be worked a week and when governments may subsidise businesses within their territories, to the maximum length of buses and the contents and labelling of food products.

An important part of European integration has taken place incrementally, by the enactment of a huge number of seemingly small decisions of the sort studied in this book. The importance of such decisions is often not appreciated, even by close observers. The former British Prime Minister, Margaret Thatcher, for example, said she did not realise the full implications of the Single European Act (SEA) of 1986, which were felt through the subsequent large collection of small decisions with the aim of strengthening the internal market.[1] A description of the EU's decision-making system given by Jean-Claude Juncker, Luxembourg's Prime Minister, also points to the importance of apparently small decisions: 'We decide on something, leave it lying around and wait and see what happens . . . If no one kicks up a fuss, because most people don't understand what has been decided, we continue step by step until there is no turning back.' Understanding the political system of the EU therefore requires analysis of the politics of everyday legislative decision-making, of the sort presented in this book.

Although the decisions studied in this book might appear small in comparison to grand landmark decisions, they have nonetheless had considerable impact upon citizens and businesses in Europe. One of the proposals selected in this study is the directive on the manufacture, presentation and sale of tobacco products.[2] The decision outcome on this directive was seen as a victory for defenders of public health interests. The directive introduced strong health warnings on tobacco products, and outlawed the use of product descriptions suggesting that the effects of certain brands are less devastating to health than others. Another example concerns the decision on a Community action programme in the field of education that reserved €1,850 million over seven years to promote cooperation, mobility and the development of a European dimension in all sectors of education.[3] In the first part of this programme, almost 500,000 students undertook a period of study in

[1] Margaret Thatcher's views on the Single European Act and the following quote from Jean-Claude Junker were cited in *The Economist*, 14 September 2002.

[2] Directive 2001/37/EC of 5 June 2001 on the approximation of the laws, regulations and administrative provisions of the member states concerning the manufacture, presentation and sale of tobacco products.

[3] Decision 2000/253/EC of 24 January 2000 establishing the second phase of the Community action programme in the field of education.

another European university, and 10,000 schools took part in European partnerships.

The present study examines the processes through which such decisions are taken. It provides insights into the processes through which actors' divergent preferences on policy outcomes are transformed into legally binding decisions contained in EU legislation. Identifying these processes requires that the investigation is informed by appropriate theories of decision-making, and that these theories are confronted with empirical evidence in a way that allows inferences to be drawn. This volume presents a range of theories of relevance to legislative choice and bargaining in many contexts, and assesses their applicability to the EU. We do so by applying our explanatory models to a large data set constructed specifically for the purposes of this study. Most of these models have not until now been tested in the context of EU decision-making, or have been applied only to very limited data sets in small pilot studies. None of the models have been tested on as large a data set as the one collected for this project. Rarely has such a range of models been tested against each other in a contest to identify their relative performance using empirical data.

The research presented in this book makes three main contributions. First, it provides answers to questions that lie at the core of understanding how the EU works in practice. How are decisions taken in the EU? How important are the formal decision-making procedures in defining decision outcomes in the EU? How important is the bargaining that takes place among the actors involved in decision-making? How can the ways in which actors interact be typified best? These questions are addressed in detail using a combination of theoretically rigorous approaches and attention to empirical detail.

Second, this book provides a unique basis for the study of decision-making in the enlarged EU by analysing decision-making in the period 1999–2001, with an EU of 15 member states. Insights gained from these patterns of decision-making will without doubt be relevant to analyses of the workings of the enlarged EU with 25 member states.

Third, it is an example of how to examine decision-making in a political system using advanced theoretical tools and an appropriate research design. In this respect, this study is also of interest to readers whose main interests are political systems other than the EU, either sub-national or national systems, or other international organisations. The present study is currently one of the most comprehensive tests of competing explanatory models of decision-making, both in terms of the range of theoretical approaches considered and the evidence examined.

In the following sections, we discuss the rationale behind the approach adopted and provide a synopsis of the stage of EU decision-making addressed in this book. The next section of this chapter identifies rational choice institutionalism as the most suitable theoretical approach for this study. This approach has the advantage that it can be applied to specific instances of decision-making, such as the ones we investigate in this book. Further, as discussed in Section 1.3, when specified in the form of testable explanatory models, this approach provides powerful tools to analyse processes of decision-making. In Section 1.4 we sketch the actors, collective bodies and procedures involved in the stage of legislative decision-making we focus on. Finally, in Section 1.5 we describe the range of models and specific approaches taken in this book, ranging from those focusing primarily on formal procedures to models emphasising the informal bargaining that takes place before decisions are taken. Given that the authors of each of the chapters provide a comprehensive overview of the literature relevant to their explanatory models, we do not provide a detailed literature review in this introductory chapter.

1.2 AN INSTITUTIONALIST APPROACH TO EXPLAINING DECISION-MAKING IN THE EUROPEAN UNION

Given our focus on explaining specific decision outcomes in the EU, the rational choice institutionalist approach is the most suitable one to use. Many other theoretical approaches have been applied to the study of the EU, but these provide relatively few insights into specific decision outcomes. Rational choice institutionalism is part of the new institutionalism, which encompasses a range of different approaches, including those that emphasise historical and sociological approaches (Hall and Taylor 1996; Peters 1999; Lane and Ersson 2000; Aspinwall and Schneider 2000; Lowndes 2002). Traditional institutionalism, from which new institutionalism developed, was an approach to study the rules, procedures and formal organisation of government, often using analytical tools from the disciplines of law or history. By comparison, new institutionalism encompasses a range of different approaches, including those that focus on the choices made by rational actors. One strand of institutionalism, for instance, argues that political institutions influence actors' behaviour by shaping their norms, values, interests, identities and beliefs (March and Olsen 1984; 1989).

Given that the explanations of decision-making proposed in this book are grounded in the rational choice approach, they share some common elements. They are similar in the sense that in all explanations used, decision outcomes are assumed to be the result of interactions among goal–orientated actors operating within institutional constraints. The goals that actors pursue in this context include the realisation of decision outcomes as close as possible to their own preferences. This does not, however, imply that preferences are always stable or that actors are always fully aware of the consequences of their actions. Unintended consequences and uncertainty about the probability of possible outcomes belong to the basic features of any decision-making process.

Despite their adherence to the basic assumptions of rational choice institutionalism, the explanations proposed and tested in this book are diverse. The models differ from each other in their propositions about the processes through which actors' policy preferences are transformed into collectively binding outcomes embodied in EU legislation. These differences in propositions lead to differences in their predictions of decision outcomes. By comparing these predictions with the actual outcomes, the explanations can be tested against each other in terms of the accuracy of their predictions. The more accurate the predictions of a model, the more the propositions of the model are assumed to be applicable in the context of European Union legislation. Some explanations (the so-called procedural models) emphasise the importance of the formal institutions in which decision-making takes place. Formal institutions are those, such as the rules that govern the decision-making procedures, which are enforceable by third parties. Among the procedural models, there are differences in interpretation of the same institutional constraints. For instance, there are different ways of interpreting the treaty articles that describe the EU co-decision procedure. Consequently, different procedural models will be tested against each other. Other explanations (the so-called bargaining models) focus on the informal bargaining during the negotiations preceding the formal adoption of legislative acts. Again, there are fundamentally different ways of conceptualising the process of political bargaining. Some models emphasise the search for an overall compromise, while others emphasise logrolling between different controversial issues or power strategies. A third group of explanations (the so-called mixed models) combine propositions about formal procedures with propositions about the bargaining process. The main research questions are the following: which of the competing models gives the most accurate predictions of decision outcomes contained in EU legislation? Under what conditions are the models' predictions more or less accurate?

In several other approaches to the analysis of the EU, the focus is rarely on how decisions are taken on specific controversial issues. Theories of European integration often aim to explain the development of European regional integration, or the institutional structure of the EU. Competing theories of the process of European integration place different emphases on the role of actors and institutions. Among the early theories of integration, neo-functionalism (Haas 1958) highlighted the role played by non-state actors and supranational institutions in the drive toward what seemed to be ever closer union. Spillover effects—functional and technical, political and geographic—were thought to determine the process of European integration. However, neo-functionalism has relatively little to say about the actual process of decision-making within the EU at any given point in time. Similarly, more recent theories of European integration that incorporate some of the tenets of neo-functionalism, such as the transactions-based theory of integration (Stone Sweet and Sandholtz 1998), aim to discover the general determinants of the demand for integration in specific policy domains, rather than explain the details of decision outcomes.

One of the major alternatives to neo-functionalist thought, intergovernmentalism, is also more relevant to examining the general course of European integration than how day-to-day decisions are taken. Intergovernmentalism places most emphasis on nation state actors' interests in defining the speed of European integration. This approach has been helpful in explaining the variable pace of European integration in the 1960s and early 1970s. Intergovernmentalism's antecedents lie in realist (e.g. Morgenthau 1948) and neo-realist thought. Mearsheimer's neorealist interpretation of international institutions holds that the policies they deliver are essentially the result of nation states exerting influence within and through them (Mearsheimer 1994). Regarding the development of the EU, intergovernmentalists have argued that integration is not the deterministic process suggested by neo-functionalists. Rather, member states are viewed as important agents in this process and have often been 'obstinate' rather than 'obsolete' in the process of European integration (Hoffmann 1966; Haas 1975). Liberal intergovernmentalism, which links a theory of domestic preference formation with the subsequent process of intergovernmental bargaining (e.g. Moravscik 1998), also appears to be more concerned with the large milestones in the process of European integration, rather than with day-to-day decision-making.

In short, studies of European integration informed by theories of international relations or of regional integration provide valuable insights into the course of European integration and the relative weight of governmental and supranational actors in the EU. However, they are not geared towards analysing the processes through which political controversies among actors are resolved in the legislative arena. For this, we must look elsewhere.

Rational choice institutionalism offers more promise in this regard, since there are many examples of studies that have used this approach to successfully formulate insights into the workings of political systems (Ward 2002). For example, the rational choice approach has been used to examine the effects of the committee system in the US Congress (Shepsle and Weingast 1987) and the more informal institutional norms of subject area specialisation (Krehbiel 1991). Comparative political studies in this tradition have investigated the effects of various institutions, including bicameralism (Tsebelis and Money 1997), the division of policy areas into ministerial portfolios and processes of coalition formation (Laver and Shepsle 1996), and the effect of multiple veto players in political systems with several stages at which actions can be blocked (e.g. Hammond and Miller 1987; Tsebelis 2002). Literature in this broad tradition provides a framework for understanding the nature of institutions and their effects, and in particular their interaction with actors' preferences to produce decision outcomes.

The existing applications of rational choice approaches to EU decision-making have also been fruitful. Researchers in this tradition have studied the consequences of legislative procedures and the relative impact of EU institutions on the outcomes of legislative decision-making (Tsebelis 1994; 1996; Moser 1996; Tsebelis and Garrett 2000; Crombez, Steunenberg and Corbett 2000). These studies are discussed in more detail in Chapter 3 of this book. Another study, to which we owe a great deal for the inspiration behind the present book, developed and applied several models of the bargaining process in the Council of Ministers (Bueno de Mesquita and Stokman 1994). The present study adopts a similar research design as Bueno de Mesquita and Stokman's 1994 book. However, we have expanded the range of explanations and institutional actors considered. We include models developed in research strategies associated with theories of coalition formation, domestic politics and legislative procedures. Moreover, the present book covers a larger number of legislative issues and proposals. This enables a more refined empirical test of alternative explanations, and an investigation of the conditions under which they are applicable.

Although this book aims to explain the process of decision-making in the EU, the relevance of the theoretical approach it employs reaches far beyond this subject area. The competing explanations offered in this book are all informed by and contribute to one of the major preoccupations of modern political science: the interplay between institutions and preferences in determining policy outcomes. Plott's 'fundamental equation of politics' (Plott 1991) posits that it is the interaction of preferences and institutions that determines policy outcomes. Preferences are understood to be measurable and reflect what individual actors want, whereas institutions provide the rules and practices conditioning actors' behaviour and through which collective choices are made. Accordingly, if preferences change, outcomes may change, even if institutions remain constant. Conversely, if institutions change, outcomes can change, even if preferences remain constant (Hinich and Munger 1997: 17). It has long been known, however, that in the absence of stabilising institutions, decision outcomes are inherently unstable when actors must agree on more than one issue (Plott 1967; McKelvey 1976; Schofield 1978). The empirical observation that such voting cycles are rare spurred the search for institutional mechanisms that prevent them. Shepsle's 'structure-induced equilibrium' is a prominent example of such a mechanism (Shepsle 1979; see also Riker 1980). The models of legislative decision-making presented in this book contain a range of other possible mechanisms. The next section describes the main features of our modelling approach.

1.3 A MODEL GUIDED APPROACH

Our models contain clear specifications of what each of us believes are the essential features of EU decision-making. The authors formulated their models before they saw the data. Moreover, all of the models are applied to study the same decisions. This enables us to compare their relative performance. Given a particular configuration of actors, their preferences and interests, the models generate predictions of decision outcomes. This allows us to test at least some of the implications of the models. An accompanying special issue of *European Union Politics* (Stokman and Thomson 2004) contains analyses of the data set that focus more on the micro-level predictions made by some of the models, for example predictions of the shifts in actors' positions during the course of decision-making. The focus on comparing model predictions with actual outcomes in real decision situations means that this book mainly considers the computational solutions to the models, rather than their more abstract analytical solutions (Morton 1999: 50). Testing the accuracy of the models' predictions over a sufficiently large number of cases enables us to make inferences on the veracity of the propositions they contain.

The use of formal models is an important methodological means to identifying the processes through which legislation is passed in the EU. This approach has been selected to achieve this aim because of its distinct advantages in terms of theory formulation and testing (e.g. Nicholson 1989; Morton 1999: chapter 2; Van den Doel and Van Velthoven 1993). When researchers set forth their ideas about EU decision-making as models, they must be explicit about the propositions they make regarding the decision-making processes at work, as well as the assumptions contained in their models. Assumptions in verbally formulated theories are often implicit rather than absent. Modelling allows the implications of the propositions to be drawn out through deductive reasoning. The number of alternative explanations we examine in this study makes the modelling approach all the more indispensable; comparing alternative models of the processes at work would be practically impossible if these were formulated verbally.

The deductive model-guided approach contrasts with more descriptive studies that have been carried out in recent years on decision-making in the EU, but has undoubtedly benefited from these studies. Our understanding of decision-making in the EU has been enriched considerably by descriptive studies, including those of Nugent (1989), Westlake (1994; 1995), Wallace and Wallace (1996), Richardson (1996), Peterson and Bomberg (1999) and Dinan (1999). While descriptive accounts are unlikely to set out with the aim of contributing to the development of formal theory, they are essential to making progress in this area. Without them, formal modellers would know little about what features of decision-making to include and emphasise in their models. Moreover, when the models prove to be deficient, descriptive studies offer ideas on how to adjust the models to reduce their level of abstraction and home in on the key elements of the complex reality.

Nevertheless, we believe that the specification of models before applying them to empirical data is essential to the search for generalisations in political science, even if such generalisations only hold when particular conditions are present. Descriptive accounts are a valuable part of this research process, but the formulation and application of models is essential to testing hypotheses about the general dynamics at work in EU decision-making.

The emphasis placed on positing and testing formal models should not detract from the fact that this is a methodological means to a larger aim: to evaluate the relative validity of different conceptions of the political processes at work. In each of the following chapters, we illustrate explanations posited by our models by referring to examples of real decision situations. These illustrations attempt to clarify the reasoning underlying each of the models. Nevertheless, the modelling approach applied in this book is certainly not intended to examine only the effects of unique events or all the intricacies of EU decision-making. Any particular case almost inevitably contains events that do not fit easily into the account provided by a model. Instead, a model contains propositions on what are thought to be the most important mechanisms explaining processes in general, across a range of cases. While the adoption of a modelling approach does not necessarily deny the importance of unique events in shaping decision outcomes, it does imply a clear stance on the issue of whether empirical research should focus on explaining specific events or on searching for regularities among different cases. Evidently, the contributors to this volume are more concerned with the latter.

Our commitment to analytical rigour in the form of a model-guided approach has affected the way in which we conducted the empirical investigation of the Commission proposals and legislative acts examined in this study. The design and process of our common data collection benefited from the clear conceptualisation required by modelling. This allowed the data collection to focus consistently on what we believe are the main elements of decision situations. To be applied, the models require a detailed and stylised description of the issues raised by the selected Commission proposals. This includes information on the decision outcomes most favoured by the actors involved, or their 'ideal points'. Finally, some of the models also require information on the levels of salience actors attach to the issues at stake and their relative capabilities in the process of EU decision-making. When collecting information on the Commission proposals selected, we focused on this information, implying that the data collection was also model-guided: it was designed to meet the requirements for the application and testing of the models. This does not, however, mean that the cases were selected as fitting examples of the processes hypothesised by the models. As will become clear in the subsequent chapters, some of the decision events, in the end, could not be accounted for by the models.

1.4 A SYNOPSIS OF EU MEMBER STATES AND LEGISLATIVE DECISION-MAKING

The present study focuses mainly on decision-making in the EU in the time period 1999–2001. Table 1.1 contains information on some of the characteristics of the 15 countries that were EU member states in this period. As the table illustrates, there are substantial differences among the member states in terms of population sizes, ranging from Luxembourg with less than half a million inhabitants to Germany with more than 80 million. Population sizes are also reflected in the weight given to the countries in the EU's decision-making procedures, as can be seen in the number of qualified majority votes each held. Substantial differences also exist regarding levels of economic prosperity. Luxembourg, with its economic concentration in the provision of financial services, has the highest per capita GDP among all EU states and, in fact, of all members of the Organisation for Economic Co-operation and Development (OECD). With impressive economic growth rates in recent years, Ireland has also surged to the top of the league table in terms of its per capita GDP. By comparison, per capita GDP figures for Portugal and Greece are lower. In addition, the 15 EU member states have rather different traditions regarding the role of the state in economic policy-making. This is illustrated in Table 1.1 by differences between the EU states in terms of tax receipts as a percentage of GDP, ranging from 31 per cent in Ireland to 54 per cent in Sweden. Attitudes toward the EU also differ widely between the member states. Support for membership is low in the UK and Sweden, where overwhelming majorities are rather sceptical of the benefits of EU membership, and highest in Luxembourg, the Netherlands and Ireland. Given these differences, and Europe's divided and troublesome history, it is remarkable that these countries agreed to give up so much sovereignty in such a broad range of policy areas. By joining the EU, member states accept the supremacy of EU law over national law. The diversity among the EU's members has only increased further with its enlargement to 25 members in 2004.

The formalities of the decision-making process through which legislative proposals become laws in the EU are well documented (e.g. Dinan 1999; Hix 1999; Peterson and Bomberg 1999; Nugent 1999). These formalities also provide an indication of the complexity of

Table 1.1. *Differences among the 15 members of the European Union in comparison with the United States in the time period studied, 1999–2001*

Country	Population (000s) in 2001[a]	Qualified majority voting weights	GDP per capita, 2001 (PPP, USD)[b]	Tax receipts as % of GDP[a]	Support for EU membership in 2000[c]
Belgium	10,226	5	27,700	45.6	62
Denmark	5,359	3	29,200	49.8	51
Germany	82,331	10	26,300	37.9	48
Greece	10,538	5	16,300	37.8	61
Spain	40,226	8	21,400	35.2	63
France	59,191	10	26,200	45.3	48
Ireland	3,839	3	30,000	31.1	75
Italy	57,358	10	26,200	42.0	59
Luxembourg	441	2	48,700	41.7	79
Netherlands	15,987	5	29,200	41.4	71
Austria	8,110	4	27,400	43.7	38
Portugal	10,061	5	17,600	34.5	61
Finland	5,195	3	26,500	46.9	39
Sweden	8,896	4	26,000	54.2	34
United Kingdom	59,756	10	26,300	37.4	28
EU15	377,514	87	25,500	–	50
United States	285,023	–	35,200	29.6	–

Notes: [a]OECD (2002) *Main Economic Indicators.*

[b]Based on current purchasing power parities; OECD (2003) *National Accounts of OECD Countries, Main Aggregates, Volume 1.*

[c]Percentage of interviewees responding positively to the question: 'Generally speaking, do you think our country's membership of the EU has been a good thing?'; European Commission (2000) *Eurobarometer, no. 54, Autumn 2000.* Brussels: European Commission.

decision-making in the EU. Figure 1.1 provides a schematic representation of the two main procedures through which legislative proposals must pass before they are adopted. In the following, we provide a brief account of the main organisational actors and steps involved before legislation is adopted in the EU.

The stage of decision-making we focus on in this book begins with the introduction of a legislative proposal by the European Commission, and ends with the final decision on that proposal: either adoption or rejection by the Council and/or the European Parliament (EP). This is not to deny the importance of events taking place before and after this stage, both in terms of their scientific relevance to testing alternative explanations, and

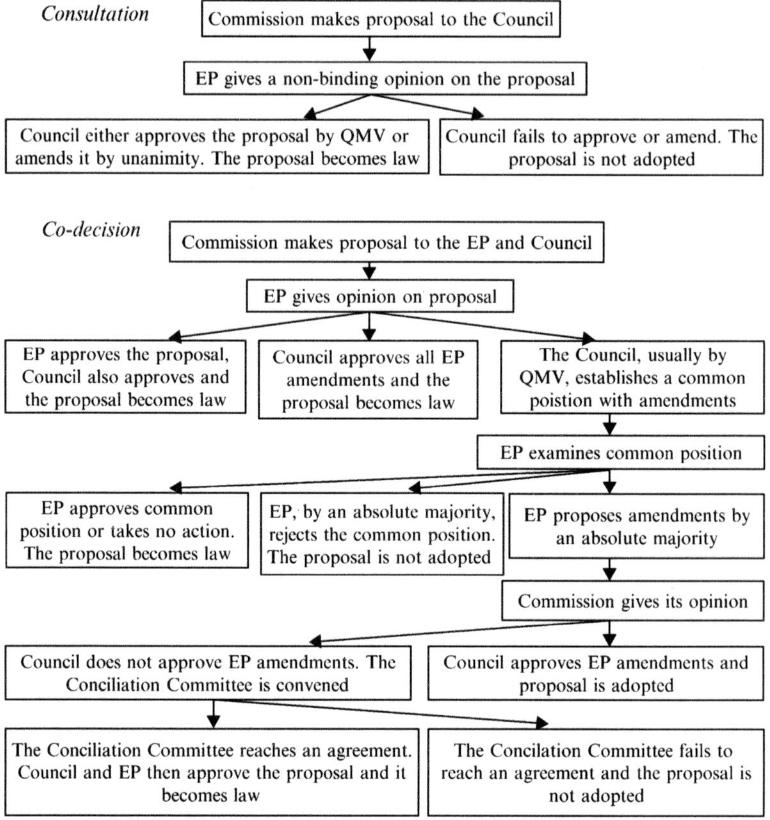

[a]The advisory rules of the Economic and Social Committee and the Committee of the Regions have been excluded in this figure.

Figure 1.1. A schematic representation of the consultation and co-decision procedures with qualified majority voting in the Council[a]

in terms of their impact on EU policies. However, given the range of models developed and tested in this project, the empirical focus of the research must be carefully specified.

The European Commission has the almost exclusive right to initiate legislative proposals. It is generally agreed that this right of initiative gives the Commission substantial authority and potential to influence decision outcomes. In practice, however, it is also clear that the Commission often acts on the basis of treaty obligations or initiatives taken by government representatives of individual member states. Nonetheless, the

Commission's proposals frame the debate within and between the Council and the EP, and it is certainly more difficult for the other institutions to amend than to accept the Commission's proposals. The support, or at least acquiescence, of the Commission is generally sought before decisions are taken. Representatives of the Commission play an active role in the discussions about its proposals; they are present in the Council meetings, consult with Members of the European Parliament (MEPs), and are also present in the Conciliation Committee, in which differences between the Council and the EP are discussed. Officials in the Commission are adept at identifying opportunities for political compromises that can pave the way for the adoption of legislative acts. The Commission's expertise in this area, and in the substance of often highly technical EU policy proposals, was often cited by the practitioners interviewed in our study as a source of its potential influence.

Events that take place prior to the introduction of legislative proposals also contribute to the Commission's authority after its proposals are presented. Before the Commission adopts a proposal, consultations may be held with stakeholders with diverse interests, including various interest groups. The Commission's proposals are approved, and if necessary voted on, by the College of Commissioners. During the time period we focus on in this book, the Commission consisted of 20 Commissioners from 15 member states; it was expanded to 25 Commissioners, one from each of the 25 member states following the 2004 enlargement. The Commissioners, each heading one or more of the Commission's Directorates-General (DGs), are selected through a process of nomination by member states and subsequent approval by the EP. The consultations that take place before the Commission's proposals are sent to the Council and EP mean that these proposals have to a large extent been tailored to the sensitivities of a wide range of affected interests. Competing interests are expressed partly by representatives of interest groups with access to the various DGs. A former Secretary General—head of the Commission's staff—commented to us that for interest groups in particular, the pre-proposal stage often offers the most fertile opportunities for exerting influence.

Commissioners are not member state representatives, but representatives of the Commission and hence supposed to act in the EU's collective interest. However, the fact that they are usually experienced politicians at the national level means that they have intimate knowledge of the issues that could raise objections in domestic politics and from decision-makers in the Council and EP.

This process through which a diversity of interests is accommodated during the preparatory stages of the Commission's proposals contributes to the Commission's authority after its proposals are sent on to the Council and EP. Its proposals are European in nature, in the sense that they attempt to take into account a range of interests broad enough to facilitate support in both the Council and the EP. In addition, the discussions at the pre-proposal stage mean that the internal divisions within the Commission have been resolved when a legislative proposal is initiated. While it is certainly true that the Commission is a fragmented body, rather than one based on unified understandings of policies, this is not an accurate description of how the Commission usually operates after a legislative proposal has been introduced. Once the Commission has adopted its proposals and sent them to the Council and EP, the factions within the Commission have usually been united around a single position, and it almost invariably speaks with a single voice in the subsequent process of EU decision-making. The common front presented by the Commission in its dealings with the Council and the EP is likely to be another source of its potential influence on EU decision outcomes.

The Council of Ministers is at the centre of the decision-making stage we focus on in this book. The Council is highly sectoralised and meets in different compositions of ministers, depending on the dossiers under discussion (e.g. Sherrington 1999). Within the Council, directly under the ministerial level, there are the groups of the Committee of the Permanent Representatives of the Member States (COREPER I and II). These groups consist of the ambassadors in COREPER II, and deputies in COREPER I, representing each EU member state (e.g. Hayes-Renshaw and Wallace 1997). These groups are responsible for preparing the ministerial meetings, and for brokering decisions that could not be reached at lower levels. Below the level of the COREPER groups in the Council there is what essentially amounts to a proliferation of working groups. These groups consist of civil servants from the permanent representations of the member states in Brussels and are often specialists in national capitals holding particular expertise. It is at this level of the Council that political agreements on large proportions of legislative proposals are reached. One report states that as much as 70 per cent of the contents of legislative acts are decided on the level of working groups (Hayes-Renshaw and Wallace 1997: 15). While this provides an indication of the importance of the working groups, it is difficult to quantify their actual input in this way. Higher institutional levels often decide on issues that are more politically contentious, and instructions from committees higher in the

Council hierarchy can be instrumental in reaching agreements at lower levels.

The Council Presidency coordinates and chairs discussions in the Council, with the Presidency, in the time period studied here, rotating every six months among the 15 member states. The Presidency's most important tasks include the facilitation of agreements on pending legislative proposals, and the representation of the Council in its dealings with the EP. The member state holding the Presidency must therefore represent its own interests in Council meetings, while also ensuring progress on pending proposals. A question that will be addressed later in this book is whether holding the Presidency allows member states to obtain decision outcomes closer to their preferences than would otherwise have been the case (see Chapter 3 by Bernard Steunenberg and Torsten Selck). Facilitating progress on pending proposals is all the more of a challenge due to the common practice of seeking broad consensus before the Council approves a decision outcome. Hence, decision-making in the Council is characterised by deliberate attempts to obtain consensus (e.g. Edwards 1996; Hix 1999; Sherrington 1999; Hayes-Renshaw 2001; Mattila and Lane 2001; Soetendorp and Hosli 2001). According to the formalities of the decision-making procedures, member states can be outvoted under the system of qualified majority voting (QMV) that applies to many policy areas. Under QMV, the distribution of votes among the member states bears a rough resemblance to the countries' population sizes (see Table 1.1)[4]. In the EU-15 we focus on in the present study, ten votes were held by the four largest member states and two by the smallest. For the Council to take a decision according to QMV, 62 votes were required. The norm of striving towards consensus means that even when only a qualified majority is required for a decision to be taken, it is common practice to continue discussions until the interests of a dissenting minority are adequately accommodated.

The European Parliament, in addition to the Commission and the Council, is the third organisational actor included in our analysis of legislative decision-making.[5] Although the EP is made up of MEPs from

[4] On relations between voting weights in the Council and member state population size, see Hosli and Wolffenbuttel (2001). The voting weights and procedures changed with enlargement, with the implementation of the Treaty of Nice and with the introduction of the provisions of the EU draft constitution (e.g. see Felsenthal and Machover 2001b; Moberg 2002; Hosli and Machover 2004).

[5] For discussions of the composition and functioning of the European Parliament, see Westlake (1994), Hix and Lord (1997), Hix (1999) or Dinan (1999).

different political groups, it is a distinct actor in the EU's legislative arena. Many issues raise inter-institutional rivalries, particularly between the EP and the Council, whereby it is not uncommon for a large majority of the EP to take a different stance to the member states in the Council. Much of the work in the EP takes place in its committees, where legislative proposals are examined and the EP's proposals for amendments to these proposals are formulated. The scrutiny of each Commission proposal is coordinated by an MEP, known as the *rapporteur.* This individual has the potential to play an important role in shaping the EP's stance on pending proposals. In the 1999-2004 term of the EP, which covers the time period we focus on here, there were seven political groups, the largest of which was the Group of the European People's Party (Christian Democrats) and European Democrats (PPE-DE); followed by the Socialist Group in the European Parliament (PSE). There is a considerable amount of cohesion within these groups and they are certainly important in structuring debate and behaviour in the EP. Nevertheless, grand coalitions between the two main groups are also common.

This book focuses on the two most prominent decision-making procedures to which EU legislative proposals are subject: the consultation procedure and the co-decision procedure. These differ with respect to the power given to the European Parliament. Consultation is the simpler of the two procedures and requires less involvement of the EP. Under the co-decision procedure, by contrast, the EP essentially co-legislates with the Council. The procedure to which a Commission's proposal is subject depends on the particular policy area the proposal is concerned with. In the year 2000, 147 pending Commission proposals for directives, regulations and decisions were subject to the consultation procedure, while 172 were subject to the co-decision procedure (European Commission 2001).

Under the consultation procedure, the EP must give its opinion on the Commission's proposal before the Council decides on it. EP opinions vary substantially in terms of their level of detail. Some opinions consist of rather general statements of approval or disapproval of the Commission's legislative proposals, while other opinions consist of detailed proposals for amendments. Under consultation, the parliament has few means at its disposal to enforce its opinions, other than exercising political pressure. Commission proposals in the subject areas of agriculture, fisheries, and justice and home affairs are among those generally subject to the consultation procedure.

The co-decision procedure provides for a more extensive involvement of the EP, as illustrated in Figure 1.1. In 1999, this procedure was amended and extended to more policy areas with the implementation of the Treaty of Amsterdam. It is this revised version of the co-decision procedure that is examined in this book. Compared to the consultation procedure, the co-decision procedure is relatively complex and provides for at least two readings of a Commission proposal if the Council and the EP cannot reach an agreement earlier. In the face of protracted differences between the positions of the Council and the EP, the Conciliation Committee is convened, consisting of representatives of the Council and the EP. However, since the Treaty of Amsterdam, the Council and the EP often negotiate an early agreement, thereby shortening the potentially lengthy co-decision procedure (see Farrell and Héritier 2003). The Commission also participates in the Conciliation Committee, although it does so as an observer. For the legislative act to be adopted, the Commission's approval of the joint text drawn up in the Conciliation Committee is not formally required. However, the text must be approved by the Council and by the EP. Internal market is one of the policy domains to which the co-decision procedure usually applies. In the selection of proposals included in this volume, this policy area features quite prominently.

Both the consultation procedure and the co-decision procedure can be combined with either qualified majority voting or the unanimity requirement in the Council. The selection of QMV or unanimity also depends on the particular policy area with which the Commission's proposal is concerned. Most proposals in the areas of agriculture and fisheries require consultation combined with QMV in the Council, while proposals in the area of justice and home affairs require consultation combined with unanimity. Co-decision is generally, although not always, combined with QMV in the Council.

Clearly, legislative decision-making in the EU involves daily interactions among the institutions and permanent representations of the member states in Brussels. As discussed in Section 1.2, many different approaches to the study of politics in the EU have been championed over the past decades. In our view, analysing the decision-making process in depth requires the formulation of clear explanations of the mechanisms through which actors resolve their differences and reach agreement on controversial issues. These explanations should be tested on the basis of systematically collected data enabling rival analytical models to be applied and tested.

1.5 OUTLINE OF THE BOOK

The models presented in the following chapters differ from each other in the relative amount of emphasis they place on formal decision-making procedures and informal bargaining. Formal decision-making procedures refer to the rules, laid down in the treaties and in practice, regarding which actors are empowered to make proposals, which actors can amend them, and the thresholds of support required before legislation can be adopted. Informal bargaining, by contrast, consists of the strategies and modes of interaction that actors engage in with a view to maximising their influence and obtaining decision outcomes as close as possible to their own preferred policies. These include entering into exchanges with each other, constructing package deals, exercising pressure, and forming coalitions with like-minded partners. Of course, such behaviour does not occur independently of the formal rules, since these strengthen the positions of some actors and provide them with leverage. Indeed, many of the explanatory models featured in our research combine elements of both the procedural and the informal aspects of legislative decision-making.

Chapter 2 presents the common research design of this study. It describes the 66 Commission proposals and 162 issues that serve as the data we use to conduct the testing of our models. The chapter discusses the reasoning behind our decision to rely heavily on key informants for the collection of the information. In addition, it describes the operationalisation of the main concepts featured in the models applied. There are some important differences between the models used in this book with respect to the numbers and types of variables they posit, which are essential to formulating valid explanations of the process of EU decision-making. Nevertheless, all the models can be applied using the same data set. All models are tested on the basis of their forecasts of decision outcomes on controversial issues raised by legislative proposals. Since the models can be applied to similar data, they can be evaluated, and also compared, using similar criteria. Such comparability is essential if progress is to be achieved through the conjecture and refutation of well-specified models and hypotheses on the basis of their relative explanatory power.

Chapters 3 to 9 contain presentations and applications of competing models of decision-making. In Chapter 3, Bernard Steunenberg and Torsten Selck offer explanations of decision outcomes that are based on formal procedural rules. They devote careful attention to how legislative rules define the extent to which actors are able to participate in the decision-making process. Procedures affect the kinds of actions actors are allowed to take and the sequence in which they may act. By excluding certain choice alternatives, these rules may induce political stability and, in combination with the preferences of the actors involved, determine the outcomes of decision-making. Although the treaties describe the legislative procedures, they leave considerable room for interpretation about how to apply these formal rules in practice. The chapter sets forth and tests a model of the consultation procedure and three models of the co-decision procedure. This allows the authors to draw inferences on the major differences between the two legislative procedures, as well as the applicability of their models.

In Chapter 4, Christopher H. Achen offers a fundamentally different view of the decision-making process to that proposed in Chapter 3. In Achen's view, informal institutions are paramount. He argues that with our current knowledge, the best forecasts of political decisions will derive from the conception that governmental institutions are the key actors in politics, and that their relative power determines political outcomes. Achen calls this classic idea of twentieth century political science 'institutional realism'. He then presents a straightforward model employing the institutional realist perspective, derived from John Nash's famous solution to bargaining games. As Achen demonstrates, the Nash bargaining solution implies that decision outcomes will be closely approximated by a simple formula for predicting EU decisions due to Jan Van den Bos (1991), the compromise model. The compromise model is simply a weighted average of actors' most-preferred points, with the weights given by the product of power and salience. In Achen's view, this modest and straightforward compromise formula embodies the best case study wisdom of the last century and is a strong candidate to dominate other forecasts based on legal and procedural views of politics.

Chapter 5 is written by Javier Arregui, Frans N. Stokman and Robert Thomson. They develop and apply models that place the spotlight on modes of bargaining among actors leading to shifts in their positions over time. The authors propose alternative models, each focussing on the ways in which actors aim to influence each other during discussions that precede final decisions. For example, the expected utility or challenge model posits that actors engage in a series of potentially conflictual encounters with each other, during the course of which some actors may be compelled to shift their policy positions. This model is based on assumptions of non-cooperative game theory, according to which actors are unable to make binding commitments in their dealings with each other. This contrasts with the type of interaction found in the position exchange model. In this co-operative view of decision-making, it is hypothesised that actors attempt to identify mutually beneficial exchanges; one actor supports the preferred policy position of its exchange partner on one issue, in exchange for the support of that actor on another issue. Procedural aspects of the legislative process do not feature prominently in these explanations. Procedural rules are treated as exogenous factors that define actors' potential to influence others using the strategies mentioned above.

Stefanie Bailer and Gerald Schneider, in Chapter 6, are the only contributing authors to examine the influence of domestic politics on decision-making at the European level. The authors develop an explanation of decision outcomes at the European level in which the ranges of opinions in each country affect member states' room for manoeuvre when negotiating in Brussels. Member states in which relatively narrow ranges of views are expressed by domestic groups have less room for manoeuvre than states in which broader ranges of views prevail. In developing this idea, they consider the relevance of domestic parliamentary committees on European affairs, which review proposals for new EU legislation. The models proposed in this chapter combine elements of formal and informal institutions. In particular, Bailer and Schneider examine whether formal institutions at the domestic level, namely domestic parliamentary committees, affect informal bargaining at the European level.

Chapter 7, by Vincent Boekhoorn, Adrian M. A. Van Deemen and Madeleine O. Hosli, employs coalition-based explanations of legislative decision-making. Like the bargaining models featured in Chapter 5 of this book, the kernel of these explanations consists of propositions about the influence process, rather than the formal legislative procedures. The models examine the dynamics of coalition formation in the EU, both within the Council and between the Commission, the EP and the Council. Considering the wide range of policy issues on which decisions are taken in the EU, it is hardly surprising that different coalitions of actors emerge. This is true with respect to the interactions among the EU institutions, and also of decision-making within the Council. The increasing use of QMV in the Council adds to the importance of this type of behaviour. In terms of its theoretical foundations, the chapter draws on models of voting in committees and on co-operative game theory.

The authors elaborate and test alternative mechanisms through which coalitions are formed in processes of EU decision-making. The formal procedures also play a role in these explanations, since they define the range and minimum sizes of possible winning coalitions.

Thomas König and Sven-Oliver Proksch, in Chapter 8, present a procedural exchange model, which combines elements of informal bargaining and procedural rules in a two-stage process. The authors point out that procedural analyses, including those presented in Chapter 3, typically consist of one-shot games, whereby a strong agenda setter makes a proposal that is subsequently voted on. Such procedural models exclude the possibility of bargaining and interaction among the actors before a vote is taken. Similarly, standard exchange models tend to disregard the EU's decision-making procedures, such as the Commission's power to initiate proposals. The model presented in this chapter consists of a first move by the European Commission, a stage of informal bargaining in the Council, and finally, a voting round that also incorporates the role of the EP in the co-decision procedure. The stage of informal bargaining is characterised by exchange. However, unlike the position-exchange model presented in Chapter 5, König and Proksch present and test an exchange model in which actors exchange power resources.

In Chapter 9, Mika Widgén and Antti Pajala posit a model of how decision outcomes are arrived at, in which actors simplify complex, multi-issue decision situations by reconstructing them as single dimensions. According to Widgén and Pajala's model, actors simplify political complexity by identifying a common dimension of conflict onto which they project their political differences and play them out. Like the authors of some of the previous chapters, Widgén and Pajala combine formal and informal institutions in their model of legislative decision-making. Once the complexity of the policy space has been reduced to manageable proportions, the formal legislative procedures determine which actors can make proposals, and what these proposals will be.

In Chapter 10, Christopher H. Achen compares the performance of the different models developed and applied in the previous chapters by comparing the models' predictions with actual decision outcomes. Achen identifies simple baseline models as benchmarks, and compares the predictions of the models with each other and with the predictions of the benchmarks. He evaluates the predictive power of alternative models by applying several alternative measures. In general, co-operative models of decision-making outperform non-cooperative ones. The compromise model generates the most accurate predictions of decision outcomes, though a few other models are close competitors. This finding highlights the importance of inclusive and co-operative informal bargaining in reaching decision outcomes in the EU.

Finally, Chapter 11, by Gerald Schneider, Bernard Steunenberg and Mika Widgrén, concludes this book by summarising the main findings of our research, and evaluating their implications for understanding EU decision-making. The relatively strong performance of the compromise model, which Achen shows to be akin to the Nash bargaining solution, is one of the most noteworthy findings. This suggests that amid the complexity of interests involved in the EU's legislative arena, decision outcomes appear to be reasonable, in the sense that they incorporate the positions of all actors, while weighting these positions by actors' power and levels of interest in the issues at stake. The implications of the findings for understanding EU decision-making, and for future research, are drawn out in detail in the concluding chapter.

2

Research design: measuring actors' positions, saliences and capabilities

ROBERT THOMSON AND FRANS N. STOKMAN

The aim of this study is to apply and compare different explanations of legislative decision-making in the European Union (EU). Two features of the research design are particularly important with respect to achieving this aim. First, the selection of cases must cover a sufficient number and variety of cases to count as a test of the explanations. Second, a way of thinking about very different decision situations has to be devised, such that they can be compared, in terms of the applicability of different explanations in any given situation, and in terms of the performance of explanations in different situations. Stating explanations in the form of models is part of the endeavour to facilitate comparison. Another part is the conceptualisation of decision situations *spatially*. Political controversies are conceptualised as *issue continua* or *scales*, with actors placed at different positions on these issues. The Commission proposal on tobacco products will be used to illustrate the data collection process. One of the issues raised by this proposal was the size of the health warning on tobacco products: see the second issue described in Figure 2.1. At one end of this issue continuum, we find the *status quo* position at that time, consisting of relatively small warnings. At the other end of the continuum, we find the alternative of very large health warnings using very strong language. Intermediate alternatives are placed on positions between these two alternatives. This way of defining issues is essential to the comparison of different explanatory models' performance. It enables us to identify which explanations generate predictions that are closer to or further from actual decision outcomes. After discussing the selection of cases, we turn to the description of decision situations in terms of issue continua with the help of policy area experts.

2.1 THE SELECTION OF COMMISSION PROPOSALS

The data set used to apply and test the models described in the following chapters contains information on 66 recent legislative proposals by the European Commission (see Appendix 1 for details of the cases selected). These proposals were selected to obtain a number of issues from a range of policy areas, sufficient to allow the predictive accuracy of alternative explanatory models to be identified. The selection of cases is certainly one of the distinguishing features of the present research. It distinguishes the present research from previous applications of explanatory models that were confined to illustrations on a few, rather casually selected cases. In addition, it differs from studies that focus on readily quantifiable aspects of decision-making, such as the percentages of adopted amendments. Instead, the cases we study are explored in more detail than the amendment approach would allow, and we identify the substance of the issues on which there were disagreements.

The Commission proposals were selected on the basis of three criteria: the type of legislative procedure to which they were subject, the time period in which they were introduced and discussed, and their political importance. As mentioned in the introduction, the Commission proposals included in this study were subject to either the consultation or the co-decision procedure. These are the most important procedures in EU legislative decision-making. The procedural models featured in Chapter 3, by Bernard Steunenberg and Torsten Selck, focus explicitly on these legislative procedures. It was therefore important to restrict the selection in this respect. Table 2.1 shows the distribution of the Commission proposals by the type of legislative procedure to which they were subject. Note that there are two variants of both procedures: one requiring qualified majority support in the Council and one requiring unanimity. Co-decision combined with unanimity voting in the Council is least common, but was nevertheless required for five of the proposals included in our selection.

The selection of Commission proposals was also confined to those that did not change legislative procedure after the Amsterdam Treaty came into effect on 1 May 1999. On this date, the legislative procedure changed for a number of Commission proposals that had been introduced earlier and were still pending on that date. For example, some proposals were introduced under the cooperation procedure, and changed to the co-decision procedure. It was decided not to include these proposals in the selection. Inclusion of proposals whose legislative

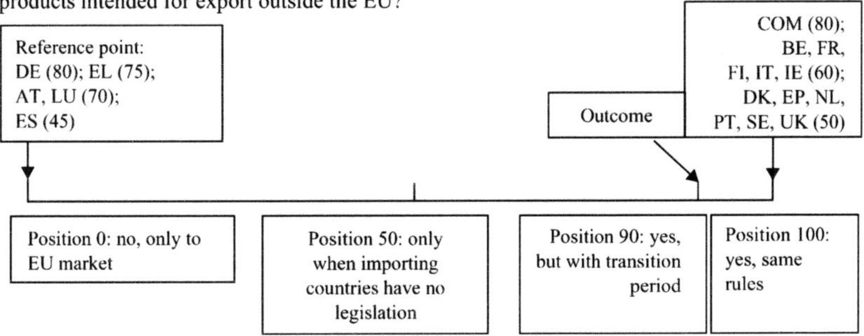

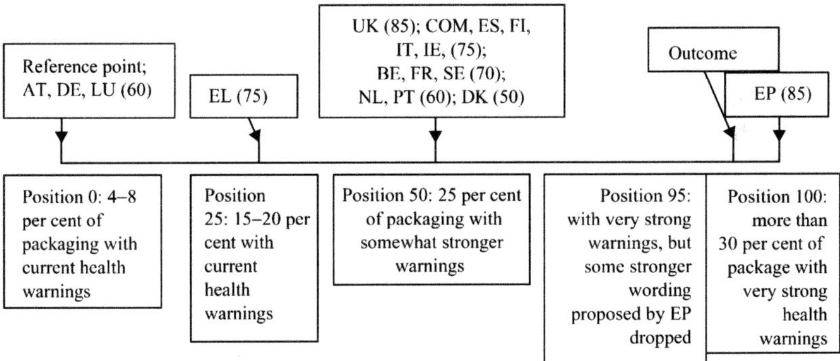

Figure 2.1. The tobacco products directive (COD/1999/244): two of the issues specified by experts. (Salience scores in brackets.)

procedure changed would have made the application of models of the decision-making process problematic. For instance, it could have raised the possibility that the poor performance of a model could be attributed to the uncertainty caused by changes in the procedure, rather than the veracity of the model. Therefore, the decision to select proposals only if their procedure did not change restricted the number of proposals available for inclusion in the selection.

As will be discussed in the following section, interviews with experts were required to collect the data needed to apply and test the models. The decision situations we asked them to describe had to be relatively recent and fresh in their memory. This had implications for the time period we could cover. We selected Commission proposals that were discussed in the Council in the period January 1999 – December 2000. Since our data collection efforts for this project ended in early 2002 (the interviews took

Table 2.1. *Distribution of 66 Commission proposals by legislative procedure and type of instrument*

EP involvement	Council voting rule	Commission proposals selected by researchers	Issues identified by experts	Type of instrument	Commission proposals	Issues
Co-decision	QMV	21	56	Directives	16	40
	Unan.	5	12	Regulations	8	24
				Decisions	2	4
Consultation	QMV[a]	22	55	Directives	10	26
	Unan.	18	39	Regulations	25	55
				Decisions	5	13
Total		66	162		66	162

Note: [a]Includes one proposal with two issues that required the support of QMV and ten member states in order for it to pass (CNS/1999/192, 2000/98/EC Council Decision of 24 January 2000 establishing the Employment Committee).

place between the Spring of 2000 and early 2002), inclusion of proposals introduced in 2001 would have resulted in the collection of data on many proposals that would not have been decided on within the time available for our research.

The third criterion for including a Commission proposal in the selection was that it had to raise some minimum level of controversy. This is the most basic requirement for the application of any of the models featured in this book. All of the models concern the transformation of actors' policy preferences into collectively binding decision outcomes embodied in EU legislation. Issues on which there was no controversy do not provide opportunities to test alternative theories of this process. Before the inclusion of a Commission proposal in the selection, it had to have been mentioned in *Agence Europe*, the main independent daily news service covering European Union affairs.[1] This news service is used mostly by specialists in EU affairs. This procedure avoided the introduction of very technical Commission proposals that were of only marginal political importance. After the identification of a report in *Agence Europe*, it was included provisionally in the selection. A policy area

[1] We included a Commission proposal if at least five lines of text were devoted to it in *Agence Europe*. This excluded proposals that were simply listed as one of the points on the agenda of a Council meeting, with no substantive reference to the proposal.

expert was then contacted and asked for advice on the proposal. If the proposal did not raise any controversy whatsoever, it was not included in the selection; if it did, the proposal was included in the selection. Despite the application of this selection criterion, there is a substantial amount of variation in the Commission proposals included in our research in terms of their levels of controversy and politicisation. This variation will be illustrated amply in the description of cases featured throughout the following chapters. As can be seen in the list of proposals in Appendix 1, the selection includes proposals that would seem rather technical, such as a directive on the manoeuvrability of buses, and ones that gave rise to years of political confrontation in the EU, such as the company takeovers directive, or the directive on resale rights for artists.

Since none of the models tested in this book refer to a specific type of legal instrument (i.e. directives, regulations or decisions), it was not necessary to confine the selection in this regard. The selection includes proposals for new and amendments to existing directives, regulations and decisions (Table 2.1). Directives stipulate a general framework or objective that must be achieved, but must be transposed into national law by member states. Regulations are generally more detailed than directives, and do not require transposition into national law. Decisions are directed toward specific member states or legal entities, and contain more detailed and often more technical provisions than directives or regulations. Because the selection included proposals that provoked some general awareness of importance and at least a minimum level of political controversy, decisions inevitably feature less prominently among the cases examined.

Likewise, none of the models featured in this book are confined to particular policy areas. The selection was not confined in this regard, and includes proposals discussed in fourteen different sectoral compositions of the Council (Table 2.2). Many of the proposals are found in the policy areas of agriculture (14 Commission proposals) and internal market (13 proposals). The distribution of the selected proposals across the policy areas is influenced heavily by the stipulation that the proposal should not have changed from one legislative procedure to another after the Treaty of Amsterdam came into effect.

The 66 Commission proposals selected for inclusion in our study are an exhaustive sample of proposals that meet the above-mentioned criteria; they are not a random sample of EU legislation. A random sample would have resulted in the selection of many technical proposals on which there were hardly any differences in the decision outcomes

Table 2.2. *Distribution of 66 Commission proposals in the data set by policy area*

Council[a]	Number of Commission proposals	Number of issues
Agriculture	14	40
Internal Market	13	34
Fisheries	7	13
ECOFIN	6	10
Justice and Home Affairs	5	15
General	6	14
Other	15	36
Total	66	162

Note: [a]Other categories include: Culture (3 proposals with 7 issues), Development (2 proposals with 4 issues), Employment (2 proposals with 4 issues), Energy (1 proposal with 2 issues), Health (1 proposal with 5 issues), Industry (1 proposal with 3 issues), Social Affairs (1 proposal with 3 issues), and Transport (4 proposals with 8 issues).

favoured by the actors involved. Such proposals do not provide opportunities to test alternative models. Decisions, as opposed to regulations and directives, often concern more technical matters, and there are fewer of these in our selection than in the population of all legislative proposals pending in the year 2000.[2] The research design decision to select co-decision proposals only if their legislative base did not change after the Amsterdam Treaty came into effect means that the co-decision procedure is somewhat under-represented. Of the proposals in our selection 39 per cent were subject to co-decision; of all the co-decision and consultation proposals that were pending in 2000, 54 per cent were subject to co-decision (European Commission 2001).

Given that the selection is confined to recent years, the ability to generalise the findings depends on the extent to which the time period examined can be compared with other time periods. Politics in the EU change constantly. This is illustrated by the recent enlargement of the EU to include many more members. Furthermore, the time period in which the selected proposals were discussed undoubtedly contains

[2] Eight of the 66 proposals in our selection (12 per cent) are decisions, while 74 of the 319 pending proposals in 2000 (23 per cent) were decisions. The percentages of directives and regulations in our selection are 39 per cent and 50 per cent compared with 39 per cent and 37 per cent of all pending proposals in 2000 (European Commission 2001).

unique events, not least the resignation of the Santer Commission and the installation of the new Prodi Commission in 1999. While the influence of such unique events on the selected proposals is difficult to gauge, with few exceptions, the experts we consulted did not attribute great importance to these events in terms of their effect on the decision-making processes on the dossiers under investigation. They did, nevertheless, emphasise the uniqueness of each of the cases included in the selection, in terms of the alignments of actors found, and the ways in which solutions were found to political problems. Generalisations about decision-making in the EU, even if they are confined to decision-making that took place within a certain time period, would be no mean feat.

There follows a summary of the three selection criteria. All legislative proposals by the Commission must meet the following criteria:

- Procedure: subject to co-decision or consultation, and no change in legislative procedure after Amsterdam Treaty came into effect;
- Time period: Commission proposals introduced during or before December 2000, and on the agenda (pending) in 1999 and/or 2000; and
- Political importance: indication of general awareness of importance, evident in reports in *Agence Europe*, and at least a minimum level of controversy revealed by interviews with key informants.

2.2 THE SELECTION OF EXPERTS

Interviews with experts on the Commission proposals we selected are indispensable. At least 150 interviews were held with 125 experts, and these interviews lasted just over an hour and 40 minutes on average.[3] These individuals are a rich source of information on the controversial issues that had to be resolved during the discussions, and the decision outcomes favoured most by the actors involved. Documents provide useful background and supplementary material. As illustrated in Appendix II, where expert judgments are compared with information found in Council documents, the written accounts of Council meetings often do not detail the positions initially favoured by the actors, but rather the

[3] This is a conservative estimate of the number of interviews carried out in this research. It includes only those interviews that related directly to the Commission proposals under investigation or to the distribution of capabilities between the actors. It does not include many interviews that were conducted at the selection stage, to identify Commission proposals that were suitable for our study (i.e. Commission proposals on which there was at least some minimum level of controversy).

alternatives they were prepared to accept, some time into the talks. We are well aware of the limitations of expert judgments. However, the way in which they were collected in this study minimises these problems. First of all, we focus on specific issues raised during the discussions on legislative proposals, rather than more abstract policy dimensions, such as a socio-economic Left-Right dimension. The meaning of these specific issues is clear, while more abstract policy dimensions may mean different things to different people. Second, we held in-depth interviews with a relatively small number of experts, rather than a survey of a large number of individuals. Consequently, we were able to monitor the effort devoted to answering the questions, and the expertise on which the experts drew when providing their estimations.

The informants' expertise was evaluated on the basis of the extent to which they were able to provide arguments to justify the estimates they provided us with. These estimates concern mainly the decision outcomes favoured most by each of the decision-making actors, and the levels of importance these actors attached to the issues at stake. Therefore, the main guiding questions in this qualitative evaluation of the informants' expertise were:

- Why did each of the actors favour the alternatives they did?
- Why did the actors prioritise the issues as they did?

Estimates from informants who could not provide convincing answers to these questions were not included in the data set.

The experts were selected on the basis of the depth of their knowledge of the dossiers under investigation. Usually they had first-hand knowledge of these decision situations, and were usually participants. We require detailed information, and there are few truly neutral and impartial individuals who had the information needed. Individuals with different institutional affiliations were included in the list of experts (Table 2.3). The largest proportion were affiliated with the permanent representations of the member states. Civil servants from all 15 states were interviewed. Usually, these were the desk officers responsible for representing their state in the Council discussions. A small number of experts were affiliated with the European Parliament and with interest groups. Due to their institutional location, these individuals are often not well placed to provide detailed information. In preparation for the data collection, many more experts from the European Parliament were contacted by phone and fax. When the nature of the questions was stated, and in particular when it was made clear that the expert would need

Table 2.3. *Institutional affiliation of experts who provided estimates for the data set*

Commission	Member state representations	Council Secretariat	European Parliament	Interest groups	Total
31	69	9	4	12	125

an overview of all actors involved in the decision situation, most indicated they did not have access to the information required. The bias toward the Council in our selection of experts reflects the view, shared by researchers and practitioners, that analyses of legislative decision-making need to examine the interactions within the Council. Although we include the Commission and the European Parliament (EP) as actors in our analyses, decision-making within these actors falls outside the scope of our study. The possibility that the institutional location of the experts influences the findings is explored in Chapter 10, where the accuracy of the models' predictions of decision outcomes is compared. In particular, it is examined whether any of the models perform significantly better on the basis of data from experts of a particular institutional affiliation.

2.3 SPECIFYING THE ISSUES AT STAKE WITH EXPERTS

As indicated by the reference to the tobacco directive and Figure 2.1 at the beginning of this chapter, controversial issues raised during the discussions are viewed as issue continua or scales. The first step in the interview process consisted of describing the political problem in these terms. The directive on the manufacture, presentation and sale of tobacco products (COD/1999/244) aimed to harmonise certain requirements that cigarettes produced in the EU must meet, such as maximum tar, nicotine and carbon monoxide levels, and to introduce stronger health warnings on tobacco products. Interviews were held with four experts on this proposal, three from the Council representations and one from a public health interest group. Five issues were identified that, in their view, capture the main elements of the discussions on this dossier. Two of these are described in Figure 2.1 (see also Appendix II for a more detailed description).

The two issues from the tobacco directive depicted in Figure 2.1 illustrate the main criteria an issue specification must meet. Each of the issues specified can be described in two ways: first, in terms of a specific policy question on which a collective decision had to be taken; and second, in terms of a scale or continuum on which the alternative outcomes of this decision could be placed. Each of the issue continua is uni-dimensional, and each actor involved in the decision-making situation who has an interest in the issue can be placed on a point on the continuum to represent the position it favours on that issue. Points on the continuum that lie further away from an actor's position are evaluated more negatively by that actor. This is related to the assumption that actors have single-peaked preference functions. This means that each actor expects to receive most value from the realisation of its own position on the continuum compared with other positions, and less from alternatives located further from its own position. The two extreme positions on each issue continuum represent the most extreme positions favoured by any of the actors. Intermediate positions represent more moderate positions and also possible compromise outcomes.

The first issue in the tobacco directive concerned the question of whether the EU rules on yield levels should apply to tobacco products intended for export outside the EU. During the early stages of the discussions on this directive, two camps could be distinguished clearly. Five member states that have substantial tobacco manufacturing industries were said to oppose the application of the same rules.[4] The others supported the Commission's proposal, that the same rules should apply. During the talks, two compromise alternatives, between these 'extremes', emerged. One was to apply the EU rules only when the importing country had no legislation; another was to apply the EU rules to exported cigarettes after a transition period. These alternatives were positioned on the continuum to reflect the experts' judgement on the political distances among them. Clearly, issue continua may be constructed to register qualitative issues. Where the issues involve choices between inherently qualitative alternatives, or where the numerical alternatives do not correspond to the political distances among the scale values, the experts are asked to place the policy alternatives on the policy scales to represent their judgement on the political distances among the alternative outcomes. In all of the analyses performed in this volume, the policy

[4] Note that the presence of a tobacco industry did not necessarily determine the positions on this or any of the other issues. The UK, for example, which is home to large tobacco companies, took a position in the public health camp.

scales are standardised so that the end points correspond with the values 0 and 100.

The criteria an issue specification must meet can be summarised as follows:

- The most basic criterion is that at least some of the actors involved in the decision-making must take different positions on each issue. If the actors take the same positions there is no political problem to be analysed.
- The points on the issue continuum must be defined in terms of the alternative decision outcomes regarding the issue. These decision outcomes may be supported by one or more of the actors involved, or may be possible compromise outcomes.
- The issues must be defined as uni-dimensional continua, on which the actors can be placed in order to represent the possible decision outcomes they favour.

The requirement that a *limited* number of issues be specified is in itself a useful exercise, because it helps the researchers and experts to distinguish between the main points and subordinate ones. The number of issues required varies between decision situations. Each of the Commission proposals in the data set contains between one and six issues, and the average number of issues in the 66 proposals is 2.5 (Table 2.1).

A distinction can be made between three different types of issues, relating to the way in which the distances between the policy alternatives referred to on the continua are conceived. The most common type of issue (109 of the 162 issues in our data set) is a ranked ordering of different policy alternatives. Both issues in the example given in Figure 2.1 can be described as ranked orderings. The experts are asked to locate the policy alternatives and the actors on the continuum so that the distances between them reflect the expert's view on the political distances among them. Positions on the continua that lie between defined points (for example, positions between 0 and 50 on Issue 1 in Figure 2.1), do not have substantive meanings, other than 'closer to' or 'further from' other points on the scale that have been given a defined meaning. When there are only two alternatives, and the outcome has to be one of these, the issues are described as dichotomous (33 of the 162 issues). Finally, some of the issues approach a scale level of measurement, such that all points on the continua have substantive meanings (20 of the 162 issues). These scale issues usually refer to the size of a budget to be allocated to a particular programme.

2.4 EXPERT JUDGEMENTS ON ACTORS AND THEIR POSITIONS

Regarding each issue, the experts were asked to:

> indicate the policy alternative *initially* favoured by each stakeholder *after the introduction of the proposal before the Council formulated its common position.*[5]

The actors were placed on the issue continua to represent the alternatives they favoured most. In Commission proposals with two or more issues, the positioning of the actors on all the issues describes the outcome they favour regarding the Commission proposal as a whole. The experts were first asked to identify the actors who took the most extreme positions on each issue continuum, and were then asked to place the actors, if any, who took intermediate positions. Returning to the issue of whether EU rules on yield levels should apply to cigarettes manufactured for export outside the EU, the experts indicated that Germany, Greece, Spain, Luxembourg and Austria were initially against this, while the other actors were in favour. Throughout the interview, the experts were asked to provide justifications for the information and estimates they provided: why did each of the actors favour the alternatives they did, and why were certain positions perceived to be closer than others? This provided much qualitative information to accompany the numerical estimates, and also allowed the interviewers to evaluate the informants' expertise. On the cigarette export issue, the opponents of the application of EU rules argued that this directive was an internal market directive (Article 95), and that goods intended for export had no bearing on the internal market. Further, it was argued that this could lead to the relocation of manufacturing outside the EU.

The actors whose most favoured positions were obtained are the European Commission, the 15 member states, and the European Parliament. The practitioners of EU affairs we interviewed found this list of actors to be an appropriate description of the constellation of actors involved at this level and stage of decision-making. If these actors are

[5] In practice, the experts used terms such as 'preferences', 'positions' and 'initially most favoured positions' interchangeably. As stated in the text, the question posed concerned the 'policy alternative initially favoured' by each actor. After posing this question, two interviewers asked in total 15 experts whether they could distinguish between these 'initially favoured policy alternatives', actors' 'preferences' or their 'initial bargaining positions'. Although the experts recognised that shifts in the positions supported by the actors did occur regularly, none of them could distinguish empirically between actors' preferences and their initial positions.

to influence decision-making in the EU, they must define their position coherently and behave, as it were, as unitary actors. The experts usually had little difficulty in identifying a single decision outcome for each actor on each issue that could be described as the outcome most favoured by that actor. Similarly, the experts elected to describe the EP as a unitary actor, and to describe the decision outcomes it favoured in terms of the positions it communicated to the Commission and the Council.[6] Clearly, the Commission and the European Parliament usually do not act as unitary actors at other stages of the decision-making process. As discussed in the introductory chapter, intense debates often take place within the Commission during the preparation of legislative proposals. Furthermore the party, and occasionally national, factions in the EP make the parliament appear anything but united. However, when interacting with the Council, these supranational institutions almost invariably take single positions, which are the result of internal discussions. Decision-making within the Commission and the EP does not fall within the scope of the present research.

The expert judgements refer to the policy alternatives actors favoured most. Experts are expected to base these judgements on their knowledge of the preferences expressed by the actors in the discussions and their knowledge of the interests of these actors. Therefore, actors' most favoured positions may differ from the positions they express in the meetings during the discussion of the issues. It is highly doubtful, however, that these estimates refer to some ideal preference, that is independent of these collective actors' judgements on the internal and external acceptability of the positions they take. The position favoured by a member state in the Council, for instance, is likely to be defined by a variety of pressures on the core executive that instructs the member state's representative on what position to take in the Council discussions. In this respect, any notion that the actors we investigate hold preferences that can be disentangled from what they perceive to be realistic would be naive.

There is a clear distinction between actors' most favoured policy alternatives and the policy alternatives they were willing to accept or

6 We explicitly asked the experts to define the most favoured positions of the party factions in the European Parliament (EP) on the issues that were said to be relevant to each Commission proposal. The experts elected to define the EP as a unitary actor in its dealings with the Council and the Commission, and to describe its most favoured positions accordingly.

eventually accepted in the form of the decision outcome. In practice, when policy experts are asked to focus on the specific issues that were at stake in a negotiation, it is possible for them to distinguish between what the actors wanted, and what they were prepared to accept. The time period is particularly important in this respect. Specifically, the experts are asked to provide information on the policy alternatives most favoured by the actors immediately after the introduction of the Commission's proposal. These most favoured alternatives usually differ from the policy alternatives the actors eventually accepted in the form of the decision outcome. There are 162 issues in the data set with information on the policy alternatives actors favoured most, and information on the policy alternative that became the decision outcome. On average 15.61 actors were attributed a 'most favoured alternative'. This means there are 2,529 'most favoured outcomes' in the data set. Of these, only 706 correspond to the alternative that became the decision outcome. Clearly, the experts were able to distinguish between the policies actors favoured, and the policy alternatives they eventually accepted as the decision outcome. This indicates clearly that the experts were able to distinguish between these concepts.

The experts frequently indicated that several actors did not have a most favoured position on one or more of the issues dealt with in a Commission proposal. As indicated in Table 2.4, on 94 of the 162 issues (58 per cent) all 17 actors had a most favoured policy alternative; on the remaining 68 issues, there was at least one actor who was said to be indifferent, or not to have participated in the decision-making for other reasons. This is a common occurrence in decision-making in the EU (see Appendix II). Nevertheless, this does pose a challenge for some of the explanatory models applied in this book: those that require that each of the actors are allocated a position somewhere in the policy space. For example, it is common that Luxembourg and Austria do not participate in discussions on fisheries dossiers, since they have little interest in this policy area. On average, 15.61 of the 17 actors took positions on each of the 162 issues in the data set. It should be noted that the term 'missing values' is misleading in this case; in principle, this does not concern information that should be there but is not, due to errors in the data collection procedure. Rather, it refers to cases where the experts indicated that certain actors did not take positions. As will be discussed in Section 2.7, on the application and testing of the models, this has implications for the way in which such cases should be handled by models that assume all actors have positions.

Table 2.4. *Numbers of actors who took positions on issues*

Number of actors with positions (max: 17)	2–5	6–10	11	13	14	15	16	17	Total
Number of issues on which the above number of actors had favourite positions	3	7	3	8	4	14	29	94	162

In addition to the actors' most favoured policy alternatives, where possible, the decision outcome that would prevail if the legislative proposal in question were not adopted was identified as a position on each issue continuum. We refer to this policy alternative as the reference point. This concept bears a close relation to the *status quo* position. The *status quo* position is the current state of affairs at a given point in time. The reference point refers to the outcome that would prevail if the legislation in question were not passed. In many cases, this will be the same as the *status quo* position before the introduction of the Commission's proposal. However, in some cases, failure to adopt the legislation would not lead to the continuation of the *status quo*. For example, failure to pass a decision allocating funds to a particular programme would not necessarily mean that the previous funding continues. Instead, such a failure may lead to no funds at all being allocated to the programme in question.

It was not possible to define a reference point on all of the issues. The absence of a reference point often has to do with the absence of a single decision outcome that would prevail for all member states if the legislative proposal were not passed. Particularly in policy areas where there is no or little EU-level regulation, there are a wide variety of national provisions (Dimitrova and Steunenberg 2001). In such cases it is often impossible to identify a single point on the issue continuum to describe the decision outcome that would prevail if the proposal were not adopted. For example, a proposal to introduce a common regulatory framework for company takeovers was rejected by the EP and was therefore not adopted. One of the controversial issues was about the degree to which management bodies should have autonomy to take defensive measures to prevent their company from being taken over. The failure of the proposal meant that different legal arrangements persisted in the EU. Models that require a single reference point cannot therefore be applied to all the cases in the data set. On 126 of the 162 issues, the experts did find it possible to define single points on the issue continua to describe the reference points; on 36 issues this was not possible.

The decision outcome on each of the 162 issues was described as a point on the issue continuum. Note that the decision outcome need not necessarily correspond to the position favoured initially by any of the actors. It may, for example, also be a point on the continuum somewhere between the actors' favoured positions, a compromise solution that was perhaps not even foreseen before the discussions took place. The models are tested by the extent to which they are able to generate accurate predictions of these decision outcomes.

Identifying the appropriate level of analysis: issues or underlying dimensions?

It was indicated that the models are tested on the basis of their predictions of decision outcomes on the issues described to us by experts. An alternative might have been to identify underlying dimensions in the preferences of the actors, and to apply our models to the actors' positions on these dimensions. For example, we might have found an 'Integration-Independence dimension', or a 'Left-Right dimension' on which the actors could be ordered consistently. This would have required that there be consistent alignments of actors on the issues, or at least on a subset of issues related to each other. Instead, we find a considerable amount of variety in the placement of actors, such that actors who support similar positions on one issue support different positions on others.

To the extent that there is a structure in the positioning of the actors' positions, it is weak. There is, for instance, a tendency for the Commission to be located at one end of the issue continua and the reference point at the other; this configuration is found in around a third of the issues. However, the issues on which this pattern is found concern all kinds of topics and themes. In addition, there is a tendency for northern and southern member states to take different positions. This tendency is also evident in around a third of the issues. For the most part, these north-south issues concern choices between free market and regulatory based solutions, whereby the northerners tend to be more in favour of free market policies. However, there are also many other issues in the data set about the strength of regulations where other alignments of actors are found. There is evidence that the weakness of the conceptual structures is due to the sectoral nature of

EU decision-making, whereby different interests are important depending on the issues at stake. The alignments of actors are discussed in an article by Thomson, Boerefijn and Stokman (2004).[7]

The lack of consistency in the alignment of actors on different issues is illustrated by the example of the tobacco products directive depicted in Figure 2.1. On the first issue, about the export of tobacco products, the Commission's most favoured position is at the extreme of the continuum: position 100, that the EU rules on maximum yield levels should apply to all products intended for export. On the second issue, about the size and strength of the health warning on tobacco products, the Commission favours a position at the centre of the continuum: position 50, that 25 per cent of the packaging should be covered with the health warning. Similarly, for example, on the first issue the Spanish delegation favoured an outcome opposite to the one supported by the Commission. But on the second issue, the Spanish favoured the same position as the Commission. So even on issues within the same proposal, we encounter substantially different alignments of actors. It was therefore decided to base the analysis on the issue scales formulated with the experts.

2.5 ESTIMATING SALIENCE

The experts were also asked to estimate the level of salience or importance each of the actors attached to each of the issues. This variable is used in some, but not all, of the models applied in this book. The models that use this variable incorporate it in different ways. These will be described in the relevant chapters. Broadly speaking, two related interpretations of this concept can be found in the bargaining models. In the first, salience is interpreted as the proportion of an actor's potential capabilities it is willing to mobilise in attempts to influence the decision outcome. In the second, salience is understood as the extent to which actors experience utility loss from the occurrence of decision outcomes

[7] The paper referred to (Thomson, Boerefijn and Stokman 2004) applies multidimensional scaling and correlation analyses to 70 Commission proposals and 174 issues. There are an additional four Commission proposals and 12 issues in our data set on which there is no information on the decision outcomes (they were still pending at the end of our study). These cases do not enable us to test models of decision-making, but they do provide information on the alignment of actors on the issues.

that differ from the decision outcomes they most favour. In the Nash bargaining framework, discussed by Christopher Achen in Chapter 4, 'salience' describes the sharpness in the curvature of the actor's loss function. Actors who attach high levels of salience to an issue are highly sensitive to small deviations from their most favoured positions, while actors who attach low levels of salience are less sensitive.

When introducing this concept to the experts, it was explained that actors may differ from each other in the salience or importance they attach to each of the issues. The policy experts were asked to estimate the level of importance each actor attached to each issue on a scale from 0 to 100. The scale was described as follows:

> A score of 100 indicates that an issue is of the highest importance to a stakeholder, while a score of zero indicates that the issue is of no importance whatsoever to a stakeholder. A score of 50 indicates that the issue has an average level of priority for the stakeholder concerned, and that it is willing to use arguments but not power politics to convince opponents. Note that it is possible for a stakeholder to attach a high level of salience to an issue on which it takes a moderate position, and a low level of salience to an issue on which it takes an extreme position.

Although it is difficult to ascribe a definite meaning to each possible salience score between 0 and 100, this description was a useful heuristic aid to the experts when providing the estimates. The relations between the estimates for different actors and between different issues for the same actors are more important than the absolute values. As with the most favoured policy positions, it was important to obtain substantive arguments for the salience estimates: why did the different actors attach different levels of salience to the same issues, and why did any one actor attach different levels of salience to the different issues?

The salience estimates on the tobacco products directive are contained in parentheses in Figure 2.1. They indicate that the first issue, on the export of cigarettes, was more important than the second issue, on the health warnings, to the actors who favoured the continuation of the *status quo*. For example, Germany attached more importance to the export issue than the health warnings issue. These actors were said to expect more negative economic effects from a policy change on the export rules than from a change to the health warnings. Applying EU rules on yield levels (of tar, nicotine and carbon monoxide) means that certain products can no longer be manufactured for export. By contrast, the introduction of large health warnings does not affect products intended for export outside the EU; the warnings need only be applied to products marketed in the EU. The EP and the UK delegation attached more importance to the issue of health warnings than the export issue. This was said to be due to the fact that the public health lobby focused most on this issue, and had particular influence over these actors. The health warnings issue was also a simple and visible issue that the politicians in the EP could capitalise on.

In the present study, the concepts of position and salience are conceptually and empirically distinct. According to the definitions and operationalisations employed here, it is possible for an actor to take a moderate or extreme position on an issue continuum and attach either a high or a low level of salience to the issue. It is perhaps intuitively plausible that actors who take more extreme positions on an issue also attach higher levels of salience to the issue concerned. However, overall, there is only a modest positive correlation between the extremity of actors' positions and the levels of salience they attach to the issues.[8]

2.6 CAPABILITIES OF ACTORS

Some of the models require a measure of actors' capabilities. This is a challenging concept to quantify. Academics and practitioners hold different views on the distribution of capabilities among the actors involved in EU decision-making. Consequently, we experimented with three alternative measures of actors' capabilities: expert judgements and two variants of Shapley Shubik Index (SSI) scores. The authors of the following chapters whose models require a measure of actors' capabilities were invited to experiment with these three measures. The second variant of the Shapley Shubik Index scores, described below, is based solely on the formal rules of decision-making; the first variant is not. As such, this second variant is in keeping with the definition of the Shapley Shubik

[8] Rank order correlations were calculated between the extremity of actors' positions and the level of salience they attached to each issue. These correlations were calculated issue by issue. The extremity of the actors' positions was measured in two ways: first as the distance to the median position, and second as the distance to the mean position. Issues on which five or more actors did not take positions and in which there was no variance in the distance between the actors' positions and the mean and median were excluded. This meant that the correlations were calculated for 137 of the 162 issues in the data set. The average correlation between the (rank order of) level of salience and the (rank order of) extremity of the positions was .31 using the mean measure of extremity and .27 using the median measure of extremity. On 28 of the 137 issues there was a negative correlation, indicating the presence of a tendency for more extreme actors to attach lower levels of salience to the issues.

Index, while the first is not. This second variant was also found to enable the models to generate the most accurate predictions. The following chapters therefore concentrate on the results based on this measure of actors' capabilities, but often refer to the results based on the other measures in footnotes. This section provides an overview of all three alternative measures of actors' capabilities.

While the expert judgements provide an interesting indication of informed opinion on the weight of the actors in the decision-making process, key informants' responses are often difficult to interpret unambiguously. This difficulty was also identified by J. LaPalombara in an early pioneering study:

> The concept of 'power' (or 'influence') is not easy to define, and, even after the interviewer suggests a definition, he cannot be certain that the respondents adhere to a specific denotation in their evaluations. (1960: 30).

The advantage of the Shapley Shubik Index scores is the transparency of the reasoning that produces the estimates. Applying alternative estimates of actors' capabilities allows us to test the robustness of the models' performance, and their sensitivity to different assumptions on the distribution of capabilities between the actors.

Expert judgements

The reason for seeking to obtain expert judgements on the distributions of capabilities among the actors has to do with the definition of this concept. In particular, the models that contain this concept are often constructed with the intention of understanding the bargaining process that takes place prior to the voting stage. This means that capabilities are not conceived of as being based solely on formal, institutionally defined powers, such as the number of votes in the Council, and the ability to introduce and amend, or propose amendments to legislation. Instead, capabilities also include informal resources, such as financial resources, access to other actors, leadership over a large number of individuals, and the efficiency and expertise of the bureaucracy at an actor's disposal. All these resources may help an actor to change the behaviour of others in a way that is advantageous to it, and to influence the decision outcome.

Experts were asked to provide judgements on the distribution of capabilities among the 17 actors. When doing so, they were asked to discuss, compare and combine different types of resources. These interviews were conducted separately from the interviews on particular Commission proposals; estimates of the distribution of capabilities were not linked to particular Commission proposals, but rather with certain policy areas or legislative procedures. In total 23 experts were selected to provide judgements on the distribution of capabilities. Five were selected due to the fact that in the interviews on particular Commission proposals, they displayed a broad knowledge of EU affairs and an ability to quantify their judgements. Most were selected on the basis of their professional position; they had been working in the EU for many years and/or had attained a position such that they had a vantage point from which to observe the effects of the relative capabilities of the actors in a range of dossiers. Again, the interviews on capabilities were held with individuals from the European Commission, the Council and the European Parliament.

It was left to the experts themselves to decide whether they wanted to discuss the distribution of capabilities in relation to a particular policy area (of the ones included in our selection), or in relation to a particular legislative procedure (co-decision or consultation). We then described the concept of capabilities to the informants. An actor's capability is its potential to influence other actors and the decision outcome, and can be based on a variety of different resources. The informants were first asked to rate the capabilities of the three institutions – the Commission, the Council and the EP – relative to each other. As with all the other variables discussed above, throughout the interviews the experts were asked to justify and illustrate their estimates qualitatively. These interviews resulted in 36 sets of estimates on the relative capabilities of the three institutions, 18 relating to the co-decision procedure and 18 relating to the consultation procedure. Most of the experts held a view of the distribution of capabilities that can only be described as supranational. They ascribed high levels of capabilities to the European Commission, and (somewhat less to) the European Parliament: the EP was judged to be almost on a par with the Council of Ministers in the co-decision procedure. A minority of experts held a different view: one that can be described as a governmentalist view. These experts ascribed modest capability scores to the Commission relative to the Council. These different views did not correspond to the institutional affiliation of the experts who provided the judgements.[9] Rather than taking the average of these

[9] For instance, the experts from the permanent representations of the member states did not provide consistently higher or lower estimates of the Commission or the European Parliament in relation to the Council compared with the estimates of

fundamentally different views, the statistical outliers were first identified and excluded; the minority governmentalist estimates were excluded, as were two estimates that were judged not to be sufficiently motivated by the experts using argumentation.

The relative capabilities of the three institutions were found to differ most between the co-decision and the consultation procedures: the rather obvious difference being that the EP was rated lower under the consultation procedure than under the co-decision procedure. The differences between the estimates relating to policy areas that fall under the same legislative procedure (for example fisheries and agriculture, which are both usually subject to consultation with the European Parliament and qualified majority voting (QMV) in the Council) were not substantial. Further, the experts made no distinction between the relative power of the institutions when unanimity was required in the Council as opposed to QMV. We therefore took the average of the estimates relating to each of the two legislative procedures. The information in Table 2.5 indicates that with regard to the co-decision procedure, on average the experts rated the capabilities of the Commission at 95, relative to the Council at 100 and the EP at 87. With regard to the consultation procedure, the average estimates of the relative capabilities of the three institutions were 92 for the Commission, 100 for the Council, and 34 for the EP.[10]

The Commission's right to initiate legislative proposals was often given as a reason behind its high capability score: in particular, its ability to formulate the contents of these proposals. Since these proposals form the basis of the policy discussions, the Commission is able to frame

experts from those institutions. On the consultation procedure, six experts from the permanent representations provided the following average estimates: Commission, 72.1 (standard deviation 50.6) and EP, 23.0 (standard deviation 29.9) relative to the Council of 100. Ten experts from the Commission provided the following capability estimates on the consultation procedure: Commission, 86.9 (standard deviation 36.8) and EP, 35.0 (Standard deviation 14.2) relative to the Council of 100. For the co-decision procedure, the experts from the permanent representations attributed on average somewhat higher capability scores to the Commission than did the experts from the Commission.

[10] For illustrative purposes, the numbers contained in Table 2.5 are standardised so that the institution with the highest capability score has 100. The experts were free to describe the relations using any numbers with which they felt comfortable and could justify using argumentation. For example, they might have said 'one-third for each of the institutions', which would be standardised as 100 for each of the institutions in Table 2.5.

the talks in the stage of decision-making after the introduction of its proposals. Its proposals have already passed through the College of Commissioners from all member states. In addition, during the pre-proposal stage, extensive consultations are often held with stakeholders in the policy area. Depending on the importance of the proposal, these consultations sometimes include the Council members and Members of the European Parliament (MEPs). This is said to give the Commission and its proposals enormous authority. At the stage of the introduction of the proposal, the Commission has almost invariably formulated a unitary position, since any dissent within the Commission has been resolved during the formulation stage. This, it was said, puts the Commission at an advantage in relation to the Council, in which a range of views is voiced by different member states. Compared to any of the other actors, the Commission was said to have some of the best expertise on the workings of the policy areas and the political system of the EU. Its adeptness at forging political deals between other actors was also listed as an aspect of its capabilities. The above-mentioned arguments were some of those used to justify the estimate that the Commission has great potential to influence decision-making during the post-proposal stage.

In the same way, the experts were also asked to rate the relative capabilities of the member states in the Council (Figure 2.2).[11] First, they were asked to identify the actor or actors with the highest level of capabilities: then, to rank the other actors relative to this score. Once again, many of the experts opted to discuss the relative capabilities in relation to a particular policy area. However, on inspection, their estimates did not vary substantially among the different policy areas.[12] The average estimates are very close to the relations among the number of votes the actors have under QMV. With regard to some countries, adjustments were made to reflect what the experts thought to be a more accurate assessment of their potential influence. In particular, while the

[11] The estimates on the relative capabilities of the Council members are based on 14 sets of estimates from experts in the Commission and the Council. The experts' estimates of the capabilities of their own member state were excluded from the calculations of the average scores. This did not, however, change the results. For a more extensive discussion of the relative capabilities of the member states using expert judgements see Bailer (2004).

[12] The most noteworthy difference concerned the capabilities of Luxembourg and Austria in the area of fisheries. As mentioned above, for obvious reasons these two actors often do not participate in discussions on fisheries dossiers. The experts estimated that they had little or no capabilities in this policy area.

number of QMV votes held by Italy would suggest that it should be on a par with France, Germany and the UK, Italy was generally judged to have a lower level of capabilities than these actors. Many of the informants attributed this to the inefficiency of Italian bureaucratic support for its permanent representation in Brussels. Germany was also judged to have a somewhat lower level of capabilities than its number of votes would suggest. This was attributed to the federal structure, as a result of which the German position on Commission proposals often only became clear relatively late in the discussions. The experts did not distinguish between the relative capabilities of the actors under qualified majority voting and unanimity in the Council. It should be noted that these estimates refer to the capabilities of the actors in the stage of decision-making prior to the final vote.

Shapley Shubik Index (SSI) scores

In addition to the expert judgements on the relative capabilities of the three institutions and the Council members, estimates of the capabilities of the actors based on Shapley Shubik Index (SSI) scores were used (Shapley and Shubik 1954; Napel and Widgrén 2002a). This is a voting power index that has been applied in many previous studies of decision-making in other settings. This index provides an approximation of the power of actors involved in a situation in which a vote must be taken before a decision can be taken. The SSI score focuses on the number of times an actor is pivotal in a coalition, in the sense that it turns a losing coalition into a winning one. It is based solely on information regarding the voting rules. To apply this index, a list is first compiled of all possible permutations of the actors involved in the decision situation. For each possible permutation of actors, the actor that turns a losing coalition into a winning one is identified, and said to be pivotal. The number of times an actor is pivotal divided by the total number of times all actors are pivotal is the actor's SSI power score.

To apply SSI to decision-making in the EU, the composition of winning coalitions must first be established, taking into account the inter-institutional nature of decision-making in the EU (Napel and Widgén 2002a). Two different ways of thinking about the composition of winning coalitions were identified, which yield two variants of the SSI scores:

- In the first variant, the Commission is always included as a member of the winning coalition under both the co-decision and the consultation

procedures. Under co-decision with QMV voting in the Council, the winning coalition consists of the Commission, a qualified majority of member states, and the EP. Under consultation with QMV voting in the Council, the winning coalition consists of the Commission and a qualified majority of member states.
- In the second variant, the Commission is not necessarily a member of the winning coalitions. Under co-decision with QMV voting in the Council, all winning coalitions require only a qualified majority of member states and the EP. Under consultation with QMV voting in the Council, there are two types of winning coalitions. The first consists of the Commission and a qualified majority of member states; the second of all Council members.

The figures in Table 2.5 show that these different assumptions result in different capability weights for the three institutions. Both variants attribute lower capability scores to the Commission and EP than the experts do. Under consultation, for example, the EP has a score of zero, since it is not pivotal to any winning coalition. Calculating the SSI scores under the assumption that the Commission need not always be present in the winning coalition produces the lowest capability scores for the Commission.

Note that the first variant of the SSI scores are not in fact Shapley Shubik Index scores in any standard sense, because they incorporate information other than that included in the formal decision rules. The reason for including the Commission in the winning coalitions in the first variant of the SSI scores is that the support or at least acquiescence of the Commission is often considered necessary before legislation can be adopted. Therefore, the SSI scores based on this assumption might bear a more accurate resemblance to the inter-institutional power relations in the EU than does the second variant. However, legally the Commission is not necessarily a member of the winning coalitions; a unanimous Council could overrule the Commission, and the Council and the EP could reach a decision under co-decision without the support of the Commission. As such, the second variant of the SSI scores, which allow for the possibility that the Commission is not a member of the winning coalition, are based more faithfully on the formal decision rules. It also turns out that the models generally predict more accurately using this second variant of the SSI scores.

Unlike the expert judgements, the SSI values for the three institutions differ dramatically between the QMV and the unanimity variants of both the co-decision and the consultation procedures. For example, while the

Table 2.5. *Relative power of EU institutions: expert judgements and Shapley Shubik Index (SSI) scores*[a]

	Commission	Council	EP
Co-decision			
Expert judgements (both QMV and unanimity)	95	100	87
SSI 1st variant—with Commission always in winning coalition			
QMV	52	100	52
Unanimity	7	100	7
SSI 2nd variant—Commission not needed in winning coalition			
QMV	0	100	45
Unanimity	0	100	7
Consultation			
Expert judgements (both QMV and unanimity)	92	100	34
SSI 1st variant—with Commission always in winning coalition (unanimous Council cannot overrule)			
QMV	45	100	0
Unanimity	7	100	0
SSI 2nd variant—Commission not in all winning coalitions (unanimous Council may overrule)			
QMV	33	100	0
Unanimity	0	100	0

Note: [a]Expert judgements on the capabilities of the institutions under co-decision are based on 11 estimates; those on consultation on 17 estimates. Scores are standardised so that the Council has a score of 100 and the other institutions are rated relative to the Council.

Commission and the EP both have a score of 52 per cent (according to the first SSI variant) of the Council total under co-decision QMV, their SSI scores under the unanimity variant are only seven per cent of the Council total.

Within the Council, the SSI scores relating to the QMV versions of both procedures bear a close resemblance to the number of qualified majority votes held by the member states (Figure 2.2). Under the unanimity versions of both procedures, however, all actors in the Council have equal weight. This is because the voting power index is based solely on the composition of the winning coalition, as defined by the voting rules.

2.7 APPLICATION AND TESTING OF MODELS

The explanatory models applied in this book differ from each other not only with respect to their hypotheses on the processes through which

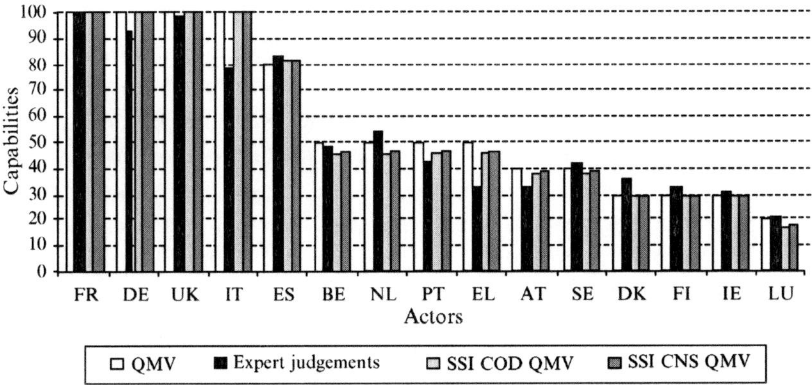

[a]QMV scores are the qualified majority voting weights multiplied by ten. Capability scores were standardised so that the Council member with the highest score has 100 and others are rated relative to that member.

Figure 2.2. Relative capabilities within Council[a]

actors' positions are transformed into collective outcomes. In addition, they also differ somewhat regarding the input variables they require, and in their conception of the political space in which actors operate. The models are tested against each other, and against baseline models, by the extent to which they are able to forecast decision outcomes accurately. The particular research design decisions that need to be taken before each model can be applied to the data will be discussed in the chapters devoted to each approach. This section aims to provide an overview of the main decisions that have to be taken in this regard.

Despite the fact that all models generate forecasts of the decision outcomes on the issue continua, there are alternative ways of conceptualising the political space in which the EU actors operate. At the simplest level, each issue continuum within each Commission proposal could be treated separately. This accords with the view, and some reports by participants of what is actually common practice in the Council, that the controversial aspects of a Commission proposal are dealt with point by point, rather than discussing all aspects of a proposal at the same time. A second way of conceptualising the political space is to allow for linkages between the separate issues dealt with in the framework of a Commission proposal. According to this conceptualisation, which is the one used for example in the exchange model discussed later by Arregui, Stokman and Thomson, actors can still make clear distinctions between the separate issues. A third possible conceptualisation is that the issues raised by a Commission proposal are conceptualised as dimensions of a multi-dimensional space. This implies that the actors evaluate other positions in the space not on the basis of the distances between their locations on the separate issues, but rather in terms of the distance between the points in the two or more dimensions that make up the space. With regard to some of the models, the conceptualisation of the space is not inherent in the theory on which the model is based. Instead, the conceptualisation of this space is a research design decision taken when applying the models to the data.

In some models, indifferent actors are regarded as simply not present, so that the decision is settled among the others. Other models, however, assume that all actors always have a preference, and need to include an assumption about the location of indifferent actors on the issue continua. Where necessary, the authors of the subsequent chapters were invited to formulate an assumption such that the indifferent actors interfere as little as possible with the logic of their model. Indifferent actors are assumed to take a position such that the decision outcome agreed on by the other actors is allowed to pass. A good solution is the assumption that the indifferent actors are located half way between the reference point and the most favoured position of the actor who is able to introduce a proposal, the so-called agenda setter. The effect of this assumption is that all proposals made by this agenda setter are acceptable to the indifferent actors.[13]

As mentioned in the previous section, some of the explanatory models presented in the following chapters require estimates of actors' capabilities. The selection of a set of capability estimates may also be considered a research design decision. The second variant of the Shapley Shubik Index scores described above, in which the Commission is not always required in a winning coalition, is preferred by all researchers whose models need such estimates. Not only is this second variant in line with the standard definition of the SSI, models loaded with this set of estimates were found to generate the most accurate predictions. The authors of the following chapters have been invited to report on the effects on their models' predictions of applying different assumptions regarding indifferent actors and capabilities. As mentioned above, not all of the

[13] Some of the authors also experimented with the assumption that the indifferent actors took the same position as the Commission. In general, when the models were applied using this assumption, they generated less accurate predictions.

models featured in this volume require estimates of the actors' capabilities. By comparing these models with those that do, we are able to test whether this additional information contributes to more accurate forecasts.

In the subsequent chapters the models' forecasts are compared with the actual decision outcomes to evaluate their accuracy. In each of the modelling chapters, a model's error on an issue is defined as the distance between the location of its prediction of the decision outcome as a point on the issue continuum, and the location of the actual decision outcome. The issue continua are standardised such that the end-points are represented by the numbers 0 and 100. Therefore, the minimum error a model can make is 0 and the maximum is 100 (providing the actual outcome is either 0 or 100). In each of the following chapters, the average of the absolute errors of each model across all issues is calculated and compared. Some of the models are not able to generate predictions on all 162 issues, due, for example, to the absence of a point on the continuum that represents the reference point. Each of the chapters reports the mean average errors by legislative procedure (whether the issues are subject to co-decision or consultation), policy area, and the type of issue (whether they are dichotomous, rank ordered or scale issues). This provides an indication of the relative performance of the models under different conditions. The main model comparison exercise takes place in Chapter 10, however. There, Christopher Achen examines alternative ways of gauging the predictive accuracy of models, and compares the best models from each of the preceding chapters against each other.

3

Testing procedural models of EU legislative decision-making

BERNARD STEUNENBERG AND TORSTEN J. SELCK

3.1 INTRODUCTION

The view that institutions are important to decision-making has led to a large number of game-theoretical models that aim to understand and explain the European Union's legislative process. As these models stress the sequential features of the legislative process as well as the differences in decision-making power of the various actors involved, they are referred to as *procedural* models. Departing from the 'older' legislative procedures, such as the consultation procedure (Steunenberg 1994a; Crombez 1996) and the cooperation procedure (Tsebelis 1994; Moser 1997a), this literature has expanded to include the more recently adopted procedures, including the two different versions of the co-decision procedure (Garrett 1995; Crombez 1997, 2000a; 2006; 2000c; Steunenberg 1997).[1] In this chapter, we focus on the procedural models developed for the European Union and test some of these models empirically.

We thank the members of the Decision-making in the European Union (DEU) group, Christophe Crombez and Antoaneta Dimitrova, for their helpful comments. We thank Leo van Nierop for research support. We acknowledge financial support from the Netherlands Organization for Scientific Research (NWO).

[1] Steunenberg (1994a), Crombez (1996), Steunenberg and Dimitrova (1999), and Laruelle (2002) present comparative analyses of different procedures. In addition, Tsebelis (1994), Moser (1996; 1997a), and Schneider (1995) discuss the cooperation procedure. Furthermore, Garrett and Tsebelis (1996), Moser (1997b), Tsebelis (1997), Tsebelis and Garrett (1996; 1997a). Scully (1997a; 1997b), and Schneider (1995) pay attention to the Maastricht version of the co-decision procedure. The Amsterdam version of the co-decision procedure is discussed by Crombez (2000a; 2003), Steunenberg (2000a; 2001), Tsebelis and Garrett (2000; 2001), and Laruelle (2002). In addition, Steunenberg *et al* (1996; 1997) have modelled

The procedural models of EU decision-making are related to a broader rational choice literature in which political outcomes are regarded as the combined result of political preferences and institutions (Shepsle 1989; Shepsle and Weingast 1995; Ostrom 1986; Dowding 2002). This literature developed as a response to studies, especially focused on the United States Congress, which approached politics as a simple account of majority rule. The main expectation from these studies was that voting cycles might frequently occur, which would make politics chaotic and arbitrary, and make it almost impossible to predict outcomes. The new literature on rational choice modelling, however, suggests that stable outcomes can be achieved as a result of structural constraints on the decision-making process imposed by existing institutions. Institutions, according to this approach, define the behavioural opportunities of political actors in the sense that they indicate who is allowed to participate in the decision-making process (the 'players', in game-theoretic terms), the decision-making rights of these players (the feasible 'strategies' available to the players), the order in which these players take a decision (the 'sequence of play'), and the way in which players' choices translate into outcomes ('aggregation rules'). This constraining effect of institutions is central to the approach that forms the basis of the concept of 'structure-induced equilibrium' (Shepsle 1979; Shepsle and Weingast 1981). Institutional rational choice theory assumes that institutions structure the decision-making process, which will be reflected in the outcome, i.e. in the policies that will be enacted. Politics is then the strategic interaction between political actors within a certain institutional setting.

The view that the institutional setting has an impact on outcome is particularly relevant to the European Union. The fact that the member states decided to establish *different* legislative procedures in the treaties suggests that they, at least, had the idea that these procedures matter and that they have an impact on outcomes. This raises questions such as how these legislative procedures affect outcomes in a context of different and possibly opposing interests, and why the member states agreed to a certain alternative. The procedural models aim to explain these outcomes as the interplay of preferences, institutions and the current state of affairs, which are assumed to constitute the key elements of politics.

Due to the view that institutions matter, the procedural models are highly sensitive to the way in which the political process is structured.

the implementation or *comitology* procedures in a similar way, while Feld *et al* (2002) focus on the Union's budgetary procedures.

Differences in the types of actors involved, the proposed sequence of play, the allocation of decision-making rights, or the translation of votes into outcomes, have an impact on the predicted outcomes. Consequently, differences in the interpretation of some of the EU's legislative procedures have triggered various theoretical debates. Moser (1996) as well as Scully (1997a; 1997b), for example, disagrees with Tsebelis (1996) and Tsebelis and Garrett (1997a) on the importance of the European Parliament and the Commission under the cooperation procedure. Crombez (1996) and Moser (1997a) disagree with Steunenberg (1994a) on whether the Commission can use its formal power of legislative initiative to block new initiatives under the consultation procedure. While Steunenberg allows the Commission to decide whether or not to initiate a new proposal in his representation of the consultation procedure, Crombez and Moser do not include this option in their models.

With regard to the co-decision procedure, as revised by the Amsterdam Treaty (1997)[2], scholars disagree with regard to the role of the Council and Parliament in shaping the final proposal. While most models now focus on the interactions associated with the conciliation committee, the question is whether the decision-making process begins with the Council proposal or amendments made by Parliament. Some authors suggest that the Council takes the lead in this procedure and submits a proposal to Parliament (for instance, Garrett 1995; Crombez 1997; Tsebelis and Garrett 1997a), while others propose the opposite by allowing Parliament to make such an offer (Steunenberg 1997; Crombez 2000a). Depending on specific preference configurations or the location of the legislative *status quo*, these theoretical specifications would lead to different predictions of decision outcomes. While there is hardly any theoretical ground to prefer the one specification to the other, only empirical work is able to decide between these interpretations. The need for empirical research is further indicated by additional discussions in the literature that are based on comparative judgments using these different interpretations. One of these discussions deals with the question of

[2] The Maastricht Treaty (1993) allowed the Council to resubmit its common position to Parliament for a 'yes-no' vote after a failed conciliation attempt. This possibility was severely criticised by Parliament. The member states formally abolished this option as part of the Amsterdam Treaty. See Steunenberg (2000a; 2002a) for a further analysis of these differences.

whether the introduction of the co-decision procedure has been 'a good deal' for Parliament.[3]

Empirical research to support the different claims made has been rather limited. Kreppel (1999), Tsebelis and Kalandrakis (1999), and Tsebelis *et al* (2001) performed tests in which the probability of successful amendments made by the European Parliament is their dependent variable. However, these success rates focus on a procedural instead of a substantive feature of the decision-making process. They do not tell us much about the extent to which models are able to predict the outcome of decision-making in terms of the actual policy set by the actors in the Union. In our view, the formal models of EU decision-making should be tested by comparing the outcomes they predict with the actual policies that result from the interaction between the Commission, the Council, and Parliament (see also Selck and Steunenberg 2004; Selck 2004).

König and Pöter (2001) present such a test for models that were developed for the cooperation procedure. They found that the models proposed by Steunenberg (1994a), Crombez (1996), and Moser (1996) predict marginally better than the ones by Tsebelis (1994) and Tsebelis and Garrett (1997a, 2000).[4] However, König and Pöter's analysis is based on only four Commission proposals. Furthermore, in order to assess the models' predictive power, they present the expected solutions only graphically and not computationally. As a consequence, their findings are rather limited and cannot be related to other legislative decisions that were negotiated under the cooperation procedure.

In this chapter, we discuss the procedural models of EU legislative decision-making and test the predictions that can be derived from these models. In view of the cases available in the data set that is used for this book, we focus on two legislative procedures. These are the consultation procedure and the new version of the co-decision procedure as introduced by the Amsterdam Treaty. With this work, we aim to determine the

[3] Tsebelis and Garrett (2000: 15) state that the change from cooperation to the Maastricht co-decision procedure disadvantaged Parliament. They base this claim on their modelling of the two legislative procedures (see also Tsebelis 1994; Tsebelis and Garrett 1997a). Crombez (2000b), Steunenberg (2000b), and Corbett (2000) question this claim and point towards the fact that Parliament explicitly preferred this procedure to the cooperation procedure. See Garrett and Tsebelis (2001a) and Corbett (2001) for replies in this discussion.

[4] In two of four cases, all four models predict the same outcome. In the other two cases, some limited differences occur between these models.

empirical veracity of the different models, and hope to increase our understanding of the European Union decision-making process as well as in the importance of legislative institutions in general.

3.2 PROCEDURAL MODELS OF LEGISLATIVE CHOICE

Current procedural models address several aspects of the EU legislative process. Although these models share common features, like the use of sequential games of complete and perfect information, they differ in important respects from each other. In particular, they can be distinguished with regard to the identification of the relevant actors (i.e. the players) and the appropriate sequence of play.[5] We now turn to these differences in as far as they are relevant to the two procedures that will be analysed, that is, the consultation and co-decision procedures.

3.2.1 *Who are the players?*

Most procedural models approach the Council and Parliament as committees consisting of a certain number of different players.[6] Combining single-peaked preferences with a one-dimensional space, the Council is conveniently reduced to its 'decisive' member in the case of unanimity or qualified majority voting, while Parliament is characterised by its 'representative' or median voter as it only applies majority voting. The Commission is mostly considered to be a unitary actor. As our data set shows, legislative decision-making in the Union is not restricted to only one issue or dimension. Most cases of decision-making include two or three issues and thus define a multi-dimensional outcome space for which we can no longer rely on these simplifying constructs. In addition, problems arise concerning the handling of multi-member voting bodies since stability in outcomes is no longer guaranteed.

In order to get around this problem, Tsebelis (1994: 138) approaches Parliament as a unitary actor in a two-dimensional outcome space. Modelling the composition of actors in this way allows him to represent

[5] The procedural models can also be distinguished between one-dimensional and more-dimensional models. As this distinction closely relates to the players that are distinguished in these models, we discuss these differences at the same time.

[6] The models by Steunenberg (1994a; 1994b; 1997), Garrett (1995), Crombez (1996; 1997; 2003), Moser (1996; 1997a), Steunenberg and Dimitrova (1999), Tsebelis and Garrett (2000), and Laruelle (2002) are based on a one-dimensional policy space.

Parliament such that it makes a unique offer to the multi-member Council.[7] Other two-dimensional models that follow Tsebelis' simplification with regard to Parliament include Moser (1997a), Hubschmid and Moser (1997), and Steunenberg and Dimitrova (1999). Laruelle (2002) pushes the actor-assumption one step further by treating all European decision-making bodies, including the Council, as unitary actors. Consequently, her model neither asks nor allows for a distinction between qualified majority and unanimity voting, a feature that other analysts consider to be distinctive for the European Union.

Regarding the Council, the question arises how this body would organise its agenda the moment that more alternatives would be possible, especially if the Commission as agenda setter is no longer included in the model. Crombez (1996: 204) suggests that the most conservative member state plays this role, which, in his model with Commission involvement, does not affect the final outcome.[8] An alternative is to introduce the Council Presidency as a 'structure-inducing' agent (Steunenberg and Dimitrova 1999), who presents a bill to the other Council members. Crombez (2000a: 44–5) also adopts this approach and lets the Presidency of each of the main decision-making bodies submit a proposal to the other members, including the Commission and Parliament.

3.2.2 *Which sequence of play is appropriate?*

The sequential nature of the games is based on a stylised representation of the decision-making process in the EU. The rules and procedures of this process, including the allocation of decision-making rights to the various players, form the distinctive features of the procedural models. As authors present different interpretations of this structure, the main differences between procedural models concern this choice.

[7] Note that Tsebelis (1994: 139) bases his analysis on the concept of the 'core' in order to identify a set of stable points in a two- or more-dimensional space. However, as indicated by Greenberg (1979), the core may not exist for qualified majority voting in a space with three or more dimensions. In the case of an empty core, Tsebelis' model is not able to predict a specific outcome for the cooperation procedure.

[8] If the Commission is the initial agenda setter in this game of perfect and complete information, it submits the final proposal that is within the Council unanimity set (i.e. no amendments are feasible), and which is accepted by a qualified majority of Council members and a majority in Parliament. Consequently, the question whether the most conservative Council member or any other member could propose an alternative that has to be preferred by all states does not affect the equilibrium.

One of these interpretations concerns the role of the Commission in the legislative process. Based on the Commission's formal right of legislative initiative, Steunenberg (1994a), Crombez (1996), and Moser (1997a) take the Commission into account in their modelling of the Union's decision-making procedures. Steunenberg (1994a: 648) takes the position that the Commission decides whether or not it will start the legislative process, and, if it chooses to do so, determines what the initial policy proposals will be. This implies that the Commission may act as a *gatekeeper*, since it could choose to maintain the current state of affairs and not issue any legislative proposals at all. Crombez (1996: 204), as well as Moser (1997a), point towards the possibility that Parliament or the Council may request the Commission to make a proposal, which in their view the Commission cannot ignore.[9] Since the Commission is not considered to have the possibility to delay or to postpone such a request, it is only regarded to be a *weak agenda setter.*[10]

Regarding the co-decision procedure, scholars disagree on the role of the Commission yet again. Crombez (2003: 111), for instance, assumes that the Commission can still shape the proposal, while most other authors argue that the Commission no longer plays a substantial role since the Council and Parliament can negotiate directly in the conciliation committee. They may change the existing proposal without any further Commission involvement.[11] Modelling co-decision as an interaction only between the Council and Parliament and without further Commission involvement, a new discussion arises concerning whether

[9] Their view seems to be informed by Art. 192 EC and Art. 208 EC, which grants the European Parliament and the Council the power to ask the Commission to initiate legislative measures.

[10] The Commission is regarded as an agenda setter in the sense that it can present a 'take-it-or-leave-it' offer to the Council if the Council is allowed to decide by qualified majority; this power of the Commission is considered weak since the Council is allowed to amend the Commission offer by unanimity. Note that under the unanimity version of the consultation procedure, the Commission will no longer be able to act as an agenda setter since the Council has to act by unanimity in any case.

[11] In another paper, Crombez (2000a: 52, 53) claims that '[t]he Commission is irrelevant under the new co-decision procedure'. This conclusion is in contrast to his view that the Commission matters as it could propose an initial proposal in the 'amendment set' (Crombez 2003: 111). In any case, the Commission itself feels that it was sidelined by the co-decision procedure. Shortly after the introduction of the co-decision procedure, the Commission 'expressed apprehension about the withdrawal of its traditional proprietorial rights over draft legislation' (Westlake 1994: 145).

the Council (or one of its members) or Parliament moves first in drafting a compromise proposal. Some maintain that the Council still holds a dominant position under the co-decision procedure and especially under the version introduced by the Maastricht Treaty (Steunenberg 1994a; Garrett 1995; Garrett and Tsebelis 1996; Tsebelis and Garrett 1996; 1997a; Steunenberg and Dimitrova 1999). Others indicate that Parliament dominates the negotiations with the Council, which applies especially to the revised co-decision procedure introduced by the Amsterdam Treaty (Steunenberg 1997; 2000a; Crombez 2000a). The question whether any of these interpretations describes the interaction between the Council and Parliament as part of the co-decision procedure best cannot be resolved by theoretical reasoning alone. At this point, further empirical research is needed.

3.3 MODELS AND THEIR DIFFERENT SPECIFICATIONS

With regard to the models developed for the consultation and co-decision procedures, we focus on those specifications in which the Council, together with Parliament in the case of co-decision, decides whether or not to pursue a new policy. The reason for this is that the data set examined here only includes proposals for which the Council has set its common position. Initiatives that did not reach the stage of being set as the Council's common position, since the Commission and/or Council members did not support these proposals sufficiently, are not included in the data set. A consequence of this choice is that we cannot test the specifications proposed by Steunenberg (1994a), who suggests that the Commission behaves as a gatekeeper and can effectively present some policy issues from getting on the Council's political agenda.

3.3.1 *The consultation procedure*

With regard to the consultation procedure, in which the Commission submits a proposal to the Council, there is no disagreement on how decisions will be made the moment the Commission releases its proposal. Whether the 'most conservative' Council member[12] (Crombez 1996: 204) or the Council Presidency (Steunenberg and Dimitrova 1999; Crombez 2000a) determines the Council agenda is not relevant to the

[12] That is, the member closest to the current state of affairs or *status quo*.

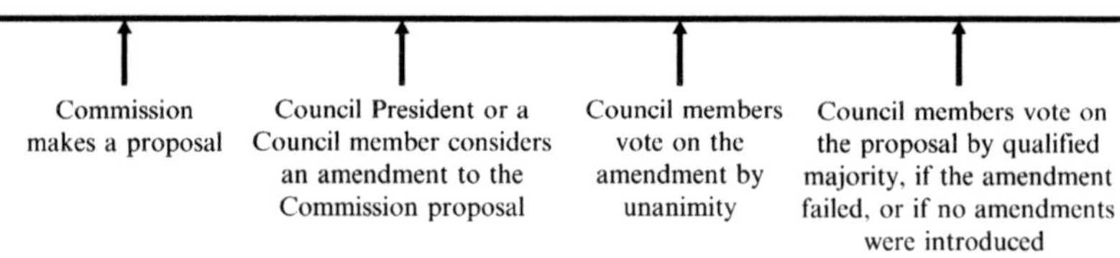

Figure 3.1. The consultation procedure

equilibrium outcome. In both cases, the Commission proposes a policy that is supported by a qualified majority and does not trigger Council amendments, i.e. it is found in the Council's unanimity set.

In this chapter we test the model proposed by Crombez (1996: 204-5) for both versions of the consultation procedure. In the qualified majority version the Council can accept the Commission proposal by qualified majority, but it requires unanimity to amend the Commission proposal. For this version, the model includes the following stages as illustrated in Figure 3.1. The line in this figure represents time and reflects the sequence of stages in the model. In the first stage, the Commission makes the initial proposal, which is submitted to the Council. In the second stage, a Council member—which could be the Council Presidency, the 'most conservative' Council member, or any other Council member—considers the proposal and decides whether or not to amend the proposal. The Commission proposal or the amended bill is then submitted to the other Council members. In the third stage, the Council considers the proposal. If the proposal is amended, the Council has to agree by unanimity. If the Council cannot agree on amendments, or if one of the Council members did not propose an amendment, the Council votes on the Commission proposal using qualified majority in the last stage. If a qualified majority cannot be formed, the *status quo* prevails.

The unanimity version forms a slight variation of this structure. In this procedure, a qualified majority in the Council is no longer sufficient to pass legislation. The Commission now has to have unanimity in the Council to have its most preferred proposal approved.

This sequential model can be solved applying backward induction, which implies that by starting at the last stage of the game, one aims to determine the proposal that will be issued by the Commission in the first stage. Since the Commission is assumed to behave strategically, it only issues a proposal that leads to the best possible result for itself. In this game, this proposal is shaped by two factors. First, the Commission has to have the support of a qualified majority of Council members in order

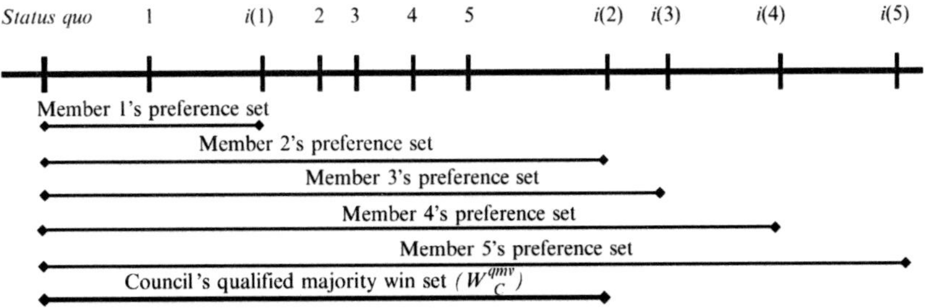

Figure 3.2. Preferences of a Council with five members

to adopt its preferred proposal as EU law, as indicated by the last stage. Second, the Commission wants to avoid its proposal being shifted away from its own preferred position by Council amendments in the third stage. It therefore drafts a proposal that cannot be changed by unanimity. Based on these two factors, the model predicts that the Commission chooses its best possible proposal which is preferred by a qualified majority, and which cannot be amended by a unanimous Council.

The basic logic of the model can be illustrated with a one-dimensional policy space as presented in Figure 3.2. For illustrative purposes, we assume in this figure that the Council consists of five members who all have a most preferred position to the right of the *status quo*. Each Council member has a (non-empty) individual *preference set*, which is the set of points a member prefers to the *status quo*. These sets are equivalent to the points in the interval between the *status quo* and the members point of indifference to the *status quo*.[13] The location of these indifference points depends on the shape of a member's utility function. As for the empirical part of this chapter, we assume that Council members have symmetric utility functions, so the distance between the *status quo* and a member's ideal position is equivalent to the distance between the ideal position and that member's point of indifference. The indifference points of the Council members are indicated in the figure as $i(1)$ for the first member, $i(2)$ for the second member and so on.

In addition, we assume for illustrative purposes that the support of four Council members is sufficient to pass legislation using qualified

[13] It is usually assumed that an indifferent player does not vote against a proposal. In that case, the preference set is equivalent to the interval including the decisive Council member's point of indifference. The *status quo* is not a point belonging to this interval and thus not an element of this set.

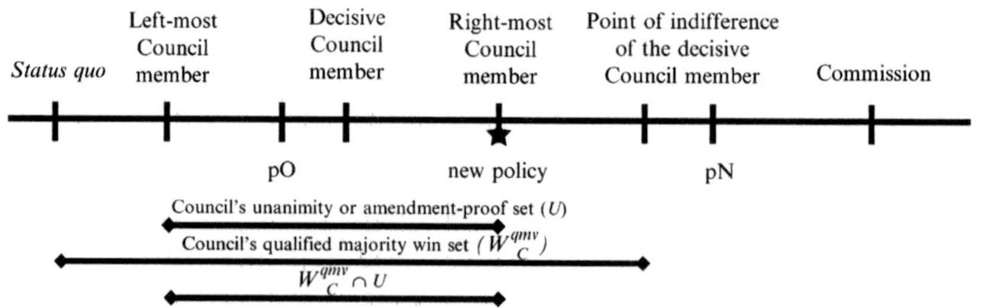

Figure 3.3. Preferences of the Commission and the Council members

majority rule. This implies that a feasible proposal has to have the support of at least four members for it to be passed. Proposals that satisfy this requirement are found in the intersection of the individual preference sets of the four most 'progressive' Council members, that is, the members most distant from the *status quo*. In Figure 3.2, these are members 5, 4, 3 and 2. The intersection of their preference sets is equivalent to the one of member 2, who is, in this case, the decisive Council member.[14] The points that are found in this intersection form the Council's *qualified majority win set*. It is the set of points a qualified majority in the Council prefers to the *status quo* (i.e. W^{qmv}_C).

The next step is to introduce the Commission. As illustrated in Figure 3.3, the Commission is assumed to have its most preferred position to the right of the *status quo*. Furthermore, only the 'critical' Council members are presented in this figure based on the configuration we used in Figure 3.2. The decisive Council member (which was member 2) is found to the right of the left-most Council member (member 1) and, of course, to the left of the right-most Council member (member 5). As indicated, the Council accepts all proposals that are in its *qualified majority win set*, which includes all points from the interval between the *status quo* and the decisive player's point of indifference. If the Commission wants to initiate a new policy away from the *status quo*, it has to choose a policy from this set. Other alternatives, which are not in this set, are not feasible.

The additional consideration is that the Council could agree on amendments if a proposal were not located in its *unanimity set*, i.e. the set of points that cannot be changed by a unanimous vote (U). Since

[14] Note that the member who is decisive depends on the location of the *status quo*. If the *status quo* is found to the right of all Council members, member 4 in Figure 3.2 would be decisive.

proposals in the unanimity set *cannot* be amended, it can be called the *amendment-proof set*. Especially for voting rules other than unanimity rule, as is the case for the models on the co-decision procedure, the term 'amendment-proof' is more suitable and will be used in this chapter. Now assume the Commission proposes a policy equivalent to *pN* in Figure 3.3. In this case, all Council members prefer a change of this policy to the left.[15] Subsequently, the Council President, or any of the other Council members, will propose amendments that change the Commission proposal. In other words, policy *pN* is not amendment-proof. However, points that are invulnerable to amendments are found *between* the extreme Council members. For any of those points at least one Council member will oppose a proposed change, since the amendment suggested by the other Council members will move the policy away from that member's most preferred position. If, for instance, the Commission proposes a policy *pO* as presented in Figure 3.3, the decisive Council member and any of the other Council members further to the right of this member prefer a change of policy to the right. The left-most member, however, will oppose such amendments, since they will move the policy away from that member's most preferred position. Policy *pO* cannot be changed by unanimity and is thus amendment-proof. More generally, all points between the left-most and right-most Council members have this property and are, as indicated in the figure, the elements of the amendment-proof set.

Finally, the Commission makes its ideal proposal so that no amendments are possible and a qualified majority of Council members prefers the policy. The policies that satisfy these two criteria are found in the subset of the qualified majority win set and the amendment-proof set (i.e. $W_{C}^{qmv} \cap U$), which is, for the configuration in Figure 3.3, equal to the amendment-proof set. Selecting its best policy, the Commission chooses a policy equal to the position of the right-most Council member, since this policy is closest to the Commission's most preferred position. The equilibrium policy is therefore the starred position indicated in the figure.

For a more-dimensional space, the same basic logic applies, although the various sets may have more complicated shapes. This also refers to the models of the co-decision procedure, which we discuss in the next

[15] This can be checked by drawing the individual preference sets of the Council members with regard to this policy *pN* and constructing the unanimity win set. This new win set is the intersection of all individual preferences, which, in this case, is not empty and equal to the preference set of the right-most Council member.

section. In the Appendix to this chapter, we provide the equilibrium outcomes for the models that are central to this chapter, and we discuss briefly the way in which the solutions of these models are derived.

3.3.2 *The co-decision procedure: who shapes the final proposal?*

For the co-decision procedure, different interpretations exist with regard to whether the Commission still plays a role under the Amsterdam version of the co-decision procedure, and whether Parliament or the Council takes the lead in the conciliation committee. Both Crombez (2003: 110–1) and Steunenberg (2001: 352–3) maintain that the Commission has agenda-setting power in the process. The proposed sequence of play is that, after the Commission has initiated a bill, the Council or Parliament considers the proposal and makes a final offer to the other.[16] A second view suggests that the Commission is not relevant under co-decision, so that a model of this procedure can be reduced to a structure in which the only players are the Council and Parliament (Tsebelis and Garrett 2000; 2001). At this point the question arises as to whether the Council takes the lead and submits an offer to Parliament, as for instance suggested by Steunenberg (1994a: 655–6), or Parliament makes an offer to the Council (see Steunenberg 1997: 220–2). Crombez (2000a: 53), in another paper, allows for both possibilities: either Parliament or the Council President is allowed to make a successful proposal to the other players.

In this chapter we test three models of co-decision, which are based on these different views. The first model starts with the Commission drafting a proposal, which is submitted to the Council and subsequently to Parliament. The Council decides on the proposal by qualified majority, while Parliament, as a unitary actor, has to approve it.[17] This version of the co-decision procedure is labelled the *Commission model* as the Commission is still regarded as a relevant actor. This sequence of play for this game is presented in Figure 3.4(a). The horizontal line in this figure represents time and indicates how the players move after each other.

[16] Note that for models of perfect and complete information in which the Commission effectively makes the proposal in the first stage, the order in which the Council or Parliament move as part of conciliation is not relevant, since the outcome is determined by the Commission in the first stage.

[17] The data set includes only one value for the preferences of Parliament, and the same for the Commission. We therefore focus on models in which Parliament and the Commission are treated as unitary actors.

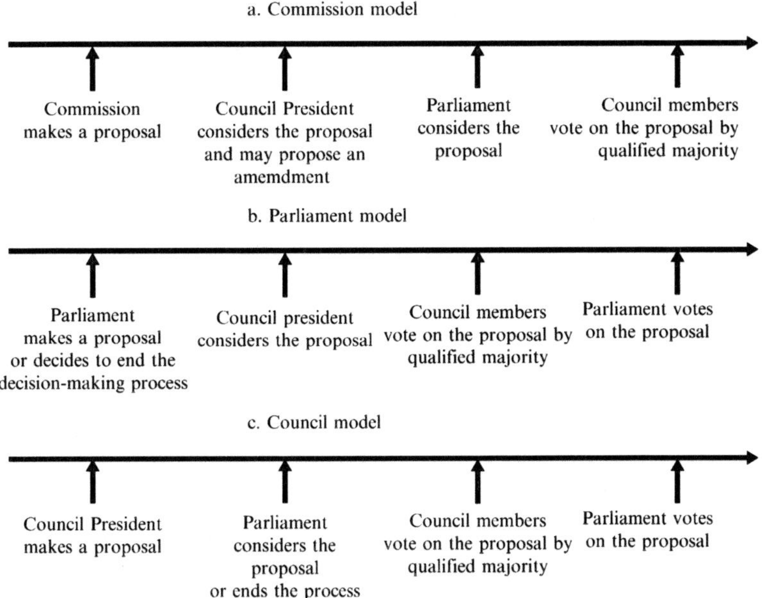

Figure 3.4. The co-decision procedure

The second model, which we label the *Parliament model* of co-decision, is inspired by another model presented by Crombez (2000a: 52–3). This model starts with the Commission making a proposal, which is submitted to Parliament. In the second stage, Parliament decides whether or not to support the proposal, or to amend the proposal (which, in the Union's terminology, is called 'proposing a joint text'). If the proposal is supported or amended, Parliament sends the proposal to the Council President. The Council President considers Parliament's proposal and may propose changes. Finally, the proposal has to be approved by a qualified majority of Council members and Parliament. In this model, both the Commission and Parliament are regarded as unitary actors. Since the unitary Parliament can always amend the proposal in the second stage and draft an alternative, and the Commission is not able to avoid this possibility, the Commission proposal in the first stage is no longer relevant for the outcome. For this reason, in this chapter we use a *reduced* form of this game in which we start with the stage in which Parliament decides on its actions. If Parliament drafts a proposal it will be submitted to the Council President (see Figure 3.4(b)).

The third model reverses the sequence of play of the second model, as illustrated in Figure 3.4(c), and is labelled the *Council model*. This model starts with the Council President drafting a proposal (or joint text), which is submitted to Parliament in the second stage. In contrast to Parliament in the previous model of the co-decision procedure, the Council President is not allowed to end the decision-making process and thus maintain the *status quo*.[18] If Parliament agrees on the proposal, it is submitted to the Council for a vote. In the last stage the Council members decide by qualified majority. Although Parliament also has to vote on the final proposal, this additional stage is redundant since the unitary Parliament already decides on the proposal in the second stage. The game can be described by its *reduced* form, which is a game with three stages as presented in the figure.[19]

The models discussed in this chapter stress the importance of a specific sequence of moves between the legislative actors. Although this sequence is based on the Union's legislative procedure, it does not strictly follow the actual procedures as described in the treaties. Some emphasise the importance of the Commission in this process, while others stress the role of Parliament, or the Council Presidency in the shaping of the final outcome. These variations are based on different perceptions of what the determining stages are in the Union's legislative process. Farrell and Héritier (2003; see also Farrell and Héritier 2004), for instance, note that for many issues introduced under the co-decision procedure agreement is reached during the initial stages of informal meetings (the so-called 'trialogues'). In these meetings the Commission discusses its proposal with the Council Presidency and representatives from Parliament. Tsebelis and Garrett (2000; 2001), however, focus on the last stage of conciliation, since they feel that members from the Council and Parliament can, at this stage, formally engage in bargaining. The different versions of the co-decision model account for these different possibilities by having one of the legislative actors take initiative and make a proposal to the others. Through empirical testing we are able to find out which interpretation fits best the actual decision-making process.

[18] Note that we assume the Council Presidency *has* to make a proposal. It does not have gatekeeping power in the sense that it can decide not to make a proposal to the other Council members. See, for instance, Tallberg (2003) and Kollman (2003) for the agenda-shaping power of the Council Presidency.

[19] If Parliament is conceived of as a multimember decision-making body for which the Parliament President considers the proposal in the second stage, the last stage is relevant. At this stage, Parliament has to decide whether or not to adopt the proposal by absolute majority.

3.4 DATA MANAGEMENT

In order to apply the models to our data set, we must now discuss some further adaptations in order to be able to test our models empirically. These adaptations concern the treatment of missing values for the *status quo*, Council members for which the expert was not able to indicate a preference, and different policy issues within the same proposal.

In the data set, the legislative reference point or *status quo* could be identified for 126 of the 162 issues which have led to legislation (or 78 per cent of the total). One possibility would be to substitute the missing value with some value so that these issues are still included in the analysis. In our view, imputing some value that applies to all cases for which the *status quo* is missing, is problematic since the results could severely undermine the logic of the models.[20] To avoid any disturbance from this coding decision we decided to drop the issues for which the *status quo* is missing.

A second issue concerns the treatment of Council members who are 'neutral', i.e. for whom the expert was not able to indicate an ideal position during the interviews. The fact that the expert did not allocate a value to these members does not necessarily imply that these values should be regarded as 'missing'. The Council members may not have had a strong opinion on these matters and might have accepted a broad range of different policies. The question is how to treat these Council members. A first solution would be to simply drop these members and lower the voting threshold for the remaining members in the Council. This strategy, however, is inappropriate since a large number of the cases concerns a two- or three-dimensional policy space. Often, an actor is 'neutral' for only one of these issues, but prefers a specific policy for one of the other dimensions. A second strategy would be to compute some value for this actor in line with an interpretation of why these actors may not have stated their preferences at the preparatory stage. At this point the

[20] Of the 126 issues that have a *status quo*, for 104 of them the value is 0. One possibility would be to impute 0 for the missing values. However, in the data set there are several cases within which a primary issue x can be identified that specifies *how much money* the EU should spend. A second issue y then specifies on what policy the Union should spend this budget. For the latter issue, the *status quo* is often missing. Assume that the allocated budget could be spent on the following policies A (coded as 0) and B (coded as 100). Imputing a value of 0 would result in assuming that the *status quo* is equal to spending the allocated budget to alternative A, which would dramatically distort the data.

question is whose preference 'neutral' Council members will follow. Taking another actor's preference as a proxy for the 'neutral' member, the imputed value has a *specific* (i.e. dependent on the method that is used) impact on the shape of the Council's win set and may affect the predicted outcome.

In this chapter we therefore opted for a more general solution, which avoids as much as possible that the way in which 'neutral' actors are treated, affects the outcome. When the interviewed expert did not record a preference, we took this as an indication that this Council member did not have a preference for that specific dimension (i.e. the actor is indifferent with regard to this dimension). Any position along this dimension is of equal importance to this actor, who, nevertheless, may prefer a specific policy on one or more of the other policy dimensions. In order to avoid the results being affected by our decision on 'neutral' actors, we decided to drop those cases with more than four 'neutral' Council members.

The last issue concerns the relationship between different policy dimensions in utility terms. In our analysis we assume that all issues are of equal salience to the actors, which is the standard assumption used in the various models. In other words, we assume that utility will decrease in the same way for every unit change in the outcome space.

3.5 DECISION-MAKING ON *SOCRATES*: AN ILLUSTRATION

On 27 May 1998 the European Commission presented a legislative proposal to Parliament and the Council to set up a new funding scheme for trans-European educational measures (COM (1998)329; COD/1998/0195). The legal basis for the so-called *Socrates* programme are Articles 149 and 150 EC, which require the co-decision procedure with a qualified majority threshold in the Council for the adoption of the proposal. During the Council discussions some countries, especially the United Kingdom and the Netherlands, took a different view on the matter than most of the other states. They felt that culture and education should be either low-key in general, or that the best political level to deal with this issue is not the European level but the national or even the sub-national level. Nevertheless, the Council was able to agree on a common position on 21 December 1998 and submitted the proposal to Parliament. Parliament disagreed with several elements, especially the amount of money reserved for the program and the possibility of renegotiating the budget after enlargement, which formed the basis of amendments. The amendments were brought into the negotiations between the Council and

Parliament during the debates in the Conciliation Committee between 27 October and 9 November 1999. On 9 November 1999, the committee reached a compromise, which was subsequently approved by Parliament and Council. On 24 January 2000 the Decision 253/2000/EC of the European Parliament and the Council establishing the *Socrates* programme was enacted.

In the negotiations on the proposal, there were three main issues at stake. The *first issue*, which was regarded as the most important one, concerned *how much money* would be spent on the programme over the time period of seven years. The expert was able to distinguish the following four positions on this dimension:

- no money should be spent for an educational programme at the European level (i.e. zero spending), which represents the *status quo* (value of 0);
- €1.55 billion, that is, no more funds than for a five-year programme (value of 62);
- €2 billion (value of 80); and
- €2.5 billion (value of 100).[21]

The positions of the players on this dimension are presented in Figure 3.5, which shows that the Council was divided on this issue, while Parliament prefered the highest budget allocation to the *Socrates* programme.

The *second issue* concered the *terminology* to be used when referring to the overall idea behind the programme. The expert identified two different positions concerning this dimension. Some Council members, fearing the evolution of future legal claims that might result from using too-strong wording, preferred the existing term of *European dimension of education* (value of 0). Parliament especially wanted the overall term *European education area* to be used (value of 100), thereby highlighting the prominence of this topic for European decision-makers.

The *third issue* dealt with the question of whether to include a clause in the programme that provided for compulsory budget renegotiations on the package after the accession of new member states to the EU (*the revision clause*). This issue was raised and brought into the negotiations during the debates in the conciliation committee. Parliament was particularly concerned about creating procedures for revising the financial

[21] The values for each issue are normalised so that their range is from 0 (which is mostly the *status quo*) to 100 (highest value).

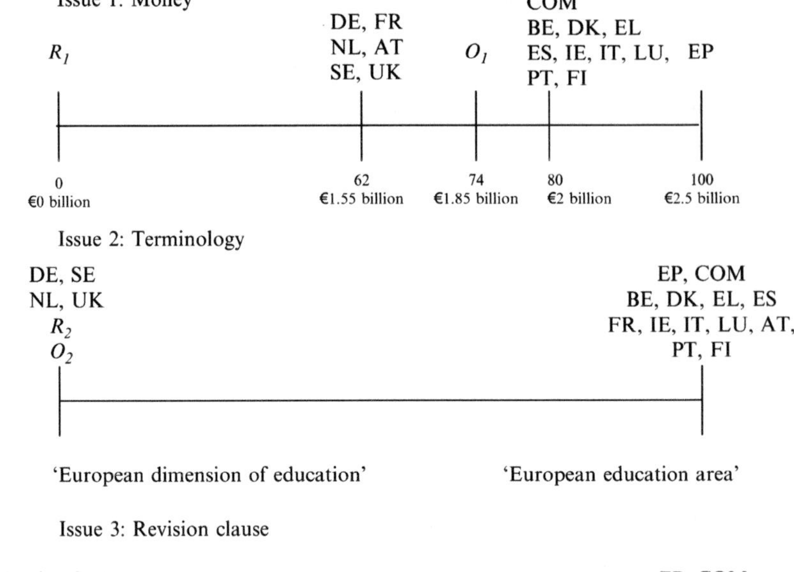

Figure 3.5. Actor positions on the three issue dimensions of the *Socrates* case

allocations for this programme, since it wanted to ensure that sufficient funds would be made available for the participation of accession countries in the *Socrates* programme. The preferences of the main actors on a compulsory revision clause can be described by two positions, as presented in Figure 3.5. The left-most position is *no revision clause*, which was preferred by all member states; the right-most position is *a revision clause* with a decision taken under the co-decision procedure, which Parliament preferred.

For two of the three issues concerning *Socrates*, the political actors, according to the expert, considered only two positions. Despite the limited number of declared positions, we will treat these issues as continuous scales. This approach is part of the joint research strategy in this book.[22] This decision can be maintained in the light of our case. In the case of the third issue, the revision clause, some member states might

[22] See the research design chapter for a discussion.

have wished to include such a clause and therefore to give Parliament some say about the allocation of funds on enlargement, but under another procedure than the qualified majority version of co-decision. If such preferences were available, it would have created more and different positions along an underlying policy dimension, possibly with the current positions as the extremes. Similarly, one could imagine different wordings for the Union's involvement in the field of education, which would increase the number of possible positions along the dimension dealing with the terminology. Maintaining the assumption of a continuous scale, we will nevertheless check in the empirical analysis whether issues that appear more discrete in nature (due to a limited number of declared positions as noted by the expert) have an effect on our predictions.

The three issues that are central to the *Socrates* programme form a three-dimensional space, which we use for the three models of co-decision. The space is illustrated by Figure 3.6. In this space, Parliament has an ideal position at the extremes of all three dimensions, while the *status quo*, indicated as *R*, is taken as the origin. The Council members are concentrated in three distinct groups. The first and largest group, which has 44 votes at its disposal, is found close to the front top right corner of this space and includes Italy (IT), Spain (ES) and most of the smaller countries. This group also contains Portugal (PT), which was the Council President at the time of the final decision-making on the *Socrates* proposal. A second group is formed by France (FR) and Austria (AT) and has 14 votes. The last group, found closest to the *status quo*, consists of Germany (DE), the United Kingdom (UK), the Netherlands (NL) and Sweden (SE). This group, which has 29 votes, is decisive for Council decision-making, since it can block the formation of a qualified majority.[23] Finally, in this space, the Commission has a position close to Parliament.

The 'decisive' group consisting of Germany, the Netherlands, Sweden and the UK primarily determines the qualified majority win set in this space. Since the other Council members prefer a more substantial change than these countries, their preferences do not constrain the set in the direction of the most preferred positions of Parliament or the Commission. The relevant part of the qualified majority win set consists of the surface of the utility contour of the 'decisive' group that cuts through the

[23] To form a qualified majority in favour of a proposal, 62 out of 87 votes in the Council are needed. This group holds the 'last' three votes necessary to have a total of 62.

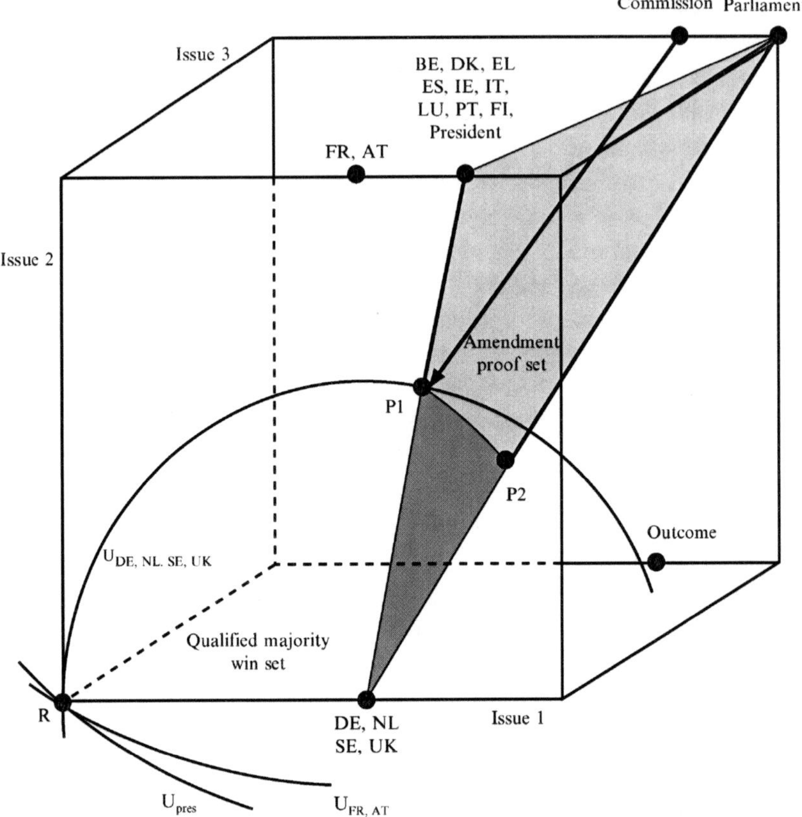

Figure 3.6. The three-dimensional space for decision-making on *Socrates*

status quo, *R*, at the origin. Based on our assumption of simple Euclidean preferences, this surface is, in this part of the space, ball-shaped.

The amendment-proof set is determined by the players necessary for the formation of a qualified majority in the Council and Parliament. It consists of points that cannot be changed by any of these players, either because such points cannot be changed using qualified majority, or because a change is not supported by Parliament.[24] These points are found within the light grey triangle formed by the most preferred positions of the group consisting of Germany, the Netherlands, Sweden,

[24] In the Parliament and the Council models of this procedure, the Council President also plays a role. Since Portugal is the Council President, it does not affect the amendment-proof set, since Portugal is part of one of the groups of Council members that is necessary to form a qualified majority.

and the UK, the group consisting of Italy, Spain and the smaller countries, and Parliament. The intersection of the amendment-proof set and the qualified majority win set contains policies that are supported by the Council and cannot be further amended. This is the dark grey triangle in Figure 3.6. The policies in this triangle are the feasible policies, which will be considered by the player allowed to make a choice within the context of the procedural model applied.

The *Commission model* of co-decision allows the Commission to select its best policy from the set of feasible policies, that is, the dark grey triangle in the figure. Minimising the distance to its own most preferred policy, which is found near Parliament's position, the Commission selects the policy that is on the surface of the qualified majority win set as it cuts through the amendment-proof set. The closest policy to the Commission position is the policy indicated by *P1* in the figure, which is equivalent to the point (72, 59, 0).

In the *Parliament model* of co-decision, instead of the Commission, Parliament chooses its best policy from the set of feasible policies. Minimising the distance between the set of feasible policies and its own most preferred position, Parliament selects the policy *P2* in Figure 3.6. This policy is equivalent to the point (76, 41, 41).

Finally, in the *Council model*, the Council Presidency makes this specific choice. During the final discussions on *Socrates*, Portugal held the Council Presidency. Minimising the distance between the set of feasible policies and Portugal's most preferred position, this model predicts the policy *P1* as the outcome.

On 24 January 2000 Parliament and the Council enacted the new *Socrates* programme. The decision established a new phase of the existing Community action programme in the field of education for the period from 2000 until 2006. The old scheme would run out at the end of 2000. The decision included the following elements:

1. The financial framework for the implementation of the programme was set at €1.85 billion for a period of seven years (a value of 74 in Figure 3.6).
2. The terminology used to refer to the overall idea behind the programme was the more conservative *European dimension of education*, which was preferred by the Council.
3. As an addendum, a revision clause was included which provided for compulsory budget renegotiations in the case of EU enlargement with the countries of Central and Eastern Europe.

The actual outcome is a policy equal to the point (74, 0, 100), which is included in Figure 3.6.

Confronting the actual with the predicted outcome, we calculated the differences between the predicted outcomes and the actual outcome. For this purpose, we first computed the *mean absolute error* (Chapter 10). For the Commission model, the mean absolute error is 41. For the Parliament model we computed an error of 34; for the Council model, the error is the greatest with 54.[25] The *Socrates* case illustrates how we apply a procedural model to the data collected. We continue by focusing on a larger number of cases and compare the results found for the different model specifications.

3.6 AN EMPIRICAL TEST: QUANTITATIVE RESULTS

We apply each of the procedural models to all of the issues subject to the legislative procedures to which the model refers. As indicated, we decided to exclude all issues for which the *status quo* is missing, or which contained four or more neutral political actors (i.e. member states which, according to the expert, did not state a position). This reduces the number of issues from 162 in the data set to 110 in our analysis.[26] We further excluded issues that were part of proposals with more than three dimensions, and issues on which the agenda setter is indifferent. The results of the comparison between predicted and actual outcomes are presented in Table 3.1.

The table presents the mean absolute error for the four different procedural models, one for the consultation procedure and three for the co-decision procedure. The mean absolute error is computed by summing up the errors of the model predictions at the issue level and dividing the total by the total number of issues involved. The results show that most models have a rather similar mean error. The model for

[25] Alternatively, we also computed the Euclidean error for the predictions based on the three models. For the Commission model, the Euclidean error is 99. For the Parliament model, we computed an error of 72, and for the Council model the error is 116.

[26] Twenty-eight issues were excluded since there was no reference point, and 11 since there were four or more indifferent actors. Due to computation capacity we were able to compute 51 issues for the Presidency version of co-decision, 50 issues for the Parliament version, but only 39 issues for the Commission version.

Table 3.1. *Mean absolute error for the four procedural models (standard deviation in brackets)*

	Mean absolute error[a]
Consultation model	32.8 (33.4)/n=57
Co-decision model: Commission version	38.0 (31.0)/n=39
Co-decision model: Parliament version	27.5 (27.5)/n=50
Co-decision model: Council version	38.3 (28.3)/n=51

Note: [a]Two-sample t-tests show that the difference between the Parliament and the Council version of the co-decision procedure is significant at the 1 per cent level.

the consultation procedure, which is based on Crombez (1996), yields an error of about 33. The errors found for the Commission and the Council models are slightly higher, but are not significantly different. With regard to the co-decision procedure, one model stands out and that is the model in which Parliament initiates the new policy in the negotiations with the Council. The mean error found for this model is smaller than the errors found for both alternatives. In other words, the predictions generated by this model reflect best the actual outcomes, which indicates that under co-decision Parliament plays a rather important role next to the Council.

A next step is to examine whether the model predictions are affected by the voting rule used by the Council. As indicated in Section 3.3 of this chapter, the Council may adopt legislation by qualified majority or unanimity, depending on the treaty requirements. The results of this analysis are presented in Table 3.2. The predictions of the model of the consultation procedure seem to improve when the unanimity rule is used, while for the qualified majority version the mean error is higher. The differences between these versions are, however, not statistically significant, which is partly due to the limited number of cases. The Parliament version of the co-decision model continues to perform best, although this performance now refers to the qualified majority version of this model.

A next step is to focus on the different policy areas and to test whether model predictions vary by area. Since for most areas the number of available measures in the data set is quite small, we make a distinction

Table 3.2. *Mean absolute error for the four procedural models based on voting rules (standard deviation in brackets)*

	Qualified majority rule[a]	Unanimity rule[a]
Consultation model	36.1 (31.5)/n=36	29.3 (37.6)/n=19
Co-decision model: Commission version	37.9 (32.9)/n=28	38.3 (27.0)/n=11
Co-decision model: Parliament version	26.4 (27.4)/n=42	33.5 (29.0)/n=8
Co-decision model: Council version	38.5 (28.3)/n=41	37.3 (29.9)/n=10

Note: [a]Two-sample t-tests show that if qualified majority voting is used the difference between the Parliament version of the co-decision procedure and the Council is significant (10 per cent one-tailed test).

between agriculture, internal market, and other sectors.[27] The results are presented in Table 3.3.

The sizes of the model errors do not seem to differ between decisions on agriculture and the internal market. However, a difference occurs for the 'other' category, which yields lower errors and thus slightly better predictions. Since this category includes some of the more recently included areas of EU policy-making, the discussion on new European measures might be more politically focused. Some of the issues on agriculture as well as the internal market might be rather technical in nature. In the case of agriculture, these measures mostly deal with the implementation of the common agricultural policy (CAP) and infectious animal diseases, while for the internal market, the measures mostly modify existing EU policy. As our models are based on the assumption that decision-making is the combined result of political preferences and the institutional features of the legislative process, the higher political importance of the issues at stake may contribute to slightly better predictions in the other areas.

[27] This category includes culture, development assistance, employment, energy, fisheries, general affairs, health, industry, justice and home affairs, social, telecommunications, and transport. A further breakdown of this category is not advisable since it would lead to rather small numbers of observations.

Table 3.3. *Mean absolute error by policy sector*[a]

	Mean absolute error[b]
Agriculture	37.5 (34.8)/n=27
Internal market	36.9 (31.0)/n=28
Other	23.1 (27.0)/n=52
All policy sectors	30.3 (30.7)/n=107

Notes: [a]Based on the combined results for the consultation model and the Parliament version of the co-decision model. The combinations which include the consultation model and the other versions of the co-decision model yield similar results.
[b]Two-sample t-tests show that the mean error for the issues in the area of agriculture and the internal market differ significantly from the one for the other policy areas; in addition, the difference in error between the group dealing with agriculture and internal market issues and those with other sectors is significant (at the 5 per cent level).

Finally, we tested whether the assumption of a continuous measurement scale underlying the different issues matters. As the *Socrates* case illustrates, the data set contains a substantial number of issues on which the actors have a rather limited number of different positions. This could indicate that some of our issues might not be continuous. If this is the case, our models may not predict well for those issues since they assume a continuous space. In order words, if the models perform differently for categories of issues that reflect differences in measurement level, the overall error might be affected by a mis-specification of the way in which the issues are measured. Our findings are presented in Table 3.4.

The results show that there is a clear difference regarding the models' predictive power if we distinguish between different measurement scales. When moving from a dichotomous to a rank order or ordinal scale, the error decreases, indicating that the distance between actual and predicted outcomes becomes smaller. When moving from an ordinal to a continuous scale, no further improvement seems to occur, partly because the number of observations for the latter scale is quite small (only 10 observations). Our findings suggest that when the measurement level of the data increases, the accuracy of the model predictions increases too. It points to possible measurement problems with regard to the dichotomous issues.

Table 3.4. *Mean absolute error by measurement level*[a]

	Mean absolute error[b]
Dichotomous	48.6 (44.8)/n=19
Rank order	26.2 (25.5)/n=78
Scale	27.9 (26.5)/n=10
All issues	30.3 (30.7)/n=107

Notes: [a]Based on the combined results for the consultation model and the Parliament version of the co-decision model. The combinations which include the consultation model and the other versions of the co-decision model yield similar results.

[b]Two-sample t-tests show that the difference between the dichotomous and the rank order issues is significant (at the 5 per cent level); in addition, the difference between the dichotomous issues and the group of issues based on the two other measurement levels (rank order and scale) is also significant (at the 5 per cent level).

3.7 CONCLUSION

In this chapter, we focused on procedural models of European Union legislative decision-making. These models, which are embedded in non-cooperative game theory and the spatial theory of voting (Enelow and Hinich 1984; Hinich and Munger 1997), stress the importance of the sequence of decision-making. For procedural models, different legislative procedures do not merely result in different capabilities or power ratios of the actors, as they do for some of the other models that are used in this book. They suggest different sequences of play as reflected in the game tree, which affect the final outcome.

In this chapter we restricted our attention to one model that was specified for the consultation procedure and three models for the co-decision procedure. The data set only includes cases for which the Council accepted a common position. Consequently, we cannot test specifications discussed in the literature that allow the Commission to act as a gatekeeper and prevent some policy issues from being placed on the Council's legislative agenda. The models we tested allow one of the Union's legislative actors (and in the case of the consultation procedure only the Commission) to make a proposal to the others, who depending on the specification can amend, accept or reject the proposal.

Applying these models to the data set, we found that most models yield rather high mean absolute errors, which indicates that their predictions often differ substantially from the actual outcome of the legislative decision-making process. In particular, Crombez's model on the consultation procedure, which we followed, and the Commission and Council versions of the model we applied to the co-decision procedure, did not perform well. The limited differences in model predictions and thus in absolute error resembles the results reported by König and Pöter (2001), who found that four different models developed for the cooperation procedure yield almost the same results. Although they focused on only four different cases, we included many more cases in our empirical analysis.

However, in our empirical analysis, one model stands out. This is the Parliament model of the co-decision procedure, which outperforms the Commission and the Council models of this procedure. The latter two models allow the Commission or the Council President to make an initial proposal, which is discussed by both Parliament and the Council. In the Parliament model, which we based on Steunenberg (1997: 220–2) and Crombez (2000a: 52–3), the European Parliament takes the lead and shapes the proposal. Parliament could take this role as part of the informal discussions between the Commission, Council and Parliament. These so-called 'trialogues' initially started as an informal preparation to conciliation committee meetings, but gradually extended to the first reading of Commission proposals (Farell and Héritier 2003: 588). These meetings provide a platform for direct negotiations between the legislative actors and it allows Parliament to shape the proposal that will be discussed in the subsequent stage of the legislative process.

Our findings suggest that Parliament has to be regarded as an important legislator in the Union next to the Council. Legislative decision-making in the Union is also based on substantive input from Parliament, which strengthens the procedural democratic legitimacy of the EU. In addition, our findings make more precise the claim from the 'revisionist approach' (Tsebelis *et al* 2001: 573), which posits that the Council is the dominant decision-making body (Tsebelis 1997; Tsebelis and Garrett 2000).

We also found that the models perform better as we move from issues with only two available positions (possibly dichotomous issues) to issues that may reflect a rank order (ordinal level of measurement) or a continuous dimension. This finding points at two possible problems related to the issues in the data set.

The first possibility is that some of the issues in the data set are indeed not divisible. In that case, the models applied in this chapter do not fit to these issues. Most procedural models assume that choices are made in a continuous space, which allows actors to select any possible proposal that will be jointly preferred. If, however, this assumption cannot be used, different models of EU legislative decision-making have to be developed to account for a more limited set of available outcomes.

The second possibility relates to data collection and concerns the question of whether the different issues or policy dimensions can be used to construct a multi-dimensional space. Especially in the case of dichotomous issues, the different positions on these issues were assigned the 'extreme' values of 0 and 100. However, whether the distance between these positions corresponds to the distances used for the other dimensions of the same space is not clear. Although in the data collection special attention was paid to the comparison of distances between positions on the *same* dimension, a check on whether distances are interpreted in the same way for *different* dimensions was not made. This is, however, crucial to the application of procedural models as tested in this chapter. Applying simple Euclidean preferences, these models assume that a unit change in any possible direction in the multidimensional outcome space yields the same change in utility. Of course, if more complicated Euclidean preferences are used which take account of the 'salience' of the different dimensions, the weighting of the different dimensions can vary for different players leading to more complicated preferences. Even if salience is introduced, the underlying policy space is assumed to be comparable. However, this property is violated by assigning somewhat arbitrary values to issue positions, as was done for the dichotomous issues. The fact that procedural models do not predict dichotomous issues or proposals that partly consist of dichotomous issues well, suggests that this problem occurs in the current data set.

Finally, we point out that we did not include differences in the salience political actors attach to the issues in our analysis. In this chapter we assumed that all issues are of equal importance. While having the advantage of keeping the analysis simpler, this assumption may also have affected our results. The impact of salience may form another line of future research in order to uncover the internal dynamics of the European Union's legislative process.

APPENDIX TO CHAPTER 3

Let q be the current state of affairs, $q \in \mathrm{R}^{\mathrm{m}}$. Let $a \in \mathrm{N}$ be a player who has simple Euclidean and separable preferences for the outcome space R^{m}, which are defined by a utility function $U_a(x)$, $x \in \mathrm{R}^{\mathrm{m}}$. $P_a(q)$, or simply P_a,[28] is the preference set of player a with regard to point q, that is, $P_a = \{x \mid U_a(x) > U_a(q)\}$. Let $W^v_C = \cap_v P_i$ be the win set for a group of players C, which is called the Council, $i \in C \subset N$, which satisfies the winning requirement of a voting rule v, which could be either qualified majority voting ($v = qmv$) or unanimity ($v = u$).

Consultation

Define the Council's unanimity set, that is, the set of points that cannot be changed using unanimity rule, as $U = \{x| W^u_C(x) = \emptyset\}$. In the last stage the multimember Council adopts a proposal if $p \in W^{qmv}_C$. In the third stage, the Council prefers the amended proposal p' to the Commission proposal p if $p' \in W^u_C\ (p)$. In the second stage, one of the Council members makes an amendment if $W^u_C(p) \neq \emptyset$. Knowing this, the Commission, *com*, releases in the first stage a proposal such that:

$$p^* = \begin{cases} \max(U_{com}(x)|x \in W^{qmv}_C \cap U) & \text{if } W^{qmv}_C \neq \emptyset;^{29} \\ q & \text{if } W^{qmv}_C = \emptyset; \end{cases}$$

which is the equilibrium outcome.

For the unanimity version of this procedure, the Commission releases a proposal such that:

$$p^* = \begin{cases} \max(U_{com}(x)|x \in W^u_C \cap U) & \text{if } W^u_C \neq \emptyset; \\ q & \text{if } W^u_C = \emptyset; \end{cases}$$

which is the equilibrium outcome.

Co-decision: Commission model

Define the amendment-proof set as the set of points that cannot be changed by a qualified majority of Council members and Parliament, that is, $A = \{x|P_{ep}(x) \cap W^{qmv}_C(x) = \emptyset\}$.[30] In the last stage Council accepts

[28] We only use the full notation when this set is defined with regard to another point than the *status quo*.

[29] See Crombez (1996: 207). If the Commission is regarded as an agenda setter, as Steunenberg (1994a) proposes, this condition would be $p = \max(U_{com}(x)|x \in P_{com} \cap W^{qmv}_C \cap U)$ if $P_{com} \cap W^{qmv}_C \cap U \neq \emptyset$, and $p = q$ if $P_{com} \cap W^{qmv}_C \cap U = \emptyset$.

[30] The question is whether this set is not the empty set, especially if the policy space consists of a large number of dimensions. For the Union's current qualified majority requirement of 62/87 or 71.26 per cent, the set $W^{qmv}_C\ (x)$ could be non-empty for policy spaces with three or more dimensions, as Greenberg (1979: 629) shows. A qualified majority core does not exist in those circumstances. At the same time,

an amended proposal p' to the Commission proposal p if $p' \in W_C^{qmv}(p)$. Parliament amends the Commission proposal if an amendment is preferred, that is, $P_{ep}(p) \neq \emptyset$, and supported by a qualified majority in the Council, i.e. $W_C^{qmv}(p) \neq \emptyset$. If $P_{ep}(p) \cap W_C^{qmv}(p) = \emptyset$, Parliament is not able to propose a successful amendment. Knowing this, the Commission, *com*, releases a proposal in the first stage such that:

$$p^* = \begin{cases} \max(U_{com}(x) | x \in P_{ep} \cap W_C^{qmv} \cap A) & \text{if } P_{ep} \cap W_C^{qmv} \cap A \neq \emptyset;^{31} \\ q & \text{if } P_{ep} \cap W_C^{qmv} \cap A = \emptyset; \end{cases}$$

which is the equilibrium outcome.

For the unanimity version of this procedure, define the amendment-proof set as $A = \{x | P_{ep}(x) \cap W_C^u(x) = \emptyset\}$. In this version, the Commission drafts a proposal such that:

$$p^* = \begin{cases} \max(U_{com}(x) | x \in P_{ep} \cap W_C^u \cap A) & \text{if } P_{ep} \cap W_C^u \cap A \neq \emptyset; \\ q & \text{if } P_{ep} \cap W_C^u \cap A = \emptyset; \end{cases}$$

which is the equilibrium outcome.

Co-decision: Parliament model

Define the amendment-proof set as the set of points that cannot be changed by Parliament, the Council President and a qualified majority in the Council, that is $A = \{x | P_{pres}(x) \cap P_{ep}(x) \cap W_C^{qmv}(x) = \emptyset\}$. In the last stage, Parliament accepts the joint text if $p' \in P_{ep}(p)$. In the third stage, the Council accepts the amendment if $p' \in P_{ep}(p) \cap W_C^{qmv}(p)$. The Presidency considers Parliament's proposal and proposes a change if $P_{pres}(p) \cap P_{ep}(p) \cap W_C^{qmv}(p) \neq \emptyset$. Knowing this, in the first stage, Parliament decides whether to draft a proposal or to end the legislative process, and it proposes:

$$p^* = \begin{cases} \max(U_{ep}(x) | x \in P_{ep} \cap P_{pres} \cap W_C^{qmv} \cap A) & \text{if } P_{ep} \cap P_{pres} \cap W_C^{qmv} \cap A \neq \emptyset; \\ q & \text{if } P_{ep} \cap P_{pres} \cap W_C^{qmv} \cap A = \emptyset; \end{cases}$$

which is the equilibrium outcome.[32]

the set $P_{ep}(x)$ is always empty for some points, at least for Parliament's most preferred position. Consequently, the amendment-proof set A, which is the intersection of both sets, is not the empty set.

31 See Crombez (2003: 111).

32 See Crombez (2000a: 53). Note that since we assume a unitary Parliament, the Parliament's preference set is equal to the majority win set of Parliament and the preference set of the Parliament President. An alternative specification allows

For the unanimity version of this procedure, $A = \{x|P_{ep}(x) \cap W^{u}_{C}(x) = \emptyset\}$. Parliament proposes:

$$p^* = \begin{cases} \max(U_{ep}(x)|x \in P_{ep} \cap W^{u}_{C} \cap A) & \text{if } P_{ep} \cap W^{u}_{C} \cap A \neq \emptyset; \\ q & \text{if } P_{ep} \cap W^{u}_{C} \cap A = \emptyset; \end{cases}$$

which is the equilibrium outcome.

Co-decision: Council model

Define, as above, the amendment-proof set $A = \{x|P_{pres}(x) \cap P_{ep}(x) \cap W^{qmv}_{C}(x) = \emptyset\}$. In the last stage the Council prefers a proposal if $p \in W^{qmv}_{C}$. Parliament considers the Council President's proposal and proposes a change if $P_{ep}(p) \cap W^{qmv}_{C}(p) \neq \emptyset$. Knowing this, the Council Presidency proposes in the first stage:

$$p^* = \begin{cases} \max(U_{pres}(x)|x \in P_{ep} \cap W^{qmv}_{C} \cap A) & \text{if } P_{ep} \cap W^{qmv}_{C} \cap A \neq \emptyset;^{33} \\ q & \text{if } P_{ep} \cap W^{qmv}_{C} \cap A = \emptyset; \end{cases}$$

which is the equilibrium outcome.

For the unanimity version of this procedure, $A = \{x|P_{ep}(x) \cap W^{u}_{C}(x) = \emptyset\}$. The Council Presidency proposes:

$$p^* = \begin{cases} \max(U_{pres}(x)|x \in P_{ep} \cap W^{u}_{C} \cap A) & \text{if } P_{ep} \cap W^{u}_{C} \cap A \neq \emptyset; \\ q & \text{if } P_{ep} \cap W^{u}_{C} \cap A = \emptyset; \end{cases}$$

which is the equilibrium outcome.

the Council President to amend Parliament's proposal, while the President cannot block it. In other words, the Presidency is not able to 'impose' its preference on the outcome of the game. In that case, define the amendment-proof set as the set of points that cannot be changed by Parliament and a qualified majority in the Council as $A = \{x|\ P_{ep}(x) \cap W^{qmv}_{C}(x) = \emptyset\}$. Parliament now proposes in the first stage:

$$p^* = \begin{cases} \max(U_{ep}(x)|x \in P_{ep} \cap W^{qmv}_{C} \cap A) & \text{if } P_{ep} \cap W^{qmv}_{C} \cap A \neq \emptyset; \\ q & \text{if } P_{ep} \cap W^{qmv}_{C} \cap A = \emptyset; \end{cases}$$

which is the equilibrium outcome. In this chapter, we follow the model as specified by Crombez since we aim to test existing procedural models.

[33] See Crombez (2000a: 53). In this case, the Council President is the one who 'successfully proposes the policy'. If the Council Presidency is regarded as a gatekeeper, i.e. could choose to maintain the *status quo*, this condition would be $p = \max(U_{pres}(x)|\ x \in P_{ep} \cap P_{pres} \cap W^{qmv}_{C} \cap A)$ if $P_{ep} \cap P_{pres} \cap W^{qmv}_{C} \cap A \neq \emptyset$, and $p = q$ if $P_{ep} \cap P_{pres} \cap W^{qmv}_{C} \cap A = \emptyset$.

4

Institutional realism and bargaining models

CHRISTOPHER H. ACHEN

4.1 THE TWO STAGES OF POLITICAL DECISION-MAKING

Close studies of governmental decisions in democracies commonly divide the process into two stages. First, the actors bargain. As Arthur Bentley (1967 [1908]: 371) put it nearly a century ago in describing the legislative process, 'It is compromise . . . It is trading. It is the adjustment of interests.' This stage may include information-gathering and exchange, as well as threats and promises. Few rules constrain the actors. The free-form interplay puts a premium on creative interpretations and skilful compromise.

Then, when deals have been struck (or the parties to the conflict are exhausted), the second stage takes place. Here the organisational regulations and legal rules shape the process, and a test of strength is carried out according to constitutional or legal procedures. Explicit voting procedures settle differences of opinion.

The two stages of political decision-making interpenetrate and influence each other. Groups with more votes in the constitutional procedures

I thank the Center for the Study of Democratic Processes, Princeton University, and the Department of Political Science, University of Michigan, for released time from teaching that made this research possible. A research fund at the University of Michigan donated by Norma Shapiro paid for the overseas trips necessary to international collaboration, and I am most grateful to her. The members of the European Union Decision-making Research Group contributed many valuable comments, and I especially thank Madeleine Hosli, Thomas König, Frans Stokman, Robert Thomson, and Adrian van Deemen. Marcel Van Assen, Larry Bartels, Simon Hug, John Jackson, Andy Moravcsik, and the graduate students in Politics 583 at Princeton in Spring Term 2004 also provided helpful additions and criticisms, as did seminar participants at the University of Michigan, National Chengchi University of Taiwan, and Rutgers University. Robert Mokken sent lengthy, constructive written comments. I have not adopted all of these suggestions, however, and thus remaining errors are my own.

have more power in the preliminary bargaining. Conversely, skilful bargainers at the initial stage may persuade other actors and build coalitions that control a disproportionate number of votes at the final stage. Manoeuvring at each stage takes account of the contending groups' power at the other stage. A sophisticated recent discussion that emphasises this two-step view of European Union decision-making is Van den Bos (1991, chapter 5). Students of domestic politics have repeatedly discovered the same process at work, particularly in studies of interest groups, 'iron triangles', policy networks, and issue coalitions. A recent colourful American example was the battle over President William Clinton's national health plan (Broder and Johnson 1996).

Contemporary formal theorists often wish to model political decisions as an extensive form game. However, coping with the two stages of decision-making, each with its own logic, presents a conundrum. Modelling the formal procedures at the second stage is difficult enough, for the law can be quite complex. To make matters worse, modelling the first stage bargaining as an extensive form game is even more difficult. The strategy spaces are staggeringly large and not known to the analyst, the information sets are poorly specified and may be determined by gossip and back channels, and the order of play is haphazard and contested. Thus expressing either stage of political decision-making in the extensive form presents troublesome challenges aplenty. At this stage of our knowledge, detailed modelling of their interconnection seems hopeless.

Sometimes (necessarily highly simplified) models of the two stages are posited without attempting a full-blown conventional game-theoretic analysis. Approaches of that kind are represented by Coleman (1966b; 1971; 1990), Bueno de Mesquita *et al* (1985), Stokman and Van den Bos (1992), Bueno de Mesquita (1994), and Stokman and Van Oosten (1994). In updated versions, all these models are represented in this book. For the assumptions of their two-stage models, see Chapters 6 and 8. In addition, Mika Widgrén and Antti Pajala present a new two-stage model of this kind in Chapter 9.

More commonly, though, theorists are daunted by the theoretical complexities, and they give up on modelling both stages. If the initial bargaining is set aside, for example, analysis can focus on the second stage. Thus, as Chapter 3 made clear, many analysts have modelled the formal legal sequencing of the various EU decision-making processes (Crombez 1996; Laruelle 1998; Laruelle and Widgrén 2001; Steunenberg 1994a; Tsebelis 1994). Typically, the Commission, the member countries represented in the Council of Ministers, and the European Parliament are each treated as unitary actors within a simplified version of the EU decision-making rules. The actors' preferences are taken to be common knowledge, so that the game is conducted under complete information. Conclusions are then derived from standard game-theoretic solution concepts for extensive form games, such as subgame perfection.[1] Models of this kind, where the legal rules are embodied in extensive form games, are called *procedural*.

Formal mathematical analyses of decision-making rules have led to important insights and debates over the consequences for EU decision-making of particular legal provisions. The great strength of taking the rules at face value is that they are relatively clear and explicit in a well-developed decision-making system like the EU. Disputes over procedures occur, of course, and not every legal rule is unambiguous. But compared to the fuzzy informality of pre-decision bargaining, the legal provisions are a model of clarity. Emphasising legalities brings the great logical power of non-cooperative game theory to bear on EU decision-making, with gains in understanding that are evident in the literature. For example, such models have demonstrated that features of decision-making often neglected in conventional analyses, such as the reversion point (what happens if agreement fails) may play a fundamental role in determining a political outcome (even if agreement does not fail).

Rational-actor models are conventionally criticised for their over-estimation of human cognitive capacity and their under-estimation of the true complexity of human choice. EU decision-making models are no exception, and critics have not been slow to complain. Experienced analysts know, however, that all good science simplifies. The only issue is the relative power of alternate simplifications.

The principal serious concern about most procedural versions of EU decision-making is not that they are simplified, but rather that they may become politically naive. For example, decisions are often modelled as unrelated even when they are closely linked. Thus the EU's 1987 decisions about emission controls on small, medium, and large cars would often be treated in extensive form models as if they occurred in complete independence from each other. Indeed, many such procedural models logically imply that no equilibrium exists if the actors consider all three

[1] An important model of this kind, directed toward legislative behaviour generally, is Baron and Ferejohn (1989).

kinds of cars simultaneously. In such cases, no prediction of outcomes is possible. Other models escape this limitation only by assuming that a particular designated actor picks the final proposal to be considered, an assumption with doubtful support in either the formal decision-making rules or the case study literature.

A great many case studies have shown that preliminary deal-making is critical to outcomes in the EU, just as they are in virtually every democratic decision-making body around the world (for example, Hayes-Renshaw and Wallace 1997: chapter 10; Wallace 2000: 526). Yet in the extensive form models of the formal rules of EU decision-making, the compromises and cross-issue deals that dominate in the initial bargaining stage are rarely discussed. Implicitly, all such activities are assumed to be unimportant compared to the legal rules.

In some procedural models, the EU constitution is treated with a reverence that would please only the legalistic political scientists of the nineteenth century. For example, the power of a dissatisfied state to impose private costs and sanctions on other states and organisations when its will is flouted is nearly always ignored in contemporary extensive form models. Similarly, intensity of preference is usually neglected because it plays no role in the legal rules. Thus when Germany feels that its fundamental national purposes are being sabotaged by some EU decision, it is assumed to behave with prissy decorum on all other EU issues, and to act in other international forums as if it did not mind having its will thwarted by the EU. It was just those sorts of legalisms that pioneering political scientists like Woodrow Wilson (1885) and James Bryce (1893) attacked so long ago.

At least since Thucydides, political analysts have understood that 'the strong do what they can, and the weak suffer what they must'. In politics, power is fundamental. To understand political decision-making is to understand the balance of political forces that were brought to bear on the decision. For centuries, students of political decision-making have taken that conclusion for granted.

Political power is different from formal voting power or the legal power of initiating proposals, and it matters more than either. The bargaining that precedes the invocation of a legal decision process is more consequential than the narrow legalities. This feature of political life holds even more strongly in international forums like the EU. Duncan Black (1958: 141), a founder of rational choice models of formal constitutional procedures, recognised the limitations of purely legal analysis in the supra-national realm:

We also know that international discussion is the stage for power politics; that behind the scenes there are promises and threats; and that 'horses are traded', or bargains struck, which do not call for mention in the conference room.

Of course, procedures and votes matter: the deal is shaped by the need to have it ratified at the legal decision-making stage. But the legal rules should not be the sole focus of analytic effort. To predict EU decisions, it is important not to characterise the process analytically as if it were a textbook collective choice problem, in which atomistic individuals, who need not speak to one another, meet in a room and try out various proposals for approval, until one alternative wends its way antiseptically through a set of legally-sanctioned procedures and emerges as a law. Instead, bargaining and power dominate.

4.2 INSTITUTIONAL REALISM AND POLITICAL POWER

The power-based bargaining that defines the first stage of policy-making belongs in analysts' models. Unfortunately, few models of the critical first-stage process exist, and none commands universal assent. Conceptually, how might such a process best be understood?

The first source of guidance is the extensive literature in political science on the policymaking process. There is no one name for so disparate a literature, but 'institutional realism' conveys its two central features—an aversion to legalism, and an emphasis on the bargaining interplay of powerful societal and governmental organisations in the formation of policy.[2] The political actors may be individuals, social groups, pressure groups, government agencies, courts, legislatures, or any other private or public organisations. The literature on policy networks and issue coalitions is part of this tradition, as are writings on how conceptions of 'the national interest' enter policymaking. Institutional realism is simply the view that politics should be seen realistically rather than legalistically, and that the key actors in politics are usually institutions of one kind or another.[3]

[2] Of course, this kind of realism is not to be identified with the state-centric analysis of international affairs, also called 'realism'. Similarly, Grafstein's (1992) 'institutional realism' is a perspective in political philosophy, quite different from its usage here.

[3] Thus both the various Marxisms and the various pluralisms are special cases of the institutional-realist view, but the category itself is much broader. On pluralism, see especially Almond 1988.

The institutional realist tradition has tended to treat political outcomes as determined by institutional power without paying much attention to the details of the legal process. This is not to say that laws are irrelevant, but rather that they are shaped by power, too. The strong get their way, not only because they can exert pressure within the rules, but also, and more importantly, because in the long run, they make the rules. Thus as Riker (1980: 445) said, 'Institutions are probably best seen as congealed tastes.' Moreover, for institutional realists, laws and organisations are not just anybody's frozen preferences. Instead, they represent the solidified desires of the powerful.

This approach does not so much ignore procedural rules as endogenise them: political forms will reflect political power, and thus the formal rules in the second stage of policy-making will support the will of powerful actors. Hence the outcomes will also reflect the desires of powerful actors, in proportion to the power they bring to bear. That is, institutional realists tend to see political outcomes at the first stage of policy-making as an agreement to be ratified nearly unanimously at the second stage. And since both the constitutional and extra-constitutional structures reflect the power relationships, the agreement struck will amount to an approximate weighted average of actor preferences, the weight being a function of the actor's power. As Banfield (1961: 349, footnote 9) puts it, the outcome of the policy-making process is 'a 'quasi-Utilitarian' conception, the utility of the individual being weighted according to his influence.' Similar statements abound in the policy-making literature. Specialised assumptions of that kind are also made frequently in applied political and economic modelling (Alesina and Rosenthal 1995: 47–48; Chong 1991: 144; Franzese 1999).

A special version of Banfield's verbal sketch has been formalised by Van den Bos (1991: 175) and by Stokman and Van den Bos (1992: 235). They call it the base model. Issues are taken to be one-dimensional. On each issue coming before them, political actors are assumed to agree to a compromise position which is a weighted average of their most-preferred (or *ideal*) positions, with the weights being their 'power'. Formally, if there are n actors, let the most-preferred position of actor i be x_i. Denote the power of i by v_i. Then the expected outcome predicted by the base model, y_B, is:

$$y_B = \frac{\sum_{i=1}^{n} v_i x_i}{\sum_{i=1}^{n} v_i} \qquad (4.1)$$

Stokman and Van den Bos were concerned with voting in the EU Council of Ministers, and so they defined 'power' as the actor's number of votes. However, an index of vote power or some other measure of political 'clout' might be substituted. In this book, as noted in Chapter 2, 'power' in the EU is measured by the actor's Shapley Shubik index value. Because of the way that value is defined, this definition of power takes account of actors' positions in the legal structure. Thus it captures in a simple way the interpenetration of the bargaining and voting stages of EU decision-making: your bargaining strength is greater when the rules favour you.

The base model is not a fully-fledged formal model, nor is it derived from such a model. It is simply a summary of other literature, such as the less subtle versions of pluralist or Marxian theory, in which only power and interests matter. It was set out by Stokman and Van den Bos not as a serious theoretical proposal, but rather as a crude but useful comparison measure, whose predictions may be matched against those of better models.

4.3 THE COMPROMISE MODEL

An institutional realism model for forecasting political decisions necessarily must take power into account, as the base model does. However, power relationships alone are not enough. Long ago, Bentley (1967 [1908]: 215–222) stressed the importance of intensity in creating influence. Much later, Lindblom (1965: 334) wrote, 'Other things being equal, the more intensely held a value, interest, or preference the heavier its weight in partisan mutual adjustment.' Similar statements about how intensity adds weight to influence have been made by Banfield (1961: 331–332) and others throughout the political science writings of the last hundred years.

Thus to the extent that one can summarise a somewhat imprecise literature extending over many decades, one might say that Banfield's 'quasi-utilitarian' conception characterises this school of thought deriving from Bentley, but with the understanding that an actor's influence depends on both the actor's potential power and on the salience or intensity of the issue for that actor. Predicted outcomes are compromises among the actors, with more powerful actors and more intense actors having more say than the weak and the apathetic. As Harsanyi (1963; 1977: 174–176, 192–195) showed, game theoretic solution concepts for bargaining games lead naturally to the same 'quasi-utilitarian' outcome, where the weight on each actor's utility is determined, not by justice, but by the actor's strength in the bargaining situation.[4]

In a parallel development, Coleman (1966a; 1966b; 1971; summarised in 1990: 769–873) developed 'exchange models' in which political actors could trade votes or positions on issues in order to achieve an 'ideal system' of social action. In one version of his framework, the ideal collective decision in a dichotomous (yes or no) choice is given by choosing the alternative that has the greatest sum of weighted preferences, where the weights are the product of power and intensity (for example, Coleman 1990: 850–851). This is again a formalisation of Banfield's version of institutional realism.

Several researchers have developed policy-making analysis in the sociological tradition stemming from Coleman. (See the review in Knoke *et al* 1996: chapter 7; a recent application to the EU is Mokken *et al* 2000.) In particular, Van den Bos (1991: 175–176) took an important step forward in that tradition by extending Coleman's decision formula to the case of continuous outcomes. He called it the compromise model.[5] In that formula, political outcomes are predicted to occur at the weighted mean of actor preferences, with the weights being the product of power and intensity. Formally, if actor i has salience s_i, and if ideal points and power are denoted as in the base model, then the expected outcome predicted by institutional realism (the compromise model) is y_C, defined as:

$$y_C = \frac{\sum_{i=1}^{n} s_i v_i x_i}{\sum_{i=1}^{n} s_i v_i} \qquad (4.2)$$

Note that if an actor does not care about a particular issue ($s_i = 0$), then that actor is dropped from both the numerator and denominator of the previous equation. In effect, the issue is resolved among the remaining actors.

The link between Banfield's and Harsanyi's quasi-utilitarian formulation, Coleman's model, and Van den Bos's formula, is easily spelled out. Suppose that the policy process works to optimise a weighted sum of

[4] Note that this version of utilitarianism is quite different from its counterpart in ethics, and thus the many axiom systems for normative utilitarianism are irrelevant here. As Harsanyi (1977) stresses, it is important not to confuse the derivations and uses of utilitarian models in the two realms. For review and discussion, see Riley (1988) and Elster and Roemer (1991), for example.

[5] Van den Bos's original wording was 'compromise specification'. In Bueno de Mesquita and Stokman (1994: 114–115), the base and compromise specifications were promoted to base and compromise 'models', and I have retained that language here.

utilities, where the weights are power times intensity, as Banfield and Lindblom suggest.[6] Suppose further that utility losses are quadratic in the distance from the actor's most-preferred alternative. Then, in the same notation as before, the policy chosen will be[7]:

$$y_C = \underset{z}{\operatorname{argmax}} \sum_{i=1}^{n} -s_i v_i (z - x_i)^2 \tag{4.3}$$

This is a simple quadratic minimisation problem in one variable, and in the case of continuous outcomes, the solution is well known from elementary calculus: it is Van den Bos's y_C as defined in Equation (4.2). Thus the Banfield formulation with quadratic loss leads to Van den Bos's compromise model.[8]

Alternately, if the possible outcomes of the decision process are discrete (for example, dichotomous), then under the Banfield view, y_C is the alternative that maximises Equation (4.3). But it is easily shown that y_C in that case is equivalent to choosing the outcome with the largest product of power times utility, as in Coleman's model. Thus Banfield's framework leads to Coleman's solution in the case that Coleman treated, and Van den Bos's compromise model also generates Coleman's prediction in that case.

In short, the compromise model is a specialised implementation of the century-old tradition of institutional realism in political science. It also incorporates the prediction models from social action theory in sociology. It is a concise and practical formula, suitable for empirical applications. No elaborate software programs are needed to compute it, and no disputable subtleties are disguised in its formula. This sophisticatedly simple equation neatly summarises much of the previous century's thought about political policy-making. For all these reasons, it appears as part of the theoretical apparatus in other models, including those in Chapters 5, 7, and 9 of this book.

As it stands, however, the compromise model lacks a certain theoretical dignity. In a fundamental sense, there is no model here: Van den Bos

6 'To the extent that the process was one of bargaining, it registered a compound of influence and intensity of interest. If it is considered appropriate to maximise 'total satisfaction' of those whose views are taken into account, then it is essential to have some indication of how intensely each value is held.' (Banfield, 1961: 332).

7 The expression, $argmax_z$, means 'the value of z that maximises the following expression'. Here z is taken to be an element of the real line; in other cases, the set of possible z's is specified explicitly.

8 Note that the base model would follow from this argument if saliences were irrelevant (or equal).

(1991: 175–176) explicitly set aside his initial formal model and imposed this equation as a better fit to EU reality.[9] The formula was proposed as an empirical summary of what is known from prior work in sociology and political science. As Equation (4.3) showed, the formula also follows from Banfield's macro-level summary conclusion about how policy-making comes to a decision. But none of these descriptive summaries is *theory* in the modern sense, that is, a derivation from fundamental axioms about the political behaviour of the actors. Even Harsanyi's (1963; 1977: 174–176) derivation of the quasi-utilitarian interpretation, while fully rigorous, is abstract, working solely with utilities and not with policy positions. Thus his framework does not connect to political outcomes and policy-making data as the compromise model does. And Coleman (1990: 868) himself expressed doubts about the theoretical legitimacy of his own formulation of the compromise model applied to the dichotomous case.[10] In short, we have no adequate micro-foundations that imply the formula. No such set of axioms currently exists.

Nevertheless, the compromise model formula gives a clear and simple, though politically sophisticated, goal for modelling. It summarises the fundamental orientation of institutional realism. Thus it is a theme or a conclusion, not the story itself. What the realist political science literature and the sociological modelling tradition have agreed on is this: if a good institutional realism model were developed, it should logically imply something like the compromise model; and if the viewpoint of institutional realism is correct, then the corresponding model should yield predictions superior to those of extensive form games that adopt a legalistic view of policy-making.

Indeed, the compromise model has enjoyed some empirical success. Bueno de Mesquita and Stokman (1994) set out seven different predictive models of EU decision-making. They focused on the Council of Ministers, by far the most powerful organ of EU decision-making at that time. Examining sixteen policy issues, they read the news agency *Agence Europe* and interviewed experts to assess the preferred policy positions

[9] Van den Bos interpreted the equation as representing an exchange of information about the actors. For further explanation and extension to other models, see Chapter 5 of this volume.

[10] In general, the sociological modelling tradition stemming from Coleman is full of political wisdom about the policy-making process, often strikingly so in comparison with its economics and political science game-theoretic counterparts, but the sociological models have struggled to attain the theoretical rigor and coherence of the game theory models. See the review in Knoke *et al* (1996 Chapter 7).

and issue saliences of each of the national actors, as was done for this book (see Chapter 2). The data were then fed into each of the models, and predictive accuracy was assessed.

In Bueno de Mesquita and Stokman's evaluations (1994, Chapter 9), the compromise model finished third, just behind the two models favoured by the authors. However, the statistical criteria used to evaluate the models differed slightly from the usual statistical measures. If more standard statistical criteria are used, the compromise model moves into second place among the models; and if an arguably more plausible scaling of saliences is employed, the compromise model is a comfortable winner, easily defeating each of the other six models (Achen 1999).

Thus in the one small dataset that has been available, the compromise model was arrayed against prominent models with good track records. It proved itself to be, at minimum, a strong competitor against the best models, and by some criteria, it did even better than that, defeating all comers. Thus as a pure statistical forecaster, the compromise model has been a serious contender.

In summary, many recent policy-making models have been animated by ideas derived from the older legalist tradition, with a potentially serious loss in political verisimilitude. A different understanding of the policy-making process, which we have called institutional realism, has dominated the political science and sociological literature of the last century. A rough weighted-utilitarian outline of its workings is visible, and it has proved itself empirically. However, the institutional realist tradition is overwhelmingly qualitative and humanist in methodology. Power-and-intensity-weighted bargaining has attracted less analytic attention than might be expected, and no formal model has been proposed which implies this standard political science view of policy-making. Without it, the case study support and statistical victories of institutional realism remain on shaky footing.

As it turns out, however, a theoretical foundation can be supplied for the compromise model. This foundation will be called the institutional realism model. The remainder of this chapter is devoted to its derivation. The compromise model then appears as a close approximation to the solution implied by the institutional realism model.

4.4 COOPERATIVE AND NON-COOPERATIVE GAME MODELS

Non-cooperative games specify the moves available to each of the players. In contemporary social science, most such games employ the extensive form, in which the sequence of moves is spelled out explicitly. Other aspects of the players' situations, such as their information sets, are included as well. Games of this kind were used in Chapter 3.

Models of the initial stage of policy-making typically do not attempt to explicitly model the full bargaining process in the manner of extensive form games. That process, with its many formal and informal channels of power and influence, cannot be encompassed in a manageable extensive form model in any case. Instead, bargaining models from co-operative game theory become the only sensible procedure for studying complex, informal bargaining processes, a point that bargaining theorists have often made (for example, Binmore 1987a: 8).

Cooperative game models make no attempt to track the full sequence of decisions in a game. Instead, they treat the decision-making process as a black box, in the manner of systems theory (Granger and Newbold 1986: 33). In the framework of this book, cooperative games take preferences, salience, and power as the inputs, and then produce collective decisions as the output. Analytic power is obtained by specifying certain conditions or axioms that the outcome of the game must satisfy, for example that the solution must not depend on strategically meaningless aspects of the game or that the players must not harm themselves for no reason. In the case of bargaining models in particular, cooperative games attempt to specify the nature of the outcome of a class of extensive form bargaining games without attempting the hopeless task of spelling out the full details of how the bargaining might be conducted in each of them.

Twenty years ago, cooperative game models were thought to be of only modest usefulness. Analysts thought of cooperative games as models in which conditions were placed on the nature of outcomes without specifying why those conditions necessary held. After all, well-known games often have counter-intuitive outcomes: how can we know what outcomes are like without solving for them explicitly? By contrast, non-cooperative game theorists insisted on spelling out the detailed choices that players face. Explicit modelling of players' choices was seen as an unmixed improvement on cooperative game models.

Most analysts no longer think about cooperative game theory in this way. Now cooperative game solution concepts are often seen as summaries of what many different non-cooperative models would produce (Mas-Colell *et al* 1995: 674). Of course, cooperative games require support from their non-cooperative counterparts. On their own, the cooperative forms do not always represent every strategic possibility well. Thus for analysts to have confidence in a cooperative game solution, it must be shown to be consistent with at least one extensive form. But that one extensive form by no means exhausts its meaning.

As Binmore (1987a: 9) puts it, the purpose of constructing extensive form bargaining games 'is *not* because it is thought that such models will replace the use of cooperative solution concepts. The purpose is to *test* cooperative solution concepts.' If successfully tested, the broad applicability of the cooperative solution may well outpace that of a corresponding extensive form game. This is especially likely to be true for free-form bargaining situations, in which any extensive form will necessarily be a rather special case substantively, leading to grave doubts about its generality as social scientific explanation. On this view, the relationship between cooperative and non-cooperative models is not competitive, but 'complementary; each helps to justify and clarify the other', as Nash himself remarked (1953: 129) long ago.

The next section, then, sets out a cooperative game foundation for institutional realism.

4.5 NASH BARGAINING AND QUADRATIC LOSSES

Institutional realism is the view that bargaining among institutional actors determines policy-making. Predicting outcomes from this perspective thus requires a bargaining model. The Nash bargaining solution (Nash, 1950) suits this purpose because it has already been suggested in one of the very best set of EU case studies as the appropriate mathematical model for thinking about EU decisions (Moravcsik 1998: 498). Moreover, as it did in the earliest days of bargaining theory, Nash theory has again come to dominate treatments of solution concepts for cooperative bargaining games (see for example Muthoo 1999: Chapter 2).

In a bargaining game, the actors have the opportunity to agree on a particular set of payoffs to each of them. The payoffs must belong to a feasible set S of such payoffs. If they cannot agree, then they must accept the disagreement outcome (or threat point), which is assumed worse for all of them than any of the other feasible alternatives.

Nash's bargaining solution for this game is implied by four axioms (set out more formally in Appendix 1 of this chapter). The first of these is the *rescaling axiom*, which simply recognises that cardinal utilities are measured only at the interval level. Hence, just as expressing a temperature in Celsius rather than Fahrenheit does not make anyone cooler on a hot day, so also re-expressing cardinal utilities on an equivalent scale should not change bargaining outcomes.

Second, the *Pareto* postulate says that when actors can all agree that one alternative is better than another, the bargaining solution will not pick the inferior one. Next, the *anonymity axiom* says that it does not matter for social choices who is called 'the first actor' or 'the *n*th actor'.

The final axiom is the only one that is seriously controversial, but even it has strong appeal. The *independence of irrelevant alternatives (IIA) axiom* states that if an alternative is chosen as the bargaining outcome in a set of alternatives, then it will again be chosen in a subset of those alternatives if it is still available.

The remarkable consequence of these simple axioms is the well-known *Nash bargaining theorem*. If we scale the utility of the disagreement outcome to zero for all actors, then we get a particularly simple form for the Nash bargaining solution: the bargainers will agree on the alternative $f(S)$ that maximizes the product of their utilities (see Appendix 1 of this chapter):

$$f(S) = \underset{y \in S}{\operatorname{argmax}} \prod_{i=1}^{n} u_i(y) \tag{4.4}$$

The strength of this bargaining solution is its foundation in non-cooperative games. The path-breaking Rubinstein (1982) extensive form game provided a micro-foundation for two-person bargaining. That game has a limiting form (for small-time intervals between offers), and that limit turns out to be the (generalised) Nash solution (Binmore 1987a; 1987b). Thus the Nash solution has the validation in non-cooperative game theory that makes a cooperative solution credible.

The Nash solution, originally developed for two-person games, also extends smoothly to the n-person case, as Equation (4.4) shows. Myerson's (1991: 417–481) text notes that the n-person Nash solution has particular appeal when the grand coalition of all players is possible, and firm coalitions among proper subsets of the players are difficult to construct. In the EU, shifting interests across issues mean that states have 'permanent interests but no permanent friends'. Moreover, the interpenetration of EU institutions by nationals of all member states makes separate, private deals among subsets of the EU actors difficult to arrange and virtually impossible to enforce. Such mini-coalitions play very little role in case studies of EU policy-making. On the other hand, the search for arrangements acceptable to all is a striking feature of those studies. Taken together, these are just the conditions in which the n-person Nash solution is theoretically attractive.[11]

Other initially attractive axiomatic two-person solutions turn out not to extend well to the n-person case. For example, the much discussed model of Kalai and Smorodinsky (1975) no longer guarantees Pareto optimal outcomes when there are more than two actors (Roth 1979: 98–107). In the remainder of this chapter, then, we consider the Nash bargaining model.

The Nash solution predicts a particular choice among *utilities* for the players, which may include lotteries. For the purposes of this book, however, actual policy-making *outcomes* must be predicted. Hence the Nash solution must be specialised further to get a form tractable for policy-making applications. We do so by assigning to each actor a quadratic loss function $u_i(z) = a_i - s_i(z - x_i)^2$ over the sure-thing alternatives, where z is a sure-thing alternative on a single dimension, x_i is the actor's ideal point on the same dimension, and a_i and s_i are constants. This postulate turns out to exclude lotteries as solutions (see Appendix 2 of this chapter).[12] Quadratic losses are, of course, the standard assumption in applied modelling on grounds of both theoretical plausibility and analytic tractability, and no alternative has acquired the same widespread acceptance.

The Nash bargaining solution, applied in the case of quadratic utilities, gives this solution over the set of sure-thing alternatives A:

$$f(S) = \operatorname*{argmax}_{z \in A} \prod_{i=1}^{n} (a_i - s_i(z - x_i)^2) \qquad (4.5)$$

Under the conditions of the Nash bargaining model and quadratic losses, then, Equation (4.5) is the predictive equation for the institutional realism model for proposals with a single issue dimension. The extension to

[11] Unfortunately, no generally persuasive micro-foundations for any n-person bargaining solutions yet exist, though several attempts have been made (Muthoo 1999: 336–338).

[12] Appendix 2 of this chapter also shows how to use the quadratic loss assumption to cope with cases, frequent in the dataset used in this book, in which only a finite number of points are meaningful outcomes. For example, suppose that 0, 30, 80, and 100 are the only substantively meaningful outcomes, yet the Nash bargaining solution applied to the full interval [0, 100] produces a forecast of 60. How is this meaningless 60 to be interpreted? Appendix 2 of this chapter shows formally that under the assumptions of this paper and to a close approximation, the forecast of 60 should be adjusted to nearest meaningful point, which is 80. Hence 80 is the approximate true Nash solution prediction.

proposals with more than one issue is obvious and is considered in Appendix 2 of this chapter.

Even in the relatively simple case of a single dimension with quadratic losses, however, the Nash bargaining solution is analytically somewhat inconvenient. First, non-linear optimisation is needed to find the predicted outcome. Second, the model requires as input the value a_i to each player of the disagreement outcome. Now the disagreement outcome is a hypothetical event whose utility is difficult for anyone to estimate, including the actors themselves. (The experts consulted for this book were not asked to evaluate it.) Moreover, these computational and data-collection challenges are compounded when decisions involve more than one issue, which occurs frequently in EU policy-making. Hence in the next section, we set out a convenient approximation to the institutional realist bargaining model which avoids both these difficulties.

4.6 THE IMPORTANCE OF CONSENSUS

As it stands, the institutional realism model requires a knowledge of the positions, saliences, and powers of the actors, along with their utilities for the disagreement outcome. Only the last of these is difficult to obtain from expert interviews. In consequence, it is tempting to solve that problem by treating the disagreement point as simply a 'reversion point'—the *status quo* or, more generally, the policy position that occurs if bargaining fails. Then the utility loss for each actor can be computed as the weighted quadratic distance to the reversion point, just as one would compute the loss for any other policy position on the same issue.

This approach to valuing the reversion point is undeniably convenient. Unfortunately, though, it emphasises the legality of the situation rather than the reality, thereby missing the point of institutional realism. It treats a woman who has just been jilted the day before her wedding as no worse off than she was before: 'After all, you aren't married today, and tomorrow you still won't be married. You haven't lost a thing. What's the problem?' That is exactly the logic of treating the reversion point as just the *status-quo* position on the issue scale.

In an ongoing relationship, a failure in negotiations is far more expensive than just a return to the reversion point. Hence EU negotiators strive intensely and indefatigably to reach an agreement that is acceptable to all parties. Lindberg (1963: 285) noted in the earliest years of the EU that:

> Each member tries to influence the content of the final decision as much as it can, but all are agreed on the necessity of mutual concession, since the normal practice is to exclude the possibility of not reaching an agreement at all.

In the same way, Hayes-Renshaw and Wallace (1997: 251) remark about the EU Council of Ministers that 'everything depends on making a proposition "yesable" to as many participants as possible'.

Once a deal has been struck, the subsequent legal stages are often no more than a formality, with all stages proceeding with the approval of very large majorities. Proposing and voting simply ratify the bargain. Hence the strikingly large number of unanimous votes in the EU Council of Ministers even under qualified majority decision rules, quite the opposite of what most extensive form games based solely on the legal rules would predict (Mattila and Lane 2001). Similar findings about the EU policy-making process appear in the case studies of other chapters of this book. Even when the rules permit a qualified majority to have its way, unanimous agreements are still sought and often attained.

Astute observers have noticed this pattern of striving for unanimity in legislative bodies for more than a century. Wilson (1885: 100–101) described the American Congressional process in this fashion:

> Indeed, only a very slight examination of the measures which originate with the [Congressional] Committees is necessary to show that most of them are framed with a view to securing their easy passage ... The manifest object is to dress them to the liking of all factions.

The same emphasis on consensus-building also appears in modern case studies of skilful committee chairs in the US Congress (Manley 1970: 111–121).

Thus in bargaining circumstances like those the EU faces, the disagreement outcome is highly undesirable. When a final agreement is at hand, a breakdown in the negotiations does not leave the parties no worse off than they were before. To the contrary, they are likely to feel deeply disappointed, even angry. Relationships with other parties are damaged, and the hard feelings carry over into other, unrelated issues. The cost to each party of the disagreement point is not the simple policy value of the *status quo*, as some models assume. Instead, the damages are the very large losses that come with broken institutional relationships.[13]

[13] There is the additional difficulty with equating disagreement outcomes to reversion points, which is that disagreement outcomes have to be worse for all actors than any feasible bargain if the logic of the Nash bargaining solution is to make sense.

Of course, these dramatic breakdowns are rarely observed; they are 'off the equilibrium path'. In practice, bargaining in the EU is characterised by a 'diffuse reciprocity'[14] rather than by threats. That can mislead researchers into thinking that the threats are relatively unimportant. However, as game theory has taught us, the frequency with which threats are used is no guide to their importance. Instead, it is precisely their availability that sustains bargaining reciprocity and makes threats largely unnecessary.

4.7 INSTITUTIONAL REALISM IS APPROXIMATED BY THE COMPROMISE MODEL

This line of reasoning has important consequences for the institutional realism model. When disagreement is highly undesirable, then a simple corollary to the Nash bargaining theorem follows (Appendix 2 of this chapter). That corollary essentially states that under the institutional realism model assumptions (the axioms of the Nash bargaining theorem hold, losses are quadratic, and the disagreement point is far in utility terms from all the possible bargaining agreements), then to a first-order approximation, the institutional realism model implies the compromise model as its solution. That is, as disagreement becomes ever more undesirable, the policy predictions of the institutional realism model converge closer and closer to the forecasts of the compromise model, and in the limit, they are identical. Moreover, when there are several issues considered simultaneously, then under an additive version of quadratic losses, the institutional realism model is approximated by the compromise model applied to each issue separately (Appendix 2 of this chapter).[15]

Thus under institutional realist assumptions, the compromise model may be interpreted as an approximation to a familiar cooperative game theory solution concept. The compromise model applied to each dimension separately gives, to a good approximation, the same answer as the

Only 66 of the 162 issues in the dataset meet this criterion. See Appendix 1 of this chapter.

[14] I owe the phrase to Andy Moravcsik.

[15] When issues are multi-dimensional, applying the compromise model on each dimension separately is a rather special case of institutional realism, based on a somewhat implausible behavioural assumption (see Appendix 2 of this chapter). However, to give the compromise model the prominent treatment and thorough test that its simplicity merits, that version of institutional realism was adopted for this book.

n-person Nash bargaining solution applied to all the dimensions simultaneously. Thus, unlike some other models of policy-making, the institutional realism model does not shatter when faced with multiple dimensions of the same decision. The saliences incorporate the information about how utility is to be traded off across issues. In addition, the difficult problem of knowing the precise disutility of the disagreement point is finessed by simply treating it as 'large' and then approximating the resulting solution.

It should be noted in this derivation that 'power' v_i is defined as the inverse of how badly off one would be in the absence of agreement: implicitly, those who have most to lose from the failure of the negotiations are the weakest.[16] On the other hand, large, rich countries that can sanction smaller and poorer countries without suffering much in return will be powerful in the negotiations. For additional details about the measurement of power and salience, see Appendix 3 of this chapter.

In summary, Nash bargaining theory has been used here to impose conditions on any solution to the collective choice problem faced by the EU. These conditions, in turn, are shown to have a solution, the institutional realism model, to which the compromise model is a good approximation. Thus the compromise model is shown theoretically to be a plausible approximation for any standard collective decision problem in which bargaining plays a central role. The prominent role of that model in case studies and empirical tests is thereby explained and justified.

4.8 AN APPLICATION

The compromise model is an approximation. There are at least four ways in which it may depart to some degree from reality, in increasing order of importance. First, quadratic losses might be a poor description of actor preferences. Second, the Nash bargaining solution might fail to describe agreements reached. Third, disagreement might be only slightly

[16] Under the approximation used to derive the compromise model, all actors have much to lose from the failure of the negotiations, and thus their power is more equal than the Shapley Shubik values imply. This argument would seem to apply most strongly to the countries voting in the Council under qualified majority rules. However, from the outset, the authors of this book agreed to use the Shapley Shubik values as the best objective measure of power, and that convention was adhered to in this chapter. For a related argument about the relative power of states, namely that 'preference outliers' are weak in EU negotiations, all else equal, see Mokken *et al* (2000).

undesirable in some negotiations, so that the quality of the numerical approximation used in the derivation might be poor. Fourth, the legal rules might allow a qualified majority to impose their will on the others and they might do so, meaning that the usual unanimity norm would not be honoured.

The EU's two 1999 decisions on reform of structural assistance in the fisheries sector (CNS/1998/347), discussed in greater detail in Chapter 5, illustrate both a predictive success and a relative failure for the compromise model. On the first issue, the number of tonnes of old fishing fleet that needed to be scrapped to qualify for new funding, the compromise model predicts that a bargaining agreement would be reached at a scaled position of 36 on a 100-point scale, meaning that approximately 110 tonnes would have to be scrapped for every 100 new tonnes. In fact, however, no agreement was reached, and the *status quo* (position 0) of 100-tonnes-for-100-tonnes scrapping was maintained. There simply was no working qualified majority for a change from the *status quo*. Although the size of the prediction error is not large in substantive terms here, this issue nevertheless illustrates the class of situation in which the compromise model may not work well. Failing to agree on this issue represented no drastic change from the *status quo*, and the blocking coalition could prevent action without great cost. Disagreement was not the divisive option that institutional realism presumes and that most case studies of the EU have found.

The second issue concerning fisheries was a measure tying EU funding to compliance with the difficult EU fisheries programme objectives. The *status quo* had no such restrictions, so that failure to agree would have had genuine consequences. On this issue, the compromise model predicts a position of 68 on a 100-point scale, while the actual bargaining outcome as scored by experts was 70. Thus the compromise model performs extremely well in this case, for which it is well suited. (For details about forecasting with the compromise model, see Appendix 3 of this chapter.)

4.9 THE STATE-CENTRIC ALTERNATIVE

In applying the compromise model or any other model based on the same inputs, thorny issues of application arise immediately. The first is that any theoretical model of politics begins by defining the relevant actors. Often this step is obvious: the actors are just who they seem to be. But in international organisations like the EU, complexities arise.

In contrast to the institutional realism of this chapter, some other perspectives see international institutions as only marginally important. Moreover, they relegate economic considerations to a minor role in decision-making compared to issues of national security. For example, in interpretations of international organisations based on 'state-centric realism' (a recent example is Mearsheimer 1994–95), the central actors in the EU are the nation-states, not the executive and legislative components of the Brussels legal structure. State-centric realism argues that national security interests pervade *all* the organs of international organisations, in proportion to state power. To a good approximation, only the preferences of the member countries (weighted by their power and intensity) matter in policy-making. As Mearsheimer's (1994–95: 13) discussion of 'the false promise of international institutions' puts it:

> Realists also recognise that states sometimes operate through institutions. However, they believe that those rules reflect state calculations of self-interest based primarily on the international distribution of power. The most powerful states in the system create and shape institutions so that they can maintain their share of world power, or even increase it.[17]

On this version of realism, the state preferences measured for this book should reflect states' evaluation of their interests in each decision, and those interests should reflect security preferences. Moreover, bargaining power in the Council—the locus of state power in the EU—should proxy for states' influence throughout the EU. Hence the best version of the compromise model would be approximated by applying it to the members of the Council only, weighting them by their power within the Council. 'Power' might be determined by the gross domestic product of each state, or even better, if the logic of state-centric realism is correct, by the Shapley Shubik index value in the Council, since the latter is determined by the institutional rules and thus should be shaped by state power. In this chapter, the latter Shapley Shubik index values are used to operationalise state-centric realism. This portrayal, based on extending Mearsheimer's arguments to our dataset, is included among the models assessed empirically at the end of this chapter and in Chapter 10.

Another prominent state-centric interpretation of the EU is given by Moravcsik (1998: Chapter 7), who argues that the most crucial EU

[17] Mearsheimer uses the word 'rules' to include both agreements and organisations. Thus he (1994–95: 8–9) defines 'institutions as a set of rules that stipulate the ways in which states should cooperate and compete with each other . . . These rules are typically formalised in international agreements, and are usually embodied in organisations with their own personnel and budgets'.

decisions are made by the member states, with supranational institutions such as the Commission playing only an intermittent role. However, he describes his viewpoint as 'liberal intergovernmentalist', not realist, since his detailed case studies indicate that the security concerns emphasized by Mearsheimer (1994–95) have distinctly secondary weight, and that economic issues dominate. The implication of his work appears to be that the more important the issue, the greater the power of national governments relative to international institutions. This is an important hypothesis.

Unfortunately, the crux of Moravcsik's arguments cannot be tested here, since the EU issues studied in this book, while consequential, are nonetheless routine, day-to-day matters, not the critical choices he studied. There are not enough major decisions in EU history to permit quantitative study, particularly since the membership and formal rules have changed every decade or two, making over-time comparison difficult. Thus at this stage, Moravcsik's case study method seems best for his purpose. With regret, we lay aside his important findings and their implications as topics deserving further elaboration and study, which we cannot undertake here.

4.10 FORECASTING COMPARISONS

For the dataset used in this book, Table 4.1 gives the mean absolute error of the institutional realism model (under three different measures of power), the state-centric realist model deriving from Mearsheimer, and the simple mean and median. As the table shows, the compromise model under the second, more plausible version of the Shapley Shubik values forecasts better than under the less plausible Shapley Shubik values, and better also than under human judges' assessments of power. In fact, the best version of the compromise model finishes first overall in the comparisons. The mean is almost equally good. The median is worst. State-centric realism falls in between: it is better than the median, but not as good as the other two models. Thus the compromise model narrowly wins this first round of competition.

The second important aspect of Table 4.1 is that state-centric realism is not as successful in predicting day-to-day policy outcomes in the EU as those models that take the full structure of EU institutions into account, including the Commission and the Parliament.[18] Knowing national

[18] Even the very conservative sign test rejects at the 0.05 level the hypothesis that the state-centric realism model is as good as the compromise model. See Chapter 10.

Table 4.1. *Compromise model, state-centric realism model, and baselines. Errors of models by legislative procedure*[a]

Model	CNS QMV $n = 55$	CNS unanimity $n = 39$	COD QMV $n = 56$	COD unanimity $n = 12$	Total max n 162
Baseline models					
Median voter (unweighted)	30.62	21.03	30.64	31.75	28.40
Mean voter	24.28	18.82	26.18	18.78	23.21
Substantive models					
Compromise modes with:					
SSI variant 2	23.31	17.33	27.28	19.24	22.94
SSI variant 1	23.84	18.79	27.70	17.62	23.50
Expert judgements	25.31	26.27	29.10	17.19	26.25
State-centric realism model (adapted from Mearsheimer)	26.79	17.33	28.04	20.75	24.50

Note: [a]CNS: consultation procedure. COD: co-decision procedure. QMV: qualified majority voting. SSI variant 1 is the set of Shapley Shubik scores in which the Commission is always a member of the winning coalition. SSI variant 2 incorporates the alternate and more plausible constitutional interpretation, in which some winning coalitions exclude the Commission (see Chapter 2.6).

policy preferences alone is simply insufficient. International institutions matter. For explaining most behaviour of an international organisation like the EU, state-centric realism is itself the 'false promise'.

State-centric realists may object that they aim to explain only major issues of war and peace, not agricultural subsidies and auto emission controls. Fair enough: an organisation like the EU has little to do with decisions of war. But then state-centric realism is sidelined into irrelevancy for explaining nearly all the actual work of international organisations. Over time, an international organisation like the EU may remake the social and economic face of an entire continent. Explaining its behaviour is deeply consequential. What the statistical evidence of this chapter shows empirically is that for that task, state-centric realism cannot help us as much as models that take seriously the internal institutions of an international organisation. By counting all institutions as separate actors, that is just what the compromise model does.

Now how impressive is the victory of the compromise model? Granted, it is superior to the median and to state-centric realism. However, the mean essentially does just as well in Table 4.1, and so does the base model with the second version of the Shapley Shubik values (results not shown). Their performances are substantively and statistically equivalent.[19] Why focus on the compromise model?

The reason for emphasising the compromise model has to do with the imprecision in the measures of power and salience. As Table 4.1 demonstrates, even well-informed human assessments of actors' power do not perform as well as the Shapley Shubik values in predicting outcomes, and the Shapley Shubik values themselves are imperfect as measures of actual power. Thus the power measures contain measurement error. Moreover, the interviewers on this project often found that assessments of salience were even more difficult for respondents, meaning that their measurement errors are probably even larger than those for power. The inevitable consequence is that noise enters any model that uses power and salience for forecasting.

Now the mean uses neither power nor salience for its predictions, while the base model uses only power. If the power measures were useless and noisy, the base model would perform less well than the mean. However, the base model performs just as well as the mean, implying that it is overcoming the additional measurement error with greater theoretical accuracy. In the same way, the compromise model uses both the Shapley Shubik values *and* the particularly noisy salience measures, meaning that if the mean or the base model were theoretically better, the compromise model should finish well behind them in predictive power. But in fact, the compromise model is just as good, indicating again that it has theoretical power that they lack. (For additional discussion, see Appendix 3 of this chapter.)

Additional confirmation of the institutional realism foundation for the compromise model appears when EU issues are separated by bargaining context and outcome. This chapter used the perspective of institutional realism to put a theoretical foundation under the compromise model. In particular, the compromise model was interpreted as a bargaining solution. From this viewpoint, actual EU issues fall into three classes: (1) classic bargaining situations in which the reversion point is either nonexistent or else falls outside the range of actor positions (that is, outside

[19] In fact, the base model finished a hair's breadth ahead of the compromise model. On the 100-point issue scale, the base model's forecasts are one-tenth of a point (0.1) better on average. In turn, the compromise model is 0.3 points better than the mean. Obviously no sensible person should rank-order models based solely on differences of this size.

the Pareto set) and a bargain was struck, (2) those issues in which the reversion point was within the Pareto set and a bargain was struck, and (3) those issues for which bargaining failed. Category (1) matches the traditional interpretation of the theoretical assumptions of the Nash bargaining solution. Category (2) may be seen as a situation in which an old bargain is being challenged by a new one, and in which the Nash solution would apply if disagreement is very undesirable. Category (3) comprises issues which cooperative bargaining models fit poorly, since they assume that some deal is always struck.

The importance of this classification is that, regarded just as a predictive formula, the compromise model should not have any more forecasting success in one of these categories than in another. The same is true for the mean and the base model. In their case, there is no obvious reason to think of them as bargaining outcomes, and indeed, the usual justification of the mean as a solution concept depends on a procedural model, not bargaining (see Chapter 10). Only if the bargaining interpretation of the compromise model developed in this chapter is correct should we see a pattern of decreasing predictive success across the three categories.

Figure 4.1 shows that the theoretical underpinnings of the compromise model are confirmed across bargaining contexts. The compromise

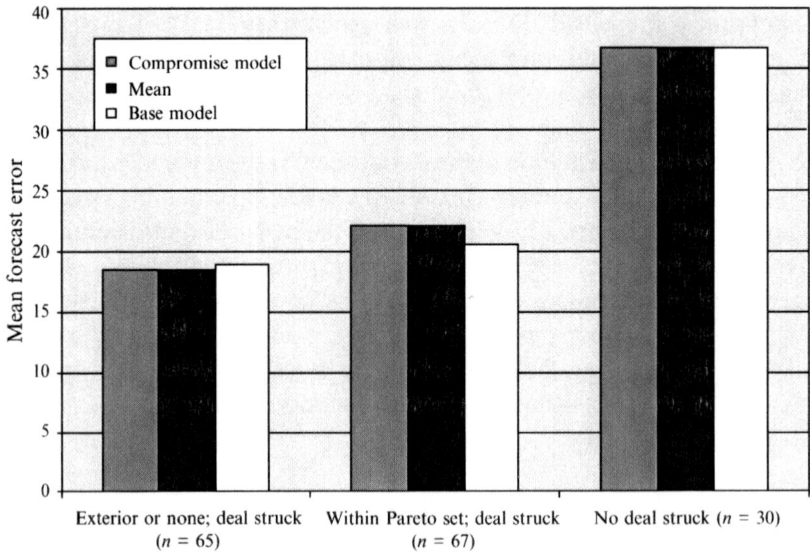

Figure 4.1. Model predictive success in bargaining contexts

model performed best in classic bargaining situations, next best in other bargaining situations, and poorly in the 18 per cent of issues for which bargaining broke down, just as the argument of this chapter implies.[20] Moreover, as Figure 4.1 shows, both the mean and the base model have precisely the same pattern of success, working well in bargained situations and not otherwise. This suggests once again that they are successful because they are approximating the compromise model and not because they capture aspects of decision-making that it neglects.

Additional discussion of these findings and comparisons with other models appears in Chapter 10.

4.11 CONCLUSION

Institutional realism is the view that institutions, including governmental organs and private organisations, are the key actors in politics, and that the relationships among them are determined by power and bargaining, structured in part by the legal framework. This chapter has argued that institutional realism provides a substantively sensible framework for thinking about government policy-making. Its intellectual ancestry traces to Thucydides, and it has been put forward independently by many authors during the twentieth century as the best description of the case studies of policy-making that they had conducted.

This chapter derived an explicit form of this framework—the institutional realism model—from a well-known and widely used solution for bargaining models, namely the Nash bargaining solution. When (1) Nash's axioms hold, (2) the failure to agree is costly, and (3) actors have quadratic loss functions on the issue scales, then Nash's solution is closely approximated by another formula, namely the compromise model, which in various guises has appeared often in both case studies and formal models in political science and sociology. It has also performed relatively well in previous empirical tests. Thus the institutional realism model has both intellectual history and contemporary theoretical and empirical support to complement its other desirable properties. The initial testing of this chapter indicated that this perspective outperforms the median and state-centric realism, and that it is as good as the mean and the base model, while having better theoretical properties than any of them.

[20] Both the first two groups are statistically significantly different from the third at the .05 level, but they are not statistically distinguishable from each other.

The procedural models of Chapter 3 emphasise the legal framework of the second stage of policy-making, de-emphasising the initial bargaining stage. The institutional realism model of this chapter does the reverse. Both approaches remain only a downpayment on a more comprehensive approach that would incorporate both bargaining and the structure of institutional rules. Nonetheless, at this stage of our knowledge, it is helpful to know which class of model is the more powerful predictor.

In other chapters of this book, alternate models of the EU decision-making process are put forward and their predictions computed. The final part of the book compares the forecasts of the compromise model with the predictions of many other models. In effect, these comparisons match the logic of institutional realism, which embodies a simple summary of much traditional social science wisdom about the bargaining process in policy-making, against other models, often more sophisticated mathematically, which are based on different understandings of politics and which derive their predictions from legal interpretations, log-rolling procedures, coalition theory, or ideas borrowed from adjacent disciplines such as economics. At the end of this book, we will ask this question: have our understandings of politics, our latest game-theoretic knowledge, and our grasp of EU legal procedures advanced far enough that our newest models can outperform a simple classic forecast like the compromise model? Chapter 10 answers that question.

APPENDIX 1: THE NASH BARGAINING THEOREM

The definition of a bargaining game begins with a set of players i ($i = 1, \ldots, n$). The players must agree unanimously on an alternative taken from a set X; otherwise they receive the *disagreement outcome* (or *threat point* or *reference point*) d. For the purposes of this chapter, we shall assume that X is the set of all possible lotteries over a finite subset A of $\Re^K$, where A is a set of K-dimensional sure-thing alternatives, including the disagreement outcome.[21] For example, A may be interpreted as the set of all possible outcomes on a particular EU Commission proposal consisting of K distinct issues. In the dataset used in this book, the possible sure-thing choices on each issue are finite in number, so that these assumptions correspond to the empirical applications in this volume.[22]

[21] Thus X is the *mixture set* defined on A (Herstein and Milnor 1953).

[22] Even those issues in the dataset treated as intervals are actually recorded only at a discrete set of points. No respondent would or could report that, on a scale of 0 to

Each player is assumed to have a von Neumann-Morgenstern cardinal utility function u_i defined on the set of lotteries X.[23] Since these utility functions are unique only up to an interval-level transformation, for convenience we set $u_i(d) = 0$ for all i. It is assumed that, for all $x^* \in X$ and for all i, $u_i(x^*) \geq 0$. That is, for every player, the possible agreements are all at least as good as the disagreement outcome.[24]

Now let S_i be the image of $u_i(X)$: $S_i = \{u_i(x^*)|x^* \in X\}$. These are the possible utility outcomes that player i could receive from points of X, including the utility of the disagreement outcome. Since X consists of all possible lotteries over a finite set of alternatives, it is straightforward to prove that any S_i defined on X is a compact (closed and bounded) and convex set. In particular, here S_i is a closed interval $[0, m_i]$ of the real line, where $m_i = \max_x^* [u_i\ (x^*)]$.

Now define the *utility profile* $u(.) = [u_1(.), \ldots, u_n(.)]$, the n-dimensional vector of the actors' utility functions over the lotteries in X. Set $S = \{u(x^*)|x^* \in X\}$. Thus S is the set of feasible utility vectors that the players might obtain from a bargaining agreement. Since each S_i is compact and convex, so is S.

With this structure (which is assumed without further mention in what follows), we may define a *bargaining game* as a pair (N, S), where N is a finite set $\{1, 2, \ldots, n\}$ of players, where S is a compact and convex subset of the non-negative orthant of $\Re^n$ containing the set of feasible utility vectors for the players, and where the utility of the disagreement outcome, the vector 0, is a member of S. A *solution* f to a bargaining game is then a map that selects a point of S for every bargaining game. Since N is unvarying, we will write $f(S)$ to denote a bargaining solution applied to a particular S, and we will refer to $f(S)$ as an *outcome*.

100, an actor's preference was 18.732, for example. Thus restricting A to be a finite set involves no substantive loss of meaning here, and it simplifies the presentation and proofs. Generalising to legitimate interval-level bounded scales of finite length (making A compact if the endpoints are included) is not difficult, however, as Nash (1950) noted.

23 Axiom systems defining preferences over lotteries and then deriving cardinal utilities to represent those preferences are well-known and are omitted here. See, for example, Mas-Colell *et al* (chapters 1–3, 6).

24 Note that this standard assumption in bargaining theory is violated when modellers assume that the disagreement point falls in the middle of the ideal points of the actors on a single-dimension issue. Then the usual mathematics supporting the Nash bargaining solution fails.

We now list the well known Nash axioms for bargaining games. Rigorous definitions of all four axioms are widely available, for example in Roth (1979: 6–8), or Mas-Colell *et al* (1995: Chapter 22E). Here we avoid full mathematical detail and state the axioms somewhat informally.

Rescaling axiom. Suppose that for a given profile u and solution f, the bargaining outcome is $f(S) = y$. Then if actor i's utility function u_i is linearly rescaled to $u_i^* = a + bu_i$ $(b > 0)$, while all other actors retain the same utility scale, then the bargaining solution chooses the same alternative y when presented with the new feasible payoff set S^*: $f(S^*) = y$.

Pareto axiom. If a lottery y_1 in S has strictly lower utility for all actors than another alternative y_2 in S, then the bargaining solution never chooses y_1.

Anonymity axiom. Suppose that for a given S, $f(S) = y$. Then suppose that the actors are renumbered, so that each utility function u_i is renumbered $u_{i'}$, creating a new profile u' and thus a corresponding new set of feasible payoffs S'. Then the bargaining solution makes the same choice with the new profile: $f(S') = y$.

Independence of irrelevant alternative (IIA) axiom. Suppose that for a given S, $f(S) = y$. Let $R \subset S$ and suppose $y \in R$. Then $f(R) = y$.

Theorem. Suppose that a solution f to a bargaining game (N, S) satisfies the rescaling, Pareto, anonymity, and IIA axioms. Then for all sets of feasible utility outcomes S:

$$f(S) = \underset{y \in S}{\operatorname{argmax}} \prod_{i=1}^{n} u_i(y) \tag{4.6}$$

A proof for the two-actor case is available in virtually any game theory text covering cooperative game theory; the n-player proof appears in Roth (1979: 8–12), and in Moulin (1988: 68).

APPENDIX 2: LEMMAS AND COROLLARY

This appendix shows how quadratic loss assumptions may be used to find the approximate Nash bargaining solution when only a discrete set of sure-thing alternatives are available (Lemma 1). It also shows that under the same assumption, lotteries will essentially never occur as solutions, so that attention can be focused on the sure-thing outcomes (Lemma 2). Finally, the appendix shows that, as the disagreement outcome becomes arbitrarily less attractive to all actors, the solution of the Nash bargaining model under quadratic loss assumptions tends to the solution given by the compromise model (a corollary to the Nash bargaining theorem).

Consider first the case when the finite set of sure-thing alternatives A lie on a single dimension (that is, A is a set of points on the real line). This corresponds to the case of an EU proposal containing a single issue to be voted on. As before, denote the most-preferred point of $\mathfrak{R}$ for actor i by x_i, let s_i be a non-negative real number interpreted as i's 'salience' for the issue, and let a_i be a strictly positive real number.[25] Then the assumption of quadratic loss is defined as follows:

One-dimensional quadratic loss axiom. For all i and all sure-thing alternatives $z \in A$, where $A \subset \mathfrak{R}$: $u_i(z) = a_i - s_i (z - x_i)^2$.

Here a_i is chosen so that at the disagreement outcome, each actor has utility 0, as in the statement of the theorem. Thus utilities are always non-negative for each actor. Note that at each actor's ideal point, where $z = x_i$, the corresponding utility is a_i. Thus a_i measures how much each actor would lose in moving from the most-preferred point to the disagreement outcome. Note also that the parameter s_i measures how quickly the actor's utility drops off on each side of the most-preferred point. It therefore expresses the actor's relative intensity or salience on the issue.[26]

Now in policy-making studies, we often find issues whose outcomes can take on only a few discrete values. Hence not all forecast values are meaningful. To cope with such cases, we formalise the notion of 'picking the nearest meaningful value'. Thus suppose that we have a continuous function f strictly unimodal over a closed and bounded real interval I. Let the point of the interval at which f attains its maximum be denoted by y^*, and let A be a finite subset of I, interpreted as the set of meaningful values. Set $h(x^*) = |y^* - x^*|$. Then define a set $Q_A(y^*)$ as follows:[27] $Q_A(y^*) = \{\text{argmin } h(x^*) \mid x^* \in A\}$. That is, Q_A picks out the point or points that are members of A and closest to y^*.

We now establish two lemmas before proceeding to the main result. Let P be the *Pareto set* of S, that is, the elements of S that are not excluded from the outcome by the Pareto axiom. In the first lemma, we consider the case in which Nash's bargaining axioms hold, there is a

[25] Note that x_i need not be feasible, i.e., it need not be an element of A.

[26] In the dataset used in this book, experts were asked to assess salience on each issue relative to other issues faced by the same actor. The assessed salience s_i plus the zero utility for disagreement establish a von Neumann-Morgenstern cardinal utility scale for each actor. Of course, nothing depends on the particular scaling chosen.

[27] The dependence of Q_A on f is suppressed in the notation: f is always the Nash bargaining solution in what follows.

single dimension of choice with a finite number of alternatives, losses are quadratic, and the disagreement outcome is very undesirable for each player compared to any sure-thing element in the Pareto set. Then the lemma shows that if only sure-thing alternatives are available, the compromise model (adjusted to the nearest meaningful point) is the approximate solution to the bargaining game.

Lemma 1. Suppose that a solution to a bargaining game (N, S) obeys the Nash axioms, and that in addition, the utility function of each actor i is described by the one-dimensional quadratic loss axiom for sure-thing alternatives $z \in A$. Assume that $a_i \gg s_i(z - x_i)^2$ for all $z \in P$. Let $T \subset S$ be the set of utility profiles in S when choice is restricted to the sure-thing alternatives A. Then to a first-order approximation, for all T and for strictly positive constants $v_i = 1/a_i$:

$$f(T) = Q_A\left[\frac{\sum_{i=1}^{n} s_i v_i x_i}{\sum_{i=1}^{n} s_i v_i}\right] \tag{4.7}$$

Equation (4.7) is, of course, the compromise model from Equation (4.2), adjusted to the nearest meaningful point. Naturally, if the sure-thing alternatives form a continuous interval in $\Re$, then all points are substantively meaningful, and we get just the compromise model itself.

Proof of lemma 1. When confined to the sure-thing alternatives on a single dimension, the maximisation problem of the Nash bargaining solution becomes:

$$f(S) = \underset{z \in A}{\operatorname{argmax}} \prod_{i=1}^{n} (a_i - s_i(z - x_i)^2) \tag{4.8}$$

Factoring out the constants a_i, taking logs, and dropping irrelevant constants from the sum yields:

$$f(T) = \underset{z \in A}{\operatorname{argmax}} \sum_{i=1}^{n} log[1 - s_i(z - x_i)^2/a_i] \tag{4.9}$$

Now, by the assumptions of the lemma and in accordance with the institutional realist logic, a_i is large relative to $s_i(y - x_i)^2$ for every actor i and each sure thing z in the Pareto set. This means that the normalised zero point (collapse of the bargaining) is far in each actor's mind from the Pareto points and thus very unattractive compared with the possible agreements.

In this case, since $s_i(z - x_i)^2/a_i$ now becomes small for all i and all z that might be agreed to, and because $\log(1 - r) \approx -r$ when r is small, to a first-order approximation in the neighborhood of the actors' ideal points, we have:

$$f(T) \approx \underset{z \in A}{\operatorname{argmax}} \sum_{i=1}^{n} [-s_i(z - x_i)^2 / a_i] \qquad (4.10)$$

If we now set $v_i = 1/a_i$ and temporarily maximise over a real interval containing A rather than A itself, then routine calculus applied to the previous equation would give the solution, denoted by y_C:

$$y_C = \frac{\sum_{i=1}^{n} s_i v_i x_i}{\sum_{i=1}^{n} s_i v_i} \qquad (4.11)$$

Finally, to restrict the solution to points of A, note that Equation (4.10) is quadratic in z, so that the solution of the Nash model must be the point of A nearest y_C, namely $Q_A(y_C)$.[28] But this is just the compromise model's forecast adjusted to the nearest meaningful point, and so the proof of the lemma is complete.[29]

The Nash bargaining solution is cast in terms of lotteries, not sure things. This seems to imply that the search for forecasts must include lotteries as well. However, the next lemma shows that under the one-dimensional quadratic loss assumption and the approximation of the previous lemma, no proper lottery will be chosen as the Nash bargaining solution. Sure-thing alternatives are always preferred.[30]

Lemma 2. Under the conditions of lemma 1, then to a first-order approximation, for all feasible utility sets S over lotteries and all feasible utility subsets T over sure things, we have:

$$f(S) = f(T) \qquad (4.12)$$

Hence under these conditions, a considerable simplification of the Nash bargaining solution is achieved when there is only one dimension: we need maximise only over the sure-thing alternatives.

[28] A concave quadratic function $f(z)$ is symmetric around the point z^* at which it attains its maximum. Hence among a set of other points on either side, the nearest point to z^* produces the largest value of f.

[29] Note, too, that a generalised version of the Nash model (for example, Muthoo 1999: 35–36), in which the social choice maximises $\operatorname{argmax}_{y \in A} \prod_{i=1}^{n} u_i^{\beta_i}(y)$, with $\sum \beta_i = 1$, would also lead to the compromise model by the same approximation, though with $v_i = \beta_i / a_i$.

[30] More precisely stated, there is always at least one sure-thing alternative among the solutions, and non-degenerate lotteries occur among the solutions only on a set of actor utilities that has (Lebesgue) measure zero.

Proof of lemma 2. When lotteries among the m sure-thing alternatives on a single dimension are the objects of choice, denote as before the sure-thing alternatives in A by z_j ($j = 1, \ldots, m$) and the corresponding probabilities that z_j will be selected in a given lottery by $\lambda = (\lambda_1, \ldots, \lambda_m)$, where $\sum \lambda_j = 1$. Let x_i again be actor i's most-preferred point. Then in this case, the Nash bargaining solution is:

$$f(S) = \underset{\lambda}{\operatorname{argmax}} \prod_{i=1}^{n} \left[\sum_{j=1}^{m} \lambda_j (a_i - s_i(z_j - x_i)^2) \right] \tag{4.13}$$

or equivalently:

$$f(S) = \underset{\lambda}{\operatorname{argmax}} \sum_{i=1}^{n} \log \left[\sum_{j=1}^{m} \lambda_j (a_i - s_i(z_j - x_i)^2) \right] \tag{4.14}$$

But factoring out the irrelevant a_i, then to the same approximation as in the previous lemma and again setting $v_i = 1/a_i$, we get:

$$f(S) = \underset{\lambda}{\operatorname{argmax}} \sum_{i=1}^{n} \left[\sum_{j=1}^{m} -\lambda_j s_i v_i (z_j - x_i)^2) \right] \tag{4.15}$$

Reversing the order of summation and setting $g_j = \sum_{i=1}^{n} - s_i v_i (z_j - x_i)^2$, it follows that the approximate Nash bargaining solution is:

$$f(S) \approx \underset{\lambda}{\operatorname{argmax}} (\lambda_1 g_1 + \ldots; + \lambda_m g_m) \tag{4.16}$$

But obviously this finite sum is maximised by assigning $\lambda_{\max} = 1$ to the quantity $g_{\max}$ with the largest value, and assigning $\lambda_j = 0$ to all the others.[31] Thus the Nash bargaining outcome here is a degenerate lottery, that is, some sure thing. Hence we must simply search over the sure things to determine which g_j is the largest. But g_j is the same maximand treated in lemma 1, and we are done.

We now move to the main result. First, we extend the quadratic loss assumption to multiple issues considered simultaneously. Here an alternative $z_j = (z_{j1}, \ldots, z_{jk})$ is a k-dimensional sure-thing vector, $x_i = (x_{i1}, \ldots, x_{ik})$ is the vector of actor i's most-preferred points on each of the K dimensions of choice, and s_{ik} is actor i's salience on dimension k:

Separable quadratic loss axiom. For all i, $u_i(z_j) = a_i - \sum_{k=1}^{k} s_{ik}(z_{jk} - x_{ik})^2$.

Intuitively, the main assertions underlying this assumption are three. The first is that losses on each dimension are quadratic, which is a

[31] If two or more g_j are tied for the largest value, then any one of them can be chosen.

reasonable approximation. The second is that losses on each dimension are *separable* from those on other dimensions, that is, that doing well or poorly on one dimension does not change one's mind about what would be the best outcome on another dimension.[32] It is, of course, possible to think of circumstances in which the separability assumption would be misleading, but these seem to be rare in practice.[33]

The third assertion embodied in the axiom is more controversial. It states that if we compare actors who won on the first dimension with actors who lost, then nevertheless, each group will be equally marginally affected by losses on other dimensions. This latter assertion is highly implausible, of course: losers are compensated with concessions on other issues because losers care more about the additional losses.[34] However, the separability assumption was maintained in this chapter because it leads to the compromise model, and that model has simplicity on its side and thus deserves to be set out prominently and tested. It should be noted, however, that the separability assumption was made purely for analytic convenience. Institutional realism does not require it, and institutional realism is not identical with the compromise model.

The next result then shows that under separable quadratic loss functions and a highly undesirable disagreement point, then to a first-order approximation, the Nash bargaining solution in the case of multi-dimensional alternatives (such as EU proposals) can be obtained by applying the Nash solution to the sure-thing alternatives dimension by dimension. That, in turn, means that under these assumptions, the multi-dimensional Nash bargaining solution is just the compromise model applied to each dimension separately and then adjusted to the nearest meaningful point. In short, this version of the Nash bargaining solution is approximated by the compromise model.

Corollary to the Nash bargaining theorem. Let $f(S) = (f_1(S), \ldots, f_K(S)$ be a bargaining solution when sure-thing alternatives consist of K dimensions. Then under the separable quadratic loss axiom plus the same

[32] More precisely, the losses on each dimension are *additive*, a strong form of separability.

[33] An actor with non-separable utilities has to feel, for example, that if emission controls on small cars are imposed, then diesel exhaust on buses not only is less aggravating now that the air is cleaner, but that it actually begins to smell better (or worse) as well.

[34] The exchange model of Chapter 5 uses precisely that logic, and its explanatory advantage over the compromise model on dichotomous issues in multi-issue proposals may stem from the use of the separability assumption here (see Chapter 10).

assumptions and the same approximation as in the previous lemmas, for all k:

$$f_k(S) = Q_A(y_{Ck}) \tag{4.17}$$

Again, when the sure things form a continuous set, we get on each dimension $f_k(S) = y_{Ck}$, that is, the unadjusted compromise model itself.

Proof of the corollary. With separable losses on each dimension, then by the same logic as before, the approximate Nash maximand for sure-thing alternatives is:

$$f(T) \approx \underset{z \in A}{\operatorname{argmax}} \sum_{i=1}^{n} \left[\sum_{k=1}^{K} (-s_{ik}(z_k - x_{ik})^2 / a_i) \right] \tag{4.18}$$

But reversing the order of summation breaks up the maximand into K independent maximands, each with the form of Equation (4.10), the single-dimension case, which have $Q_A(y_{Ck})$ as their respective solutions by lemma 1. Lemma 2 then applies to eliminate non-degenerate lotteries, and the proof is done.

APPENDIX 3: APPLYING THE COMPROMISE MODEL TO DATA

As discussed in Chapter 2, two versions of Shapley Shubik values were computed for this book, along with expert judgments of institutional power. For the latter, informants were simply asked to assess each actor's power directly, in the same way that saliences were assessed. These measurement procedures have the appeal of straightforwardness, but they raise a concern. What is 'power'? What is 'salience'? And how can they be accurately assessed? These challenging issues of measurement arrive immediately when theoretical models are taken to data.

A pleasing feature of the quadratic loss/Nash bargaining framework is that power and salience have clear meanings. Both describe features of the actors' loss functions. 'Power' describes the relative distance of the disagreement outcome from the actor's bliss point, and 'salience' describes the sharpness in the curvature of the actor's loss function. Thus in principle, standard methods for interviewing actors to learn their loss functions (for example, Keeney and Raiffa 1993) might be used to make the necessary measurements.

In practice, of course, the top political actors in major international institutions like the EU are rarely available for interviews of any kind, much less for the kind of detailed, somewhat technical interviews necessary to construct utility functions. Their preferences, power, and saliences over issues must be assessed by other participants or by outside experts and observers familiar with them, as was done in constructing the dataset used in this book.

Sometimes external assessment is straightforward. An actor's 'most-preferred point' is a clear idea and relatively easy to measure. Even for more difficult concepts such as power and salience, external assessment, done with care, can often be very effective. For this book, elaborate precautions were taken to ensure the accuracy of the judgements. However, as in any interviewing technique, some error is inevitably introduced. Moreover, there is no guarantee that experts used the measurement scales in precisely the same way that any one interpretation of the theory might require. As mentioned in Chapter 2, LaPalombara (1960: 30) put the point clearly in a pioneering early study:

> The concept 'power' (or 'influence') is not easy to define, and, even after the interviewer suggests a definition, he cannot be certain that the respondents adhere to a specific denotation in their evaluations.

Similar remarks might be made, perhaps with even more force, about the concept of 'salience'. Indeed, since there is no canonical question to ask informants in either case, and no standard scale on which their answers are to fall, different studies would inevitably arrive at different measures of power and salience even when interviewing exactly the same informants about exactly the same political events.

Good science requires taking measurement issues seriously. Thus in testing the models in this book, we were alert to the possibility that *measured* power or *measured* salience were not identical with *actual* power or *actual* salience. Either measure might need to be transformed to meet the theoretical demands that models place upon it. In particular, since both power and salience are presumably ratio-level variables, the natural class of transformations to consider is exponential.[35] Thus if s_i is true salience and $\hat{s}_i$ is measured salience, it makes sense to consider transformations of the form $s_i = \hat{s}_i^k$, where k is a parameter to be determined (Achen 1999).

Several such checks were carried out with the current data. However, there was no systematic evidence in favour of any transformation, and the untransformed versions of power and salience appeared to work

[35] Also called 'power transformations', an inconvenient expression when applied to measures of political power.

best. Hence all reported results were done with untransformed values. Moreover, the Shapley Shubik values performed better than the expert judgements in forecasting policy-making decisions, and so the Shapley Shubik values were used in constructing forecasts. Additional discussion of this point appears in Chapter 10 and in Achen (1999).

No matter how much care is taken in collecting measures of power and salience, however, they remain unavoidably somewhat noisy. It is important to understand why the noise can disguise the relative performance of different models. Consider the simple case of two actors of equal power, positioned at 0 and 100 on the issue scale. Suppose that we select a sample of such cases, assigning each actor a true salience of either 40 or 60, drawn with probability .5 each, independent of the salience of the other actor. Assume that the true model is the compromise model with the correct saliences, so that we may compute the true outcomes in each case.

Now suppose that the true saliences are unknown to the researcher, as usual, so that respondents are used to estimate them. Imagine that the respondents always report the saliences with 20 point errors (on a 100 point scale), either too high or too low, each error drawn with probability .5, independent of the error in the salience estimate for the other actor. Now we may compare the forecasts from the compromise model using the respondents' estimates of the saliences with the forecast errors using the mean (which always predicts 50 in this example).

It is easy to show that the average errors from the compromise model will be more than twice those of the mean in this case, even though the compromise model is the correct model and the mean is not.[36] Thus noisy saliences degrade model performance considerably, and the errors are approximately proportional to the amount of noise. For example, if the respondents' salience errors are cut in half in this example, the compromise model and the mean perform similarly, and if the respondents' salience errors are eliminated, of course, the compromise model is much better than the mean. Thus there is a trade off in predictive success when theoretically more accurate models require data we do not measure well. Most importantly, models that overcome noisy inputs are usually theoretically superior to simpler models using more reliable inputs, even

[36] The point here is exactly parallel to the advice in econometrics texts that estimating a correct first-order serial correlation or heteroskedasticity model may be worse than using ordinary regression if the additional parameters are estimated with considerable noise.

if the two models predict equally well. This argument was set out informally in the text of this chapter to explain why the compromise model is likely closer to the theoretical truth than the mean or the base model, even though all three predict equally well.

The other issue that arises in applications of the compromise model is that the corollary of this chapter requires its predictions to be adjusted to the nearest meaningful point on each issue scale. When the issue scales are virtually interval-level measures (for example, when the values 0, 1, 2, . . ., 100 on a one-hundred point scale are all meaningful), the adjustment is essentially irrelevant and can be ignored. At the other extreme, when the issues are dichotomies (yes/no), then only the positions 0 and 100 are meaningful, and forecasts of 45 or 51 will be adjusted very far indeed—to 0 and 100, respectively.

The mathematical results in the appendices to this chapter assume that all positions, saliences, and power values are measured perfectly. In practice, measurement error inevitably enters to blur the predictions. What appears to be a prediction of 45 on a dichotomous scale (and is therefore rounded to zero) may be a measurement error for a prediction of 55 or 65, which should be rounded to 100. Simply using 45 and rounding it to zero takes no account of the statistical character of the data. The best unbiased forecast should average the rounding decisions over the possible measurement errors, perhaps yielding a result such as 40 (meaning a 40 per cent chance of 100 and a 60 per cent chance of 0). The value 40 is not a meaningful position on the issue scale, but it is the unbiased model forecast nonetheless. Unfortunately, the distribution of measurement errors is unknown, and so this calculation cannot be done.

To avoid these insoluble complexities and to approximate the unknown unbiased forecast, therefore, the compromise model was simply applied to each issue in the dataset, whether dichotomous, rank-ordered, or continuous, without rounding. If the model forecast 45, for example, that forecast stood as the prediction, even if 45 was not itself a possible outcome on the issue.

5

Compromise, exchange and challenge in the European Union

JAVIER ARREGUI, FRANS N. STOKMAN AND ROBERT THOMSON

5.1 INTRODUCTION

According to the account of European Union (EU) decision-making proposed in this chapter, this is a bargaining process during which actors shift their policy positions with a view to reaching agreements on controversial issues. Formal institutions, such as the procedural rules explored in Chapter 3, matter in this process. They define the set of actors included in the process and their relative weight or power. The observation that actors shift their positions, and cajole or compel others to shift theirs, is central to our conception of political bargaining. Practitioners of European affairs reported that flexibility in actors' initial policy positions is an important feature of the decision-making process. During one interview an informant was asked why the actors were so polarised in terms of the policy alternatives they 'favoured most' at the outset of the discussions. He responded: 'That's not so unusual. At the start of the negotiations, the positions tend to be more extreme. As the discussions get underway, we realise what is politically feasible, and converge gradually toward those points'.[1] In this chapter, we compare two different models of the bargaining process in which actors shift from the policy positions they favour most at the outset of the discussions.

The models we focus on in this chapter are the position exchange model (Stokman and Van Oosten 1994) and the challenge model (in

We thank Bruce Bueno de Mesquita, René Torenvlied, Ignacio Sanchez-Cuenca and the editors, Christopher Achen and Thomas König for their valuable and encouraging comments on this chapter.

[1] Interview by Robert Thomson on 26 July 2000 on the Directive relating to cocoa and chocolate products intended for human consumption. For more details of this dossier see the illustration in Chapter 6 by Bailer and Schneider.

other studies this model is also referred to as 'the expected utility model', Bueno de Mesquita 1994). These models belong to a class of rational choice models of collective decision-making that distinguish between two stages of the decision-making process. The first is the *influence* stage, and the second is the *final decision* or *voting* stage. During the influence stage, actors attempt to influence each other with a view to realising decision outcomes that are close to the policy alternatives they favour. The models differ with respect to their propositions about what *influence strategies* actors use in the first stage, and with respect to actors' expectations of the final decision outcomes in the second, final decision stage. In the position exchange model, for instance, effective influence depends on cooperation between actors; the challenge model assumes an orientation towards non-cooperative behaviour. Although the actors are assumed to be goal-oriented, they may not recognise the full implications of the strategies they employ to influence others. For instance, the challenge model includes the possibility that while attempting to build an effective coalition around their positions, actors might provoke opposition, as a result of which their positions are weakened, rather than strengthened. Further, in the position exchange model presented here, actors do not consider the full implications of their influence strategies on other actors, who are not the target of their influence attempts. This is the subject of our discussion on 'externalities' that we will turn to later (Section 5.2.3).

The focus on the informal means through which actors exert influence is what distinguishes the bargaining approach to explaining decision-making from some of the other approaches adopted in this book. Much of the best-known literature on legislative decision-making in the EU focuses on the formal procedural rules laid down in the Treaties (see Chapter 3 by Steunenberg and Selck, and the references therein). According to our conception of decision-making, formal rules still matter, but in ways different to those supposed in procedural models. First, these procedures partly define the capabilities that actors can deploy during the execution of their influence attempts. These capabilities are exogenous to the bargaining models considered here. The bargaining approach focuses on how these capabilities are deployed through the particular modes of interaction between actors: the use of *exchanges* or *challenges* through which actors' initial positions are transformed into voting positions in the final voting stage. Second, formal procedures determine the voting rule and actors' weights in the final voting stage in which the actors' final positions, possibly after being influenced by other actors, are transformed into collective decision outcomes.

The research approach adopted in the present chapter is one that was used in a previous study of European level decision-making. Bueno de Mesquita and Stokman (1994) applied these bargaining models to decision-making in the Council of Ministers of the European Community. That volume included a careful specification of the models and applied them to five dossiers containing sixteen issues. The challenge model was found to generate the most accurate predictions of the outcomes of Council decision-making. The authors concluded that, 'overall, the two best models are the expected utility (or challenge) model and the compromise position exchange model'[2] (Bueno de Mesquita and Stokman 1994: 225). It was not, however, possible to distinguish between the alternative models statistically, nor to investigate the conditions under which they might produce more or less accurate forecasts. We aim to do so in the present chapter. Further, we now have a better theoretical foundation for the compromise and position exchange models, and are able to derive and compute the externalities of bilateral exchanges. These externalities are gains or losses experienced by actors not involved in the exchanges of voting positions. Finally, this chapter also includes the analysis of a much larger number of issues and more actors, including the Commission and the European Parliament (EP).

In other decision situations, researchers have applied this approach to make inferences on the prevailing modes of interaction among political actors. For example, the position exchange model was applied to the analysis of decision-making on the European Union's Structural Funds in Ireland (Payne 1999; Mokken *et al* 2000). The challenge model has been extensively applied within the field of international relations. An overview of the applications of Bueno de Mesquita's challenge model can be found in Ray and Russet (1996; see also Thomson *et al* 2003). The position exchange model has also been applied to other decision situations: for example, in local authority decision-making in the Amsterdam City Council (Berveling 1994) and, together with the challenge model, to negotiations between employers and trade unions (Rojer 1999). Similarly, on the basis of the accuracy of the models' forecasts of decision

[2] In addition to the 16 issues on which most of the models were applied and tested in the 1994 volume, data were also collected on an additional six issues on the creation of the European Central Bank. Note that some of the statistical tests applied in the 1994 book, in particular the t-tests and correlations, are highly questionable. Nevertheless, the challenge model did generate predictions with somewhat lower errors on average than the other models, but these were not significantly smaller than those of the simple compromise model.

outcomes, we make inferences about the relevance of the influence strategies they posit.

In Section 5.2 we describe the alternative models. This also includes a discussion of the compromise model, elaborated by Christopher Achen in Chapter 4. This discussion is important because the compromise model is a component part of the position exchange model and, moreover, there is an interpretation of the compromise model that links it to a particular type of influence process. Section 5.3 describes a few aspects of the research design not covered by the general discussion in Chapter 2. Section 5.4 provides an illustration of the models with a case study on a regulation on fisheries infrastructure. Section 5.5 presents the results, and Section 5.6 summarises the findings and conclusions to be drawn from these analyses.

5.2 MODELS

We begin by describing the challenge model, and then introduce the position exchange model and our interpretation of the compromise model. The final part of this section considers some conditions under which each of the models might be more or less applicable.

5.2.1 The challenge model

According to the challenge model (Bueno de Mesquita *et al* 1985; Bueno de Mesquita 1994; 2002), actors attempt to strengthen the coalition surrounding their own policy positions by compelling or persuading other actors to change the positions they take. The variables required as input for the challenge model are actors' bargaining positions,[3] their capabilities, and the levels of salience they attach to the issues concerned. Differences between the actors in terms of their capabilities and salience scores drive the process of challenge. Power dominance matters more than convincing arguments according to this conception of political bargaining. Influencing others according to this mode of interaction is a precarious business; even when an actor has been compelled or persuaded to shift its position toward that of a challenger, it might shift its position in the opposite direction during a subsequent round of the

[3] The challenge model uses current bargaining positions rather than ideal points. The challenge model assumes that the stated bargaining positions reflect a strategic trade off between the policy outcome the actor most desires and the expected outcome.

negotiations if that brings it back closer to its initial bargaining stance. Thus, the commitments actors make to shift their positions are not binding, and the challenge model is therefore a non-cooperative model of decision-making.

The decisions faced by each of the actors involved in this bargaining process are modelled explicitly. Each actor has to decide whether or not it will challenge the position taken by each other actor on a certain issue. This decision is based on the expected outcome of either challenging or not challenging the other's position. The value of the expected outcome of each challenge is calculated in terms of its expected effect on the decision outcome. Challenges that are expected to bring the decision outcome closer to an actor's position will tend to be waged by that actor. It is assumed that the position of the *weighted median voter* is perceived by all actors to be the likely decision outcome, whereby the positions are weighted by the actors' capabilities and the levels of salience they attach to the issue (Bueno de Mesquita 1994: 77–82). Therefore, actors are engaged in a struggle to pull the position of the weighted median closer to their favoured policy alternative. The model assumes that actors bargain on the issues separately.

Figure 5.1 illustrates the choices each actor, in this case actor *i*, faces with respect to each other actor, in this case actor *j*, on any given issue, in this case issue *a*. Actor *i* may challenge actor *j*, or may decide not to do

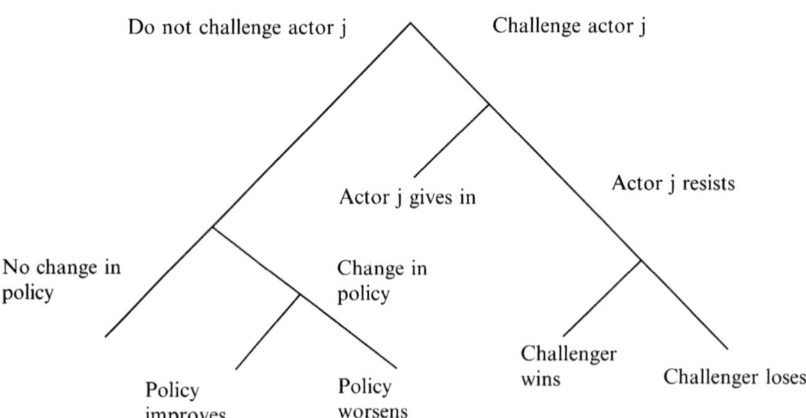

Figure 5.1. Bueno de Mesquita's challenge model (the expected utility model)

so. If actor i challenges j (the right side of Figure 5.1) then actor j can either give in or resist the challenge. If actor j gives in, then it will have to support the policy position of the challenger (actor i). If, however, actor j resists, there are two possibilities: the challenger (actor i) wins or the opponent (actor j) wins. Alternatively, actor i might decide not to challenge j (the left part of Figure 5.1). In that case, actor j will not move due to challenges by actor i. However, due to challenges by other actors, j may move, resulting in a better or worse policy outcome from the perspective of actor i. These computations also take into account the support actors i and j receive from other actors. Each of the actors calculates the utility of each alternative and the likelihood of its occurrence. This calculation requires an estimate of the utility and the likelihood of occurrence from the perspective of the opponent. With respect to actors' calculations of their opponents' expectations, the model simulates misperceptions, because actors do not consider the possibility that some actors are more risk-acceptant and others risk-averse.

The expected utility for i of challenging j is computed as follows. The likelihood that actor j will resist a challenge by i is estimated by the salience actor j attaches to issue a, denoted by s_{ja}. The likelihood that actor j will give in is equal to $(1 - s_{ja})$. In the latter case, actor j will support the actor i's policy position. The utility for actor i of this move by actor j is denoted by $u^i \Delta x_{ja}{}^{+}$. If actor j resists the challenge, then actor i can either win or lose. In the first case, the shift of actor j's position toward that of actor i has a utility of $u^i \Delta x_{ja}{}^{+}$ for actor i. If actor i loses, it is forced to support j's position. The negative utility for actor i of that move is denoted by $u^i \Delta x_{ja}{}^{-}$. The likelihood of success or failure for actor i in such a dispute depends on the relative powers of stakeholder i and j, denoted by p_{ij}. This value depends on the leverage (capability times salience) each of the actors is willing to invest and the support each of them receives from third actors. The expected utility for actor i of challenging actor j on issue a is equal to:

$$E^i u^i \Delta x_{ja} | No\ Challenge = s_{ja}\{p_{ij}[u^i \Delta x_{ja}^{+}] + (1 - p_{ij})[u^i \Delta x_{ja}]\} + (1 - s_{ja})[u^i \Delta x_{ja}^{+}] \quad (5.1)$$

In a similar way, we compute the expected utility for actor i of not challenging the policy position of actor j. If j is not expected to shift its position due to challenges from other actors, then j is expected to remain on the same position. The utility for actor i of no change in the current positions of the stakeholders on issue a is denoted by $u^i \Delta x_{ja}^{o}$. The expected utility of not challenging another actor, *j*, is then simply:

$$E^i u^i \Delta x_{ja} | No\ Challenge = u^i \Delta x^o_{ja} \quad (5.2)$$

The total expected utility for actor *i* with respect to the challenge of actor *j* is now equal to:

$$E^i u^i \Delta x_{ja} = E^i u^i \Delta x_{ja} | Challenge - E^i u^i \Delta x_{ja} | No\ Challenge \quad (5.3)$$

The challenge model is an iterative model consisting of a number of bargaining rounds (usually around three). At the end of each round, each actor receives a set of challenges from others. If the set contains more than one challenge, the recipient actor selects the one that requires the smallest shift in its policy position (relative to the original starting position rather than its current position). The result of this challenge is either conflict (if the recipient also made a challenge to the actor from whom the challenge came), or that the recipient is compelled to shift its position toward that of the challenger. The shift may reflect a compromise that falls between the two actors' positions, or a capitulation by one to the other. These position shifts occur at the end of each round of bargaining and create a new constellation of positions. These new positions are taken at the start of the subsequent round of bargaining. In that new setting, actors repeat the same process. This continues until none of the actors shift their positions (substantially) or until all converge on the same position.

The forecast of the decision outcome is generated on the basis of the policy positions after the final round of bargaining. It is assumed that the *weighted median voter rule* also determines the outcome *in the voting stage*, but now based on the *final*, rather than the *initial* positions. The transformation of the final positions into the outcome could conceivably be based on another rule, perhaps one based on the formal procedures in the European Union.[4] The core of the challenge model concerns the

[4] Future research might consider transformation rules other than the weighted median voter for the challenge model and the weighted mean for the position exchange model. Applying the procedural models featured in Chapter 3 to these final positions would be possible candidates. In their present form, however, these procedural models generate predictions on the basis of the assumption that there are no shifts in positions after the agenda setter introduces its proposal. The procedural models could be reformulated so that the actors vote on the agenda setter's proposal, not on the basis of their initial positions, but on the basis of their voting positions. If such a model were to generate more accurate predictions than current procedural models, this would be evidence that informal bargaining is an important part of the process that takes place between the introduction of the proposal and the formal adoption of the legislation.

transformation of initial into final positions, *not* the final transformation of these positions into an outcome. During the influence process, actors use the weighted median voter rule to form their expectations on the effects of their challenges.

5.2.2 *The position exchange model*

According to the position exchange model (Stokman and Van Oosten 1994; Stokman *et al* 2000), the influence process is defined by agreements between pairs of actors on pairs of issues, whereby one actor agrees to shift its position on an issue of relatively lower importance to it in return for concessions from the other actor on an issue of relatively more importance to that actor. For exchange to be profitable, both potential exchange partners must take opposing positions on both issues, and attach different relative levels of salience to the two issues. When actors agree to shift their positions as part of an exchange agreement, these shifts are binding and cannot be reneged upon. The position exchange model is therefore a cooperative model of political bargaining.

The compromise model introduced in Chapter 4 is essential to understanding the workings of the position exchange model. Recall that the compromise model is the mean average of the actors' positions on each issue considered separately, weighted by their effective capabilities (capabilities times salience). The forecast of the compromise model is important to the workings of the position exchange model in three respects. First, it is assumed that exchanges take place between pairs of actors who take positions on opposite sides of the compromise model's forecast on each of the two issues involved in the exchange. Second, actors evaluate the gains from exchange in terms of their effects on the expected decision outcomes, as defined by the forecast of the compromise model on the basis of the revised policy positions after exchange. Third, after the exchanges have been realised, and the actors have moved to new positions as a result of these exchanges, the compromise model is used to transform these final voting positions into a decision outcome. There are several theoretical reasons for incorporating the compromise model in the position exchange model, rather than, for example, the weighted median voter, as is the case in the challenge model.

Van den Bos (1991) proposed the compromise model in the context of his study of European Community decision-making. When introducing this model, he referred to the strong pressure to reach decision outcomes that are acceptable to all, in combination with the special role of the Presidency of the Council, probably in collaboration with the Commission, in proposing solutions. Van den Bos assumes that such a solution 'takes all positions of member states into account, weighting these by the resources[5] a member state can apply during the negotiation and the importance each attaches to the decision at hand' (Van den Bos 1991: 176).

The specific interpretation given by Van den Bos in the context of European decision-making corresponds to more general interpretations of influence processes in which actors' *common interests*, based on functional interdependencies, are more important than their *diverging interests* (Lindenberg 1997). The mechanism by which agreements are achieved in such situations is mutual persuasion. Information-based influence processes are often represented in contagion models (Friedkin and Johnsen 1990; 1997; 1999; Marsden and Friedkin 1993; Leenders 1995; 2002) and in repeated games. These models represent social influence in the form of an influence network, reflecting the dyadic influence actors have on each other. In their two-stage model of decision-making, Stokman and Van den Bos (1992) connect such influence processes to collective decision-making, by integrating political influence networks with the most important elements of decision situations: the positions actors take on issues, the salience they attach to those issues and their relative capabilities. The two-stage model is a network-based model of political influence, in which actors adjust their positions on the basis of the influence of other actors to whom they are connected in the network. This influence takes into account the actors' capabilities and saliences. If the network is complete, a common position results that is equal to the predicted outcome of the compromise model. The solution of the compromise model is therefore related theoretically with influence network models, representing processes based on persuasion. The type of adaptation of policy positions posited in information-based network models is distinct from that proposed in the exchange and challenge models considered here. On the basis of persuasive information, the shifts in actors' positions may be conceived of as being akin to shifts in their preferences. By contrast, in the position exchange model, actors who shift their policy positions find it expedient to do so. In the challenge model, they can be compelled to shift their positions.

[5] While Van den Bos uses the term 'resources' we use the similar term 'capabilities'. As will become clear in the research design section of this chapter, we operationalise the concept of capabilities using the Shapley Shubik Index (SSI) scores.

In Chapter 4 it was shown that the predicted outcome of the compromise model is an approximation of the *n*-person Nash bargaining solution, when disagreement is much less desirable than any of the other alternatives being considered. This strengthens the interpretation of the compromise model as a cooperative, information-based network solution: an outcome that incorporates divergent interests as much as possible. The compromise model does not, however, provide an analysis of the process through which decisions are reached, something that both the exchange and the challenge models do. By incorporating the compromise solution into the position exchange model, we connect a cooperative position exchange model with a cooperative influence model. The position exchange model (in which positions are exchanged) can thus be understood as an intermediate stage in the compromise model (in which information is exchanged). If no exchanges are possible, compromise is assumed to take place on the basis of the initially favoured positions; if exchange is possible, such compromise will take place on the basis of the new voting positions.

According to Arrow's theorem (1951[1963]), there are many decision situations in which transitive individual preferences cannot be aggregated to produce collective equilibrium outcomes. In the case of the position exchange model, this means that bilateral exchanges of voting positions can produce outcomes that are sub-optimal for other actors that are not involved in the exchange. When pairs of actors exchange voting positions, this can produce negative externalities for other actors on those issues in which they exchange voting positions. Therefore, there will be cases in which the position exchange model does not provide the most optimal solution for the whole set of actors. We will explore this possibility further in our discussion of externalities.

Actors can engage in mutually beneficial exchanges if two criteria are met (Stokman and Van Oosten 1994). First, they must take different positions on two issues, such that they are located on opposite sides of the expected outcome (as defined by the compromise model) on both issues. Second, they must attach different relative levels of salience to the two issues. Figure 5.2 describes the most important exchange possibilities in terms of positions held by the stakeholders. Four groups of actors can be distinguished. Actors in group 1 (*G1*) are located on the left side of the expected outcome on both issues; actors in group 4 (*G4*) on the right side. They take opposing positions on both issues and are therefore potential exchange partners. The same holds for group 2 (*G2*) and group 3 (*G3*). Since *G1* and *G2* have the same position on issue *a*, they cannot exchange. *G1* and *G3* cannot exchange as they have the same

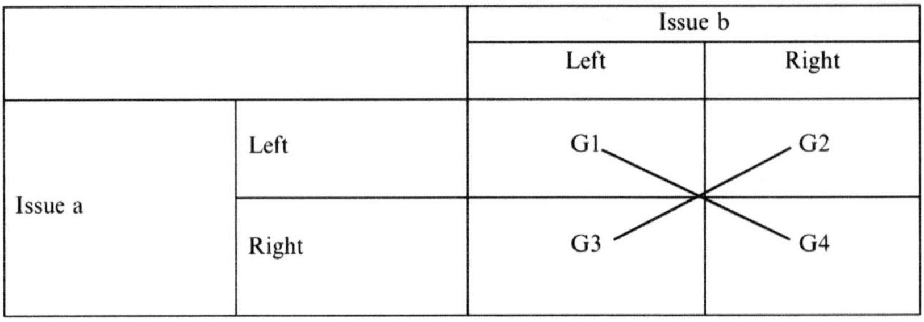

		Issue b	
		Left	Right
Issue a	Left	G1	G2
	Right	G3	G4

Figure 5.2. Position exchange possibilities

position on issue b. Each actor, in this case actor i, evaluates utility gains from exchanges on the basis of shifts in expected outcomes on the issues, using the following loss function:

$$L_i = \sum_{a=1}^{m} -s_{ia}|x_{ia} - O_a| \tag{5.4}$$

where x_{ia} and s_{ia} are defined as above and O_a denotes the expected outcome on issue a with $0 \leq x_{ia}, O_{a,} \leq 1$ and $0 < s_{ia,} \leq 1$.

Our model of exchange assumes that exchanges are carried out at one particular exchange rate contained in the core, namely equal utility gain for both stakeholders involved.[6] For the exchange partners to obtain the maximum possible utility gain from the exchange, at least one of the actors shifts its voting position completely to the position of the other, while the other shifts its position only partly towards the position of the first actor.

When the position exchange model is applied, a list of all potential exchanges between all pairs of actors and all pairs of issues within a Commission proposal is generated.[7] The potential exchanges are ordered on the basis of the potential utility gains experienced by the

[6] The exchange rate of equal utility gain involves a comparison of utilities between individuals. Alternative exchange rates include the Raiffa-Kalai-Smorodinski (RKS) solution (Friedman 1990: 218–23) or the Nash bargaining solution. Van Assen (2001) compares the three solutions. Only under certain conditions do RKS and Nash differ from equal utility gain. A comparative analysis of the three exchange rates in empirical applications resulted in only marginal differences in the predicted outcomes. An exchange rate based on equal utility gain makes the ordering of potential exchanges easier, since their order in terms of utility gains is the same for the two actors involved in the exchange.

[7] The position exchange model would be able to generate a list of new exchanges between pairs of actors as a consequence of the shifts in positions generated by previous exchanges. However, this more elaborate model does not provide additional theoretical insights or more accurate predictions in the present application.

two exchange partners. Exchanges are realised in that order. Each actor's position shift on its supply issue is binding, in the sense that it cannot move back toward its initial position. Therefore, the realisation of an exchange often excludes certain exchanges ranked lower down the list. However, if an actor does not shift completely toward the position of its exchange partner, it may shift further in that direction in a subsequent bilateral exchange. The whole process ends when no potential exchanges remain. The final outcome is determined on the basis of the voting positions of the stakeholders after the exchange process, applying the compromise solution to the voting positions.

5.2.3 Conditions favouring compromise, exchange and challenge

The compromise model and the challenge model represent contrasting influence processes (Stokman 2004; 2005). When the conditions favour the search for compromise, we would expect the challenge model to be less relevant. The compromise model's connection with information-based influence processes implies that the compromise solution might be the preferred solution when an issue is less polarised. In such a situation, we would expect divergent interests to be accommodated in favour of the common interests. The polarisation of an issue depends not only on the distribution of the positions, but also on the location of actors with high capabilities that attach great importance to the issue. We operationalise issue polarisation as the average distance between actors' initial positions and the expected outcome (as defined by the forecast of the compromise model), whereby these distances are weighted by the product of actors' capabilities and the level of salience they attach to the issue. Issues are less polarised if the effective power is concentrated around the same point on the issue scale. While we expect the compromise model to perform well on issues of low polarisation; the challenge model is expected to perform poorly in such situations.

The effects of exchanges in terms of the benefits or losses that accrue to actors not directly involved in the exchange are referred to as externalities. Such externalities may encourage or discourage the realisation of exchanges. Equation 5.4 makes it possible to measure directly whether exchanges of voting positions result in better or worse outcomes for actors than the compromise solution. Because issues are combined with each other, it is possible that all actors might be better off supporting a decision outcome other than the compromise model's solution on two issues. The consequences of all exchanges on any combination of two issues for actor *a* can be divided into three components. First, the utility gain as a consequence of actor *a*'s *own exchanges*. Since actors only engage in exchanges in which they gain, this component has to be positive. The second component consists of changes in utility experienced by actor *a* resulting from *exchanges in its own group*. If, for example, actor *a* is a member of *G1* (see Figure 5.2) exchanges between all other *G1* and all *G4* actors feature in this component. This component could either be positive or negative, depending on the direction of the exchanges realised by the other *G1* and *G4* actors. The third component consists of changes in actor *a*'s utility following *exchanges in the other group*. The 'other group' of an actor contains all other stakeholders: for example, for a *G1* actor, all actors of type *G2* and *G3* are members of the other group. Utility changes as a result of exchanges between other actors represent externalities. Negative externalities (negative utilities) signal conflict. Therefore, the sum of utilities resulting from exchanges in the other group and from exchanges in its own group are denoted by measures of *between group conflict* and *within group conflict* respectively (Van Assen *et al* 2003).

We assume that exchanges of voting positions are more likely in Commission proposals when there are higher utility gains for the actors involved in the exchanges (own utility gains), when there are higher positive externalities, and when there are lower negative externalities. Bilateral exchanges between actors promote common interests if they have positive externalities. Bilateral exchanges with negative externalities promote parochial interests, and may well endanger the process of finding common solutions (Stokman 2004; 2005). Sometimes, negative externalities are unavoidable. This is the case if all four cells in Figure 5.2 are filled. *G1*-*G4* exchanges then have positive externalities for *G2* and negative for *G3*, if issue *a* is the demand issue for actors in *G1* and issue *b* the demand issue for actors in *G4*. Exchanges can have negative externalities within an actor's own group if the priorities within the own group differ. In that case, for example, issue *a* may be the demand issue for one stakeholder in *G1* and supply issue for another.

Table 5.1 summarises the two models that are confronted with each other, the principles on which they are based, and the input data that they require.

5.3 RESEARCH DESIGN

Most of the research design decisions have been discussed in Chapter 2. Here, we simply report on the measure of actors' capabilities used in

Table 5.1. *Summary of models applied and their required input variables*

Model	Prediction	Input data
Challenge model	Iterative bargaining model based on non-cooperative game theory that models challenges of positions	Positions of the actors, the levels of salience they attach to issues and their relative capabilities
Position exchange model	Bargaining model based on cooperative game theory that models exchanges between pairs of actors across pairs of issues	

this application, and on the selection of issues for inclusion in our analyses.

We report the results of the analyses based on the second variant of the Shapley Shubik Index scores described in Table 2.5 of Chapter 2. According to these scores, the Commission does not feature in the co-decision issues; the bargaining takes place between the Council members and the European Parliament. Although the Commission may be a member of the coalition that supports the final decision outcome, it is assumed not to be essential to the success of that coalition. The European Parliament has a score of 45 relative to the Council's capability score of 100 under the qualified majority voting (QMV) variant of co-decision, and a score of seven under the unanimity variant. This low score under the unanimity variant is due to the fact that all 15 member states and the EP have to support the decision outcome for it to be adopted. Under consultation, the EP never features in the decision-making process. Under the QMV variant of consultation, the Commission is equal to a third of the total Council's capability score, and has a score of zero under the unanimity variant. This score of zero is due to the fact that a unanimous Council is assumed to be able to overrule the Commission under the consultation procedure. We also experimented with the other two sets of scores described in Chapter 2 that ascribe higher scores to the Commission and EP. These yielded poorer predictions. The errors of the models using other capability scores will be reported in footnotes.

The position exchange model is applied to all Commission proposals. On the legislative proposals with just one issue, the position exchange model's forecast is the same as the predictions of the compromise model. We therefore have 162 issues to which we apply the challenge, the compromise and the position exchange models.

5.4 AN ILLUSTRATION: REFORM OF STRUCTURAL ASSISTANCE IN THE FISHERIES SECTOR

To illustrate the application of these models, we refer to the example of a proposal for a regulation on fisheries policy. The proposal was an attempt by the Commission to reconcile a perceived contradiction in EU policy. On the one hand, the European Union has an ongoing programme to control the size of fishing catches (in the framework of the Multi-annual Guidance Programme, MAGP). On the other, the EU provides subsidies for the renewal of fishing fleets. Because new ships are more efficient than older ones, this contributes to larger fishing catches. The legislative proposal was introduced by the European Commission in December 1998 (OJ C 1999/16/12), and after debate in the Council of Ministers, adopted in December 1999 (OJ L 1999/337/10). Two issues had to be resolved before the proposal could be adopted (see Figure 5.3).

The first issue concerned the size of the scrap-build penalty. This issue refers to the question of how many tonnes of old fishing fleet should be scrapped in relation to new fishing fleet to qualify for subsidy. This issue was contested for both environmental and budgetary reasons. The actors in favour of a large scrap-build penalty argued that this would restrict the demand for subsidies for fleet renewal. This would mean that newer, more efficient boats with higher 'killing power' would be introduced at a slower pace. In the proposal, the European Commission called for a scrap-build penalty of 130 tonnes of old ship for every 100 tonnes of new ship. The UK favoured the most extreme position, a scrap-build penalty of 150–180 tonnes of old ship for each new ship of 100 tonnes. On the issue continuum, the scale position of 100 was used to represent this position. The other extreme, scored as 0, was the *status quo* position at that time, requiring a penalty of 100 tonnes for every new 100 tonnes. Most member states favoured the continuation of the *status quo* when the proposal was introduced.

According to an expert who provided information on this proposal, the Commission's most favoured outcome on this issue (a scrap-build penalty of 130 tonnes) should be scored as 90 on our scale, much closer to the UK's position than to the *status quo*. Two member states, Denmark and Austria, were placed between 90 and the most extreme score. The Dutch delegation was said not to have participated in the discussions on this issue, and was therefore not attributed a position. We were informed that this had to do with a disagreement between the Dutch Ministry of Fisheries and Agriculture on the one hand, and the Ministry

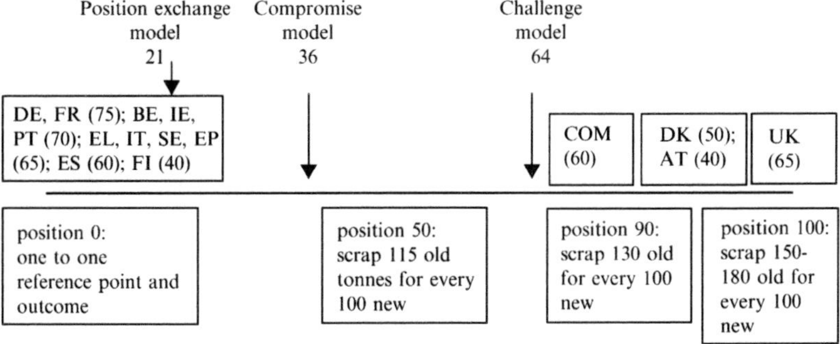

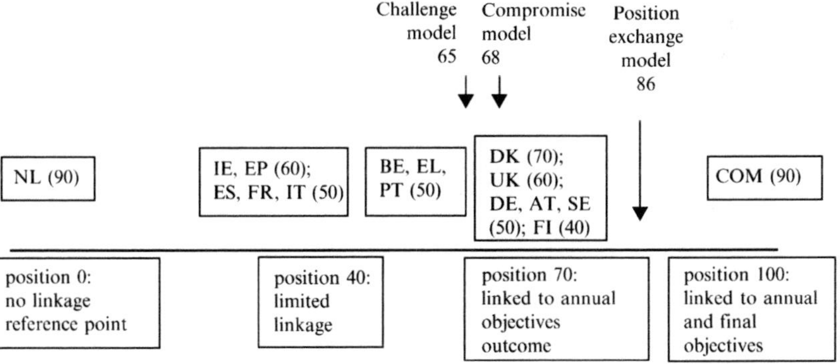

Figure 5.3. Illustration of model predictions on Commission proposal for a Council regulation, laying down the detailed rules and arrangements regarding the Community structural assistance in the fisheries sector (CNS/1998/347). (Salience scores in brackets)

of Environment on the other. As a result of this disagreement, the Dutch did not formulate a coherent position. During the course of the negotiations, a compromise proposal was made that then received the support of some member states, but this was not incorporated into the final decision outcome: the key informant located this compromise position half way along the continuum, at position 50. According to this expert, the final outcome could best be described as a continuation of the *status quo* on that issue, corresponding with position zero on the first issue scale.

The second controversial issue was the proposed linkage of the subsidy with the extent to which member states achieved their annual and final objectives in the MAGP. The specific policy question addressed here was the extent to which member states must achieve their objectives to qualify for subsidy. Most member states had some difficulty meeting the MAGP objectives. Introducing strict adherence to these objectives as a necessary condition for obtaining subsidy would have had negative financial consequences for the sector. The European Commission took the position that strict adherence to all MAGP objectives should be a condition for receiving subsidy for fleet renewal. This position was scored as 100 on our scale. The Netherlands was said to have had most difficulty meeting the MAGP objectives, which caused the Dutch to take the most extreme position on the other side of the continuum. They would have preferred no linkage at all between the subsidy for building new boats and the extent to which MAGP objectives had to be met, which was the *status quo* position at that time. Most other member states took intermediate positions. The UK, Germany and four other delegations were in favour of linking the subsidies to annual objectives only (position 70). France, along with three other member states, favoured a more limited linkage (position 40). Belgium, Greece and Portugal were said to favour a somewhat stronger linkage than France, but considerably less than the UK and Germany. They were placed at position 50 on the scale to represent this. The actual outcome is described by position 70 on the issue scale: linked to the annual but not final MAGP objectives.

As described above, in the position exchange model it is posited that actors identify mutually beneficial exchanges of voting positions on pairs of issues. Such an exchange process is expected to be particularly prominent when actors who take very different *positions* on the two issues also attach very different levels of *salience* to the two issues. In particular, the first criterion that must be met before an exchange is possible is that the pairs of stakeholders engaged in the exchange must take positions on opposite sides of the expected outcome on the two issues. The expected outcome is defined by the prediction of the compromise model (the average of the positions weighted by capabilities times salience).

The predictions of the compromise model are positions 36 on issue 1 and position 68 on issue 2. Table 5.2 shows the positions of the actors in relation to these expected outcomes, and identifies which actors might be able to engage in exchanges of voting positions. On the basis of the actors' initially favoured positions, it is clear that the only possible exchanges that could take place are between actors to the left of the expected outcome on both issues, and those to the right of the expected

Table 5.2. *Potential exchange partners in Commission proposal on structural assistance in the fisheries sector. Positions in relation to expected outcome*[a]

		Issue 2: linkage to MAGP	
		Left	Right
Issue 1: scrap-build penalty	Left	BE, ES, EL, FR, IT, IE, PT, EP	DE, FI, SE
	Right	None	COM, AT, DK, UK

Note: [a]Luxembourg did not take a position on either issue. The Netherlands took a position on the linkage issue only.

outcome on both issues. The three actors to the left on issue 1 and to the right on issue 2 (DE, FI and SE) have no potential exchange partners.

The second criterion that must be fulfilled before an exchange can be realised is that the actors involved must attach different relative levels of salience to the two issues. Only if there is a difference between the relative levels of salience attached to the two issues will the exchange be of benefit to both actors engaged in it; otherwise they cannot exchange. The comparison of the relative levels of salience also determines the direction of the exchange: which actors will move in which direction during the exchange.

In this example, exchanges involving the Commission drive the predictions. The Commission attached a higher level of salience to the linkage issue (issue 2) than to the scrap-build penalty issue (issue 1). This linkage issue was said to be more strongly related to the main objective of the proposal from the perspective of the Commission: namely, dismantling the apparent contradiction between fleet renewal and conservation. It was estimated that the Commission attached a salience score of 60 to issue 1 and 90 to issue 2. According to the logic of the position exchange model, the Commission would have been interested in an exchange whereby it shifted its position on the scrap-build penalty issue (issue 1) in return for the support of other actors on the linkage issue (issue 2). The question is whether the actors, who were in a position to engage in such an exchange, would find this proposition attractive. As it happens, all of the actors to the left of the expected outcome on both issues, the Commission's potential exchange partners, attached more importance to the scrap-build penalty issues than the linkage issue. This is the opposite prioritisation to that of the Commission.[8] For example, the French representation was estimated to attach a salience of 75 to the scrap-build penalty issue, and 50 to the linkage issue. According to the position exchange model, this is indeed the first exchange realised. The Commission moves leftward on the scrap-build penalty issue, and occupies a position closer to the *status quo* (position 73 on the continuum to be exact). In return, France shifts its position to 100 on the linkage issue. In subsequent exchanges, the Commission continues to drift toward the *status quo* on the scrap-build penalty issue, and to receive the support of other member states on the linkage issue. As a result of these shifts, the expected outcome generated by the position exchange model is close to the left of the issue continuum representing the scrap-build penalty issue (on issue 1 the prediction is 21), and close to the right of the right of the continuum representing the linkage issue (on issue 2 the prediction is 86).

The predictions of the challenge model in this example are influenced greatly by the differences between the stakeholders in terms of their risk propensities. An actor's risk propensity determines whether it will seek out conflict with other stakeholders and defend its policy position vigorously if it is challenged by another. In the challenge model, the risk propensity is influenced by the distance between an actor's policy position and the expected outcome. The challenge model defines the expected outcome as the median average position (weighted by the product of the actors' capabilities and salience). In the scrap-build penalty issue in the example, the weighted median position is zero on the scale, which accords perfectly with the actual outcome. In the challenge model, the expectation of this outcome induces the actors who support this position to be risk-averse, and those who are distant from it, namely the Commission, Denmark, Austria and the UK, to be risk-seeking. According to the model, these four stakeholders are successful at demolishing the support for the continuation of the *status quo*. Within a few rounds of simulated negotiations, there are no stakeholders left supporting the *status quo*; they all shift their positions to the right half of the continuum representing the scrap-build penalty issue. This is not an accurate description of the events leading to the actual decision outcome.

The illustration makes clear that models containing the same information can make substantially different predictions of decision

[8] Exchanges are feasible when the level of salience actor *i* attaches to the first issue relative to the second issue differs from that of actor *j*. Exchanges may therefore also occur between actors who both attach the highest level of salience to the same issue.

Table 5.3. *Summary of error of models on issues*[a]

Model	Error of models on all issues
Compromise model	22.9 (n=162)
Position exchange model	23.9 (n=162)
Challenge model	28.0 (n=162)

Note: [a]The forecasts examined in this and the following tables were made using the Shapley Shubik Index scores (version 2, which includes the possibility of a winning coalition without the Commission) described in Chapter 2.

outcomes, as the comparison between the predictions of the challenge and the position exchange models' predictions on issue 1 makes clear. The position exchange model performed rather well in this particular case. The illustration provided in this section is of course just that; it was intended to clarify the workings of the models, and should not be seen as a substitute or alternative to the quantitative analyses performed in the following section.

5.5 ANALYSIS

Which model generates the most accurate forecasts of decision outcomes in the EU?[9] Table 5.3[10] provides the first cut answer to this question. It contains the average absolute distances between the actual outcomes and the model forecasts on the 100 point issue scales of the sort referred to in the illustration. The compromise model performs best with an average error of 22.9. The position exchange model is slightly worse with an error of 23.8[11], and the challenge model is the least accurate with an

[9] Note that our models can be tested in two different ways. First, as in the present chapter, the models can be tested at the collective (or macro) level by identifying the accuracy of their predictions of decision outcomes. Second, our models can also be tested at the actor (or micro) level, by comparing the accuracy of their predictions of the shifts in actors' policy positions. This second type of analysis has been published in the special issue of European Union Politics (Arregui *et al* 2004).

[10] On the basis of expert judgements of capabilities the errors are: compromise model 26.2 (n = 162); position exchange model 26.1 (n = 162); challenge model 31.2 (n = 162).

[11] Note that the predictions we show in Table 5.3 make reference to the analysis of 162 issues. The Commission proposals in the data set with two or more issues contain 137 issues. The predictions of the position exchange model can only differ from those of the compromise model on these 137 issues. The error of the position exchange model on these 137 issues is 25.2.

Table 5.4. *Summary of error of models by type of issues*

	Dichotomous	Rank order	Scale
Compromise model	33.0 (*n* = 33)	21.0 (*n* =109)	16.7 (*n* = 20)
Position exchange model	26.2 (*n* =33)	23.3 (*n* =109)	23.4 (*n* =20)
Challenge model	34.2 (*n* = 33)	27.0 (*n* = 109)	23.3 (*n* = 20)

error of 28.0. The difference in the level of accuracy of the compromise and challenge models is relatively large.[12]

Table 5.4[13] contains the errors by the type of issue: dichotomous, rank order or scale. There are substantial differences between the performance of the compromise and challenge models across the types of issues. The errors of these models are considerably higher on dichotomous issues. The errors of the position exchange model appear to be relatively unaffected by the type of issue, so that it has the lowest error for dichotomous issues.

Table 5.5[14] contains the errors of the models on issues subject to different legislative procedures. For the consultation issues, the most

[12] A non-parametric test, Wilcoxon's signed rank test, indicates that the challenge model's predictions are significantly worse than those of the compromise model (p = .008). This test also indicates that the challenge model's predictions are worse than those of the position exchange model (p = .096). Finally, the differences between the accuracy of the predictions made by the compromise and the position exchange model are not significant.

[13] The error of the compromise model using the first version of the SSI scores is 33.8 for dichotomous issues, 21.2 for rank order issues, and 18.6 for scale issues. For dichotomous issues the mean errors of the position exchange model become smaller using the first version of SSI scores: the average error for dichotomous issues is 25.0, for rank order issues 23.1, and for scale issues is 24.4. The challenge model makes an average error of 33.4 on dichotomous issues with the first version of SSI scores. It has the same error regarding scale issues (23.2) and has a higher error for rank order issues (29.7).

[14] A similar pattern of errors as that reported in Table 5.5 is found when the first version of SSI scores for the power estimates is used. The average errors of the compromise model with the first version of SSI scores are the following: under consultation qualified majority votting (QMV) 23.9, under consultation unanimity 18.7, under co-decision QMV 27.7, and under co-decision unanimity 17.6. The position exchange model also shows similar error patterns to those reported: under consultation QMV 26.2, in consultation unanimity 20.4, under co-decision QMV 24.8, and under co-decision unanimity 17.4. Finally, when we used the first version of the SSI scores in the input data for the challenge model the errors were 30.6 under consultation QMV, 24.1 in consultation unanimity, 32.2 under co-decision QMV, and 27.5 under co-decision unanimity.

Table 5.5. *Summary of error of models on issues by legislative procedure*

	CNS QMV	CNS una.	COD QMV	COD una.
Compromise model	23.3 (n=55)	17.3 (n=39)	27.3 (n=56)	19.2 (n=12)
Position exchange model	26.1 (n=55)	18.7 (n=39)	26.3 (n=56)	19.3 (n=12)
Challenge model	30.1 (n=55)	23.9 (n=39)	29.8 (n=56)	23.6 (n=12)

Table 5.6. *Summary of error of models on issues by policy area*

	Agriculture	Internal market	Other policy areas
Compromise model	26.6 (n=40)	31.2 (n=34)	18.0 (n=88)
Position exchange model	29.8 (n=40)	28.7 (n=34)	19.3 (n=88)
Challenge model	30.1 (n=40)	33.8 (n=34)	24.9 (n=88)

accurate model is the compromise model. For the co-decision issues, the position exchange model generates the most accurate forecasts for the QMV variant of Council voting, while for the co-decision unanimity variant, the compromise and the position exchange models have the same level of error.

Table 5.6[15] reports the errors of the models on issues in different policy areas. A division is made between agriculture, internal market and 'other policy areas'. The last category includes issues relating to a number of areas, including fisheries, culture, and transport. These categories were placed together because each contained relatively few issues. In agriculture and 'other' policy areas, the most accurate model is the compromise model. In issues dealing with internal market policies, the most accurate model is the position exchange model with an average error of 28.7. There appears to be a substantial amount of variation between policy areas, especially between the 'other' category and the first two policy areas.

[15] The errors by policy areas using the first version of the SSI scores are the following: the compromise model has an average error of 27 in agriculture, 30.4 in issues related to internal market, and an average error of 19.2 for the issues in other policy areas. The position exchange model has an average error of 28.9 on agriculture issues, 29.7 on issues in the internal market area, and 19.0 for the other issues. The challenge has an error of 31.2 for agriculture issues, 33.7 for internal market issues and, finally, an average error of 26.8 for issues in other policy areas.

Table 5.7. *Distribution of utility gains from bilateral exchanges within Commission proposals*

	n	Minimum	Maximum	Mean	Std. deviation
Own gains	49	.00	.41	.11	.10
Negative externalities	49	−6.75	.00	−1.28	1.62
Positive externalities	49	.00	3.14	.70	.80
Total gains and losses	49	−4.75	1.47	−.47	1.11

Equation 5.4 makes it possible to compute the effects of exchanges on each actor's expected utility. As discussed earlier, these changes in utility can be divided into different components. These are the possible gains as a result of exchanges in which each actor itself is involved, and the utility changes from the positive and negative externalities from the exchanges involving other actors. Since these utility gains concern exchanges between pairs of issues, aggregation of the utility gains per issue would result in issues being counted more than once. We therefore aggregated them at the level of Commission proposals, which avoids double counting.

Table 5.7 provides these figures for the 49 Commission proposals to which the position exchange model was applied that contained more than one issue. This table reveals two remarkable things. First, the externalities are substantially higher than the own gains. This is due mainly to the large number of actors involved. Second, the negative externalities are twice as large as the positive ones. There are only a few Commission proposals in which exchanges are possible without negative externalities. This suggests why the position exchange model is unable to improve significantly on the predictive accuracy of the compromise model in the present application. We expect that exchange possibilities without negative externalities are more easily realised than those that have large negative effects on the utility of other actors. When exchange possibilities have high negative externalities, these bilateral exchanges will be discouraged. They will be seen as serving the *parochial interests of the two exchange partners*, rather than *contributing constructively to a common solution*. This also implies that exchanges are not the primary solution for resolving controversies in legislative decision-making in the European Union. Consequently, the position exchange model is not the best model to predict outcomes in this context.

Our expectation is that the position exchange model works predominantly in exchange situations without (large) negative externalities. However, we are unlikely to find strong statistical effects in our subset of issues with high negative externalities, due to local stochastic independence. In addition, we face a second statistical problem (see Table 5.8). The size of the gains is expected to depend strongly on the number of pairs of issues in a Commission proposal. The correlations in Table 5.8 show that the sizes of the gains and losses indeed correlate very highly with the number of (pairs of) issues. The correlations between the own gains and the positive and negative externalities are also very high. Therefore, we face a problem of multicollinearity. This cannot be solved by multilevel regression analysis as we are dealing with three levels (proposals, issues and pairs of issues) of which the lowest level (pairs of issues) is not nested in the higher levels. When applying multilevel regression with two levels (proposals and issues, and gains defined at the proposal level), we encountered many estimation problems. Thus, we show two statistical analyses. The first is a regression of the errors of the position exchange model on the issues from Commission proposals with only two controversial issues (Table 5.9). These errors are regressed on the 'own gains' and the negative externalities present in those proposals. The second analysis is an OLS regression at the issue level over all proposals to give some indication of the statistical effects (Table 5.10).

Table 5.9 shows that high 'own gains' improve the predictions of the position exchange model significantly, but that negative externalities do not matter. However, the coefficients in Table 5.10 indicate that high negative externalities indeed increase the errors of the position exchange model.[16] This effect is statistically significant and supports the expectation that negative externalities discourage the realisation of exchanges. Own gains matter less (and the small effect is in the direction opposite to that expected). Externalities had no effect on the errors of the compromise and challenge models. We did not include these effects in the reported regression analyses for those models.

The OLS regression analysis shows three important sets of findings. First, the reported differences in errors between the different legislative procedures do not result in significant effects of the co-decision and unanimity dummies. Table 5.10 also reveals that the compromise model

[16] Note that the OLS regression analysis includes 137 issues for the position exchange model. This is because externalities cannot be calculated for the legislative proposals with just one issue.

Table 5.8. *Product moment correlations between utility gains and number of (pairs of) issues*

	Own gains	Negative externalities	Positive externalities	Total gains and losses	No of issues	No of pairs of issues
Own gains	1	−.612[a]	.738[a]	−.265	.873[a]	.858[a]
Negative externalities	−.612[a]	1	−.747[a]	.855[a]	−.637[a]	−.598[a]
Positive externalities	.738[a]	−.747[a]	1	−.299[b]	.700[a]	.701[a]
Total gains and losses	−.265	.855[a]	−.299[b]	1	−.340[b]	−.286[b]
No of issues	.873[a]	−.637[a]	.700[a]	−.340[b]	1	.951[a]
No of pairs of issues	.858[a]	−.598[a]	.701[a]	−.286[b]	.951[a]	1

Notes: [a]Correlation is significant at the 0.01 level (2-tailed).
[b]Correlation is significant at the 0.05 level (2-tailed).

Table 5.9. *Effects of own gains and negative externalities on the error of the position exchange model for proposals with two controversial issues (n=38)*[a]

	b	Standard error	t	Sig.
Constant	33.19	5.66	5.86	0.00
Own gains	−225.03	109.02	−2.06	0.05
Negative externalities	2.44	7.50	0.33	0.75

Note: [a]Adj. R Square .08.

Table 5.10. *OLS regression analysis of the errors of the models (standard error in brackets)*

	Compromise model (SSI2)	Position exchange model (SSI2)	Challenge or expected utility model (SSI2)
Constant	24.55[a] (6.13)	19.39[a] (6.03)	25.22[a] (8.63)
No. of (pairs of) issues			
No. of issues	.82 (1.26)		.14 (1.78)
No. of pairs of issues		1.48 (1.03)	
Legislative procedure			
Co-decision	2.43 (3.13)	−1.47 (3.77)	−1.87 (4.40)
Unanimity	−4.29 (3.48)	−3.06 (3.90)	−2.47 (4.89)
Issues			
Rank	−16.12[a] (4.05)	−5.18 (4.50)	−10.64[c] (5.7)
Scale	−17.00[a] (5.76)	−8.02 (6.64)	−11.59 (8.1)
Polarisation	.10[a] (.03)	−0.06[c] (0.035)	0.136[a] (0.04)
Externalities			
Own		19.7 (32.75)	
Total negative		1.97[c] (1.19)	
Adj. R Square	.17	.09	.07
F	6.32[a]	2.68[a]	2.8[b]
N	154	137	154

Notes: [a]Significant at .01 level.
[b]Significant at .05 level.
[c]Significant at .10 level.

is most sensitive to the measurement level of the issue continua (with regard to the distinction between dichotomous, rank order and scale issues), while the position exchange model is least sensitive. Finally, the table illustrates that the higher the polarisation in the positions, the more accurate are the predictions of the position exchange model.[17] For the other two models the reverse is true, although we expected that the challenge model would do better on polarised issues. The accurate predictions of the position exchange model on dichotomous and polarised issues can be explained by the fact that exchanges of extreme positions yield the highest utility gains.

5.6 CONCLUSIONS

In this chapter we applied models in which actors attempt to build coalitions behind or close to their positions. According to these models, actors are willing or feel compelled to shift their positions during the stage of informal bargaining before decisions are formally adopted. Three processes though which actors might reach agreement were distinguished. If actors' common interests are high relative to their divergent interests, as reflected in their positions and saliences on the issues, actors may change their initial positions on the basis of convincing information and persuasion by others. The compromise model introduced in Chapter 4 represents this process. The exchange and challenge models take the initial positions as given and fixed, but assume that actors might be willing or forced to support other positions at the final voting stage. The position exchange model assumes that shifts in actors' positions result from pairs of actors taking advantage of mutually profitable exchange opportunities across pairs of issues. Such exchange opportunities are present when actors have opposing positions on both issues, and attach different relative levels of salience to the issues. Both actors involved in the exchange stand to gain relative to the outcome if the compromise model were applied to the initial positions. While exchanges have positive effects on the utilities of the actors that execute them, they may have serious positive or negative externalities for other actors. Finally, the challenge model is based on non-cooperative processes,

[17] Recall, we measured the polarisation of the positions on each issue by the average distance between each actor's position and the prediction of the compromise model, whereby the distances were weighted by the product of the actors' capabilities and the level of salience they attached to the issue.

through which some actors are compelled or persuaded to change their voting positions due to challenges from others.

The first conclusion to be drawn from these analyses is that the more complex challenge and position exchange models do not improve on the accuracy of the compromise model's predictions. On all issues in the data set to which we applied the models, the average error of the position exchange model is 23.9 points while the challenge model has an error term of 28.0. The compromise model improves on both models, with an error of 22.9. Thus, computational sophistication is no guarantee of accuracy. So what has changed since the previous study of Bueno de Mesquita and Stokman (1994), in which the challenge model was found to be the best predictor of decision outcomes? The previous study contained an analysis of 22 issues, and most of the statistical analyses were performed on just 16 issues. In the present analysis, 162 issues have been included. This could make a difference. Furthermore, the analysis performed for the 1994 book included a smaller number of actors; then, there were only twelve Council members, and the analysis excluded the Commission and the EP. The current analysis includes fifteen member states, the Commission and the EP. A larger number of actors makes the decision-making process more complex, which makes it more difficult for the bargaining models to predict accurately.

A second important finding is that bilateral exchanges between pairs of actors tend to induce large externalities for other actors in the European Union. The negative externalities are about twice as large as the positive ones, and much larger than the utility gains expected by the potential exchange partners. When this is the case, exchanges between pairs of actors will be seen as serving parochial interests, rather than contributing to common solutions that would be acceptable to all actors. Negative externalities are present in almost all Commission proposals in the data set. This makes it difficult to test whether the position exchange model generates more accurate predictions when there are low negative externalities (the problem of local stochastic independence). Despite the apparent inapplicability of the position exchange model, it does generate more accurate forecasts than the challenge model. This is true in terms of the overall performance of the models, and also within most of the subsets of issues we investigated. Furthermore, the position exchange model's forecasts do not appear to be statistically worse than those of the compromise model. Given that bargaining in the EU involves repeated interaction between the same players, it is plausible that models based on cooperative assumptions are more applicable than the challenge model, based on non-cooperative assumptions.

The third conclusion is that we have made some progress in specifying the conditions under which the three models are more or less applicable. The position exchange model is the only model that is insensitive to the level of measurement of the issues. Moreover, its predictions are more accurate when the issues are more polarised. The position exchange model's predictions improve slightly when the negative externalities from exchange are lower. The other two models perform worse on issues that are highly polarised. The compromise model is particularly sensitive to the level at which the issues are measured, and generates poor predictions on dichotomous issues. The bivariate analyses suggested that the accuracy of the three models varied across legislative procedures. Under the consultation procedure (both QMV and unanimity voting in the Council) the compromise model generated the most accurate predictions, while under the co-decision procedure (both QMV and unanimity) the position exchange model performed best. In the multivariate analyses these effects disappeared, however.

The main conclusion to be drawn from this chapter is that the results support to some extent to the compromise model. This gives credence to the view that legislative decision-making in the European Union is based on processes in which information and persuasion are central, and in which actors are willing to compromise for the sake of reaching common solutions. However, while the exchange and the challenge models provide an account of the actor level process by which choices are made, the compromise model does not. Furthermore, as we have shown in Section 5.5, the differences in predictive power among the three models are very small compared with the standard errors. Therefore, it can be concluded that each of these models incorporates some aspects of the reality of European Union decision-making that the other two models miss.

6

Nash versus Schelling? The importance of constraints in legislative bargaining

STEFANIE BAILER AND GERALD SCHNEIDER

6.1 INTRODUCTION

When the Council of Ministers had to decide on the so-called chocolate directive in 1999, its plan to allow vegetable fat in the production of candy products met with fierce opposition from Belgium, France, and the Netherlands. These three member states objected to the usage of vegetable fats other than cocoa in chocolate. Although they advanced some consumer-friendly arguments, continental manufacturers also tried to avoid competition from the British chocolate industry and to protect some of their traditional trading partners in the African, Caribbean and Pacific (ACP) countries.[1] They particularly protested against the proposed derogations that would have allowed the United Kingdom and Ireland to continue the production of 'household milk chocolate', which contains a large amount of milk. While the Belgian government spoke of 'à la carte harmonisation' benefiting 'the industries of only certain

We would like to thank the editors, reviewers and seminar participants at the universities of Twente and Mannheim as well at the Netherlands Institute for Advanced Study (NIAS) meetings for their comments. Research support by the German Research Foundation is gratefully acknowledged. We received valuable assistance throughout the research process from Stefanie Börst, Simone Burkhart, Helen Callaghan, Han Dorussen, Dietrich Drüner, Daniel Finke, Nikolaus Hautsch, Stefan Klotz and Nadine Warmuth. The detailed and encouraging comments by the two chapter reviewers—Simon Hug and Robert Pahre—greatly improved our theoretical argument and empirical analysis. While this article focuses on the accuracy of two-level game predictions, Schneider *et al* (2004) also consider other bargaining models and offer a more detailed discussion of the substantive implications.

[1] This became particularly obvious in statements by the Belgian, French and Luxembourg delegations after the last vote was cast in the Council in May 2000. Press release: Brussels (25 May 2000), Press: 180 No. 8829/2/00, 2265th Council Meeting Internal Market, 25 May 2000.

member states' (*Europe Daily Bulletins*, No. 7583, 29 October 1999), French chocolate makers demonstrated against the measure during the plenary session of the European Parliament in January 2000. The massive lobbying by the Belgian and French interest groups was, however, only partially successful. The European Parliament accepted the common position of the Council, allowing some sorts of vegetable fats in chocolate as well as the derogations favouring British and Irish 'family milk chocolate'. The legislature nevertheless added a 'fair trade' requirement. This successful amendment granted the industry the right to sell chocolate containing up to six sorts of vegetable fat everywhere in the European Union, as long as these ingredients came from developing countries (*Europe Daily Bulletins*, No. 7677, 16 March 2000).

The compromise found illustrates that domestic interests considerably shape the negotiation mandates of member states. At a theoretical level, the influence of sectoral interests in the negotiations on the chocolate directive is in line with the conjecture that domestically constrained and therefore supposedly weak negotiators, like the Belgian and French ministers under pressure from the chocolate industry and development countries, often possess disproportionate bargaining power. These two countries were able to postpone the directive for many years. Thomas Schelling (1960: 22) enthroned this hypothesis with the status of a 'paradox' and suggested that a commitment to a demanding negotiation position might be a useful bargaining device. He wrote, 'that the power to constrain an adversary may depend on the power to bind oneself; that, in bargaining, weakness is often strength, freedom may be freedom to capitulate, and to burn bridges behind one may suffice to undo an opponent.'

Although the strategic analysis of such commitment tactics did not really take off until the early 1990s, Schelling's 'paradox of weakness' has enjoyed considerable popularity in descriptive and normative bargaining theory. Robert D. Putnam's (1988) influential article on 'two-level games' reinforced the status of the counter-intuitive conjecture. According to him, constrained governments might try to exploit their constraint to advance their own interests. It was especially this idea that has encouraged empiricists and formal modellers to dwell on the 'paradox of weakness'.

This chapter evaluates the empirical relevance of the Schelling conjecture, showing that two-level game models do not predict much better than standard models of multilateral bargaining. We embed the Schelling conjecture within a conventional multi-actor Nash bargaining game.

Our assessment of the 'paradox of weakness' relies on different criteria to account for the possible influence that domestic institutions, diverging ideological stances, and the behaviour of the negotiators exert on the final outcome. We compare the predictive power of the different Schelling bargaining games with the accuracy of the symmetric Nash bargaining game. Our results show that the model that simultaneously considers institutional and ideological constraints fares the best by comparison. The models that try to measure domestic constraints through ideological constraints alone or the occurrence of threats have, by contrast, a rather low predictive accuracy. The chapter is structured as follows: we first introduce the Schelling conjecture and embed it within a multi-actor Nash bargaining model. Next, we outline our research design. The empirical section presents the model comparison and analyses the conditions under which the assumption of domestically constrained governments makes sense in the analysis of EU decision-making.

6.2 BARGAINING WITH DOMESTICALLY CONSTRAINED ACTORS: THE BASELINE MODEL

Most introductions to the literature on international negotiations describe bargaining as both a cooperative and a conflictive endeavour in which negotiators share an interest in solving a common problem, but disagree on the appropriate settlement (e.g. Wagner 2004). Since no formal bargaining protocol exists for most international negotiations, government leaders possess ample possibilities to influence the outcome through strategic means. This implies that formal power considerations or, to put it more bluntly, the international pecking order does not suffice to understand the final allocation of resources among the negotiators. While psychological research most often focuses on the varying ability of individual negotiators to strike a deal, political scientists and economists believe that such advantages will cancel out on average. In their view, the deal that the negotiators probably strike is, by and large, a consequence of the varying bargaining constraints and the way in which the negotiators manipulate them.

One important and non-trivial generalisation in this vein is the 'paradox of weakness'. With this metaphor, Schelling (1960: 24, italics suppressed) describes a manoeuvre whereby one side 'can accept the irrevocable commitment in a way that is unambiguously visible' to the other. Through this commitment tactic the first negotiator can 'squeeze the range of indeterminacy down to the point most favourable to him'.

The credibility of a commitment thereby often depends on the possibility of manipulating one's own constituents: 'If a binding public opinion can be cultivated and made evident to the other side, the initial position can thereby be made visibly final" (Schelling 1960: 28). In other words, international negotiators who have to seek the ratification approval of a conservative audience back home can credibly threaten that the negotiations will fail unless they receive some concession to appease their principal. Fearon (1994) as well as Schneider and Cederman (1994) have taken up this argument and formally shown how the costs of committing oneself domestically to a particular negotiation position (so-called audience costs) can influence international bargaining outcomes.

Although Schelling in his informal discussion also listed some limitations to this tactic, the conventional wisdom was soon reduced to the deterministic hypothesis that the constrained side almost always possesses a bargaining advantage. An influential manifestation of this trend was Putnam's (1988; 1993) article on 'two-level games', in which he tried to establish the Schelling conjecture as an empirical law of international negotiations:

> 'The larger the perceived win-set of a negotiator, the more he can be 'pushed around' by the other Level 1 negotiators. Conversely, a small domestic win-set can be a bargaining advantage: 'I'd like to accept your proposal, but I could never get it accepted at home'. (Putnam 1993: 441)

With the two-level game approach, Putnam tried to overcome a lacuna that he had identified in the theory of international relations. In his view, both the 'liberal' and 'realist' research traditions in international relations unnecessarily reduce the interaction between the international system and the nation state to a one-way street.[2] He claims rather that his two-level game approach provides a conceptual framework for building 'general equilibrium' theories that pay systematic attention to the possibility of reciprocal causation. Although Putnam (1988: 435) only sketched his conjectures, his call for a more rigorous 'algebra' of the nexus between domestic and international politics did not remain unheard. Yet, Putnam's popularisation has mainly triggered off sophisticated formal work and isolated case studies whose implications are hard to generalise. Some 15 years of intellectual investment in the two-level

[2] Moravcsik terms Putnam's approach 'interactive', to distinguish it from 'additive' approaches in which the two sets of constraints—domestic interests and international bargaining—are treated as superimposed (Moravcsik 1993: 17).

game approach have, in short, led to the typical mismatch between theoretical ambition and empirical confirmation that unfortunately still characterises many subfields in political science. Although a multitude of models probe the limitations of the 'paradox of weakness', only a very limited number of studies explores the empirical relevance of the Schelling conjecture in a systematic fashion.

Most formal models examine how domestic constraints shape international interactions.[3] The consensus is that the Schelling conjecture has to be qualified. Yet, this agreement does not reach much beyond the sober assessment that much of the early excitement about the 'paradox of weakness', and especially the two-level game metaphor, was not warranted. Iida (1993), Schneider and Cederman (1994), Mo (1995) and Tarar (2001) show situations in which negotiators benefit from domestic constraints. But they all condition the conjecture in one way or the other. One implication of this work is, for instance, that negotiations risk breaking down if the non-constrained governments are not well-informed about the constraint of the other side.

Milner (1997; see also Milner and Rosendorff 1996, 1997) as well as Hammond and Prins (1999), by contrast, argue that the Schelling conjecture is most often not true. In the view of Milner (1997), negotiators suffer rather than profit under domestic constraints. Hammond and Prins (1999) examine all possible preference configurations and conclude that the 'paradox of weakness' may be practically irrelevant. Martin (2000) argues in a similar vein that opposing legislatures may make cooperation between states easier on some occasions, because they render a commitment more credible. Yet, the positive impact of the legislature depends on the utility of the reference point. As Pahre (2001) points out, a conservative legislature is willing to go along with international agreements when the distance between its ideal point and the one of its government grows.

We believe that several modelling assumptions have sharpened the disagreements over the Schelling conjecture. A first important difference in the models is the attribution of agenda setting power. Milner (1997), and Milner and Rosendorff (1996; 1997), for instance, 'translate' the Nash bargaining solution into a spatial setting by introducing a direct distance utility measure. This produces a corner solution with the effect that the actor closest to the *status quo* controls the bargaining protocol

[3] Lohmann (1997) is one of the few studies that rigorously examines the impact of international bargaining on domestic politics. For ratification games see also Schneider and Weitsman (1996) and Hug (2002).

(Butler 2004). It follows quite naturally in a situation of complete information that domestic constraints would hurt this actor, because they prevent the negotiating governments from 'agreeing' on the agenda setter's ideal point.[4] Hammond and Prins (1999) are able to overcome the arbitrariness of endowing one actor with the agenda setter power by placing a possible outcome within a much larger bargaining set. Their exhaustive analysis of all preference configurations points out the possible exceptionality of situations in which negotiating governments can profitably use domestic constraints. This conclusion, however, crucially hinges on the assumption that the different preference configurations are uniformly distributed. Because we do not know how likely certain profiles are, we are not able to firmly reject the Schelling conjecture, but might have to concede that it depends on certain preference configurations. A second difference between the models is the interpretation of what constitutes the fall-back position in international negotiations, and which actors control it. Pahre (2001) convincingly argues that two-level game applications should focus on the reversion point, and thus the outcome that would result in the case of a negotiation failure. He also demonstrates that the model implications become ambiguous if either the government or the opposition is allowed to control the reversion point.

A third assumption, which crucially affects the scope of some theoretical claims, refers to the information level of the actors under consideration. The spatial exploration presented by Hammond and Prins (1999), for instance, excludes the possibility that informational asymmetries lend a particular claim credibility. In the descriptive literature on two-level games, Moravcsik (1993: 159) similarly maintains that a negotiator is only seldom able to bluff that a domestic constraint is binding. In his view, the other governments might be able to predict the actions of the cheater, '. . . among modern information-rich democracies, it is extremely difficult for negotiators to mask their true domestic win-set, even in a sensitive area of national security like weapons procurement'.[5]

[4] Note that this assumption is not necessary and that a quadratic transformation would not result in endowing one specific actor with the agenda-setting power (Butler 2004). For a controversial discussion about other aspects of this model, see the exchange between Dai (2002) and Mansfield *et al* (2002) that the Mansfield *et al* (2000) extension of the Milner/Rosendorff model provoked.

[5] In his assessment of the evidence assembled by the contributors to Putnam, Evans and Jacobsen (1993), Evans (1993: 409) states that leaders 'did try to strategically misrepresent their own polities, but not as often as expected, and with much less success'.

However, to assume informational asymmetries away borders on a hapless attempt to throw the baby out with the bathwater: why should fully-informed negotiators bother to bargain at all, instead of agreeing on the supposedly easily foreseeable bargaining outcome in the first place?

Differences between models, such as the ones we discussed here, are partly necessary because of varying ambitions and applications. But we believe that some of the judgements made on the validity of the Schelling conjecture depend too much on the implicit and explicit assumptions that guide the theoretical work. We consequently believe that the debate on the relevance of the 'paradox of weakness' is far from being settled.

This inconclusiveness also explains why the literature on two-level games is still growing. This holds particularly true for the application to the European Union which has traditionally been one of the main testing grounds for the Schelling conjecture. Schneider and Cederman (1994), Schneider (1994), Bräuninger *et al* (2001), and Hug and König (2002) explore how real or feigned constraints affect the negotiation outcome in the purely intergovernmental context of European Council deliberations. Schneider and Weitsman (1996), Hug and Christin (2002), and Hug (2002) examine how the government tries to convince domestic constituents in referendum debates, while König and Hug (2000) focus on ratification in the parliamentary setting.

The frameworks used in these studies are, however, not directly applicable to an analysis of European Union legislation. One key reason for this limitation is obviously that these applications of the two-level literature focus on the intergovernmental arena, be it the bargaining rounds in the European Council or the ratification of treaty amendments, while our cases are drawn from the legislative rather than the constitutional arena. Because we examine day-to-day decision-making rather than the grand bargains, we need to consider how domestic actors, and especially the national parliaments, condition the negotiation mandates of their governments. In a pioneering study, Martin (2000: 168) lists three factors that increase the credibility of a state's commitment to a particular bargaining position. First, in her view, early parliamentary involvement in the negotiation process reduces parliamentary opposition toward an international bargain. Second, ministers are more likely to negotiate well if they are accountable to the parliament. Third, a government is more likely to be taken seriously if the implementation is transparent and the actors who are involved in this decision-making phase are identifiable.

However, not all parliamentary oversight mechanisms will directly affect government behaviour as in the US system where the executive is not formed out of the legislative parliamentary bodies. According to Pahre (1997: 148), domestic constraints may only matter if the scrutinising committee also includes members of the opposition parties:

> Models that treat executive preferences as exogenous are appropriate for a directly elected executive but exclude the government formation problem that is central to parliamentary government.

This is the main reason why we focus in this examination on the possible influence that powerful and ideologically independent legislatures are able to exert on government negotiation behaviour. We embed our analysis of two-level bargaining games within the parsimonious framework that the Nash bargaining solution (NBS) offers. The NBS stands for an axiomatic approach to bargaining that finds widespread application throughout the social sciences. Several reasons justify the reliance on this static approach. First, we can extend the NBS, which Nash (1950) originally developed for the analysis of bilateral negotiations, to the analysis of multilateral bargaining situations. Non-cooperative bargaining models, by contrast, can only be extended to a multi-actor world on the assumption that the actors adhere to a strict bargaining protocol, or that the size of the pie alters stochastically over the bargaining rounds (Merlo and Wilson 1995). Yet, in the European Union and especially within its most important legislative actor, the Council of Ministers, the rules that guide the interactions between the negotiators are so sparse and feeble that every commitment to a particular negotiation mode is incredible. Furthermore, many legislative negotiations are guided by a shortened time horizon, rendering assumptions about multiround interactions tenuous. If we were using a non-cooperative framework, such as the signalling game used by Schneider and Cederman (1994), we would thus be forced to reduce the number of players to two or possibly three actors or to assign agenda setting power to one member state. Schneider *et al* (2004) test how relevant extensions of the Rubinstein sequential bargaining model (Baron and Ferejohn 1989; Merlo and Wilson 1995) are in comparison to the NBS. Yet, their application is still static, as they have to use the saliency measure of the DEU data set as a proxy for the time preference.

Our second motive for relying on a cooperative approach is empirical. To our regret, the DEU data set does not contain sufficient information on the dynamics that characterise the negotiations on the legislative proposals under consideration. To give full justice to a non-cooperative model, it would be essential to identify the sequence of moves. But even if we had this information, it would not be guaranteed that we could interpret it meaningfully. Interestingly, the spatial literature still disagrees on which institutional actor possesses agenda-setting power under certain legislative procedures and would thus be the first mover (see Steunenberg and Selck, chapter 3 of this volume). The only information that we possess on the behaviour of the negotiators – whether or not an actor issued a threat – will be used in one of the operationalisations of domestic constraints. A third and final reason why we rely on the NBS is its parsimony. The canonical version of this tool allows us to calculate point predictions by only including information on the preferences of all relevant actors. If one assumes like us that Ockham's razor is a useful yardstick to evaluate a model, the NBS possesses a major advantage over more baroque models of EU decision-making.[6]

Technically, the NBS maximises the product of the differences between the outcome and their so-called disagreement points. In our application, the reference point is the common disagreement point of the actors. Binmore (1998: 66) criticises that applications in industrial relations often equate the *status quo* with the disagreement point, although the *status quo* might not necessarily coincide with the outcome that is realised in the case of a bargaining failure. We follow this line of logic and assume that the reference points represent the common fallback position of the actors.

If the actors are domestically constrained, their disagreement point is assumed to be closer to their ideal point than the reference point. In other words, we assume in line with the literature on two-level games that some governments are able to credibly restrict their bargaining zone (or 'win set', as Putnam put it in reference to spatial models of legislative choice). In the logic followed here, it is always profitable to be constrained because the distance between the ideal point and the disagreement value shrinks.

Note that we assume in contrast to some existing limited information applications (e.g. Iida 1993; Schneider and Cederman 1994) that a member state's reference to a domestic constraint is always credible. Although the assumption of perfect credibility is certainly unrealistic, it is in accordance with some of the contributions to the literature on two-

[6] For an early application of the NBS to the EU decision-making see König (1997).

level games discussed above. More importantly, our focus is empirical, and we will explore the relative importance of the Schelling conjecture by comparing the average predictive power of the NBS without constraints to several extensions of the NBS in which some actors are supposed to be domestically constrained. This gives us some leverage to decide whether the Schelling conjecture is relevant in contrast to the standard bargaining tool of cooperative game theory. Our evaluation will also help us decide which domestic factors contribute to the bargaining leverage of EU actors.

We assume in line with the literature that the set of Pareto-improving outcomes Θ is non-empty. If the bargaining space contains the outcome and the disagreement value, the NBS amounts to the following maximisation problem for negotiations among n players:

$$\max_{O \in \Theta} \prod_{a=1}^{n} (u_a(O) - u_a(Q)) \tag{6.1}$$

where O is the predicted bargaining outcome and Q the reference point.[7] In this and the following equation, the subscript n stands for players, i for issues. We add to the standard NBS setup the distance between the actor's ideal point and the final negotiation outcome. We assume that the further away a bargaining outcome x is from the bliss point x_{ia} from each player, the larger the utility loss. If we use Euclidian distances to calculate these utility changes, the NBS amounts to the following:

$$\max_{O \in \Theta} \prod_{a=1}^{n} \left(-\sqrt{(O_i - x_{ia})^2} + \sqrt{(Q_{ia} - x_{ia})^2} \right) \tag{6.2}$$

Our issue-per-issue calculations of the NBS are based on equation 6.2.[8] Because the canonical version of the NBS does not consider power differentials among negotiators, we only have to know the outcomes the actors favour the most and the location of the reference points.[9] We use the symmetric NBS as the baseline model and compare its relative predictive power against three different interpretations of the two-level game. The first two-level variation of the NBS refers to a situation in which a government faces a powerful European affairs committee, while the second measures the interaction effect between this institutional

[7] Muthoo (1999) offers a recent introduction to the Nash bargaining solution and other standard tools in negotiation analysis.

[8] The calculation of the NBS at the level of the proposal and at the level of each issue coincide as long as the utility of a proposal has a multiplicative form and the actors attribute equal weight to the issues.

[9] Bailer and Schneider (2002) evaluate whether or not differences in the capabilities of the actors are important.

variable and the occurrence of a preference divergence between the government and its European Affairs Committee. The third definition of a constraint is more behavioural and considers the impact that the threat of an actor has on the bargaining outcome.

6.3 RESEARCH DESIGN

In this section we outline how we operationalised the key variables and how we implemented the four permutations of the Nash bargaining solution. We use different measures to operationalise domestic constraints because the literature stresses either institutions, preferences or threats as the key resources on which governments rely in international bargaining processes (Bailer and Schneider 2002). This allows us to assess whether domestic constraints make a difference at all, and which of its components influence the average bargaining behaviour.

The first domestic constraint is purely institutional. To assess the power of the EU affairs committees, we quantify the four categories Bergman (1997) used in his comparative evaluation of these parliamentary institutions. The first consideration in our operationalisation is whether or not the EU affairs committee is involved in pillar I, II, and III decisions of the Maastricht Treaty. The extent of involvement in the three pillars is in our view a direct indicator of committee influence. All national committees have a say in the Common Market Pillar, whereas only half of them have the possibility to give opinions on Justice and Home Affairs and the Common Foreign and Security Policy. This is, for instance, the case for the French EU committee.

The second criterion is whether the committee can submit the proposals under deliberation for plenary debate. This right grants parliamentarians the opportunity to open the debate on issues that otherwise could pass without notice by the public. The Swedish EU affairs committee is the most restricted in this sense and has no right to bring topics to the plenary fore. All other EU-committees, however, may do so.

A third criterion assesses the degree to which the opinions of the committee bind the government. To develop this scrutiny measure, Bergman (1997) assigned the EU countries to three categories. A committee exerts little influence if it can only exchange information with its government and if the executive side can easily ignore the advice of the legislative body (e.g. Greece, Ireland, Italy, Portugal, Spain). Moderate forms of influence exist when the government follows the opinion of the committee (e.g. Finland, Sweden). A high level of influence is characteristic of a situation in which the committee is able to make binding recommendations (e.g. Austria, Denmark, Germany).

We measured the different subcategories on ordinal and dummy scales and created an additive index of these powers.[10] We considered an additive index useful because the three criteria represent different facets of the relationship between the executive and the domestic legislature. A committee can for example be powerful if it submits issues to the parliament and has a say in all three Community pillars even if it does not include Members of European Parliament (MEPs) in its meetings.

To make our NBS calculations more transparent, we only consider four degrees to which European affairs committees are able to reduce the zone of agreement of their negotiating government. The institutional constraint is large if the additive index exceeds six points. This is the case for Austria and Denmark. We consider a constraint to be above the average if the additive index amounted to five (Finland, Germany). We coded an institutional constraint as average in the event that the additive index equalled four (Ireland, the Netherlands, Sweden, Luxembourg), and a government is not institutionally constrained in its negotiation behaviour if the index ranged between zero and three (Belgium, France, Greece, Italy, Portugal, Spain, United Kingdom). Operationally, we reduced the bargaining range and moved the disagreement point closer to the ideal point if an actor is institutionally constrained. We reduced the bargaining zone by 75 per cent for highly constrained, 50 per cent for member states with an above-average constraint and 25 per cent for an actor with an average constraint.

The second operationalisation of domestic constraints builds on this indicator and adds the possibility of a preference divergence between the government and the domestic legislative committee to it. Relying on the index developed by Hix and Lord (1997), we identified the ideological

[10] *Degree of bindingness of EU affairs committees*: a case receives the scale weight 2 if the degree of bindingness is strong, while it obtains a scale weight of 1 if the corresponding value is moderate. A value of 0 finally results if the degree of bindingness is low. *Plena*: this category is coded as 1 if the EU affairs committee has the opportunity to submit issues under deliberation to the floor for plenary debates. A case gets the scale weight 0 if this is not allowed. *Pillar*: a country receives the value of 3 if its EU affairs committee is involved in debates on pillar I, II, or III. The category 2 refers to cases where the committees are only allowed to participate in pillar I and II decisions, while a value of 1 corresponds to partaking in pillar I only. The zero code is reserved for countries in which the committees are not allowed to participate in the deliberations on any decisions within one of the three Maastricht pillars.

position of the cabinet and committee members on a left-right scale by subtracting the mean of the party positions of the members in the national cabinet from the mean of the party positions of the members in the EU committee.[11] We obtained the second constraint measure by multiplying the absolute value of these distances with the ideological constraint and by reducing the variance to three categories: no constraint (range of values 0–1.9), average constraint (2.0–3.9), large constraint (4.0–7.5). If a member state fell into the last category, we reduced the bargaining zone 66 per cent (Belgium, Germany, Sweden, Finland, Luxembourg). A reduction of 33 per cent was made in case of an average constraint (Italy, Greece, France, Spain, Austria). No changes were made if there was no constraint (the Netherlands, United Kingdom, Ireland, Denmark, Portugal). We acknowledge that our preference measure is rather crude. However, the left-right dimension is the dominant cleavage in the European Parliament (Noury 2002), and we therefore have some reason to assume that it is also important in the Council of Ministers (Zimmer *et al* 2005). Since the delegations of the member states in the Council are formed by the national representatives of ministries which makes them directly dependent on the executives and their respective party orientation, we consider party profiles as valid variables to estimate the political orientation of the negotiating actors.

The third and final operationalisation of domestic constraints is purely behavioural and relies on the usage of threats by a member state government. Information on threats was also obtained in the DEU interviews. The theoretical rationale for using this indicator is the expectation that domestically constrained actors are more likely to signal their commitment to a specific solution than other negotiators. We admit that threats are relatively rare events and that only governments whose credibility is reduced will utter them. We are only able to report threats that were put forward openly enough for our interview partners to notice, even if they were not from the party of the threatening or the threatened side. It was not possible to take into account all possible bilateral threats issued on an informal basis. We also acknowledge that experts responded very differently to our question of whether or not they were able to observe threats.

11 Austria (0.4), Belgium (−2.4), Denmark (0.32), Finland (−1.5), France (−1.7), Germany (−1.05), Greece (−1.4), Ireland (0.2), Italy (1.3), Luxembourg (1.82), the Netherlands (−0.2), Portugal (−0.43), Spain (1.96), Sweden (−1.95), United Kingdom (0.93). Hix and Lord (1997) use mainly the data developed in Huber and Inglehart (1995) and fill in values for countries not covered by Huber and Inglehart with data from Mavrogordatos (1984) and other sources.

While some interview partners completely negated the existence of such stratagems, others claimed that there are so many implicit or secret threats and promises going on between the 15 delegations, that they could not even be reliably counted. Nevertheless, we have data on 23 explicit threats that occurred during the negotiations.[12] We asked for the intensity of threats during the interviews and measured them with three categories: low (no reduction of the bargaining space), average (reduction of 33 per cent), high (reduction of 66 per cent).

We used the library constrained optimisation of GAUSS, the programming language, in order to optimise our function and to constrain our result to the bargaining space between 0 and 100.[13] We assumed that the reference point lies at the position 0. The reference point was already at this position in 104 of 162 issues. If $0<Q<100$, we calculated the absolute distance of the actors from the reference point. We used the position of the Commission as a substitute for those cases in which the interview partners were not able to identify a common reference point. Although this might appear to be a considerable assumption, we consider it justified if one considers the Commission's initial position as the point from which the discussion started. In some situations, there were 15 different national situations since there had been no EU legislation in this policy field before. As we are not able to identify these 15 reference points, we work with the crude approximation of the Commission position as reference point. Similarly, if the rare event occurred that there was no Commission position, we filled the reference point in at that place.

The Newton algorithm served as our optimisation method. We employed the mean as the starting vector in all models. The mean was calculated from all positions of the member states and the Commission in the case of proposals under the consultation procedure and all member states, the Commission and the European Parliament in the case of proposals under the co-decision procedure. Table 6.1 summarises the models, the parameters used, and the implicit modelling assumptions.

We imputed the positions of actors whose positions are missing in the data set because the experts stated they were indifferent. We located these actors half way between the reference point and the position of the

[12] On 23 occasions an actor formulated a threat towards his or her counterparts. As we measured threats only at the proposal level, these 23 threats are spread over 30 issues.

[13] The source code used for calculating the model predictions is available at the homepage of the second author (www.uni-konstanz.de/FuF/Verwiss/GSchneider/).

Table 6.1. *Models, parameters and assumptions*

Model	Variables	Assumptions
Symmetrical NBS (NBS)	Preferences	All bargaining models: – starting vectors for all calculations: mean – optimisation method: Newton – procedure: constrained optimisation (calculated in GAUSS, library co.src)
Two-level symmetrical NBS (institutional constraints) (NBS Two1)	Preferences, power of EU affairs committee	
Two-level symmetrical NBS (interaction model) (NBS Two2)	Preferences, institutional constraints, preferences of EU affairs committees	
Behavioural model (threats)	Preferences, threats, intensity of threat	

Commission. This indicates that these delegates simply did not care whether the *status quo* or the Commission proposal would result from the negotiation. As the NBS is static, our model does not take any agenda setter considerations into account.[14] Actors were included in our calculations, even if they were at risk of being made worse off by the decision outcome in comparison to the *status quo*. Although such players could be treated as inessential, we assume that they are trying to minimise their utility loss.

6.4 THE CHOCOLATE DIRECTIVE AS AN ILLUSTRATION

We illustrate the predictions of our models with the decision on the chocolate directive. This internal market proposal gave rise to four controversial issues. The goal of this proposal was to create common rules for the composition, manufacturing, specification, packaging and labelling of cocoa and chocolate products. Because the chocolate industry in the member states followed different traditions, the main issue was the wish of the United Kingdom and Ireland to continue to use vegetable fats other than cocoa butter in the production of chocolate. Belgium and

[14] We did not include the position of the European Parliament for the consultation cases.

the Netherlands voted against the common position while Luxembourg abstained.

The proposal had a long history. The Commission had already introduced its ambition to harmonise the rules that structure the chocolate market in the 1970s. These intentions were, however, to no avail since the Belgian, French, Dutch and Luxembourgish diplomats successfully prevented vegetable fat chocolate from entering their national markets. The resistance of the candy protectionists had the effect that British chocolate was practically banned from the continent until the mid-1990s. The discriminated producers, especially the large, export-oriented manufacturer, Cadbury, had, however, a strong interest in entering the continental market. The cocoa coalition of the small chocolate producers in Belgium, France, the Netherlands and Luxembourg protested strongly against this sort of 'impure' chocolate. Yet, the opposing faction considered not only the interests of their own industry. The diplomats of these member states also tried to appease cacao producers in their former colonies, especially from the Ivory Coast.

A related bone of contention was the question of how to label chocolate containing vegetable fat. The British delegates considered this issue nearly as important as the permission to use vegetable fats. This issue provided ample opportunity for the Belgians to block the directive by suggesting that chocolate containing vegetable fat should be labelled so that cocoa-fat chocolate would be easily recognised as 'quality chocolate'. French chocolate producers helpfully suggested that vegetable fat chocolate should receive the brand name 'végécao' (*Europe Daily Bulletin*, No. 7634, 14 January 2000). The British, in return, objected that this label would amount to a severe trade barrier for their manufacturers.

An intensive discussion also arose over the derogation that the Commission wanted to grant to Great Britain and Ireland. In spite of its mission to guarantee common market rules, the Commission supported the idea of extending an existing derogation to allow the British and Irish industry to produce chocolate with a higher milk content than stipulated for the fabrication of regular chocolate. This exemption was important for the two member states because a complete harmonisation might have affected the production of the popular 'Cadbury's dairy milk'. The expert whom we interviewed on that proposal pointed out that the British delegates would have even been prepared to block other legislation in order to receive this exception. In the end, the other delegations accepted the labelling of the British chocolate as 'family milk chocolate' and granted the derogation. This compromise constituted, at least in the eyes of our interview partner, a major surprise. The new label could potentially make the British chocolate more attractive than the Belgian or French milk chocolate.

The final outcome, which also found the support of the European Parliament, allows the use of vegetable fat up to five per cent and the sale of vegetable fat chocolate everywhere in the European Union. Yet, it simultaneously grants continental producers the right to label cocoa-fat chocolate with 'pure cocoa' or 'guaranteed traditional specialty', and requires that vegetable fats are denoted close to the list of ingredients. Furthermore, the delegations agreed on six tropical vegetable fats such as palm oil which are from now on to be used in vegetable fat chocolate in order to soften the negative effects for developing countries.

The key member states in the legislative negotiations were the United Kingdom, Belgium, Luxembourg, the Netherlands and France. The institutional constraints of these states are average to low. The institutional-ideological constraint category indicates a high restriction for Belgium and Luxembourg, an average restriction for France and no restrictions for the Netherlands and the UK. Judging from these measures alone, we would expect the more constrained states to be more successful. Empirically, however, this does not apply to the British negotiators, who were rather successful. The highly constrained negotiators from Belgium and Luxembourg, conversely, had to make considerable concessions.

Interestingly, the member states for which legislation in this domain was important experienced all considerable pressure from interest groups: Cadbury Limited had a strong interest in finally getting access to the continental market and lobbied the British government. Chocolate producers in Belgium and France feared this competition. They received support from cocoa-producers in the developing world, especially the Ivory Coast. Demonstrations of Fair Trade Associations in Brussels and 'chocolate tasting sessions' of a group of MEPs interested in consumer issues are examples of this pressure (*Daily Bulletin*, Agence Europe, No. 6608, 18 November 1995).

Our expert identified four issues on which the stakeholders disagreed. Figure 6.1 illustrates that the coalitions acted quite homogeneously across these topics. The member states are, however, relatively polarised on whether or not they should follow the Commission proposal, or the proposal favoured by the Benelux countries and most of the southern member states. Note that the Commission and the Parliament were initially divided over whether or not the United Kingdom and Ireland should obtain derogations.

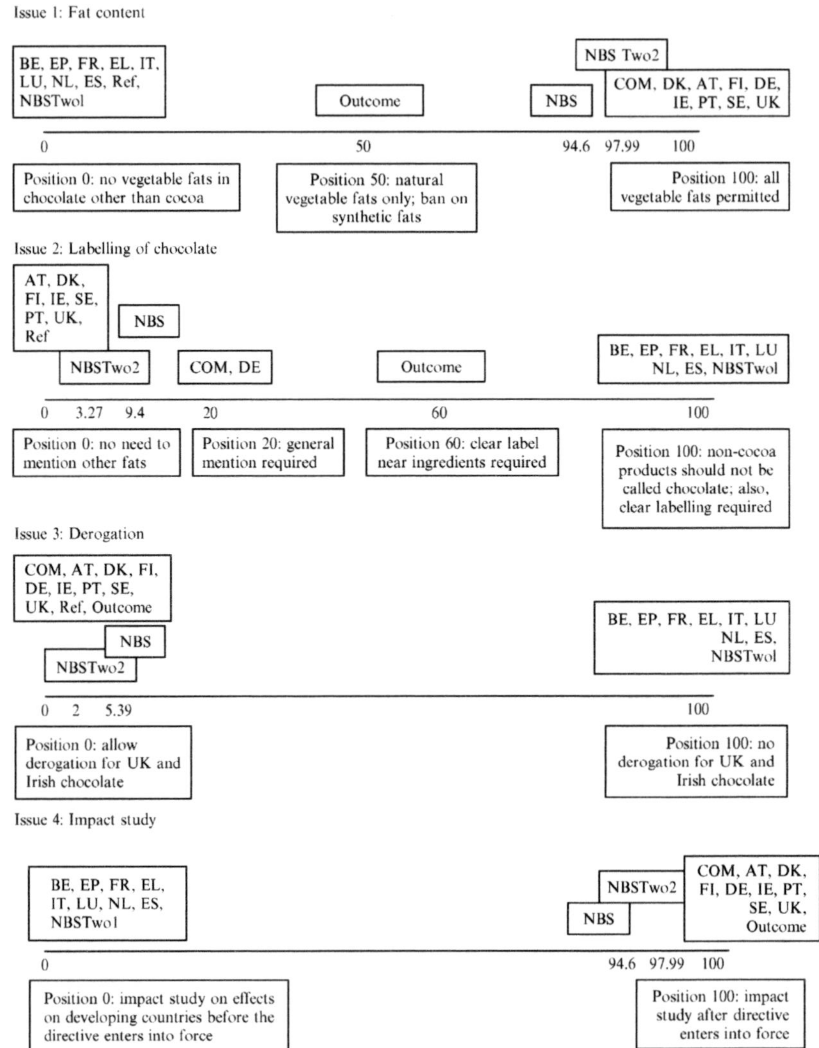

Figure 6.1. The negotiations over the chocolate directive[a]
[a]For details of the models NBS NBSTwo1 and NBSTwo2, see Table 6.1.

The bargain finally struck by the EU actors on the first two dimensions is a typical consensus both sides could live with. The decisions made on the two other issues is much more majoritarian by contrast. Overall, the northern camp, the Iberian states and the Commission are closer to the solution that the Council of Ministers adopted against the opposition of Belgium and France. These two member states appear to have been unsuccessful in finding sufficient support in the coalition often derogatorily called the 'club méditerranée'.

Figure 6.1 shows that the predictive accuracy varies a lot across the issues. The preferences on all issues were rather polarised. The models typically predict outcomes that are close to the preferences of one of the leading coalitions. This explains why some of them predict rather well on issues three and four. When the decision-making process results in a compromise, the accuracy of all models conversely suffers. Interestingly, the Commission is part of both winning coalitions on issues three and four. This could indicate that the supranational agent possessed some sort of informal agenda setting possibilities in these contests, while it did not have a privileged position on the other issues.

The institutional model (NBSTwo1) performs, relatively speaking, quite badly. This model, which only takes institutional constraints into account, has an error of 100 issue scale points on issues three and four. The more refined model (NBSTwo2) that also takes the preferences of the domestic stakeholders into account is much more successful. The forecasts of the NBS without constraints (NBS) are quite similar. To commit oneself to a specific stance seems thus only to make a marginal difference. In the following sections we will analyse whether the Schelling conjecture has an empirical relevance to the average legislative decision within the European Union.

6.5 THE PREDICTIVE ACCURACY OF FOUR VERSIONS OF THE NASH BARGAINING SOLUTION

This section evaluates whether or not the two-level versions of the NBS yield better forecasts than the NBS without constraints. We will also explore the reason why the accuracy of the forecasts differs from one issue to another. As the case study suggests, the predictive accuracy differs among the classes of models. We will evaluate why and when this happens.

Although average measures can be misleading to some extent, we start the analysis by comparing the mean error of the models. It should be noted that the benchmark for predictions of the two-level NBS with threats are the forecasts that were obtained for the very same issues with alternative NBS models. We report thus in parentheses the corresponding NBS predictions.

The general result of our evaluation is that the move from the symmetrical NBS to more complicated models does not really pay off (see

Table 6.2. *Average predictive accuracy of the NBS models (average absolute error across issues)*

Model	All issues (n=162)	CNS QMV (n= 55)	CNS unan. (n=39)	COD QMV (n=56)	COD unan. (n=12)
Median[a]	27.21 (28.04)	30.55 (30.62)	17.83 (21.03)	30.38 (29.90)	27.58 (31.75)
NBS model	25.8	27.13	17.33	30.8	23.84
NBS institutional constraints	29.28	33.8	18.41	34.24	20.76
NBS instit. constraints × preferences	25.76	27.08	19.27	30.04	20.81
Two level NBS with threats	25.58 (n=30)	21.9 (n=13)	24.2 (n=9)	50.0 (n=5)	4.94 (n=3)

Note: [a]Median of the data version with imputed values (original median in brackets).

Table 6.2). The symmetrical Nash bargaining solution predicts better than the model with institutional constraints, whereas the model with institutional and preferential constraints is slightly better than the symmetrical one. This suggests that countries in which the preferences of government parties and the EU affairs committees do not coincide possess a slight bargaining advantage. The importance of the ideological constraint is rather surprising, given the fact that we measured it crudely on a left-right dimension only. Facing a powerful EU affairs committee back home does not, by contrast, make a government more successful in the negotiations within the Council of Ministers. If a negotiator makes an explicit threat, it can also not move the outcome closer to its ideal point in comparison to the NBS. We should, however, add at this point that the active usage of such strategic means is rather rare.

A comparison of the accurate point predictions of the two-level models and the threat model shows that different measures of predictive accuracy can tell us different stories. In 39 of 162 issues the symmetric Nash solution predicted the outcome exactly, this is the case for the two-level models in 35 issues and for the threat model in three of the 30 cases.

If we soften the criterion of accurate point predictions to a prediction around five points plus or minus the actual outcome position, we find that the symmetrical NBS predicts the outcomes of 56 (34.6 per cent) issues correctly, the institutional NBS forecasts 51 (31.5 per cent) issues correctly, and the model with institutional and preferential constraints only 57 (35.2 per cent) issues correctly. That means that the criterion of point predictions sheds a similar light on the predictive accuracy of the models.

Next, we explore the conditions under which some models predict better than others using a multivariate OLS regression. In particular, we examine whether issue and proposal characteristics are key to understanding variation in the predictive accuracy of the models. One key explanatory variable that could play a role is the number of issues under contestation. The more dimensions a proposal has, the more difficult it generally is to forecast the outcome because the possibility of trading votes grows. A second variable that has to be considered is the variance in the preferences. We expect a higher variance to decrease the predictive accuracy of the models. Our measure is the standard deviation of the preferences. If the preference distribution is skewed, however, we expect that the outcome is easier to predict, because it will be closer to the larger coalition than to the smaller one. We include the skewedness of the preference distribution as an explanatory variable. A related factor is whether or not the preferences among the actors are polarised. We use the Herfindahl-Hirschman index of concentration to account for this influence.[15] A final consideration is whether or not the imputation method affects the predictions. The corresponding dummy variable accounts for all the cases in which we imputed the reference point.

Table 6.3 reports the results of the OLS regressions with the absolute issue level error as the dependent variable. Note that we do not report the impact that decision-making rules and the policy domains have on the predictive accuracy of the four models under evaluation (see additional tables at the end of this chapter). Nor do we include scale measures in the multivariate analyses, because we believe scale to be largely a consequence of the perceived nature of conflict, rather than of a pre-given conflict space.

The table shows that the number of issues does not significantly influence the dependent variable which is the distance between the prediction and the actual outcome for any of the models. The same holds true for the skewedness of the preference distribution. The variables that

[15] The Herfindahl-Hirschman (HH) index of concentration equals the sum of the squares of each position's percentage share. The larger this index, the higher the concentration of positions. See Ray and Singer (1990) for a political science application.

Table 6.3. *Determinants of the predictive accuracy of four NBS models*

	Median	Symmetric NBS	Institutional constraint NBS	Institutional preference constraint NBS	Threat constraint NBS
Number of issues	1.38	0.01	0.02	0.02	−0.04
Standard deviation	0.92[a]	0.01[a]	0.01[a]	0.01[a]	0.01
Skewedness	0.95	0.01	0.01	0.01	0.08
Concentration	16.47	0.21[b]	0.17	0.23[b]	0.37
Imputed reference point	−10.11[c]	−0.13[b]	−0.09	−0.13[b]	0.13
Constant	−14.20	−0.16	−0.25[b]	−0.17[c]	−0.14
n	162	162	162	162	30
Adj. R Square	0.10	0.11	0.17	0.12	0.26

Notes: [a]significant at a 0.01 level.
[b]significant at a 0.05 level.
[c]significant at a 0.10 level.

Table 6.4. *Average absolute error across policy areas*

Model	Agriculture (*n*= 40)	Internal market (max *n*=34)	Other policy areas (*n*=88)
Median[a]	29.85 (=33.29)	34.68 (=39.60)	23.13 (29.13)
NBS model	28.19	35.34	21.02
Two-level NBS with institutional constraints	36.86	39.22	22.0
Two-level NBS with institutional and preferential constraints	27.90	33.44	21.82
Two-level NBS with threats	30.0 (*n*=4)	4.94 (*n*=3)	27.50 (*n*=23)

Note: [a]Median of the data version with imputed values (original median in brackets).

take the variance and the polarisation of the ideal points into account, conversely, have a significant impact on the accuracy of our predictions. The standard deviation exerts a significant influence in all models except the threat model. We measure the polarisation of preference through the Herfindahl-Hirschmann index, which is an instrument widely used to

Table 6.5. *Average absolute error across issues*

Model	Dichotomous (n=33)	Rank order (n=109)	Scale (n=20)
Median[a]	31.82 (=30.30)	27.34 (=29.42)	18.9 (=19.7)
NBS model	31.02	25.6	18.24
Two-level NBS with institutional constraints	38.13	26.63	29.13
Two-level NBS with institutional and preferential constraints	31.37	25.3	19.03
Two-level NBS with threats	50.0 (n=4)	24.49 (n=23)	1.4 (n=3)

Note: [a]Median of the data version with imputed values (original median in brackets).

assess different forms of concentration. Note that this concentration measure differs considerably from the skewedness variable. The correlation coefficient between the two measures only amounts to −0.10. Quite remarkably, the concentration measure is significant for nearly all models and accounts for the largest part of the adjusted R^2. As the case study already indicated, a high degree of polarisation worsens the accuracy of the model predictions. If the number of powerful factions decreases, the outcome is more likely to shift radically, increasing the error in the model predictions. The cases in which we imputed the reference point provide better forecasts than the ones where such an imputation was not necessary. Because we imputed the reference point through the position of the Commission, this result indicates once again how important the formal and informal agenda setting by this actor is.

6.6 CONCLUSION

Interstate bargaining in the European Union is often seen as a form of interaction where the domestic constraints negotiators face back home prevent cooperation-minded governments from concluding far-reaching agreements. Illustrative evidence from the meetings of the European Council and the Council of Ministers support the contention that meetings within the European Union are affected strongly by the strategic moves of laggard governments. At the moment, all the evidence that we possess on EU negotiations is, however, largely descriptive and not based on any systematic comparative assessment.

This chapter has moved closer toward a systematic examination of EU negotiation processes. We have analysed whether domestic constraints influence the process of legislative bargaining in the European Union. Our analysis adds to a still-growing literature, that has up to now largely focused on the influence of domestic constraints on purely intergovernmental bargains within the European Union (Schneider and Cederman 1994; König and Hug 2000; Hug and König 2002). In particular, we explore the impact that the European affairs committees in the national legislatures have on the negotiation behaviour of their ministers. We can show that governments can profit to some extent at the international level if the preferences of the domestic actors differ substantially. Our application also demonstrates that the NBS is a largely under-exploited tool to explain decision-making in the European Union. While it does not account for institutional factors, it yields reasonable forecasts based on a firm axiomatic foundation. Although its static nature and the reliance on cooperative considerations could be seen as a drawback, it is relatively easily tested and parsimonious compared with competing bargaining models. Future applications will compare its predictive accuracy with other bargaining models.

Yet, it has to be admitted that the differences in the predictive accuracy of the baseline NBS model and the two-level versions of the NBS are not large. This underlines, in agreement with the early descriptive literature and the contribution by Hammond and Prins (1999), that the active usage of domestic constraints as a bargaining mechanism is probably an infrequent event and restricted to high-stake negotiations. In day-to-day policy-making within the European Union, such events are obviously rare. The practical implication of our results is that domestic control mechanisms do not really function. Governments often strike deals in Brussels irrespective of the demands of the domestic stakeholders. This problem will persist as long as ministers are able to mask their behaviour in Brussels. Our analysis thus reveals an important aspect of the 'democratic deficit' that could be easily solved by increasing the transparency of decision-making in the Council of Ministers. We have only little hope that the enlargement process has increased the quality of decision-making in the Council. Extensions of our research show unambiguously that preference distributions have become more polarised and that producer interests are the main winners in the legislation arena of the EU (Dobbins *et al* 2004; Zimmer *et al* 2005). The increased importance of protectionist and structurally conservative forces increases the incentive for governments to shield their behaviour in Brussels against domestic public scrutiny. Institutional reforms could alleviate this problem. Yet, the current wave of Euroscepticism makes it highly unlikely that the European Union will adopt convincing decision-making rules in the near future.

7

A cooperative approach to decision-making in the European Union

VINCENT BOEKHOORN, ADRIAN M. A. VAN DEEMEN AND MADELEINE O. HOSLI

7.1 INTRODUCTION

An essential ingredient of politics is winning. What counts in politics is the passing of a bill, the amendment of a proposal, getting a policy accepted, or the enforcement of a decision. However, in general, it is impossible to win by staying alone. In politics, including European politics, it is necessary to form winning coalitions in order to enforce decisions.

Surely, in any political system, individual preferences with respect to a decision-making problem will diverge. Consequently, conflict will be at the heart of politics. However, this does not mean that coalitions are not important. In order to resolve conflict in political decision-making processes, cooperation and hence coalition-formation is essential. Conflict and cooperation are different sides of the same coin. Indeed, even if conflict is so strong that no resolution is possible, coalition-formation is still essential: in the extreme, it is necessary in order to revolutionise the system itself.

Since cooperation is an essential ingredient of politics, coalition-building cannot be neglected in the modelling of political decision-making. A framework that explicitly deals with cooperation and coalitions is cooperative game theory. In this chapter, we will use cooperative game theory to analyse decision-making in European politics.

However, cooperative game theory has a serious drawback: it is mainly geared towards solving games in terms of payoff structures, not in terms of coalitions. For quite some time, political scientists have been aware of this fact (e.g. see Riker 1962). Due to this disadvantage, some authors have developed a number of coalition-formation theories, each of which is rooted in *n*-person cooperative game theory (for an overview, consider De Vries 1999 or Van Deemen 1997). In this chapter, we follow this theoretical line. The aim, therefore, is to model decision-making in the EU from a coalition-formation perspective.

In this chapter, we present two multi-dimensional models of coalition-formation which are closely related. Both models predict policy outcomes and the winning coalitions that are associated with these outcomes. The basic idea of the two models is that distances between players' preferences contain information about the extent of conflict existing between them.

In the first model, the notion of the expected policy centre of a winning coalition is essential. The expected policy centre of a winning coalition is the convex combination of the policy preferences and the weights of its members. It is a kind of gravity centre for the coalition which may be interpreted as the policy that coalition will implement when formed. Conflict in a winning coalition S is defined as the variance of the distances of the members of S to the expected policy centre of S.

The second model takes another route. In this model, the notion of 'reference distance' is central. It posits that players in a decision-making committee have different, subjective notions about the level of conflict existing within a coalition. The extent of conflict depends on their interpretation of pairwise distances between their own policy position and the policy preferences of other players. This subjective conflict notion is based on two reference points for each player, namely one of absence of conflict and one of maximal conflict. This model is close to the original conflict of interest model as formulated by Axelrod (1970).

The models in this chapter differ in at least two respects from more traditional theories of coalition-formation. First, coalition-formation so far mainly has been described in terms of solution concepts for spatial voting games. Among the more well-known concepts are the competitive solution, the ϵ-core, the Copeland set, the uncovered set, the yolk and the minimal response point (Owen 1995). Our models differ from these concepts in the sense that they are built on two parts, namely, a descriptive and a solution part. The descriptive part of the model focusses on the policy positions of the players, the formation of individual coalition preferences, and the rules that define winning (and hence also losing). On the basis of the descriptive part of the model, the solution part then formulates predictions. The distinction between the solution and the description part is due to Shubik (1982).

The second difference as compared with more traditional models of coalition-formation is that players' preferences for coalitions are taken into account. In almost any model of coalition-formation, the preferences of players for coalitions are either assumed to be exogenously given or simply neglected. In our models, by comparison, coalition preferences are treated endogenously. Both models explain the formation of individual coalition preferences in terms of their policy preferences and the expected policy positions of the coalitions that may form.

Both models are multi-dimensional elaborations and variations of the conflict of interest model as presented by Axelrod (1970). Also, both models predict coalitions in combination with their policy position. A discrete version of the models was developed by Van Deemen (1997). The aim of this chapter is to test the two multi-dimensional models of coalition-formation on the basis of data about decision-making and policy outcomes in EU politics.

The chapter is organised as follows. In Section 7.2, the basic concepts of spatial voting games and of conflict models of coalition-formation are presented. In Section 7.3, we discuss the research design for the application of the models to the data set. Section 7.4 illustrates the models on the basis of a concrete example of the decision-making process: reform of the subsidy regime for cotton producers in the European Union . In Section 7.5, the models are tested using data on EU decision-making. The final section evaluates the research results and discusses possible avenues for future research.

7.2 CONFLICT MODELS OF COALITION-FORMATION

7.2.1 *Voting games*

Our models are based on the theory of voting games. These games are discussed in more detail in, for example, Owen (1995) and Van Deemen (1997).

Consider a nonempty, but finite set N of players. Any subset S of N is called a *coalition*. A *voting game* or *simple game* is an ordered pair of sets $G = (N, W)$ where N is the players set and W is a set of coalitions such that

- W is not empty, i.e. there is a winning coalition
- The empty set $\emptyset$ is not in W
- If a coalition S is in W and coalition T is a subset of S, then T is in W.

Coalitions in W are called *winning*, coalitions not in W are *losing*. The set of losing coalitions is denoted by L. The first axiom implies that the game is not trivial. There is a winning coalition. The second says that the empty set is not winning. The third axiom is a monotonicity assumption. It says that adding players to a winning coalition cannot turn that coalition into a losing one.

The complement of a coalition is the set of all players not in that coalition. A voting game G is

1. *proper* if the complement of any winning coalition is losing
2. *strong* if the complement of any losing coalition is winning
3. *decisive* if G is proper and strong.

A *minimal winning coalition* (MWC) is a coalition in which each member is necessary for the coalition in order to win. Leaving out any one of the players turns such a coalition into a losing one. The set of MWCs is denoted by W^{min}.

In voting games, there can be a number of special players, such as veto players or dummies. A *veto player* forms part of every winning coalition. This implies that no coalition can win without a veto player, that is, a veto player is necessary for a coalition to win. Any coalition without a veto player is losing. Although a veto player cannot win on its own, it can block a decision. In an essential game, players have an incentive to form coalitions. Its counterpart, an inessential or dictatorial game, contains a dictator, i.e. a player who does not need other actors to win. Clearly, dictatorial games are strong.

An essential game with a veto player is called *weak*, i.e. not strong, since the complement of any losing coalition with a veto player is itself losing. Several analyses applied to EU decision-making, and more specifically analyses of a priori voting power in EU institutions, are dealing with weak games. In the Council of the EU, for example, a winning coalition has to encompass 62 out of the total of 87 votes. Losing coalitions are coalitions with less than 62 votes. In most cases, their complements are not winning. For such analyses, e.g. see Hosli (1993; 1995), or König and Bräuninger (1998).

A *dummy* is a player who is in no minimal winning coalition. Hence, a dummy player can never render a losing coalition winning or vice versa. In this sense, it is a powerless player. An example in European decision-making is Luxembourg in the first constellation of membership in the EU: it held just one vote, whereas the other Benelux countries had two and Germany, France and Italy had four votes. The qualified majority threshold being 12 out of 17 votes, Luxembourg could never turn a winning coalition into a losing one or vice versa. See, among others, Brams and Affuso (1985) and Hosli (1993).

An important class of voting games are *weighted voting games.* Let $w_i \geq 0$ denote the voting strength or weight assigned to player a i in N. A *weighted voting game* is an $n + 1$ tuple

$$(q; w_1, w_2, ..., w_n)$$

where q denotes a threshold. A coalition S is winning if the sum of the weights of its members is at least as large as the threshold q. Formally:

$$S \in W \Leftrightarrow \sum_{i \in S} w_i \geq q.$$

In some instances, different thresholds may apply simultaneously. This will be true, for example, for decision-making in the Council of the EU after ratification of the Treaty of Nice, e.g. see Hosli (2000), Hosli and Van Deemen (2002), Felsenthal and Machover (2001b), or Leech (2002). Evidently, a weighted voting game belongs to the category of voting games.

7.2.2 *Spatial voting games*

An m-dimensional spatial voting game G is a voting game together with n points x_i, $i \in N$, in an m-dimensional Euclidean space R^m.

Formally, a *spatial voting game* G is an ordered triple

$$G = (N, W, \{x_i\}_{i \in N})$$

where

1. $G = (N, W)$ is a voting game
2. $x_i \in R^m$ where R^m is an m-dimensional Euclidean vector space.

Points in R^m are termed *policy points.* Point x_i is the *ideal point* or *bliss point* of player i. Spatial voting theory is used frequently in both political science and economics. Helpful expositions of the theory are Enelow and Hinich (1984), Hinich and Munger (1994), and Owen (1995).

There are neither theoretical nor empirical reasons to use the Euclidean norm. However, currently, the Euclidean is the standard norm. We are not aware of literature in political science or in economics using alternative norms.

Define

$$n(x, y) = \{i \in N : d(x_i, x) < d(x_i, y)\}$$

and

$$n(x \sim y) = \{i \in N : d(x_i, x) = d(x_i, y)\}$$

where d denotes Euclidean distance. In words, $n(x, y)$ is the set of players who are closer to x than to y and $n(x \sim y)$ is the set of players with an equal distance to x and y. A policy point x *dominates* policy point y if $n(x, y)$ is winning, that is, if $n(x, y) \in W$. A point x is *un-dominated* if there is no other point y that dominates x. The *core* of a voting game G is the set of un-dominated points.

As is well-known, a necessary and sufficient condition for the existence of a nonempty core for a spatial voting game is the existence of a median hyperplane in all directions. That is, all median hyperplanes have to pass through one same point (Davis, *et al* 1972, Owen 1995). Since this condition is very demanding, the core of a spatial voting game will, in general, be empty. In order to meet the problem of the emptiness of the core, a number of other solution concepts have been developed for spatial voting games. For an excellent review of these solution concepts, consider Owen (1995).

7.2.3 *Theory of conflict*

The conflict models of coalition-formation presented in this chapter will use the theory of spatial games as a point of departure. The assumption used in these models is that the larger the distance between two points in policy space, the larger is the extent of conflict among players advocating these points.

We assume that conflict occurs over a number of issues which can be represented as continua on which decision-makers have single-peaked preferences. Since conflicts are an important determinant of the coalitions to be formed, we will associate an issue space to the formation game. In this issue space, players report to each other their most preferred positions on the issues constituting the decision-making problem. We denote this set of issues within a decision-making situation by $M = \{1, 2, \ldots, m\}$ with a, b as typical elements. In some collective decision-making situations, players must decide on only one issue ($m = 1$), whereas in other situations, they decide on a set of issues ($m > 1$). Each of these issues can be seen as a major controversial point among the players. In other words, issues are specific policy questions on which players take different positions and which consist of at least two policy alternatives placed on a one-dimensional policy scale. The *status quo* and the actual outcome of decision-making can also be located as points in an m-dimensional space with metric properties.

In spatial voting games, the set of alternatives corresponds to an m-dimensional subset of the Euclidean space and the committee's task is to choose a point in this subset (McKelvey *et al* 1978). The idea is that we use a limited number of independent dimensions to describe objects (locations) that could serve as the outcome of the decision-making situation. If we denote the set of alternatives on an issue a by X_a, then the issue space is given by the Cartesian product

$$X^m = \prod_{a=1}^{m} X_a.$$

Defined in this way, X^m is a subset of R^m.

This description is necessary in order to clarify the structure in which decision-making takes place. The basic idea of our models is that conflict among individual players, or among players and coalitions, is the degree of dissimilarity of their preferences. Hereby, dissimilarity will be defined in terms of policy distances. Situations of conflict, evidently, arise when two interacting players cannot simultaneously attain their most preferred policies (Axelrod 1970). In order to find coalitions with the lowest conflict index, and hence to predict the occurrence of certain coalitions, a spatial conflict index has to be defined.

7.2.4 *Conflict indices*

Consider a spatial voting game $G = (N, W, \{x_i\}_{i \in N})$. A conflict index assigns to each subset of policy points $\{x_i\}_i \in N$ a real number indicating the extent of conflict among the players concerned. A conflict index must satisfy at least two conditions: first, it cannot be negative. Second, if a subset of players take identical positions, then there is no conflict within their coalition, that is, the conflict index for this coalition must be zero (see Van Deemen 1997).

Formally, a *conflict index* C is defined to be a mapping from the power set of $\{x_i\}_i \in N$ into the set of real numbers such that for all $S \subseteq N$:

1. $C(\{x_i\}_i \in S) \geq 0$,
2. $C(\{x_i\}_i \in S) = 0$ if for every $i, j \in S : x_i = x_j$.

The real number $C(\{x_i\}_i \in S)$ is called the *conflict index of* S. For convenience, we write $C(S)$ instead of $C(\{x_i\}_i \in S)$. Of course, other axioms can easily be added. Defined in this way, many conflict indices are possible in practice.

The two models we present here each elaborate conflict in their own particular way. The first model uses the concept of the expected policy centre of a coalition, which is a convex combination of the policy positions and the weights of the players in that coalition. It is a kind of 'focal point' for the players. Clearly, the dispersion of the policy positions of the players in the coalition around its expected policy centre can be interpreted as the extent of conflict existing within the coalition. A dispersion measure at hand is, of course, the variance of the distances to the policy centre, which reflects the differences in the extent to which the several members had to 'give in' with regard to their most preferred policy position in order to achieve the coalition's policy centre. Hence, a suitable measure for the extent of conflict is the variance of the policy positions with respect to the expected policy centre of a coalition.

In precise terms, the *expected policy centre* x_S of a coalition S is defined to be the vector

$$\frac{\sum_{i \in S} w_i x_i}{\sum_{i \in S} w_i}.$$

Evidently, if players exert different degrees of influence on the various issues that shape the decision-making situation, w_i is no longer a scalar, but an m-vector (w_i1 ... w_{im}) instead. In accordance with this, the policy centre of a coalition S is the vector x_S such that for all $a \in M$, $xs_a \sum_{i \in S} w_{ia} x_{ia} / \sum_{i \in S} w_{ia}$.

The expected policy centre of a coalition is the balance point where the momentum (weights times distances from the centre) is zero, that is, where $\sum_{i \in S} w_i(x_i - x_S) = 0$. The essence of the notion of expected policy centre of a coalition lies in the fact that expected policy proposals enforced by *winning* coalitions have the character of a public good. Members of a losing coalition, without exclusion, have to accept the enforced proposal. Certainly, the concept of expected policy centre is applicable to one player ('solo coalition') or to two players. In the case of one player, the centre simply is the policy position of this player. Furthermore, it can be proven that in the case of two players i and j, the centre lies on the line segment connecting the policy positions x_i and x_j. In general, it can be proven that the expected policy centre x_S of a coalition S in an R^m space is on the hyperplane spanned by the ideal points of the members of that coalition.

As mentioned above, a conflict index can now be defined as the variance of the weighted Euclidean distances of all members of a coalition to the policy centre of that coalition.

Formally, let G be a spatial game. Let $S \subseteq N$ be a coalition and x_S be the policy centre of coalition S. Let $d(x_i, x_S)$ denote the Euclidean distance between player i and coalition S. The *variance conflict index* of S, $\sigma(S)$, is

$$\sigma(S) = \frac{\sum_{i \in S}(d(x_i, x_S) - \sum_{i \in S}(d(x_i, x_S)/|S|)^2}{|S|}.$$

Here, $|S|$ denotes the number of players in S. It can be verified that this definition satisfies the conditions for a conflict index as defined above.

The second model we use in this chapter is closer to Axelrod's original model of conflict of interest (see Axelrod 1970, also cf. De Swaan 1973). It is based on the notion of ' conflict range'. In contrast to the first model outlined above, this model allows for conflict to be a non-symmetric measure. Players in this second model may have different perceptions about the extent of conflict existing between them.

In order to determine the extent of conflict between two players, we formulate two reference points. Each reference point visualises an extreme situation, namely, one of maximal conflict and one of absence of conflict. Clearly, situations of conflict arise when two interacting players cannot attain their most preferred points simultaneously (Axelrod 1970). Defined in this way, player i finds herself in a situation of maximal conflict with another player j if that player takes a policy position x that is the most distant within the policy space. The line segment connecting the bliss points of i and j is the set of Pareto optimal agreement points. This is the region of the policy space where the interests of i and j are strictly opposed to each other. Assuming single-peaked preferences, utility losses will be smaller the closer players are to each other, that is, the smaller the region of the conflict of interest.

Formally, let G be a spatial game. Let i and j be players and x_i and x_k be their ideal points. Let $d(x_i, x_k)$ denote the distance between player i and player k. The *maximal conflict reference distance* (MaxCRD) for player i is defined as

$$MaxCRD_i = \max_{k \in N}\{d(x_i, x_k)\}$$

The other reference point is the policy position of the ideal coalition partner for player i. Being rational, player i wants to establish a policy outcome x as close as possible to her own policy position x_i. Then, i's ideal coalition partners would be the set of players with the exact same position in the policy space as player i herself has. In other words, it is expected that player i has no conflict with players that take the same position as player i does. The distance between a player's bliss point and the reference point MaxCRD can be interpreted as the range of possible conflict for a player in the game. Using this conflict range and the players' capabilities to influence decision outcomes, we can determine the extent of conflict between any two players in the game. Conflict of a player i with player j is asymmetric because of differences in maximal reference distances and weights. Keeping this in mind, we arrive at the following definition.

Consider a spatial voting game G. Let players i and j be members of coalition S, and let x_i and x_j be their ideal points. Let $MaxCRD_i$ denote the maximal conflict reference distance for player i and let w_j denote the weight of player j. Then the extent of asymmetric *conflict* player i experiences with player j is defined as:

$$\rho(i,j) = \left\{ \begin{array}{ll} 0 & \text{if } \max_{k \in N}\{d(x_i, x_k)\} = 0 \\ w_j \dfrac{d(x_i, x_j)}{MaxCRD_i} & \text{otherwise.} \end{array} \right\}$$

Note that the definition of asymmetric conflict of player i with j weights the relative distance between i and j by the size of j. This takes account of the fact that a player i, who evaluates two equidistant players j and k, will experience more conflict with the more influential player of the two (defined in terms of weights), because this player will have a larger potential to shift the decision outcome towards his or her own bliss point.

As a consequence of the subjective evaluation of pairwise distances, players may have different evaluations regarding the extent of conflict in a coalition. This leads to the following definition of subjective coalition conflict—the extent of conflict a certain player experiences within a coalition.

Formally, let G be a spatial game. Let players i and j in coalition S and let $\rho(i, j)$ be the asymmetric degree of conflict player i experiences with player j. Then, *subjective coalitional conflict* of player i with regard to S is defined as:

$$\rho_i(S) = \sum_{i \in S,\ i \neq j} \rho(i,j)$$

Regarding the extent of conflict among a set of players, we assume that conflicts with a larger player are more important than those with smaller players (Axelrod 1997). The total extent of conflict within a coalition is the weighted sum of the subjective extents of conflict experienced by its members.

In formal terms, let G be a spatial game. Let player i be a member of coalition S, let $\rho_i(S)$ be i's subjective coalitional conflict, and let w_i denote the weight of player i. Then, the *maximum reference distance conflict index* of S is defined as:

$$\rho(S) = \sum_{i \in S} w_i p_i(S)$$

The idea behind weighting the extent of conflict by the size of players is as follows. When members of a coalition have to reach a final decision, they all want to establish an outcome as close as possible to their own preferred positions. Clearly, the larger the weight of a player, the more power this player will have to shift the outcome into the direction of its most preferred outcome. An influential player will only be accepted as a coalition member if her position is not too far away from that of the other players; otherwise she could shift the outcome too strongly into the direction of her preferred position. By comparison, a less influential player with the same peripheral position in the issue space will be accepted more easily, because she does not possess the same leverage to shift the outcome in her favour.

7.2.5 Models of conflict: description

Subsequently, we elaborate the descriptive part of the conflict model. The model is based upon a number of assumptions: first, coalition-formation takes place in a setting that may be modelled by means of spatial games. Second, each actor has complete information about the policy positions, capabilities and salience of all actors involved in the decision-making process. Third, conflict in a coalition can be measured by means of a conflict index. Fourth, there is a behavioural rule stating that each actor strives to be a member of a minimal conflict coalition. Note that we formulate the descriptive part of the models generically in terms of C. The advantage of this general approach is that we do not need to specify the several models for each separate conflict index.

The coalition preferences of the players will be based on both perspectives for winning and the extent of conflict existing within the coalitions.

All the following definitions apply to a spatial voting game $G = (N, W, \{x_i\}_{i \in N})$.

Let coalitions S and T be winning, let $i \in N$ and let C be a conflict index. Hence, $C(S)$ denotes the degree of conflict in coalition S.

1. *i strictly prefers* S to T, notation $S \succ_i T$, if
   a. i is both in S and in T and the conflict index for S is smaller than for T, i.e. $C(S) < C(T)$; or
   b. i is a member of S but not of T.
2. i is *indifferent* between S and T, notation $S \approx_i$, if
   a. i is neither in S nor in T, or
   b. i is both in S and in T and $C(S) = C(T)$.
3. i weakly prefers S to T, notation $S \succeq_i$, if $S \succ_i T$ or $S \approx_i T$.

Part (1a) of the definition states that if a player is a member of two winning coalitions, she will prefer the winning coalition with the lower conflict index. Part (1b) states that a player prefers a winning coalition to any coalition T she does not belong to. Clearly, $\succeq_i$ is complete and transitive for every $i \in N$. Therefore, the set M_i of $\succeq_i$-maximal choices, that is, the set of all coalitions for which there are no better ones for player i, is not empty.

7.2.6 *Models of conflict: solutions*

In order to determine a solution for a spatial voting game in terms of coalitions and their policy positions, we have to determine a dominance relation among the coalitions. We do this by investigating the preferences of the members only in the intersection of two coalitions. The members of the intersection of two coalitions are called *critical players*. Hence, we only analyse the coalition preferences of the critical players, an idea due to McKelvey *et al* (1978). By the definition of individual coalition preferences we know that if S and T are both winning coalitions, then for all $i \in (S - T)$ we have $S \succ_i T$ and for all $i \in (T - S)$ we have $T \succ_i S$. Hence the preferences of the critical players are decisive.

For the formation of coalition S, the non-critical players in $S - T$ (the non-critical players in S) are dependent on the critical players' choice of coalition. Coalition S is viable against T if there is at least one critical player that weakly prefers S to T. From this, it follows that coalition S is not viable against T if *all* critical players find coalition T strictly better than S. Or equivalently: coalition S is *viable* against T if it is *not* the case that *all* critical players have a strict preference for T. Two coalitions S and

T are *mutually viable* if S is viable against T and vice versa. From this, it follows that one indifferent critical player is sufficient to make the two coalitions it belongs to viable against each other. Finally, we define *strict viability* of coalition S against T as a situation where coalition S is viable against T but not vice versa. In this case, all critical players have a strict preference for S. More formally, we define:

In formal terms, let G be a spatial game and let $S, T \in W$.

1. A coalition S is *viable against* a coalition T, notation $S \trianglelefteq T$, if there are critical players $i \in S \cap T$ such that $S \succeq_i T$.
2. A coalition S is *strictly viable against* a coalition T, notation $S \triangleright T$, if $S \trianglelefteq T$ but not $T \trianglelefteq S$.
3. Coalitions S and T are *viable with respect to each other*, notation $S \simeq T$, if $S \trianglelefteq T$ and $T \trianglelefteq S$.

Expressed in words, a coalition S is viable against T if there is at least one critical player weakly preferring S to T. Coalitions S and T are viable against each other if S is viable against T and vice versa. Finally, a coalition S is strictly viable against T if S is viable against T, but T is not viable against S.

As usual, we take the set of $\trianglelefteq$-maximal elements as the prediction set. The *coalition core* of a spatial game $G = (N, W, \{x_i\}_{i \in N})$, notation $Core(G)$, is defined to be the set of $\trianglelefteq$-maximal elements of W. That is,

$$Core(G) = \max(W, \trianglelefteq) = \{S \in W : \neg \mathrm{T}[\mathrm{T} \trianglelefteq S]\}.$$

An element of $Core(G)$ is called a *core coalition*.

Clearly, no individual player or coalition of players can improve upon a core-coalition. It now remains to prove under which conditions a core-coalition as defined above exists for a spatial game. The next theorem states that if we are dealing with a proper spatial game, the coalition core will not be empty.

Theorem 1: *Let G be a proper spatial game. Then*

$$Core(G) \neq \emptyset$$

Note that according to this theorem, properness of a game is a sufficient condition. The proof of this theorem is based on Van Deemen (1997: 203).

Let G be a spatial game, S be a coalition, and C be a conflict index. S is a *minimum conflict coalition* in G if for all T in W, $C(S) \leq C(T)$. The set of all minimum conflict coalitions in G is denoted by $W^{mc}(G)$. That is, a minimal conflict coalition is a winning coalition with the lowest conflict index. The next result expresses the fact that *Core*(G) equals the set of minimal conflict coalitions in G.

Theorem 2: *Let G be a proper spatial game. Then*

$$Core(G) = W^{mc}(G)$$

Again, the proof of this theorem follows the proof given in Van Deemen (1997: 202). According to this theorem, in order to compute the coalition core of a game, it suffices to calculate the conflict index for every winning coalition and, subsequently, to determine the coalitions with the smallest index.

The core solution as presented here, however, is not the only applicable solution concept. Another possibility is, for example, to use the Nash bargaining solution (NBS). According to this approach, the solution is based on the maximum of the products of individual utilities for coalitions. However, in order to use this concept, we would need to be able to represent coalition preferences on an interval measurement level.

7.3 RESEARCH STRATEGIES AND DESIGN

This section describes the research design for the application of the cooperative models used in this chapter. For most parts, the design is based on the general research design for this book, as described in Chapter 2 of the volume. Hence, we will subsequently mainly focus on a number of additional assumptions needed in order to apply the cooperative approach to the common dataset. As input variables, the models require the actors' most favoured positions, salience scores, Shapley Shubik Index (SSI) measures of capabilities, but not the reference point. First, we will define the set of winning coalitions under each of the legislative procedures and Council voting rules. We also discuss the capabilities of the actors to influence the outcome of decision-making, and how we will deal with indifferent actors.

7.3.1 *Winning coalitions in EU decision-making*

The cooperative approach to EU decision-making is strong, but simple: it takes into account the preferences of actors and their capabilities and salience, but it does not consider other bases of power, such as the capacity to set the agenda, i.e. to make suggestions on the basis of own preferences that make the realisation of the preferences of others more difficult. Incorporation of such forces might make the picture more realistic, but also more difficult and messy to analyse.

In our cooperative approach to EU decision-making, we do not focus on procedural legislative aspects, but mainly on the question of *whether it is numerically possible for some set of players to form a winning coalition*. The question of *how to coordinate strategies* is beyond the scope of our approach as presented here. Expressed in simple terms, this means that we focus on the question of *whether a set of players is able to approve a legislative proposal, should its members wish to do so*. How and at which point in the legislative process they reach such an agreement to form a coalition, is beyond our concern here.

Each of the legislative proposals in the common data set is subject to one of the following procedures and requirements:

Consultation qualified majority voting (QMV): QMV in the Council in order to adopt a Commission proposal, unanimity in the Council in order to amend a Commission proposal.

Consultation unanimity: unanimous vote in the Council in order to adopt or amend a Commission proposal.

Co-decision QMV: proper coordination of the action of the European parliament (EP) and the Council may lead to the adoption of a legislative proposal. In this case, the Council needs a qualified majority in support of the proposal, whereas the EP needs a simple majority.

Co-decision unanimity: proper coordination of the action of the EP and Council may lead to the adoption of a legislative proposal. In this case, the Council needs unanimity, whereas the EP needs a simple majority.

In addition, we assume that in each one of these procedures, the Commission is a part of every minimal winning coalition, that is, it is a veto player. In principle, this description allows us to define the set of winning coalitions for these four procedures. The following observations are important, however. If a legislative proposal is subject to the consultation procedure with QMV, the EP is always a dummy player, whereas under the co-decision procedure, both the EP and the Commission are veto players. In reality, the treaties specify the conditions under which the EP can exercise its veto power, on the basis of simple majority votes. But unfortunately, we cannot model the sub-game within the EP, because our data set does not contain information on the policy positions of the various party grouping in the EP: it only contains information on the position of the EP as an entity. Hence, accordingly, we will treat the EP as a unitary actor in our analysis.

7.3.2 Solutions to the problem of indifferent actors

Another limitation of the DEU data set is that for some of the decision-making situations, the data set does not include specific information on the policy positions of the main actors (on this issue, also see Chapter 2 on the general research design). The importance of indifference regarding the outcome emerges from the fact that the combination of an actor's issue positions, and the importance attached to these issues, indicate the level of interest for the decision outcome. Moreover, the combination of the actor's capability to achieve policy preference and the salience attached to an issue, determine the effective influence exercised on the outcome of this issue. That is, the more salient an issue is to an actor, the more resources will be employed to influence the decision outcome. Therefore, an actor's weight in definition of policy centre is defined as the product of capability and salience.

Activeness and inactiveness—the formulation or not of a policy position—on the one hand, and interest or the lack of it on the other, lead to the following classification of actors: an actor who does not take a position on an issue and does not attach any salience to it may be described as a 'normal' indifferent actor. This actor does not care what the outcome is on the issue at hand. Moreover, the actor may not even recognise the issue as such. Instead, if the actor attaches some salience to an issue, the actor recognises that it needs to be resolved, independent of *how* this will be done.

An actor taking a position, but not attaching salience to it, considers it to be unimportant that this issue be resolved. Regarding the outcome, the actor itself is not indifferent, but does not care whether there is an outcome on the issue at all. However, this situation, although certainly possible in practice, does not occur in the common data set. The most common situation, generally, is one in which an actor takes a position and attaches some salience to it.

For the cooperative models we test in this chapter, indifferent actors need not constitute a problem, however. First, it is important to note that indifference of an actor is defined in relation to the outcome of a certain issue, and not with respect to a policy point (which constitutes a vector of issue positions). An actor is indifferent regarding a policy point when it is indifferent with respect to all issues that make up the respective decision-making situation. Formally, let M be the set of issues constituting a decision-making situation. Let $K_i \subseteq M$ be the set of issues player i is indifferent about (not precluding the possibility, of course, that $K_i = \emptyset$). Two different situations are then relevant:

situation 1: $K_i = M$: player i is indifferent on *all* issues regarding the policy outcome;

situation 2: $K_i \subseteq M$ but $K_i \neq M$: player i is not indifferent on all the issues at stake.

How do the conflict models deal with these two situations in cases when there is some difference among them? In the case when a player is indifferent regarding *all* issues in the game, and therefore indifferent with respect to the policy outcome of the game, it is assumed that there will be no incentive to block legislation (or give its support to any coalition of players). Nor will the player exert any influence in an attempt to shift the policy outcome in any specific direction. Therefore, we will simply exclude such a player from the game. We will do this by reducing the winning threshold of the game by the sum of the weights of the players that are indifferent with regard to all issues, and by setting their formal voting weights to zero. This way, the indifferent players are transformed into 'dummy players'. They should not be conceived as powerless players, however, but rather as players who have no incentive to exert any power in the game. Consider a situation where 15 players have to come to an agreement on a decision-making problem by, for example, unanimity, and that one of them is indifferent regarding the outcome. The 14 players who are not indifferent assume that when it comes to a vote on the outcome during the last meeting of the decision-making committee, the indifferent player will go along with them (after all, this player was indifferent). Via backwards reasoning, the '14' know that they have to reach an agreement among themselves before the last meeting. Therefore, the weighted voting game could be modelled by a 15-tuple [14; 1,1,...,1] where each player holds equal voting weight. In the terminology of voting game theory, the 15th player—the indifferent player—is not a powerless player, because the player has the same formal voting weight as the other players, but will never use this 'veto power' because of the very fact that the player is indifferent.

Second, a player can be indifferent regarding some issues, but not regarding all of them. Analytically, this means that this player is interested in some parts of the decision outcome, the issues that are salient. We assume that indifferent actors do not exercise any influence on the establishment of a position on any of the issues (as part of the policy position) on which they are indifferent. For example, let $M = \{a, b, c\}$ and i, j, $k \subset N$, and $K_i = \{a\}$ and $K_j = K_k = \emptyset$. Then only the salience, capabilities and positions of players j and k will be taken into consideration when we calculate the position on issue a (as part of the policy position) of $\{i, j, k\}$ in the *variance model*.

Subsequently, the distances between the policy centre of a coalition and the members' bliss points, which are key determinants for the measurement of conflict in the *variance model*, are based on the issues that are salient for the respective players. In our example, this means that the distance between x_i and $x_{\{i,j,k\}}$ is calculated on the basis of the positions of i and $\{i, j, k\}$ on issues b and c (evidently, in combination with the salience i attaches to these issues). In the *reference distance model*, the conflict index of a coalition is based on the subjective coalitional conflict indices of its members. To compute the subjective indices, we need to calculate the maximal conflict reference distance. If we want to determine the maximum conflict index for an actor i who is indifferent with respect to some issues, we only take into account distances on issues that are salient for i and for each of the other players. (Note that this does not preclude the possibility of asymmetrical pairwise conflict indices.) For example, let $M = \{a, b, c\}$ and $i, j, k \subset N$, and $K_i = a$, $K_j = b$, and $K_k = \emptyset$. In order to determine the maximal conflict reference distance for player i, we evaluate the distances between i and j on issue c (i is indifferent regarding issue a, whereas j is indifferent regarding b), and the distances between i and k on issue b and c (i is indifferent regarding issue a, whereas k is not indifferent regarding any of the issues at stake). If $K_i \cap K_j = M$, if there are no issues on which the distances between i and j may be calculated, then we assume that there is no conflict of interest between i and j.

7.3.3 The measurement of capabilities

With respect to the determination of a policy centre of a coalition which could serve as the final policy outcome of the game, we assume that the capabilities of the stakeholders to influence the decision outcome depend on the membership composition of winning coalitions. In particular, we use the Shapley Shubik indices of the stakeholders as an estimate of their capabilities. As regards the treatment of indifferent actors, we assume that stakeholders that are completely indifferent regarding the policy outcome have no capability to influence the decision outcome, since they are simply excluded from the game. Our calculations are based on the first variant of the SSI scores described in Chapter 12. These are the ones in which the Commission is always included in a winning coalition. They are, however, not identical to the ones used in the other chapters, since they are based on the set of actors that took positions.

Besides exclusion from the game as a consequence of indifference regarding the policy outcome, players might also be excluded because they have no formal voting rights in some of the decision-making situations.

There are three decision-making situations in the data set where some of the stakeholders indeed do not possess voting power: in COM(2000) 27—a Proposal for a Council Regulation listing the third countries whose nationals must be in possession of visas when crossing the external borders and those whose nationals are exempt from that requirement—*Denmark, the UK*, and *Ireland* have no voting power. In COM(2000) 303—a Proposal for a Council Regulation listing the third countries whose nationals must be in possession of visas when crossing the external borders and those whose nationals are exempt from that requirement—and COM(1999)686—a Proposal for a Council Regulation creating a European Refugee Fund—this is the case for *Denmark*. All three of these proposals were subject to consultation and unanimity.

In these cases, we have adjusted the structure of the games by setting the voting weight of the players without voting power to zero, and by reducing the winning threshold by the number of votes held by the excluded players. Subsequently, the capabilities of the stakeholders were estimated by calculating Shapley Shubik indices within the structure of the adjusted voting game.

7.4 CASE STUDY: PRODUCTION AID FOR COTTON

In this section, we will apply the conflict models to the legislative bargaining which occurred over a Commission proposal for a Council Regulation on production aid for cotton, introduced at the end of 1999. In the preceding years, the world price for cotton had fluctuated greatly and the price was low when the Commission proposal was introduced. In situations of low world prices, cotton producers have to receive relatively large subsidies in order to bring the price they receive up to the level of a guaranteed price. The general aim of the Commission proposal was to keep expenditures for the cotton regime under control, and to protect the environment by means of a number of measures designed to curb environmental damage and discourage the emergence of a mono-culture in some regions of the world.

The revision of the cotton aid regime the Commission envisaged was based on increased penalties for exceeding the National Guaranteed Quantities (NGQs) allotted to producing countries, while the guide price level would be kept constant, as well as the level of NGQs. The penalty rate is the percentage of the guide price by which aid is reduced if the NGQs are exceeded by 1 per cent. The Commission proposed to increase the penalty from 0.5 per cent to 0.6 per cent. This means that if NGQs were exceeded by 1 per cent, the guide price would be reduced by 0.6 per cent.

As an illustration, consider the following computation example: according to the Commission proposal, if the national quantities were exceeded by 1 per cent, aid would be reduced by 0.6 per cent of the guide price (instead of 0.5 per cent as in the past). At the time of the proposal the guide price for cotton was set at €1.063 per tonne. The NGQ for Greece, together with Spain, the only cotton producing member states in the EU, was 782,000 tonnes. At the time, Greece overran its NGQ and penalties were imposed. Now suppose Greece's actual production was 1,275,000 tonnes, an overrun of 493,000 tonnes or 63 per cent of its NGQ. If a penalty of 0.5 per cent is set, this means that under the regime proposed by the Commission the guide price would be reduced by 63 per cent × 50 per cent = 31.5 per cent. The reduced guide price would then become 1.063 − (31.5 per cent × 1.063) = 1.063 − 335 = €728 per tonne.

Legislative bargaining on this proposal mainly focused on two aspects: *the level of the penalty rate*, which is the percentage of the guide price by which aid is reduced if NGQs are exceeded by at least 1 per cent, and the *level of the NGQs*, which at the time of the introduction of the proposal were set at 782 K tonnes for Greece and 249 K tonnes for Spain. The underlying reasons for disagreement on these issues were that the decision outcomes would affect the amount of subsidies to be received by cotton producing countries (Spain, Greece, and to a very limited extent, Portugal). The environmental aspects of the proposal did not feature in the issues as specified by the interviewed experts, however.

On the first issue, four distinctive policy positions can be defined, ranging from the reference point of a 50 per cent penalty to a 100 per cent penalty in case NGQs were be exceeded (Table 7.1). These positions were scored as 0 and 100 by the experts. In between, and closer to the reference point, experts scored the Commission proposal of a 60 per cent penalty as lying at position 20 and a 70 per cent penalty at position 40.

Table 7.1. *Positions, saliences and capabilities in an illustrative case*

Stakeholder	Position issue 1[a]	Position issue 2[b]	Salience issue 1[a]	Salience issue 2[b]	Capabilities
Commission	20	0	90	80	0.310299
Belgium	40	0	90	80	0.037683
Denmark	100	0	90	80	0.024230
Germany	20	0	90	80	0.080979
Greece	0	100	50	70	0.037683
Spain	0	100	50	70	0.066210
France	20	0	90	80	0.080979
Ireland	20	0	90	80	0.024230
Italy	20	0	70	70	0.080979
Luxembourg	40	0	90	80	0.014107
Netherlands	100	0	90	80	0.037683
Austria	40	0	90	90	0.031023
Portugal	0	0	70	70	0.037683
Finland	40	0	90	80	0.024230
Sweden	100	0	90	80	0.031023
UK	40	0	90	80	0.080979
EP	0	100	90	50	0

Notes: [a]Issue 1: level of the penalty rate:
0 = 50 per cent penalty;
20 = 60 per cent penalty;
40 = 70 per cent penalty;
100 = 100 per cent penalty.
[b]Issue 2: level of the NGQs:
0 = NGQs of 782 and 249 K tonnes for Greece and Spain respectively;
100 = NGQs of 1200 and 300 K tonnes for Greece and Spain respectively.

Greece and Spain, supporting the reference point, certainly acted on the basis of domestic self-interest: Portugal supported this position largely in order to secure an eventual future development of domestic cotton production. Portugal only had one domestic cotton producer, which conducted its processing in Spain, however. During the stage of legislative bargaining Portugal did not face penalties and therefore regarded this issue as of low importance regarding its own priorities.

The Commission held the preference it did largely due to a desire to find a balance regarding the interests of the cotton-producing countries and its own concern to keep the EU's agriculture budget under control. In the stage before the proposal was introduced, the Commission provided calculations indicating that penalty rates lower than 70 per cent would lead to an increase in budgetary expenditure if the NGQs remained unchanged. Because Spanish and Greek delegations pressed the Commission to lower its initial penalty rate of 70 per cent, emphasising the economic and social importance of cotton production in the regions producing it, the Commission proposed a penalty rate of 60 per cent. EU states who argued for an increase in the penalty rate—especially those located in the EU's north—did so because of the argument of budget neutrality.

The EP, however, did not agree to increase the co-responsibility levy by 20 per cent—from 50 per cent to 60 per cent of the overshot—as had been suggested by the Commission. Instead, the EP argued that the percentage reduction in the guide price applying at the time the proposal was introduced had proven to be an effective budget stabiliser and enabled Community cotton production to be maintained despite major fluctuations in world market prices for cotton fibre. In addition, an increase in penalties would force the smallest holdings to go out of business, thus causing social hardship, while, paradoxically, expenditure would rise due to the fact that prices paid increase when production decreases.

The issue of NGQs was raised by Greece and Spain, who claimed that their current NGQs were set at a time when a particularly bad harvest for cotton had occurred, and that the NGQs did not reflect real production capacity. The Commission, however, stated that NGQs were assessed on the basis of three normal harvest years. The other EU states supported the position of the Commission on the issue.

The EP was opposed to maintaining the *status quo*. It argued that NGQs should be increased in order to bring them up to the level at which actual production stabilises (1200 K tonnes in Greece and 300 K tonnes in Spain). According to the EP, the imbalance between those amounts and NGQs in effect was the key cause for the structural penalties.

As indicated above, cotton is produced in two EU countries only: Spain and Greece. These two countries were certainly not enthusiastic about the reforms envisaged for the cotton sector. Although other EU member states could easily have outvoted them, since the proposal was subject to the decision rule of QMV, the Council demonstrated its tendency to account for the concerns of individual member states and aimed at reaching a decision by consensus. All the experts interviewed for this proposal stated that this behaviour of the Agriculture Council is rather common in situations in which some individual states hold pronounced interests. This is mainly due to the fact that other member states realise they may have to draw on the support of these states in future negotiations on agricultural production on issues in which they, in turn, may have special concerns ('log-rolling'). Overall, the outcome of the decision-making is most important for Greece and Spain, but since the outcome has financial consequences for the other member states too, all member states have a substantial interest in the proposal. That is to say, the other member states do not care that much how the budget restriction is brought about, as long as it is established.

Together, the NGQs and the penalty rate determine the budget expenditure in the cotton sector. A reduction in the budget expenditure could be established by keeping the NGQs at their present level and increasing the penalty rate. But it could also be established by both increasing the NGQs and the penalty rate at the same time, although this would be more difficult. Therefore, most member states were only prepared to give on their position on the NGQs if a penalty rate near 60 per cent were established. The southern member states—Greece, Spain, Italy, and Portugal—attached a lower level of salience to the issue of the penalties. Spain and Greece acknowledged to some extent that their demands were infeasible and that they must be willing to give up their position before other member states, especially because at the same time this proposal was discussed, other agriculture products were the subject of discussion. Furthermore, Spain and Greece had already established a lower penalty rate than the Commission planned to introduce in its proposal, and they were aware of the fact that an increase in the penalty rate was unavoidable. Therefore, it was more worthwhile for Spain and Greece to invest in the issue of the NGQs.

Until the end of the decision-making process, Spain continued to oppose the Commission proposal, despite the fact that a large majority of member states favoured the suggested reforms of the cotton sector. Hence, it tabled an alternative proposal: the proposal aimed at a 50 per cent penalty rate for production between 1,031,000 tonnes and 1,600,000 tonnes, and an increase of 1 per cent per 20,000 tonnes above 1,600,000 tonnes. Basically, this proposal was equal to the *status quo*, as long as production would not exceed 1,600,000 tonnes.

Analysing the configuration of policy positions on this issue, we can observe a large group of actors taking more or less the same positions regarding both of the issues: on the first issue, they either supported the 60 per cent penalty as proposed by the Commission, or the suggestion of a somewhat larger penalty of 70 per cent. Regarding the level of the

NGQs, all of them supported the Commission proposal, which was equal to the reference point. The coalition of these ten actors (the Commission, Belgium, Germany, France, Ireland, Italy, Luxembourg, Austria, Finland, and the UK) did, however, not have the required legislative majority to get a common policy position accepted: the coalition included nine member states with a total number of 57 votes. In order to be winning, this coalition needed support of a number of member states with a total weight of at least five votes.

One possible solution to achieve this aim would have been to include Portugal in this coalition. The inclusion of Spain or Greece was less likely, however, because of their rather extreme positions on both issues. Portugal, by comparison, only took a different position regarding the issue of the penalties. The same held for the Netherlands, Denmark and Sweden, who each strived for maximum penalties, while favouring maintenance of the *status quo* regarding the NGQs.

Let us illustrate the respective coalition-formation process and subsequent calculations on conflict indices. Inclusion of Portugal leads to a minimal winning coalition with a policy centre of (24.09, 0). To illustrate how this policy position is obtained, the following information regarding the issue positions, saliences and capabilities of all actors is relevant:

According to its definition, the policy centre of the above-mentioned 10-member coalition plus Portugal, which we will denote by S, is a vector x_S, such that

$$x_{S1} = \frac{w_{COM1}x_{COM1} + \dots + w_{UK1}x_{UK1}}{w_{COM1} + \dots + w_{UK1}}$$

and

$$x_{S2} = \frac{w_{COM2}x_{COM2} + \dots + w_{UK2}x_{UK2}}{w_{COM2} + \dots + w_{UK2}}.$$

The extent of influence the Commission exerts on the first issue, w_{COM1}, is estimated here by the product of its power in the game, approximated by its Shapley Shubik index of 0.310299, and the salience it attaches to the first issue, namely 90. Similarly, for the second issue, its influence is estimated by the product 0.310299 × 80.

This allows us to derive the policy centre of the above-mentioned coalition, which is (24.09, 0). For each member, we can subsequently compute the Euclidean distance to the policy centre, and obtain both the average weighted distance to the policy centre and the variance of this distance, which can serve as an estimate of the conflict level of a coalition (see the section on conflict indices above). For this decision-making situation, the coalition mentioned above is the coalition with minimal conflict in the sense that the variance of the distances to the policy centre are minimal. According to Theorem 3, a core coalition is a minimum conflict coalition. Since {*Commission, Belgium, Germany, France, Ireland, Italy, Luxembourg, Austria, Portugal, Finland, UK*} is the coalition with the lowest conflict, this coalition forms the core. We will now focus on the reference distance conflict model.

The maximal conflict reference distance of the Commission—and in fact that of almost all EU states—is its distance to Greece and Spain (see Table 7.2). Spain and Greece have maximal conflict of interest with Denmark, the Netherlands and Sweden in terms of the political distance between their policy positions points on both issues. The EP, a dummy player under the consultation procedure, supports Spain and Greece on both issues, but the distances to players with no capabilities are not taken into account when reference distances are determined. From Table 7.1, it can be seen that distance and conflict between two players are asymmetric measures. Consider, for example, the distance between France and Greece. This distance is given by:

$$d(F, EL) = \sqrt{[(20-0)(0-100)]\begin{bmatrix} 90 & 0 \\ 0 & 80 \end{bmatrix}\begin{bmatrix} (20-0) \\ (0-100) \end{bmatrix}} = 914.3$$

whereas for Greece, the respective distance is given by

$$d(EL, F) = \sqrt{[(0-20)(100-0)]\begin{bmatrix} 50 & 0 \\ 0 & 70 \end{bmatrix}\begin{bmatrix} (0-20) \\ (100-0) \end{bmatrix}} = 848.5.$$

The general formula for weighted Euclidean distance (WED) between i and j in an m-dimensional policy space is defined as follows (see Enelow and Hinich 1984; Hinich and Munger 1994; 1997): Let x_i and x_j be (column) vectors representing the policy positions of i and j. Let S_i denote a salience matrix of dimension $m \times m$ for i. The main diagonal elements in this matrix, s_{aa}, s_{bb}, *et cetera*, are the salience terms, i.e. the relative value i attaches to issue a, b, *et cetera*. The off-diagonal elements are called *interaction terms*. These interaction measures s_{ab} reflect how much evaluation of changes on issue a depends on the position of issue b. (Note that in this project, we assume that there are no interaction effects.) Hence, S_i is obtained by multiplying a $1 \times m$ row vector of i's salience with an identity matrix of order m. Then, we obtain:

Table 7.2. *Pairwise distances between actors and maximal reference distances*[ca]

	COM	B	DK	D	EL	E	F	IRL	I	L	NL	A	P	FIN	S	UK	EP
COM	0.0	189.7	758.9	0.0	**914.3**	**914.3**	0.0	0.0	0.0	189.7	758.9	189.7	189.7	189.7	758.9	189.7	914.3
B	189.7	0.0	569.2	189.7	**971.6**	**971.6**	189.7	189.7	189.7	0.0	569.2	0.0	379.5	0.0	569.2	0.0	971.6
DK	758.9	569.2	0.0	758.9	**1304**	**1304**	758.9	758.9	758.9	569.2	0.0	569.2	948.7	569.2	0.0	569.2	1304.0
D	0.0	189.7	758.9	0.0	**914.3**	**914.3**	0.0	0.0	0.0	189.7	758.9	189.7	189.7	189.7	758.9	189.7	914.3
EL	848.5	883.2	**1095**	848.5	0.0	0.0	848.5	848.5	848.5	883.2	**1095**	883.2	836.7	883.2	**1095**	883.2	0.0
E	848.5	883.2	**1095**	848.5	0.0	0.0	848.5	848.5	848.5	883.2	**1095**	883.2	836.7	883.2	**1095**	883.2	0.0
F	0.0	189.7	758.9	0.0	**914.3**	**914.3**	0.0	0.0	0.0	189.7	758.9	189.7	189.7	189.7	758.9	189.7	914.3
IRL	0.0	189.7	758.9	0.0	**914.3**	**914.3**	0.0	0.0	0.0	189.7	7589	189.7	189.7	189.7	758.9	189.7	914.3
I	0.0	167.3	669.3	0.0	**853.2**	**853.2**	0.0	0.0	0.0	167.3	669.3	167.3	167.3	167.3	669.3	167.3	853.2
L	189.7	0.0	569.2	189.7	**971.6**	**971.6**	189.7	189.7	189.7	0.0	569.2	0.0	379.5	0.0	569.2	0.0	971.6
NL	758.9	569.2	0.0	758.9	**1304**	**1304**	758.9	758.9	758.9	569.2	0.0	569.2	948.7	569.2	0.0	569.2	1304.0
A	189.7	0.0	569.2	189.7	**1022**	**1022**	189.7	189.7	189.7	0.0	569.2	0.0	379.5	0.0	569.2	0.0	1022.0
P	167.3	334.7	**836.7**	167.3	**836.7**	**836.7**	167.3	167.3	167.3	334.7	836.7	334.7	0.0	334.7	836.7	334.7	836.7
FIN	189.7	0.0	569.2	189.7	**971.6**	**971.6**	189.7	189.7	189.7	0.0	569.2	0.0	379.5	0.0	569.2	0.0	971.6
S	758.9	569.2	0.0	758.9	**1304**	**1304**	758.9	758.9	758.9	5692	0.0	569.2	948.7	569.2	0.0	569.2	1304.0
UK	189.7	0.0	569.2	189.7	**971.6**	**971.6**	189.7	189.7	189.7	0.0	569.2	0.0	379.5	0.0	569.2	0.0	971.6
EP	732.1	802.5	1183	732.1	0.0	0.0	732.1	732.1	732.1	802.5	1183	802.5	707.1	802.5	1183	802.5	0.0

Note: [a]Maximal reference distances are indicated by boldface type.

$$WED(x_i, x_j) = \sqrt{(x_i - x_j)^T S_i (x_i - x_j)}$$

where T denotes the transpose.

In this decision-making situation, France can be seen to have maximal conflict of interest with Spain and Greece, whereas, as indicated above, Spain has maximal conflict with Denmark, the Netherlands and Sweden. In order to compute the extent of conflict within this coalition, based on reference distances, we take the weighted sum of the subjective coalitional conflict levels of the members. For France, for example, this subjective coalitional conflict level is given by:

$$\begin{aligned}\rho_F(S) = \rho(F, COM) + \rho(F, B) + \rho(F, D) \\ + \rho(F, IRL) + \rho(F, L) + \rho(F, A)\rho(F, P) \\ +\rho(F, FIN) + \rho(F, UK).\end{aligned}$$

The first element of this sum—the level of conflict with the Commission—is given by: $w_{COM}(d(x_F, x_{COM})/d(x_F, x_E))$ which is 0, because France and the Commission take the same position on both issues. Hence, the relation between the Commission and France does not contribute to the level of conflict within this coalition.

With regard to the levels of conflict with two member states that are equidistant from France, e.g. Belgium (second element) and Luxembourg (fifth element), we can observe that France has more conflict with Belgium than with Luxembourg, because Belgium has more capabilities to influence the decision outcome than Luxembourg does. France and Belgium attach the same level of importance to the issues, but Belgium is stronger than Luxembourg in terms of its Shapley Shubik index.[1]

The level of conflict for all coalitions can be calculated in a similar way. It turns out that the coalition mentioned above was a minimal conflict coalition for this decision-making situation, and therefore a core coalition.

The example in this section only had one core coalition as a solution for each of the models. This is not necessarily the case in all decision-making situations, however. In particular, situations where we encounter identical players, i.e. players with the same policy positions, salience and voting weights, can easily give rise to more than one core coalition. Consider a decision-making situation where a coalition needs a qualified

1

$$w_B \frac{d(x_F, x_B)}{d(x_F, x_E)} = 0.037683 \times \frac{189.7}{914.3} \text{ and } w_L \frac{d(x_F, x_L)}{d(x_F, x_E)} = 0.014107 \times \frac{189.7}{914.3}$$

majority in order to pass a proposal. If a given coalition T, of which player i is a member, is in the core, and there is an identical player j in the complement of T in N, then player i can be exchanged for j, so that the resulting coalition T' will be in the core as well. Note that it is common for many game theoretical solution concepts, for transferable utility games, to provide a set of outcomes as a solution rather than a single outcome.

7.5 PREDICTIVE ACCURACY OF THE MODELS

The data set to which the conflict models described in this chapter have been applied consists of information on 66 Commission proposals containing a total of 162 issues. No proposals or issues were excluded from the analysis as presented here: in contrast to other models, the conflict models do not require reference points and, in addition, they can deal quite easily with the issue of indifferent actors.

The first question that will be answered here is which of the models provides the most accurate predictions for outcomes of the EU decision-making process: the conflict models or the unweighted median base-line model. The accuracy of the models can be assessed by comparing the predicted outcome of the models and the information on the outcome as described by the experts. Note again that the models may predict more than one core-coalition. However, to each coalition one and only one position is assigned. See the definition of policy centre. In our empirical application, the occurrence of multiple coalitions did not lead to different predictions in terms of decision-outcomes. Table 7.3 presents the average error at issue level for each of the models under each combination of

Table 7.3. *Average absolute error across issues*

	All issues (n=162)	CNS QMV (n=55)	CNS unan. (n=39)	COD QMV (n=56)	COD unan. (n=12)
Unw. median model	28.4012	30.6182	21.0256	30.6429	31.7500
Reference distance model	26.2571	28.6415	18.8662	30.5910	17.6192
Variance model	24.6874	25.3829	18.9435	29.5191	17.6192

legislative procedure: consultation (CNS); co-decision (COD); voting rule in the Council (qualified majority voting, QMV); and unanimity (U). The model that performs best is the conflict model in which conflicts within coalitions are based on the variance of the distances of the members to the policy centre of the coalition. The performance of the conflict models is quite similar, but all clearly perform better than the median model.

Under all combinations of legislative procedures and Council voting rules, the conflict models hence perform better than the unweighted median model which relies on the policy positions of the players only.

The differences in the predictive accuracy between the different procedures, however, are striking. All models yield better predictions for the procedures where a unanimous Council is required in order to pass legislation. Under these procedures, the preferences of all players having a voting weight are taken into account, whereas in the QMV procedures, a winning coalition can easily neglect the preferences of players on the losing side.

Under unanimity voting procedures, the set of winning coalitions is quite small compared with the set of winning coalitions under QMV. When the legislative procedure is consultation, the set of minimal winning coalitions consists of a unanimous Council in addition to the Commission. Addition of the EP would expand the size of this minimal winning coalition. The EP, however, has no capacity to influence the policy centre, but it could choose to join a coalition, and thereby possibly affect the level of conflict within the coalition. Note that in the reference distance model, players with no capabilities do not affect the extent of conflict in a coalition.

Under the co-decision procedure with QMV in the Council, minimal winning coalitions consist of the Commission, together with a qualified majority in the Council, and the EP. Adding more member states could expand the size of winning coalitions, and affect the level of conflict within a coalition. In the reference distance model, adding more members necessarily leads to more conflict, because conflict is defined as the sum of subjective interpretations of the level of conflict within a coalition. In the variance model, adding a player could lead to either a reduction or increase in conflict.

Tables 7.4 and 7.5 compare the performance of the models by policy issue and by type of issue, respectively. As can easily be seen, the reference distance model performs better than the baseline model when issues are categorised according to policy areas. However, the performance of

Table 7.4. *Average absolute error across issues by policy area*

	Agriculture (n=40)	Internal market (n=34)	Other policy areas (n=88)
Unweighted median model	33.2875	39.6029	21.8523
Reference distance model	31.7065	34.8496	20.4603
Variance model	28.4527	33.2985	19.6488

Table 7.5. *Average absolute error by type of issue*

	Dichotomous (n=33)	Rank order (n=109)	Scale (n=20)
Unweighted median model	30.3030	29.4220	19.7
Reference distance model	35.6819	23.9750	23.1439
Variance model	33.9738	24.2324	22.6635

the reference distance model appears to be best when applied to issues that are rank-ordered. When measurement is on the scale level, or when issues are dichotomous in nature, performance on the basis of this model is much less satisfying. Similarly, the variance model outperforms the baseline model (but not the reference distance model) when issues are rank-ordered, but it actually performs worse in the case of dichotomous issues or issues measured on scale level.

Peripheral players which are powerful are able to generate larger shifts of the policy centre, which in turn could result in a substantial increase in the sum of the distances between the bliss points of the other members and the new policy centre. If this increase outweighs the positive effect of adding an extra member to a coalition, i.e. the conflict is spread out over more members, conflict is higher within the coalition. For the variance model, the effect of adding an extra member is clearly dependent on the configuration of the policy positions of the players the additional member is about to join. Note that the variance model in essence describes the balance in terms of dissatisfaction with a policy outcome among a set of players who form a winning coalition, and that the model clearly differs in this respect from the model envisaged by Axelrod (1970), who advocates taking into account the dispersion of policy positions when the level of conflict in a coalition is to be measured. The policy outcome will only coincide with the preference of each individual player if all players have identical policy positions and the game reduces to a partnership game, otherwise it still has the property of being a balance point where the momentum is zero. Basically, this means that all coalition members have to give in to reach a compromise outcome, but that some players have to accept greater losses than others, which are dependent on their preferences and their potential to influence decision-outcomes. This leads to the observation that the more inequalities there are in terms of losses, the more conflict there will be in a coalition. If the differences in the distances to the policy centre among the players are smaller due to enlargement, the level of conflict will decrease. By comparison, if the differences increase, conflict will be higher.

Since the compromise model appears to make better predictions than the conflict models, one may ask, however, whether conflict as defined in our models is indeed such an important determinant of the outcome of the EU decision-making process. One could, for example, raise the question whether excluding some of the players with peripheral policy positions in order to derive a predicted coalition with even less conflict might be a sensible strategy to embark upon. Alternatively, one might focus on the level of conflict within the total player set, rather than the level of conflict within a specific coalition. Generally, it appears that the compromise model more or less predicts the policy centres of core coalitions for decisions taken under unanimity (identical to the solutions proposed in this chapter), whereas it seems to provide more accurate forecasts in the case of decisions under QMV. The errors for QMV are substantially higher than the errors of the compromise model for QMV. One reason may be that EU actors may try to get unanimity solutions under QMV as well. The basic assumption of voting game theory is that the winner takes all, and therefore any player wants to be on the winning side. However, by neglecting the preferences of players on the losing side, in order to minimise internal conflict, members of the winning coalition could easily burn their fingers in a next game with the same player set, but with a different configuration of policy preferences. That is, players may realise that they might have to draw on the support of other players during future negotiations in which they hold a peripheral policy position. Therefore, a tendency to give in to the concerns of individual players and aim to reach a decision by consensus, may be characterised as rational behaviour in the framework of repeated games.

7.6 CONCLUSION

In this chapter two models of coalition formation in collective decision-making processes have been presented. Both models are confronted with data about decision-making in the European Union. The models are to be placed in the tradition of the cooperative game theoretic approach to political coalition formation. This tradition in political science is initiated by the seminal works of Riker (1962) and Axelrod (1970). The two models are based on the behavioural assumption that each player strives to form a coalition with minimal conflict. In this, we closely follow the work of Axelrod (1970). Conflict minimisation and consensus-building are dual sides of the same coin. If conflict is minimised, consensus is maximised. Therefore, both models also can be interpreted as consensus maximisation models. In this sense, both models aim at explaining and describing consensus building in politics.

This chapter posits that as in many other real-world situations, coalition-formation is at the core of the decision-making process in the EU. We claim that the relevant institutional actors—which, according to this volume, are assumed to be the European Commission, the European Parliament and the members of the Council of the EU—do not affect policy outcomes individually, but that cooperation and the formation of (winning) coalitions among them is central to the determination of respective decisions.

In order to demonstrate our claim, we apply two spatial models of coalition-formation to the data collection forming the empirical basis to this volume. Our theoretical approach builds upon earlier work by DeSwaan (1973); McKelvey *et al* (1978); and Axelrod (1970; 1997). We use two models in this chapter which are both based on a notion of possible conflict within a coalition. Both models constitute a multi-dimensional elaboration of the conflict of interest model as presented by Axelrod (1970). The models follow mainstream research by measuring 'distance' as Euclidean distance (although other approaches might be justified). Both are based on the behavioural assumption that actors strive to form coalitions with minimal conflict. However, both models measure conflict in a different way. The models predict coalitions and their respective policy outcomes.

In the empirical application of the models, we consider the weights of the players as the product of capability and salience. We use Shapley Shubik indices as capability scores. For the Council, we distinguish between qualified majority and unanimity as voting rules. These rules, together with the consent of the Commission, determine the set of winning coalitions under the consultation procedure, whereas for decision-making subject to co-decision, the consent of the EP is also required. The policy outcomes predicted by our models are simply the balance points of the winning coalitions with minimal conflict.

The results of the application of the models to European politics show that in this field of politics consensus building indeed is important. Both conflict models provide relatively accurate forecasts of EU policy outcomes indeed.

8

A procedural exchange model of EU legislative politics

THOMAS KÖNIG AND SVEN-OLIVER PROKSCH

8.1 INTRODUCTION

In mid-1996, the Commission initiated a package of proposals on food products known as the 'breakfast directives', proposing regulations on honey, preserved milk, certain sugars, fruit juices and jams. Aiming to facilitate the free movement of these products in the internal market, the breakfast directives were typical examples of regular European Union legislative decision-making. The Commission sought to simplify existing legislation by harmonising the labelling of food products in the EU. Due to three disputed issues, the directive relating to honey was the last one of the package to be the object of political agreement. The final decisions on the three contested issues were taken at the working group level of the Internal Market Council. One of these issues was about the scope of implementing powers to be conferred upon the Commission through the comitology procedure, raising particular concerns by the United Kingdom and the Nordic countries. The other issues referred to the labelling and denomination of low quality honey. In the end, mutual concessions were made to member states on some issues to ensure their agreement on the directive as a whole. For instance, Germany and the UK obtained generous exceptions regarding the labelling of their products, while the other member states attached less importance to this issue because of the progress made on the other parts of the directive.

Similar examples have often been observed by case studies, which reveal two characteristics of EU legislative decision-making:

1. Member states and the Commission link issues within proposals in particular policy areas (Mattila and Lane 2001). This multi-issue packaging is promoted by the ministerial resort principle in the Council of Ministers, which establishes sectoral relationships

with mutual exchange opportunities (Hayes-Renshaw and Wallace 1997).

2. While political exchanges on issues of a Commission proposal are facilitated at the sectoral level, the vertical decision-making structure of the Council of Ministers shifts the real lawmaking work to the committee system at the working group level (Van Schendelen 2002). This suggests that the roughly 300 working groups induce stability by breaking up complex multi-issue packages into issue-by-issue voting (Shepsle 1979).

Although these features are often cited in the literature, it is a different question whether a formal approach can accurately model this sectoral two-stage decision-making process, in which member states and the Commission first exchange their views at the proposal level, and then take decisions on the issue outcomes through their experts in these working groups. Compared to our structural induced equilibrium view of the Council's committee system, other studies have used either a strong agenda-setter perspective (Crombez 1996; Steunenberg and Selck in Chapter 3 of this book), or introduced a bargaining view in their procedural analysis in order to find an equilibrium solution (Tsebelis and Garrett 2000; Tsebelis 2002; Widgrén and Pajala in Chapter 9 of this book). In this chapter, we present a procedural exchange model that first considers proposal-specific exchanges between member states and the Commission and then the final issue-by-issue voting on outcomes. We examine whether our two-stage model better predicts the final outcome of the issues than the exchange model of Coleman/König (König 1997) and the procedural model of Tsebelis/Garrett (Tsebelis and Garrett 2000).

One major goal of our analysis is to test our procedural exchange model against the predictive power of alternative sophisticated explanations of EU decision-making. Like Widgrén and Pajala in Chapter 9, we also intend to increase the accuracy of our modelling by using a two-step approach. This might reduce the risk of procedural analyses of over-emphasising the one-shot, inter-institutional power relationship between the Commission, the member states and the European Parliament (EP).[1]

[1] Procedural models assume that actors act as if they were in a one-shot game and reach decisions instantaneously: depending on the agenda-setter's proposal, they are reduced to either voting for changing the *status quo* or rejecting the proposal (Crombez 1996; Moser 1996; Steunenberg 1994a; Tsebelis 1994). Under these closed-rule conditions, identifying the agenda-setter and the reference point is the most crucial step in the procedural analysis (see Steunenberg and Selck in Chapter 3).

Following Coleman (1990) we assume an open-rule process, in which actors enhance their welfare by optimising the allocation of those resources that control the issue outcomes. Our model, however, differs from other exchange models in two important ways. First, unlike Coleman (1990) and König (1997), we explicitly consider the procedural aspects of EU legislative decision-making, such as provisions for agenda-setting and veto powers in the legislative framework of the EU. Second, and in contrast to the model of exchanging policy positions forwarded by Arregui, Stokman and Thomson in Chapter 5, we refer to the exchange of resources, which control the outcomes of the issues. According to Coleman (1990), we conceive the right to vote as partial control of an issue outcome that can be exchanged in relation to the actors' interests. This allows us to derive equilibrium solutions for the final control distribution with respect to the budget of the actors and the price of resources for controlling the issue outcomes.

Our two-step perspective introduces a new conception of EU legislative decision-making. We assume that the Commission makes the first move by initiating multi-issue proposals, which raise member states' expectations on the issue outcomes.[2] These expectations motivate member states and the Commission to exchange their resources in the Council deliberations, because actors are better off when controlling those issue outcomes they are more interested in. In order to model this two-step process, we conceive of preferences as being multi-issue, which are transformed into exchange expectations with respect to the actors' (weighted) distances to the Commission's first-mover proposal. In the final voting stage, we refer to the committee system of the Council and apply the one-dimensional spatial model of legislative choice to assess whether our exchange model predicts the issue outcomes more accurately than the procedural model of Tsebelis and Garrett (2000) and the extended exchange model of Coleman (1990). Hereby, we distinguish between qualified majority voting (QMV) and unanimity in the Council in the consultation procedure. In the co-decision procedure, the EP and the Council determine the issue outcomes, because the result must find the approval of a majority in the Parliament and the required qualified majority of votes in the Council.

[2] In contrast to our first mover concept, procedural scholars either provide the Commission with strong gate-keeping powers (Steunenberg 1994a) or exclude it from the legislative process (Garrett and Tsebelis 1997).

The chapter is structured as follows: in Section 8.2 we present our approach and introduce our procedural exchange model as well as the two competing models. Following this we outline our research design in Section 8.3 and explain how we used and coded the key variables. In order to provide intuitive insight into our approach, we illustrate the preconditions and logic of our procedural exchange model in a case study of the honey directive proposal. Finally, we discuss the predictions of our procedural exchange model, comparing them to the Coleman and Tsebelis/Garrett models, and draw some conclusions on the analysis of EU legislative decision-making.

8.2 EXCHANGE AND VOTING: COMBINING COLEMAN/KÖNIG AND TSEBELIS/GARRETT

Our motivation for combining the Coleman/König exchange model with the Tsebelis/Garrett procedural model is twofold: in the EU literature, many empirical reports point to exchanges in EU decision-making as well as to the multi-level committee system of the Council of Ministers. This committee system includes the Council meetings of ministers at the top level, the committee of permanent representatives (COREPER) at the intermediate level, and the working groups at the lower level. Usually, exchanges on Commission proposals do not result in a solution, but indicate a possible compromise among member states and between them and the Commission (Mattila and Lane 2001; Van Schendelen 2002: 77). Lewis (2000) calls these meetings a dealing room for exchanges.[3] Instead of being outvoted, some countries may offer to compromise on another policy issue in return for the others' votes (Brams 1975; Tollison and Willet 1979). Such exchange processes are often-cited strategies for situations in which a procedural one-shot view would predict rejection (Baron 1991; Gilligan and Krehbiel 1995; Stratmann 1997).[4] However,

[3] Empirical studies on EU decision-making often describe such exchange processes and criticise the procedural models for overestimating the supranational influence of the Commission and/or the EP, while outcomes are often located in the consensus set of the member states (König and Pöter 2001). In their quantitative analysis, Mattila and Lane (2001) observe that member state consensus is much more frequent than expected. They conclude from this that exchanges are particularly likely in the Council. Member states favouring policy change have an incentive to bargain with others.

[4] Theoretical studies on constitutional logrolling have already discussed how chamber size and voting rule affect the member states' ability to exchange votes (Carrubba and Volden 2000), and whether exchanges may explain Commission appointments (Crombez 2000c).

exchanges do not necessarily lead to advantages for all the actors under majority rule (Riker and Brams 1973; Tullock 1959). Therefore, we examine whether exchanges can better explain EU legislative decision-making than existing approaches do.

8.2.1 The Tsebelis/Garrett spatial model

One of the most established of these approaches is the spatial model of legislative choice. Due to its relative simplicity and versatility, scholars of the European Union and of US Congress alike have applied it to legislative decision-making processes. The spatial model of legislative choice is a useful tool for analysing the impact of institutions on legislative decision-making outcomes (see Chapter 3 by Steunenberg and Selck). To apply this approach, it is necessary to characterise the nature of the policy choices, to identify the policy positions of the actors, to make assumptions about their behaviour and their information level, and to define the equilibrium solution (Krehbiel 1988: 260). The policy choices are uni- or multidimensional, and each actor has an ideal policy position in the policy space, that is, this policy choice yields greater benefits to the actor than all other policy choices. Each actor's preferences are single-peaked, meaning that as policy choices move away in any direction from his ideal policy position, then the utility for this actor never increases. For convenience, utility functions are assumed to be symmetric, that is, for any two policy choices y and z in the policy space, an actor prefers the policy which is closer to his ideal policy position.

Compared with voting models, the spatial model of legislative choice considers the agenda-setting and veto rights of legislative decision-makers. These rights can vary across procedures, and EU procedures can be distinguished by their different distribution of agenda-setting and veto rights. The major institutional actors of EU legislative decision-making are the Commission, the Council and the European Parliament. Since the Rome Treaties in 1957, the Commission and the Council interact in the consultation procedure, either by unanimous or qualified majority voting of member states in the Council. The Commission initiates all legislation, but the Council, even when deciding by qualified majority voting, can amend the proposals by unanimity. This is why Tsebelis and Garrett (2000) focus on the unanimous reversion point in the case of qualified majority voting in the Council. The Commission makes proposals, which are not only closest to its preferences and adopted by at least a qualified majority in the Council, but which also take into account a possible counter-proposal by the unanimity of the member states. The second prominent legislative procedure is the co-decision procedure, which was introduced by the Maastricht Treaty in 1992 and modified by the Amsterdam Treaty in 1997. In this procedure, the Council and the European Parliament must adopt the Commission's proposal. According to Tsebelis (2002: 265), the Council and the European Parliament bargain on equal footing over the final outcome.

8.2.2 *The Coleman/König exchange model*

The starting point for Coleman's exchange model (Coleman 1966a; 1990) are general situations of social choice: multiple actors have to commonly decide whether or not to adopt a proposal. At the micro level, Coleman assumes that each individual actor has a relative interest in the issues of the proposal and that their outcome is uncertain. At the macro level, no actor alone can control the outcome of the issues. Under these conditions, actors can exchange their partial control of issues they are less interested in for control of issues they are more interested in.

The model's basic variables are actors' preferences on issues and their resources controlling the outcomes of them (see Appendix, equations 8.1–2). This draws our attention to the definition and measurement of preferences and resources. In order to derive the control resources of legislative actors on issue outcomes, Knoke *et al* (1996) combine formal and informal resources in a comparative analysis of legislative systems (see Appendix, equations 8.3–5). They conceive a voting arena with issues a that includes all actors i having the formal right to vote on issue outcomes O_a. Since the formal voting resources are part of the exchange process, the idea is to model them as endogenous parameters of decision-making, which are fixed (a priori) parameters with possible effects on outcomes (Snidal 1994: 456).[5]

In addition to resources, other extensions of the original Coleman model have focused on actors' preferences with respect to the external costs of majority voting, which are an endogenous element of actors' exchange considerations (König 1997; Pappi and Henning 1998). According to König (1997), who includes actors' policy positions and saliencies, the likely decision outcome of the original Coleman model is

[5] They are initially given exogenously as voting resources, but since they can be exchanged, they are endogenous parameters in the process.

determined by the relative majority of the control resource distribution (see Appendix, equations 8.6–7). These are the external costs of majority voting, and actors consider these costs by deriving expectations on behalf of the weighted distances between their policy positions and the likely outcomes (see Appendix, equation 8.8). In our model, these expectations refer to the weighted distances between the actors' policy positions and the Commission proposal (see Appendix, equation 8.9).

According to Coleman (1990), two aspects are crucial for actors' simultaneous exchange choices: the individual budget of an actor and the value of the issues. The values of the issues result from the saliencies of the controlling actors: the more actors are interested in an issue, the higher is the relative value of the resources that control the issue's outcome (see Appendix, equations 8.11–13). Under these conditions, the equilibrium is determined by the total weighted demand, assuming that actors use their individual budgets to maximise their utility by exchanging resources in relation to the issues' values (see Appendix, equation 8.14). Since all elements of exchange – actors' interests, their individual budget and the value of issues – are standardised, the total final resource allocation for each issue also sums up to 1 ($\Sigma_a R^*_{ai} = \Sigma_a s'_{ia}(p_i / w_a) = 1$, see Appendix). The policy position with the relative majority of the final resources is the predicted outcome.

8.2.3 A procedural exchange model of EU legislative politics

Both approaches, the Coleman/König exchange and the Tsebelis/Garrett spatial approach, conceive EU decision-making as a one-step process: actors either exchange or vote on the issues of a Commission proposal. In our procedural exchange model, we propose to model EU decision-making as a two-step process. In the first step, we argue that the Commission makes the first move and that the Council of Ministers and the Commission engage in a subsequent exchange of issue control resources. At this stage, we introduce a first-mover exchange model of actors' resources, which control the outcome of contested issues. In the second step, we focus on the procedural aspect of EU legislative decision-making, contending that member states (under co-decision together with the EP) vote on the final issue outcome. Sophisticated procedural analyses are non-cooperative models, which are applied to either one-dimensional or multidimensional policy spaces (Moser *et al* 2000; Tsebelis 2002; Selck and Steunenberg, Chapter 3). As mentioned earlier, we apply the one-dimensional variant of the spatial model with cooperative features in the co-decision procedure as proposed by Tsebelis/Garrett (Tsebelis and Garrett 2000; Tsebelis 2002).

Resource exchanges in the Council. In our procedural exchange model, the Commission is the first mover by initiating a multi-issue proposal. Member states derive expectations on the basis of their policy positions and the Commission's proposal. Each actor may also weight the different issues by his salience, which is individually distributed over the issues of the proposal. We assume that member states derive their expectations from their distances to the Commission proposal. These Euclidean distances are weighted when member states have different saliencies on the issues of the proposal. Furthermore, we assume that actors' exchange behaviour is risk-averse. Thus, we attribute higher expectations to member states whose policy positions are similar to that of the Commission.

On the basis of their expectations, member states exchange resources, which control the multi-issue outcomes. In a simple world with two member states and two issues, such exchanges may offer easy coordination: if two member states have different saliencies on two issues, they may make concessions on their less salient issue in order to gain support on their more salient issue. In more complex situations with many actors and issues, such exchanges depend on simultaneous choices made by the actors interested in the issue outcomes. The exchanges lead to a final resource allocation that is used to identify pivotal member states for qualified majority voting in the Council.[6]

Structure-induced equilibrium: one-dimensional voting in the working groups. Decision-making in the Council has become an increasingly specialised process. Ministers meet only a few times a year, and the real decision-making work is done at the working group level (de Zwaan 1995). COREPER and ministers usually transfer decision-making to the roughly 300 working groups made up of civil servants from the member states.[7] Even if the ministers or the COREPER discuss an open issue, they

[6] In one-dimensional Commission proposals, member states and the Commission do not exchange resources. Here, we calculate their initial average of (formal and informal) resources according to which they finally vote in the Council.

[7] The COREPER puts a so-called A-mark on a single proposal or group of proposals if it believes that the ministers, given the required procedure, can accept it. This acceptability of the dossier, however, is explored by the working groups which put a roman I on the dossier. The large majority of COREPER A-dossiers are I-dossiers from the working groups (van Schendelen 2002).

finally send it back to the working groups in order to decide on it. The working groups usually meet once or twice for a straightforward proposal, but for complex and controversial dossiers it can take several months before they are transferred back from the working group to COREPER and the ministers (Council of the European Communities 1990: 25). Hayes-Renshaw and Wallace estimate that around 70 per cent of the legislative business is agreed at working group level, while COREPER decides on 15–20 per cent of the issues and ministers on the remaining 10–15 per cent (Hayes-Renshaw and Wallace 1995: 562). At the working group level, we observe that issue outcomes are predictable and stable, while the multidimensional analysis would predict instability (McKelvey 1976; 1979). This suggests that the working group system induces structural equilibrium by partitioning the multi-issue policy space into subsets of single issues that are voted on one at a time (Shepsle 1979).[8]

In our study, we identify the pivotal actors for each issue according to the procedural setting in play. We derive equilibrium solutions (issue-by-issue core) with respect to the institutional provisions (assignments of issues to the working groups). They define the requirements for finding member state approval in the consultation procedure, or, in the co-decision procedure, a common position after exchange. In the consultation procedure, we consider the unanimous member state as the reversion point, because the Council can overrule the Commission proposal by unanimity (Tsebelis and Garrett 2000, Tsebelis 2002). In the co-decision procedure, the EP and member states determine the final outcome, which must improve both a qualified majority of member states and a parliamentary majority.

Pivotal member states. Our procedural exchange model and the Tsebelis/Garrett model identify the pivotal member states in the Council under qualified majority voting differently. Using the share of the weighted votes, member states are pivotal in the Tsebelis/Garrett model if they control the 26th (for a blocking minority) and the 62nd weighted vote (for a qualified majority) out of the total 87 votes. Correspondingly, the procedural exchange model considers member states to

[8] This also means that preference outlying working groups may lead to inefficient policies that favour special interests (Shepsle and Weingast 1984; Weingast and Marshall 1988).

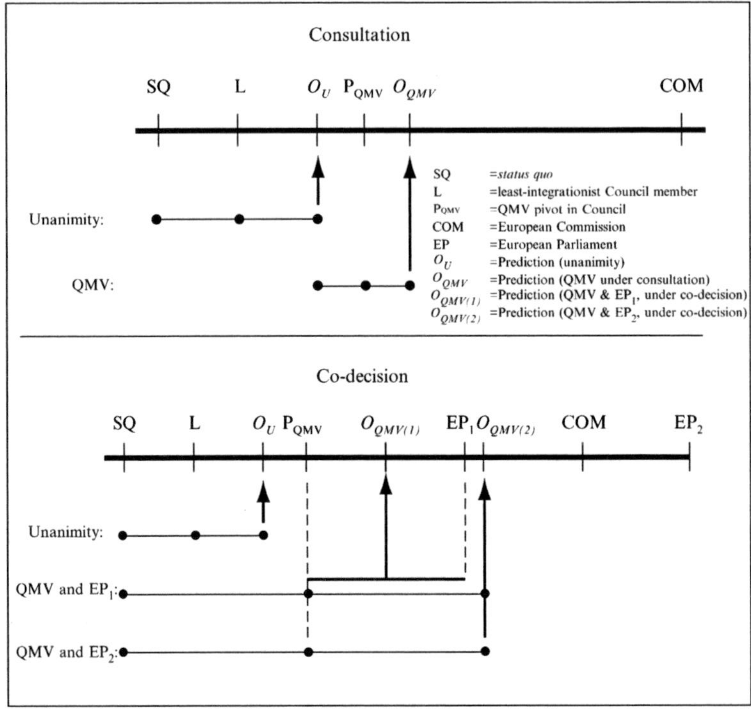

Figure 8.1. The one-dimensional model

be pivotal if they control a 26/87 and a 62/87 share of the final allocated resources.[9]

In Figure 8.1, we present the one-dimensional model, which we use for predicting the issue outcomes. It differs from other spatial analyses in the conception of the reference point (König and Pöter 2001).[10] We compare the consultation procedure with the more complex co-decision procedure, assuming that the Commission and the European Parliament are unitary actors, or can be represented by the median Commissioner and the median member of parliament respectively. The Council is a collective actor consisting of the 15 member states with weighted votes.

[9] We use the definition of qualified majority voting (QMV) that applied to the period of our data sample. Our model could easily be modified to take into account alternative definitions of QMV (as set by the Nice Treaty or the EU Constitution) as well as an enlarged Council of Ministers.

[10] Tsebelis/Garrett use the unanimous win-set because member states can unanimously modify a qualified majority, while others define the *status quo* as being the reference point.

All actors have Euclidean preferences and, like Tsebelis and Garrett (2000: 15), we assume a supranational preference scenario in our example in Figure 8.1. This means that the Commission and the European Parliament are more integrationist than any member of the Council and the *status quo* is to the left of the least integrationist member state in the Council.[11]

Consultation. The consultation procedure is the standard legislative procedure and involves only the Commission and the Council in the decision-making process. As the agenda setter, the Commission (COM) seeks to move the *status quo* as close as possible towards its own ideal position. Under qualified majority voting (QMV), the Commission must consider a unanimous overrule by the member states. Hence, the Commission proposal takes into account the preference of the pivotal Council member (P_{QMV}) and a potential unanimous counter-proposal of the Council. The pivotal member state only accepts a solution until point O_{QMV}, where it would be indifferent to the unanimity outcome O_U or the Commission proposal. Thus, the model predicts O_{QMV} as the final outcome. Under unanimity, both models assume that the Commission makes a proposal closest to its policy position taking into account the least-integrationist member state. Thus, the final outcome prediction is point O_U: it makes the least-integrationist Council member (L) indifferent to the *status quo* (SQ).

Co-decision. Following Tsebelis and Garrett (2000), we conceive of the co-decision procedure as a bargaining game between the Council pivot and the European Parliament. In our procedural exchange model, the Commission initiates a proposal as in the consultation procedure, and member states and the Commission agree upon a common position by exchange. After this common position has been agreed upon, the European Parliament and the pivotal member state bargain on the final outcome. However, they must consider the bicameral support by the EP and the Council, under either unanimity or QMV.

Under qualified majority, the model predicts the outcome half way between P_{QMV} and EP_1, ascribing equal bargaining power to both institutions in the Conciliation Committee. The prediction in this case is $O_{QMV(1)}$. The bargaining space ends when the 'split-the-difference'

[11] The alignment of actors on the single dimension in Figure 8.1 is not part of the model, but just one possible configuration.

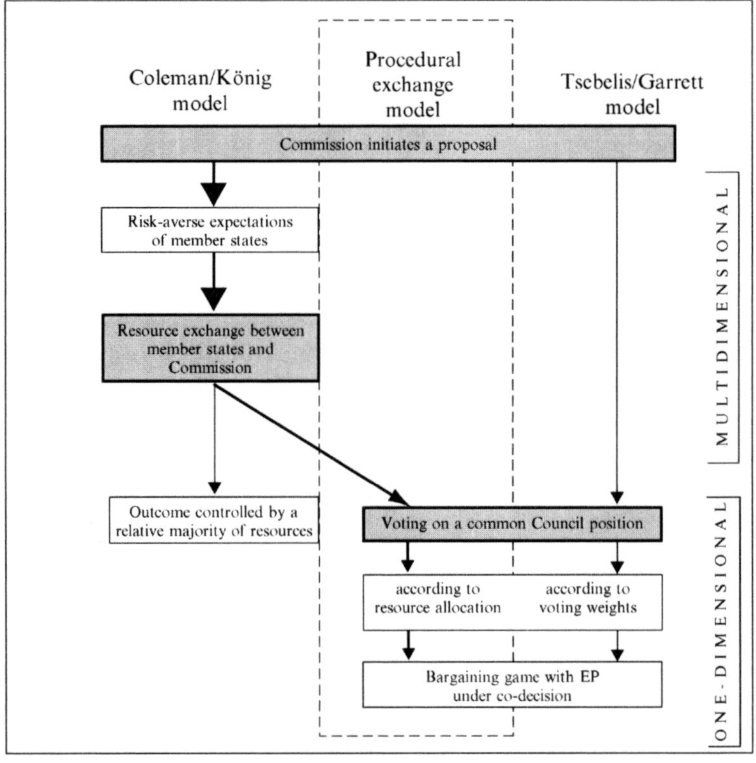

Figure 8.2. Sequences of the procedural exchange model and the reference models

solution makes the Council pivot worse off than the *status quo* (in the second example with EP_2). Then the prediction is located at $O_{QMV(2)}$. Under unanimity, any solution must make the member state closest to the *status quo* better off or at least indifferent (O_U).

In Figure 8.2, we outline the differences between our procedural exchange model and the Coleman/König model as well as the procedural model of Tsebelis/Garrett. After the Commission has made the first move by initiating a proposal, member states derive their expectations about the likely outcome. Given these expectations, we examine whether member states and the Commission exchange their (formal and informal) control resources. The exchange processes lead to an optimised allocation of control resources among member states. The Coleman model only captures this exchange process and does not take account of these procedural provisions. On the other side, the Tsebelis/Garrett spatial model does not capture the step of exchanging control resources. Instead, the model assumes that issue outcomes are decided by member states' vote shares in a one-shot voting game. The procedural exchange model thus combines the two: *voting in the Council occurs according to the issue control resource shares which have been allocated by mutual exchanges.*[12]

Our procedural exchange model and the Tsebelis/ Garrett model base their predictions on the location of actors' policy positions and use the same procedural algorithm to identify the pivotal actors in the different procedures.[13] The main difference between the models concerns the member states they identify as being pivotal.

While exchanges seem uncontroversial if not incontrovertible, there is little empirical knowledge about what is exactly exchanged and what is gained in decision-making. For examining this exchange theory, we must therefore specify what kind of resources are exchanged and the conditions under which the Commission and Council members will and will not adopt a specific allocation of resources. This draws our attention to the concept and measurement of actors' preferences and resources, or more generally, the research design on the key variables of the models.

8.3 RESEARCH DESIGN

Despite their different conceptualisations of the various stages of the decision-making process, the procedural exchange model, the Coleman/ König model and the Tsebelis/Garrett model offer explanations of the final outcomes of the contested issues. Their point predictions are related to the dependent variable of issue outcomes, which have been indicated by the experts. In the following section, we show how we specified and operationalised the independent variables of the models. Subsequently, we outline our case selection strategy and present our data sample used for the empirical tests of the models.

8.3.1 Independent variables

The key variables of the two models are listed in Table 8.1. The *status quo* is relevant for the procedural exchange and the Tsebelis/Garrett

12 If a member state has not allocated resources due to the absence of any salience for an issue, it receives its original (pre-exchange) resource share in the voting stage.

13 They also identify the member states with the left-most or with the right-most policy positions (in case of unanimity) and the left- or right pivotal member state (in case of QMV).

Table 8.1. *Variables included in the models*

	Procedural exchange model	Coleman/ König model	Tsebelis/ Garrett model
Dependent variable: policy outcome	X	X	X
Independent variables:			
Status quo	X	–	X
Preferences	X	X	X
Decision rule	X	–	X
Saliencies	X	X	–
Resources	X	X	–
Voting weights	–	–	X

model in the voting phase of the game. As for the outcomes, the *status quo* is located on the policy scale which has been described by the interviewed experts. Actors' **policy positions** are the crucial variable for (a) deriving member states' expectation values in the exchange phase, and (b) determining the pivotal member states in the voting phase of the game.[14]

In addition, the procedural exchange model and Tsebelis/Garrett model take into account the **institutional decision rule**, differentiating between legislative procedures (consultation, co-decision) and the voting rule in the Council (QMV, unanimity). The procedural exchange model and the Coleman/König model also consider actors' saliencies, resources and the dimensionality of the Commission proposal. The latter constitutes an essential element of boundary specification in our model, for we contend that resource exchanges take place only within **Commission proposals.** Multiple issues offer member states and the Commission opportunities to exchange their resources.[15] **Saliencies** are an indicator for an actor's relative interest in the multiple issues of a Commission proposal.

[14] We do not differentiate between dichotomous, rank order or continuous issues. For reasons of increased variance, we rescale the preference values from the original scale (0–100) to a scale ranging from 0 to 1 when calculating the expectation values.

[15] An alternative boundary specification, which we tested as well, is policy area. The argument would run as follows: member states and the Commission meet regularly in specialised Council configurations and therefore have the opportunity to exchange their resources across the issues of several legislative proposals within the same policy area (i.e. agriculture, internal market, etc). However, we believe that the proposal level offers the more convincing conceptual framework for our exchange analysis.

Hence, we standardise them across each proposal, which means that actors can weigh the importance of the proposal issues.

Concerning **resources**, we follow Knoke *et al* (1996) and consider both formal and informal resources. We operationalise this dual concept by a combination of a voting power index and the expert evaluations of capabilities. With regard to formal resources, we apply the Shapley Shubik Index (SSI) for measuring the *ex ante* inter-institutional voting power distribution between the Commission and the member states. Informal resources are measured by the expert judgements on the distribution of actors' capabilities. As for saliencies, we standardise both the formal and informal indicators and assume that actors share their control resources over the issues of each Commission proposal. We exclude the Parliament from our resource calculation because it does not participate in the Council deliberations and hence the resource exchanges.

8.3.2 *Case selection: strategies and samples*

The data set examined here includes 162 issues spread over 66 Commission proposals. We decided to use a sample of 113 issues because we encounter a number of indifferent actors who did not take positions on all issues and missing *status quo* points, which do limit the examination of the predictive power of both approaches. In order to apply the models to reliable data, our strategy to solve the missing value problem was threefold: first, we deleted four issues for which the Commission does not have a policy position, the reason being that the Commission initiates all proposals and is the first mover in the game.[16] Second, we excluded 11 issues with more than four missing values for actors' policy positions; otherwise, recoding would have risked affecting the qualified majority threshold in the Council. Third, in order to recode the remaining missing values, we assumed that actors are indifferent between the legislative *status quo* and the newly introduced Commission proposal. In these cases, we replaced missing values with the mean value between the *status quo* and the Commission's position, which makes actors *de facto* indifferent to either solution.

Another problem concerned missing *status quo* points. Missing *status quo* points may result from either newly introduced policies (at the EU

[16] The interview reports on the four issues on which the Commission did not take a position suggest that member states added these issues to the negotiation after the legislative proposal had been tabled.

Table 8.2. *Case selection: strategy and sample*

	Data sample
Initial number of issues	162
Missing Commission preferences	−4
More than four missing preferences	−11
Remaining missing preferences	[recoded to indifference value]
Missing *status quo* points	−34
Σ =	113

level) and/or the fact that interviewees found it difficult to identify them. We decided to delete issues with a missing *status quo* point and had to remove another 34 issues from the analysis. Table 8.2 summarises our strategies and the final sample. In sum, after removing 49 issues, our final sample contained 113 (instead of 162) issues.

The sample provides the data for our empirical tests of the procedural exchange model and we can now calculate the point predictions for each of the issues. Since the procedural exchange model is a combination of two well-known models in the literature, we compare their results to the predictions of our own model.

8.4 MODEL ILLUSTRATION: EXCHANGES AND VOTING IN THE HONEY DIRECTIVE

In this section, we illustrate our approach with a sample of the three issues of the honey directive proposal. This case illustration intends to introduce the logic of our model. Table 8.3 displays our key variables and predictions for the three contested issues. The first column contains the issue labels. In the subsequent columns, we list the qualified majority pivots for the Tsebelis/Garrett model and for our procedural exchange model. In case of unanimity, actors with the most extreme policy positions are relevant for predicting the outcome in the two procedural models. Moreover, we show the Commission position, the *status quo* point, the position of the European Parliament, the type of procedure and the Council voting rule being used. In the last column, we list the actual issue outcomes and the corresponding model predictions.

Exchange opportunities and voting in the honey directive proposal. In May 2000, after almost three years of debate, the Internal Market

Table 8.3. *The honey directive proposal: pivots, procedures and predictions*[a]

	QMV pivots position									Point predictions		
Issue	Procedural exchange model	Tsebelis/ Garrett model	Unanimity pivot position	COM	SQ	EP	Procedure	Voting	Outcome	Procedural exchange model	Tsebelis/ Garrett model	Coleman model
1	0	20	0	100	0	50	CNS	QMV	60	**0**	40	100
2	40	20	0	80	0	40	CNS	QMV	80	**80**	40	80
3	0	0	0	100	0	50	CNS	QMV	0	**0**	0	100

Note: [a]Proposal introduced as CNS/1996/114.

Council reached political agreement on a proposal concerning honey. As one of the so-called 'breakfast directives', the honey directive proposal had been presented in June 1996 by the Commission. Its aim was to simplify existing legislation by making the rules on the conditions for the production and marketing of honey more accessible, and by bringing them into line with general Community legislation on foodstuffs (Agence Europe 2000). The honey directive had been initiated under the consultation procedure and was subject to a qualified majority vote in the Internal Market Council (European Commission 1996). We therefore concentrate on the events in the Internal Market Council and disregard the European Parliament.

The proposal contained three contentious issues. Figures 8.3a through 8.3c display the preference configurations on the issues as well as the *status quo* (*SQ*), the relevant qualified majority pivots identified by our procedural exchange model (P_{PEM}) and the Tsebelis/Garrett model ($P_{T/G}$), and the most extreme member state position (L). The first issue concerned the inter-institutional relationship (comitology). The Commission, favouring a prominent role in controlling the implementation of the directive, placed great importance on this issue and proposed the advisory committee procedure, which would have granted it the widest implementing powers. However, member states were somewhat reluctant, with the UK and the Nordic countries being most opposed to the introduction of a comitology procedure. They preferred that the Commission would have to introduce new legislation when updating the directive in the future. Other member states took more moderate policy positions on this issue. We have visualised the different policy positions of the actors on this issue in Figure 8.3a.

The second and third issues were of a food-technical nature and were contested due to different member state practices on the production and consumption of honey products. On the second issue, concerning the listing of the origin of the honey on the label, the northern member states preferred the international standard, which does not label the place of origin of honey. In contrast, the southern member states favoured a regional label with certain quality types of honey. Located in between those two extremes were the smaller member states, which supported the country of origin label. We have displayed this preference configuration in Figure 8.3b.

The third issue related to the denomination of low quality honey that may be used for industrial production. Countries in which a relatively high quality industrial honey is produced (such as the UK,

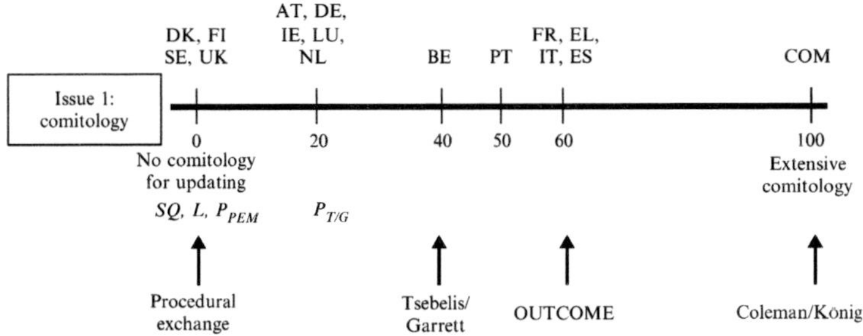

Figure 8.3a. The 'comitology' issue of the honey directive

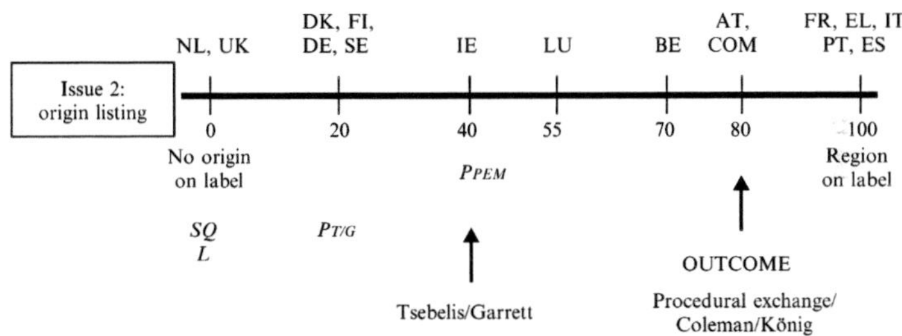

Figure 8.3b. The 'origin listing' issue of the honey directive

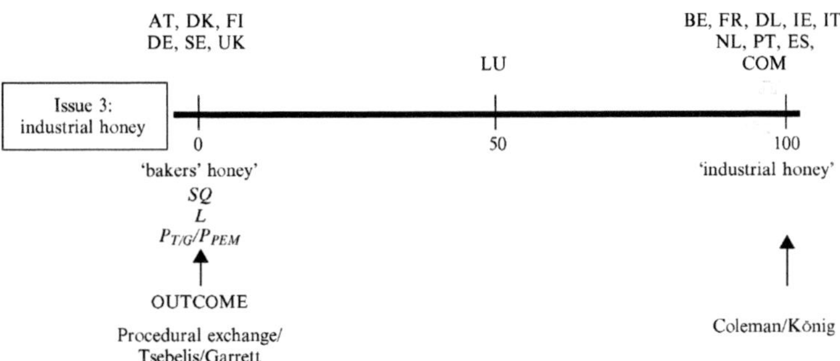

Figure 8.3c. The 'industrial honey' issue of the honey directive

Germany or Austria) insisted that this kind of honey should be referred to as 'baker's honey'. They were supported by the Nordic countries, which did not have a particular interest in this issue, but considered this as a case for applying the subsidiarity principle. Opposed to this solution were the southern and smaller member states (and the Commission) who wanted to make industrial honey clearly distinguishable from consumers' honey. The preference distribution for this issue is shown in Figure 8.3c.

Resource exchange. Did member states and the Commission have the opportunity to exchange their resources? In order to assess our assumption on exchange possibilities, we calculate actors' individual demand for and supply of issue control resources. In equilibrium, the total demand values equal the total supply values for each issue (König 1992). Thus, a positive value indicates that an actor has excess demand for issue control, whereas a negative value refers to an actor's excess supply. According to Table 8.4, the Commission had clearly the greatest excess demand for control on the issue of comitology. The countries most opposed to the Commission proposal also demanded issue control, since they were very interested in the issue but unable to control the issue outcome. All the

Table 8.4. *Control demand and supply for issues of the honey directive proposal (Internal Market Council)*

	Honey directive[a]		
Comitology	Origin listing	Labelling of industrial honey	
Austria	−358	52	305
Belgium	−742	46	696
Denmark	127	−310	182
Finland	445	−104	−341
France	−448	907	−459
Germany	530	−1112	582
Greece	−557	601	−44
Ireland	−346	−282	629
Italy	−657	978	−321
Luxembourg	85	392	−476
Netherlands	−402	136	267
Portugal	−671	541	129
Spain	−753	503	250
Sweden	562	−131	−431
United Kingdom	−277	−617	894
Commission	3461	−1600	−1861

Note: [a]A positive value indicates an actor's excess demand for issue control and a negative value an actor's excess supply of issue control. This effective demand of actor i for issue a results from the difference between the expectation s'_{ia} weighted by influence p_i, and the control r_{ia} weighted by the price w_a for issue a: $d_{ia} = ((s'_{ia}\ p'_i) - ((r_{ia}w'_a)'))\times 100000$ (the multiplication is for illustrative purposes).

other member states had excess supply. The situation is different for the second issue, where Germany, the UK and the Commission had excess supply of control resources. The other member states, by contrast, were demanding issue control, with Italy and France having the greatest excess demand values. Regarding the industrial honey issue, the values are similar to those of the first issue. Again, the Commission could offer many resources, whereas the UK, Belgium, Ireland, and Germany were among those demanding control over the issue outcome.

Thus, we find a number of exchange opportunities for the Commission and member states. In the context of the honey directive proposal, Germany, for instance, could use its excess supply on the second issue to get control over the first and last issue outcome. Similarly, the Commission could make concessions on the last two issues to receive control over the comitology issue. Confirming this, the qualitative data in the interview report indicates that member states were aware of these opportunities. In particular, other member states were quite prepared to grant the UK and Germany the concession they needed in order to ensure their support on the other issues and on the directive as a whole (interview with official from a permanent representation, 5 October 2000).

Voting in the Council. In the next step, we determine the pivotal policy positions for each issue. We do this by summing up the resources, i.e. issue control shares, until we have reached the necessary qualified majority threshold of 71.3 per cent (62 out of 87). The data structure of the issues collapses the differences between the models. The preference configurations on the issues cause similar *pivotal policy positions* despite dissimilar *pivotal member states* (Table 8.3).

Supporting our assumption of one-dimensional voting at the lower Council level, the COREPER dealt with the honey directive proposal and sent it to the working group to work out a compromise (Council of the European Union 2000). The arrows in Figure 8.3a-c indicate the point predictions generated by the procedural exchange model, the Tsebelis/Garrett model, and the Coleman/König model. On the first issue of comitology, the Tsebelis/Garrett model predicts closest to the final outcome. On the second and third issues, the procedural exchange model is the correct predictor of the outcomes. Note that the Coleman/König exchange model predicts the Commission position as the final outcome in all three cases.

In short, our illustration reveals two important aspects of decision-making. First, member states and the Commission do have exchange opportunities in the Council. We find incentives for exchanges with respect to excess demand for and excess supply of issue control. Second, resource exchanges can lead to a resource allocation of control with different pivotal member states but similar pivotal policy positions. Thus, similar pivot and outcome predictions of the Tsebelis/Garrett and the procedural exchange models are likely to be caused by the structure of the policy positions found in the data.

8.5 RESULTS: PREDICTIVE ACCURACY OF THE PROCEDURAL EXCHANGE MODEL

This section presents our findings from the empirical tests of the models. We apply our procedural exchange model and the two reference models (the Tsebelis/Garrett spatial model and the Coleman/König exchange model) to the sample of 113 issues from the data set. Table 8.5 shows the predictive power of the models in the form of average absolute errors across the issues.[17]

Overall, the procedural exchange model has the lowest error of all three models, with an average deviation of about 30 points on the 100-point scale. Yet the difference between this and the other models is quite small. Once we control for the different legislative procedures and voting rules being used, we find more differences between the models.

We first control for issues which were subject to **qualified majority voting.** Here, the two procedural models may determine different pivotal

Table 8.5. *Average absolute error: procedures and voting rule*

Model	All issues (n=113)	CNS QMV (n=38)	CNS unan. (n=19)	COD QMV (n=45)	COD unan. (n=11)
Procedural exchange model	30.01	30.87	28.79	29.09	32.91
Tsebelis/Garrett Model	31.28	30.21	28.79	32.84	32.91
Coleman/König model	32.50	34.26	20.89	36.49	30.18

[17] We also tested an alternative version of our procedural exchange model, which assigns the agenda-setting power to the Council Presidency and not to the Commission. However, our final results remain stable and we therefore do not report these additional findings here.

positions in the Council, and hence predict different outcomes. Under the consultation procedure, the Tsebelis/Garrett model and the procedural exchange model are good predictors of the issue outcomes. Again, the Coleman/König model has the highest average error. The results for the more complex co-decision procedure, which involves the European Parliament as an additional legislative actor, underscore the high explanatory power of our two-stage model *vis-à-vis* the reference models. The predictions of the procedural exchange model are on average closest to the final outcomes. These numbers suggest that our combination of resource exchange and voting provides a better understanding of the complex bicameral legislative decision-making procedure in the European Union.

We move on to scrutinise the **unanimity** procedures. To reiterate, the procedural exchange model and the Tsebelis/Garrett model make the same predictions for issues subject to unanimity, because the most extreme positions in the Council are pivotal. The results in Table 8.5 show that the Coleman/König exchange model performs exceptionally well under this consensus rule. This is in contradiction to our expectation of the lowest common denominator.

These findings suggest two conclusions. First, the procedural exchange model and the Tsebelis/Garrett model have a similar predictive power, with the latter model performing slightly better under consultation and the procedural exchange model performing best under the co-decision procedure. Second, the modelling of veto rights under unanimity does not sufficiently capture EU legislative decision-making. The Coleman/König exchange model outperforms both procedural models for the issues subject to member state unanimity.

How do these results change when we control for specific policy areas? None of the models makes specific assumptions about the nature of a policy area. Table 8.6 compares the predictive power of the models for the two largest policy areas in the dataset, agriculture and internal

Table 8.6. *Average absolute error: policy areas*

Model	Agriculture (*n*=27)	Internal market (*n*=29)	Other policy areas (*n*=57)
Procedural exchange model	29.07	31.90	29.49
Tsebelis/Garrett model	30.67	35.21	29.58
Coleman/König model	36.22	46.72	23.51

Table 8.7. *Average absolute error: level of measurement*

Model	Dichotomous (n=20)	Rank order (n=83)	Scale (n=10)
Procedural exchange model	40.00	27.93	27.30
Tsebelis/Garrett model	35.00	30.87	27.30
Coleman/König model	40.00	31.33	27.30

market. In agriculture, the procedural exchange model and the Tsebelis/ Garrett model do better than the Coleman/König model, although the values are again quite similar. For the internal market issues, we find more deviation and the procedural exchange model has again the highest predictive power.

Regarding the scaling of the issues, we would expect that our models perform better on continuous (scale) than on dichotomous issues. Table 8.7 confirms our expectation, and all the models significantly improve their predictions of outcomes on rank order and continuous issues.

8.6 CONCLUSION

In this chapter, we introduced a procedural exchange model and tested its predictive power against the accuracy of competing approaches, the Tsebelis/Garrett spatial model and the Coleman/König exchange model. We developed our two-step procedural exchange model along the lines of the EU decision-making literature and the institutional arrangement of the Council committee system. Together, these suggest exchanges among member states and the Commission in the first stage, and issue-by-issue voting at the working group level in the second stage. We operationalised this model with respect to further claims on EU decision-making, in particular on the proposal boundaries of this process. Our model contains the *status quo*, actors' policy positions, their saliencies and resources, which control the issue outcomes in each Commission proposal. In total, we were able to apply our approach to the outcomes of 113 issues.

The pros and cons of our approach were illustrated before presenting our final results. The example of the honey directive issues showed that member states and the Commission had considerable exchange opportunities. However, we found large similarities between all models. Even though the models identified different member states as being pivotal, their policy positions were often the same. This suggests that our model comparison is dependent on the structure of actors' policy positions found in the data.

Our final results confirm our hunch. The most notable restriction on the models' accuracy is the scaling level. Unfortunately, many issues are dichotomous, and the error term drastically increases with a lower level of measurement. This does not mean that the models cannot correctly predict the issue outcomes. By contrast, the models perform quite well in their predictions, but the data seem to restrict the comparative evaluation of the models. The model predictions only differ in quality when looking more closely at the institutional settings. Outcomes in the consultation procedure are best explained by the Tsebelis/ Garrett model. The procedural exchange model is the best predicting model for the more complex co-decision procedure. Furthermore, majority voting issues can be better captured with procedural models, whereas unanimity issues are better explained by the Coleman/ König exchange model.

On the one hand, these findings seem to confirm the scepticism about empirical research in general and comparative testing of models in particular. Of course, we spent time and effort in the development of the models and the operationalisation of their key variables. We certainly expected to provide more evidence for one of the examined approaches, or at least to find particular insights into their performance. While we cannot provide a final answer on the better (or even best) approach for the study of EU legislative decision-making, we find that procedural models do perform better in complex institutional settings, while the type of policy area plays a minor role in explaining issue outcomes. However, since the scaling level limits our findings, in particular in the case of dichotomous issues, more research has to be done on measurement instruments of empirical research.

APPENDIX: THE COLEMAN/KÖNIG EXCHANGE MODEL

A.1 The original Coleman model and extensions regarding the type of resources

Let actors i distribute their salience s across all issues a of a Commission proposal k, where $i = 1, \ldots, n$ and $a = 1, \ldots, m$. For each proposal, any actor i is assumed to distribute his salience over all issues a:

$$\sum_{a=1}^{m} s_{ia} = 1, \text{ and} \tag{8.1}$$

the outcomes O of issues a are completely controlled by the resources r of actors i:

$$\sum_{i=1}^{n} r_{ai} = 1. \tag{8.2}$$

This matrix of issue control can be decomposed into a matrix, in which actors i have formal *a priori* voting resources v:

$$\sum_{i=1}^{n} v_{ai} = 1. \tag{8.3}$$

Informally, all actors i may also have capabilities to influence the issue outcomes, i.e. due to their reputation. This is measured by the interviewees' indications of actors' capabilities c on issue outcomes a.

$$\sum_{i=1}^{n} c_{ai} = 1. \tag{8.4}$$

We combine both elements, the formal voting power v_{ai} and the amount of capabilities c_{ai}, to actors' overall resources r_{ai} to control the outcomes of issues a in the first stage:

$$r_{ai} = \frac{v_{ai} + c_{ai}}{2} \text{ with } \sum_{i=1}^{n} r_{ai} = 1. \tag{8.5}$$

The inclusion of policy positions into the original Coleman model

In the original Coleman model, the policy position x_{ia} on issue a of actor i were exogenously given and decided by a probabilistic voting rule.[18] In order to include policy positions, let Y define the issue space of a Commission proposal k. The probability of an issue outcome, which is

[18] Because additional votes lose their value once a simple majority has been reached, the outcome is randomly selected by a legislator (Knoke *et al* 1996: 154). This turns the partial control of an indivisible issue into full control of a portion of the consequences (Coleman 1990: 117).

weighted by resources r_{ai}, is $y \in Y$:

$$P(Z = y) = \prod_{a=1}^{m} \sum_{i=1_{x_{ia}=y_a}}^{n} r_{ai} \tag{8.6}$$

Without the exchange assumption, the likely issue outcome y and actor's i utility loss are:

$$\begin{aligned} &y = y \text{ with } \quad P(Z = y) = \max\{P(Z = y|y \in Y\}, \text{and utility} \\ &u_a(y) = (1 - |x_{ia} - y_a|)^{s_{ia}}. \end{aligned} \tag{8.7}$$

On behalf of their initial preferences and the likely outcome actors i derive expectations s'_{ia}:

$$s'_{ia} = \sum_{y \in Y} P(Z = y) \frac{s_{ia} \frac{1}{e^{|x_{ia} - y_a|}}}{\sum_{a=1}^{m} s_{ia} \frac{1}{e^{|x_{ia} - y_a|}}} \tag{8.8}$$

Under the assumption of risk aversion, a monotone transformation 1/exponential function corresponds to the Maximin principle, according to which actors expect the most unfavourable alternative (König 1997: 158). In the context of the EU, another assumption is that the Commission proposal k is the likely outcome $y \in Y$. In this case, actors i derive their expectations on behalf of their initial preferences and the Commission proposal k_{ia}:

$$s'_{ia} = \frac{s_{ia} \frac{1}{e^{|x_{ia} - k_{ia}|}}}{\sum_{a=1}^{m} s_{ia} \frac{1}{e^{|x_{ia} - k_{ia}|}}} \tag{8.9}$$

Having derived the expectations of actors s'_{ia}, the exchange follows the steps described in Coleman (1990; 682). In a competitive equilibrium, the total supply L_a of resources equals the value of the issues w_a:

$$L_a = \sum_{i=1}^{n} r_{ai} w_a = w_a. \tag{8.10}$$

Considering the budget p_i of an actor i as its share of weighted control resources

$$p_i = \sum_{a=1}^{m} w_a r_{ai}, \tag{8.11}$$

the total weighted demand D_a for control results from the proportional resource allocation

$$D_a = \sum_{a=1}^{m} r^*_{ai} w_a = \sum_{i=1}^{n} s'_{ia} p_i. \tag{8.12}$$

The equilibrium is determined by L_a and D_a with p_i

$$w_a = \sum_{l=1}^{m} w_l \Big(\sum_{i=1}^{n} r_{ai} s'_{ia}\Big). \tag{8.13}$$

Exchange is accordingly based on expectations s'_{ia}regarding power p and values w with final resource distribution R*

$$R^*_{ai} = s'_{ia} \frac{p_i}{w_a} \text{ by the Cobb – Douglas – function } U_i = \prod_{a=1}^{m} r_{ai}^{s_{ia}}. \tag{8.14}$$

9

Beyond informal compromise: testing conditional formal procedures of EU decision-making

MIKA WIDGRÉN AND ANTTI PAJALA

9.1 INTRODUCTION

Quantitative analysis of European Union decision-making can be divided into two distinct traditions. First, there is a camp representing the cooperative approach; this includes the power index approach, the compromise model and cooperative bargaining and coalition formation models.[1] A common feature of these models is that they do not consider explicitly how the outcome of the decision-making process is arrived at. Instead, it is assumed that a compromise among the actors is reached that is a result of their formal or informal capabilities, their information-gathering capacities, and/or the interaction and coalition formation among them. Using rather general assumptions about these elements, the cooperative approach derives solution concepts that also give predictions of decision outcomes.

As noted in Chapter 4, many studies of governmental decisions divide the process into two stages. The first stage is that of compromise-seeking or coalition-formation and has very few formal rules. The second stage consists of the application of the decision-making procedure, where there are explicit written rules and the sequence of moves is specified. The cooperative approach corresponds roughly with the first stage. It makes either no assumptions concerning the second stage at all, or it (implicitly) assumes

The authors thank all members of the DEU research group for helpful comments and interaction during the project and especially Adrian Van Deemen, Sven-Oliver Proksch and the editors of this book for more detailed comments on earlier drafts.

[1] For applications of power indices to EU decision-making see Widgrén (1994), Kirman and Widgrén (1995), Laruelle and Widgrén (1998), Baldwin *et al* (2001), Felsenthal and Machover (2001b), Leech (2002), Baldwin and Widgrén (2004a; 2004b) and the references therein.

that all aspects of the second stage of relevance to compromises or coalition formation have been taken into account during the first stage of the process. This approach also presumes that the compromises made in the first stage are binding.

The other approach is, not surprisingly, based on non-cooperative game theory, and often (procedural) spatial voting theory.[2] The main focus of analysis in this approach is the formal decision-making procedure. It therefore focuses on the second stage of decision-making. The approach does not rely on binding contracts or compromises during the first stage of the decision-making process; instead, it requires that these be self-enforcing. The key elements of the non-cooperative approach are actors' preferences and formal procedural rules.

In this chapter, we aim to combine elements from both approaches in a model which is essentially a non-cooperative procedural spatial voting game, but which makes use of co-operative elements at the preparatory stage of decision-making.[3] These co-operative elements are assumed to reduce a multi-dimensional policy space in preparation for the formal voting game, which is then played on a modified uni-dimensional policy space. More specifically, we use the base model and the compromise model presented in Chapter 4 to modify the set of possible outcomes in the formal decision-making procedure.

There are at least two rationales behind this kind of model. First, one might suppose that in their pre-play negotiations, the actors want to rule out certain alternatives and simplify their choice set. Quite naturally, the simplification reflects actors' capabilities and the importance of the issues at stake. The reduction of the dimensionality of the policy space might also be due to the fact that decision-makers find it too difficult to handle all the information associated with a multi-dimensional conflict.

[2] An extensive survey of (procedural) spatial models can be found in Chapter 3. Examples are Steunenberg (1994a; 1997; 2000a), Crombez (1996; 1997; 2001), Tsebelis (1994), Moser (1997a), Tsebelis and Garrett (1996; 1997a; 1997b). For a discussion between proponents of cooperative and non-cooperative approaches, see Garrett and Tsebelis (1999a; 1999b; 2001b), Holler and Widgrén (1999) and Felsenthal and Machover (2001a).

[3] There is also a literature in which cooperative solution concepts, like the Shapley value or Nash bargaining solutions, are justified with underlying non-cooperative game forms. For the former see e.g. Gul (1989) or Hart and Mas-Colell (1996) and for the latter Rubinstein (1982). The so-called unified approaches investigate actors' power or success in non-cooperative game forms, but by randomising actors' preferences make the analysis *a priori* (see Steunenberg *et al* 1999; Napel and Widgrén 2004a).

This compels them to take positions on a single conflict dimension. The reduction of the policy space to a single dimension implies that all dimensions or issues in a proposal are handled together. This means that decision-making is assumed to take place at the proposal level. Within each proposal, actors' power, their issue-by-issue policy positions and the levels of salience they attach to those issues are assumed to determine the basis for the formal proposal-level game.

We believe that this approach provides an accurate picture of decision-making in the EU, where the decisions are essentially made on proposals, and the issues in a proposal taken together form the basis of the negotiations. We do not, however, want to rely completely on pre-play negotiations as predictions of outcomes. For this reason, we incorporate the formal non-cooperative approach in the model. This incorporation makes the formal game, corresponding with the second stage of decision-making, conditional on the pre-play stage.

In the literature, the impetus to our model is the logic behind the Shapley-Owen power index.[4] The index assumes multi-dimensional spatial voting. The model behind the index presumes that actors' ideal policy positions are projected on to a line. This is referred to as the *issues line* and essentially indicates a way in which the dimensions (issues) of a proposal can be combined. The projections of actors' positions on to the issues line gives actors modified policy positions. The actors' positions on the issues line also determine their ordering. In each possible ordering, there are two pivotal players, depending on the direction in which one counts.[5] Pivotal players are assumed to exert power. Considering all lines (directions) in the multi-dimensional policy space, we obtain several orderings of actors. Each actor's *a priori* power is then defined as its share of pivotal positions of the total number of pivotal positions.

In this chapter, we modify the Shapley-Owen approach to suit our purposes. Like the Shapley-Owen approach, we use the issues line as the policy space in which the formal game is played. We project actors' ideal policy positions on to a line, and a spatial voting game is then played using these modified positions. An important difference between our

[4] For the theory, see Shapley (1977) or Owen (1995). An application to the US presidential elections is contained in Rabinowitz and MacDonald (1986) and to the EU Council of Ministers in Barr and Passarelli (2004).

[5] Note that these two pivotal players could in fact be the same voter. If the number of voters is odd and each voter has one vote, the absolute majority rule makes one player pivotal, regardless of the counting direction.

approach and that of Shapley and Owen is that in our case the issues line is not random. Rather, we assume that the co-operative stage of the game, i.e. the base model or the compromise model, determines the direction of this line. We also use the reference points from the dataset. The issues line is the line that goes through the reference point and either the base model or compromise model prediction.

The reasoning behind our issues line is the following. We assume that the pre-play bargaining does not necessarily provide the final solution, but rather a general direction towards which the solution is moving. This direction is determined by actors' policy positions, power and salience, and determines the way in which the issues are weighted in the final decision. In the spirit of non-cooperative games, the base model and compromise model predictions are not necessarily binding, and that is why they are not used as predictions. Nevertheless, these predictions do contain information about the factors relevant to determining the direction towards which the final solution is moving, relative to the legislative *status quo*.

In the first of our models, players' ideal points weighted by power determine the direction of a solution. In the second, their ideal points weighted by power and salience on each issue together determine the direction. We use these *a priori* compromises first for predictive purposes, and then as constraints in the second stage of the game, which is a spatial voting game. Our first model can be seen as a modification of the Shapley-Owen approach, which works here as a way of restricting the procedural spatial voting game. The second model uses the same idea, but takes salience into account.

Both our models consist of two stages. One possible interpretation of these two stages is the following. During the first preparatory stage, we assume that the issues are known. Actors represent their ideal policy positions and these are weighted by their power. The actors want to shift the current state of affairs (the reference point) in the direction of their own ideal points, resulting in a compromise direction, which is the power-weighted average of these directions. Power gives each actor the capability of moving this compromise direction towards its own ideal point. Note that this does not require that actors observe the exact ideal points of the other actors, since any multiple of actors' ideal points could give the same issues line. The actors are, however, assumed to represent either their true preferences or the same multiple of them. The resulting direction is also assumed to be binding in the sense that the policy change, if any, is supposed move towards that direction from the reference point. In our first model, the ideal points are weighted by the Shapley Shubik Index (SSI) values and this gives the issues line. Let us refer to this as the SSI-IL model.

Actors typically attach different levels of salience to the issues in each proposal. Incorporating salience gives us the second alternative direction. If an actor attaches more importance to one issue than another, he is supposed to put more weight on the more salient issue when attempting to shift the *status quo* towards his ideal point. In our second model, we assume the salience-weighted ideal point determines the desired direction in which an actor wants to shift the policy outcome. The compromise prediction is used as the power and salience-weighted average of these directions. Let us refer to this as SSSI-IL model.

The second stage of the game is supposed to be played on the issues line. For this reason, the originally preferred policy positions are projected orthogonally onto the issues line, and the procedural voting game is played using these modified ideal points. The issues line, therefore, simply reduces the issues of a proposal to a modified uni-dimensional policy space. The shortest distance between a player's ideal point to his modified ideal point is inversely related to his own power and also luck, in the sense that other players' ideal points might position the compromise line, from his viewpoint, in a desirable direction.

Our model has links to five other models presented in this book. First the determination of the issues line uses the base model and the compromise model (see Chapters 4 and 5). The determination of the issues line is also based on coalition formation possibilities and implicitly on the ideal points of the actors. This links our approach to the cooperative approach applied in Chapter 7. The second phase of our model is a simple uni-dimensional procedural spatial voting game, which links it to Chapter 3 on procedural models. The difference lies, however, in modelling the Conciliation Committee. In terms of modelling spirit, the most similar model to ours is the procedural exchange model of Chapter 8, which is also a two-stage model. The difference is that in our model the first stage is driven by power rather than exchange. Also, the spatial model differs since, although we have a uni-dimensional spatial voting game, it is not run at the issue level, but at the proposal level.

9.2 THE MODELS

The models presented in this chapter are either purely cooperative models or combinations of the cooperative and non-cooperative modelling traditions. In Section 9.5, we give four model predictions. The first is simply the base model and the second the compromise model prediction. The other two models belong to the non-cooperative tradition, since decision-making procedures are modelled as procedural spatial voting games. They do, however, contain an element of the cooperative approach since the policy space of the spatial game is restricted using the base model or the compromise model. The predictions of these models are neither long-run power index estimates nor point predictions of procedural spatial voting models. Instead, they aim to include elements of both. We denote these models by SSI-IL and SSSI-IL.

The Council is modelled as a 15-player voting game in which actors' resources are their voting weights. The European Parliament (EP) and the Commission are assumed to be unitary actors. For illustrative purposes, suppose that member states hold the numbers 1–15, the Commission is numbered by 16 and the EP by 17.

The consultation procedure is modelled in a common way. In the unanimity version, a Commission proposal can be accepted by unanimous agreement in the Council and also amended by a unanimous Council. In the qualified majority version, 62 votes out of 87 are needed for the acceptance of a Commission proposal, and unanimous agreement in the Council is required to pass amendments. In the co-decision procedure, we assume that the procedure can be reduced to Nash bargaining in the Conciliation Committee. This is because the Commission is not able to overrule amendments proposed either by the Council or EP.

In our models, we adopt the following two-stage procedure. We assume that decision-making procedures in the EU can be divided into two phases. The first phase determines the issues line. In practice, this part of the game takes place before the draft proposal is written and it involves all preparatory legislative work. We assume that during that phase, players' capabilities play the most important role. The reference point is normalised to the origin.[6] If the issues line is based on actors' power and policy positions, it is defined for each actor as in equation (4.1) in Chapter 4, i.e. the base model, and hence the issues line is defined as the n-vector of these elements. If we add salience to the determinants

[6] Note that in the original data reference points were not always at the origin. Before our computation we modified these data by subtracting the reference point from ideal points, which moves the origin to the reference point. The equilibrium analysis was carried out using these data. After that, we added the original reference points to the modified predictions in order to return to the original scale.

of the issues line, it is defined as the n-vector of the elements presented in equation (4.2) in Chapter 4 above, i.e. the compromise model.

Concerning the first stage of our models, we argue that actors' ideal policy positions are not known exactly, or that players have incentives to hide or manipulate their ideal points. The direction of their ideal points is, however, observable by all actors. Although the base and compromise model predictions require exact knowledge of actors' ideal points, and these also form the basis of our models, the same issues line can be constructed by any set of ideal points that are multiples of the true ideal points. We thus assume that policy positions or salience-weighted policy positions have an impact on the determination of the issues line. However, this does not require that the exact ideal points are common knowledge; common knowledge consists of the direction in which each of the actors wishes to move the decision outcome relative to the reference point.

Alternatively, one could have argued that a single player, like the Commission as the agenda-setter, is able to select the issues line and even change it during the process. This alternative is, however, subject to criticism. The optimal choice of the issues line then requires exact information on other players' preferences. For this reason, and also due to our desire to add some aspects of bargaining to the preparatory stage, we assume that the issues line cuts through the reference point that is normalised to the origin, and that it also cuts through either the base or compromise model prediction.

By fixing the issues line, we also assume that the outcome lies on this line. We assume that after the issues line has been fixed, actors play a procedural spatial voting game on the issues line, which essentially reduces the dimensionality of the policy space to one. It also means that decision-making is assumed to take place at the level of the proposal, as the issues line is simply a convex combination of all issues in one proposal.

There are two important aspects of the issues line. First, consider a player who is a dictator and an agenda-setter. Then, his ideal point would determine the issues line by his dictatorship. In spatial models, when the other players are in effect dummy players, the optimal proposal of an agenda-setter does not lie on a line connecting the reference point and his ideal point. The dictator agenda-setter simply passes his ideal point. If other players have influence on the outcome they exert power, and the issues line does not necessarily go through agenda-setter's ideal point. If an actor exerts power, the issues line rotates in the direction of that

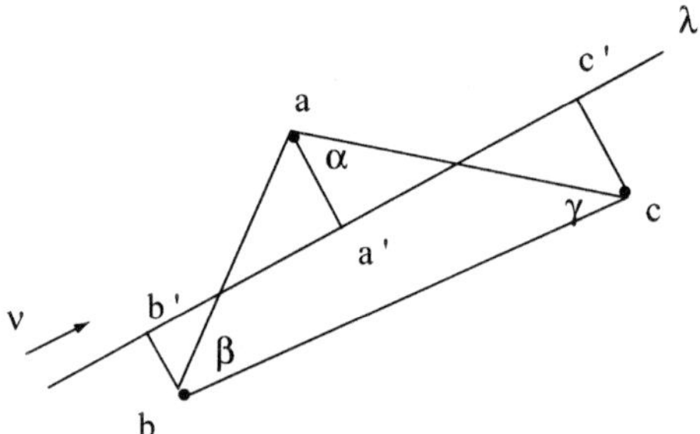

Figure 9.1. Projecting ideal points on to the issues line

player. Since the outcome must lie on the issues line, this means that the outcome also shifts in the same direction. Thus, despite the fact that we measure power using the SSI of coalitional form games, the impact of influence is a shift in equilibrium outcome.[7] The overall effect is a simultaneous shift towards Council members' and the EP's ideal points.

Second, the players are assumed not to be able to renegotiate the issues line. If this were possible, under the consultation procedure the Commission would only take into account the Council pivot whose ideal point is closest to its ideal point. This would correspond with the idea that the pivot is always unique in a single vote. In co-decision, the issues line would be the one connecting the EP and some Council pivot. As the EP has a major role in amending proposals in that procedure, one might suggest that the EP simply picks the pivot closest to its ideal point, but there are also other alternatives.

Figure 9.1 gives a graphical illustration on the first phase of our models. More formally, let λ denote the issues line. We get the modified ideal points x' on the issues line for the players as perpendicular projections of the original ideal points x in a proposal on to the issues line. This means that for each actor we pick the closest point to his ideal point at a proposal level from the issues line as the modified ideal point. These can be found by taking the shortest distance from the original proposal level ideal point to the issues line, i.e. the orthogonal projection. Formally this can be written as follows

[7] This is also how Napel and Widgrén (2002b; 2004a) approach *strategic power.* It is worth noting, however, that the SSI overestimates Council members' power and underestimates the Commission's power in the consultation procedure, since they are credited with power even when the Commission is able to pass its ideal point. In the co-decision procedure the Commission is credited with substantial power despite the fact that its impact on the equilibrium is very limited.

$$x' = \frac{\langle x, \lambda \rangle}{\|\lambda\|^2}\lambda(\text{in SSI-IL}) \text{ or } x' = \frac{\langle x, \lambda^S \rangle}{\|\lambda^S\|^2}\lambda^S(\text{in SSSI-IL})$$

where $\|.\|$ denotes the Euclidian norm and $\langle . \rangle$ is the usual inner product.[8] It is worth noting that the individual rationality constraints regarding the modified ideal points and original ones are the same as far as the outcome is restricted to the positions on the issues line. The equilibrium outcomes can, however, be expressed more directly using modified ideal points. Note that the modified ideal points are only seemingly at a proposal level since the restriction to the issues line weights all issues in one proposal into one direction and the game with modified ideal points is essentially a uni-dimensional spatial voting game.

As an example, consider a three-player spatial voting game with ideal points a, b and c, and suppose there is an issues line λ as in Figure 9.1. Then, the projected ideal points are simply the feet of the projection a', b' and c'. By changing the direction of λ we get different realisations of modified ideal points.

In the spirit of rational choice models, the choice of the issues line is a strategic choice. In the consultation procedure, the obvious stakeholder to make this choice would be the Commission and, in the co-decision procedure, either the Commission or the Council and the EP together, or even the EP alone. In our models we do not follow this approach, but rather adopt the cooperative approach in determining the issues line. This means that all stakeholders have an impact on the direction of the issues line via their capabilities and the levels of salience they attach to the issues. For that, we need one fixed point relative to which the direction is determined. A natural choice for this is the reference point since it represents the current state of affairs that the actors try to change. This immediately implies that our analysis needs a reference point.

Figure 9.2 illustrates the determination of the issues line in a simple three-player, two-issue example. The original ideal policy positions of the actors are denoted by x_1, x_2 and x_3 and their projections by x'_1, x'_2 and x'_3 respectively. The latter are the modified ideal points. The issues line goes through the reference point that is normalised to 0. The determination of the issues line can be understood as a three-step

[8] Let $x=(x_1, x_2)$ and $y=(y_1, y_2)$ be vectors. The Euclidian norm $\|x\|$ of vector x is $\|x\| = |x| = \sqrt{x_1^2 + x_2^2}$ and the inner product of x and y is $\langle x, y \rangle = x_1 y_1 + x_2 y_2$.

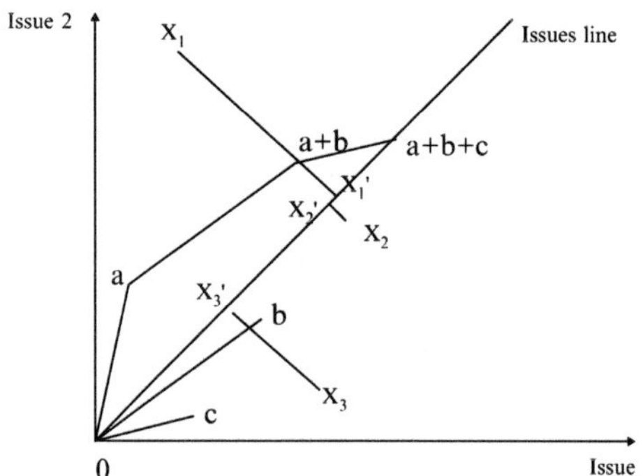

Figure 9.2. The determination of the issues line

procedure. Take the first actor x_1. The line from the origin to point a gives his SSI- or SSSI-weighted ideal point. For player x_2 we get a similar line from 0 to b, and for x_3 from 0 to c. To fix the second point on the issues line we use the sum of these, i.e. $a+b+c$, which is also the base or compromise model, depending on the weight used. The issues line now goes through 0 and point $a+b+c$. When we project the original ideal points on to the issues line we get the modified ideal points x_1', x_2' and x_3' that are used for the second stage of the game.

EU procedures on the issues lines

On the basis of the existing literature on EU procedures as spatial voting games (e.g. Steunenberg 1994a), we identify four types of equilibrium outcome (point prediction) at the proposal level, one for each variant of the two variants—unanimity and QMV—of the two legislative procedures—consultation and co-decision. Let us start with the consultation procedure and define the concept of the Council pivotal player on the issues line. Denote his modified ideal point by $x'_{(p)}$. Since the Commission makes a proposal in the consultation procedure, we can use its modified ideal point x_c' to find the pivot. The Commission's modified ideal point on the issues line can be expressed as

$$x_c' = \frac{\langle x_c, \lambda \rangle}{\|\lambda\|^2} \lambda$$

where λ is either the base or compromise model prediction that determines the issues line and $\|.\|$ denotes the Euclidian norm and $\langle . \rangle$ is the usual inner product as above. Now,

$$x'_i = \frac{\langle x_i, x'_c \rangle}{\|x'_c\|^2} x'_c$$

defines an ordering of Council members on the issues line. Next, define an order statistic (i), $i = 1,\ldots,15$ for the modified ideal points of the Council members on the issues line as follows: $(i) < (j) \Leftrightarrow \langle x_i, x'_c\rangle < \langle x_j, x'_c\rangle$. In the example presented in Figure 9.2 above, $(x_3) < (x_2) < (x_1)$. A player with modified ideal point $x'_{(p)}$ is now pivotal if

$$\sum_{15-(i)=0}^{15-p+1} w_{(i)} \geq Q$$

where Q is the Council vote threshold, i.e. 62 in the majority version and 87 in the unanimity version of the consultation procedure, $w_{(i)}$ is the voting weight of the ith player in the ordering induced by the projection of original ideal points on to the issues line. The predictions at a proposal level depend now on the position of $x'_{(p)}$ relative to the modified ideal point $x'_{(c)}$ of the Commission. If the pivotal player and the Commission's modified ideal points are on opposite sides of the reference point on the issues line, the prediction is the reference point. If they are on the same side and if $\|x'_c - x'_{(p)}\| \geq \|x'_{(p)}\|$, the outcome prediction is $\Omega = 2x'_{(p)}$. In this case the modified ideal point of the pivotal player is closer to the reference point than to the modified ideal point of the Commission. If $\|x'_c - x'_{(p)}\| < \|x'_{(p)}\|$ we obtain the modified ideal point of the Commission as the prediction. In that case, the pivotal player's modified ideal point is closer to the Commission's modified ideal point than to the reference point and hence better in spatial sense. Finally, let $x'_{(1)}$ and $x'_{(15)}$ denote the left-most and right-most modified ideal points in a given ordering. If $\|x'_{(1)}\| > \|x'_c\|$ we get $\Omega = x'_{(1)}$, and if $\|x'_{(15)}\| < \|x'_c\|$ we get $\Omega = x'_{(1)}$ and $\Omega = x'_{(15)}$ respectively. In that case, all Council members' modified ideal points are either further away from or closer to the reference point than the Commission.

In the co-decision procedure, the equilibrium outcome depends mostly on either the position of the extreme or pivotal player in the Council and the modified ideal point of the EP. By backwards induction, bargaining among the Council and EP at the last stage of the procedure, i.e. the Conciliation Committee (CC), determines the sub-game perfect Nash equilibrium outcome. There are several alternative ways to model the CC. Here we simply assume that the outcome in the CC is simply the

Nash bargaining solution in a bargaining game among the median voter in the EP and the Council pivot.[9] The Commission affects the outcome only if the reference point is closer to its modified ideal point than the Nash bargaining solution in the Conciliation Committee. Suppose that the reference point is normalised to origin, let us denote the outcome by Ω, and assume that voters have quadratic utility functions, i.e. $U_i = -(x_i - \Omega)^2$ where x_i refers to the (modified) ideal point of actor i and Ω to the equilibrium outcome. Now, let

$$\Delta U_i = -(x_i - \Omega)^2 + x_i^2$$

denote the difference between actor i's utilities when the utility he receives from the *status quo* prevailing is subtracted from the utility he receives from the actual outcome materialising. The former gives actor i's reservation utility. In the majority version, the Nash bargaining solution is the outcome Ω^* that maximises the Nash product

$$NP = |(x_c')^2 - (x_c^i - \Omega)^2||(x_p')^2 - (x_p^i - \Omega)^2|.$$

where x_e' denotes the modified ideal point of the EP and x_p' is the modified ideal point of the Council pivot. Solving this gives

$$\Omega^* = \frac{3}{4}(x_e' + x_p') - \frac{1}{4}\sqrt{9x_e' - 14x_e'x_p' + 9x_p'}$$

The reference point r prevails if $\|x_c'-r\| < \|x_c'-\Omega^*\|$ and if $\|x_e'-x_p'\| > \|x_e'\|$ or $\|x_e'-x_p'\| > \|x_p'\|$. The first case refers to the Commission's power to prevent action, but as the bargaining solution in the CC shows, this is the only way the Commission affects the outcome in this model. The latter two cases in which the reference point prevails refer to the situation in which the CC cannot find a compromise. Then, the CC does not meet at the equilibrium.

Note that the Nash bargaining solution in the CC is biased towards the reference point, and towards the crucial preferred policy of the actor (the EP or the Council pivot in the majority version, or the extreme Council member in the unanimity version) who is closer to the reference point. Due to the use of qualified majority voting and unanimity voting in the Council, the Council pivot or extreme is more likely to be closer to the reference point on the compromise line than the EP, which uses

[9] For a quantitative assessment, see Napel and Widgrén (2004b) and for a qualitative and different treatment Tsebelis and Garrett (2000).

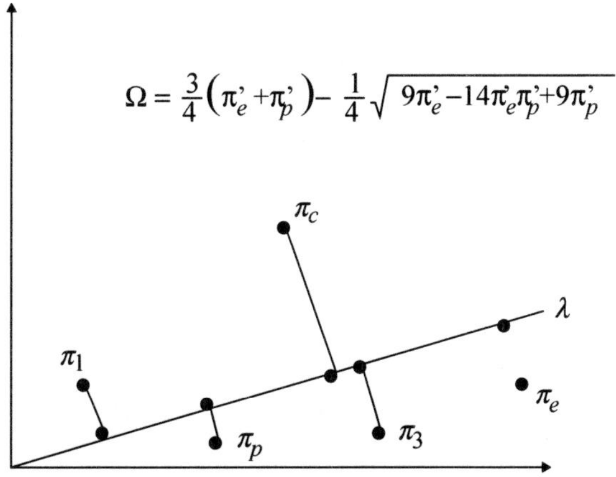

Figure 9.3. A simplified co-decision procedure

absolute majority voting (for details of this point see Napel and Widgrén 2004b). Moreover, the utility of the player who is closer to the reference point decreases relatively faster than the utility of the player who is further away from the reference point. The Nash product is, therefore, maximised at a point closer to the ideal point of a player who is closer to the reference point (see Figure 9.3).

In both procedures our models give predictions at the proposal level. They are located on the issues line. In the original policy space, they are vectors from the origin to one point on the issues line. The issue level predictions are simply the elements of these vectors.[10]

9.3 RESEARCH DESIGN

The data set consists of 162 issues contained in 66 Commission proposals. Because of some missing variables in the data set, which bias the examination of the predictive power of the model, we chose a sample of 113 issues. In more detail, we adopted a similar strategy to that used in Chapter 8 to solve the missing value problem. First, we deleted the few issues where the Commission did not have a policy position. Second, we did not consider issues with missing reference points. Missing reference points occur in policies that are so new that there is no reasonable reference, or in cases where the interviewees could not determine them.

[10] Or more technically, the issue level predictions are orthogonal projections of the proposal level prediction on to the axes of the policy space.

Of the 162 issues, the reference point was missing on 36. Missing salience values did not reduce the sample size as they were simply assumed to be zeros. Third, in terms of missing policy positions, we draw a line at four, and excluded the issues with more missing policy positions than that. The exclusion of issues on which the Commission did not have a position is obvious, since in the procedural model it makes the first proposal. In terms of missing policy positions in the Council, the threshold is less obvious. One alternative would have been to recode missing policy position with an indifference assumption. This suggests the mean of the Commission ideal point and the reference point serves as a proxy. The average number of votes in the Council is 5.8. In issues with more than four missing policy positions, any assumption would imply that on average we would assume the policy position of a blocking minority (29 votes). For the issues with four missing policy positions or less, we supposed that actors are indifferent between the reference point and the Commission proposal, and replaced missing values with the mean of the Commission's position and the reference point. The number of issues excluded due to missing policy positions was 15.

9.4 AN ILLUSTRATION

As an illustrative example of our models, we refer to the proposed directive COM(1999)296 titled 'Energy efficiency requirements for ballasts for fluorescent lighting'. The proposal is a good example of a rather technical directive, which is still able to raise controversy because of its economic effects. The proposal also illustrates nicely the predictive behaviour of the models. The directive, introduced in mid-June 1999, was decided using the co-decision procedure and qualified majority voting in the Council. The original proposal was followed a little less than a year later, on 3 April 2000, by an amended proposal COM(2000)181. The final act was taken some months after that on 18 September 2000.

The main purpose of the proposal was to create common rules for the market, as the impetus for the directive originally came from the industry. Another purpose was to move towards more energy efficient type B ballasts, a component of fluorescent lighting. The energy savings are, however, rather modest.

The energy efficiency requirements refer to the use of different types of ballasts. Ballasts are little gadgets found in fluorescent lighting systems. Currently, there are three types of ballasts: B, C, and D. Type B is the most recent and efficient electric ballast; types C and D are older and less efficient. The most inefficient type D ballasts are not produced in the Community, but are imported from third countries.

The underlying controversy was mainly between ballast producers. The biggest producer of electric ballasts is Phillips in the Netherlands. In turn, the biggest producer of magnetic ballasts is Helvar in Finland. Other ballast producers in the EU are located in Austria, Germany, Italy, Portugal and Spain. It is noteworthy that Greek industry had special difficulties in adapting to the new (and costly) legislation. In general, the EP suggested somewhat tighter conditions than those contained in the Commission proposal. Hence, there were differences in opinion between the member states in the Council and the EP.

The proposal raised two issues. The first relates to the transition period in which the switch from magnetic to electric ballasts should take place. Quite expectedly, some member states wanted to see a shorter transition period than others. The formulation of the 9th article of the proposal constitutes issue 2. This is a question of whether the magnetic ballasts should be phased out completely, or whether magnetic ballasts should be permitted under some special conditions. It was argued that in certain conditions only magnetic ballasts are usable (in very cold conditions or in trains).

With respect to the first issue, all actors (except Ireland) took a position. The reference point is zero and is defined as a situation in which magnetic ballasts would not be phased out at all. Next to the reference point was point 33, supported by the Greek delegation that opposed the adaptation of the proposal due to costs. Magnetic ballast producers supported a one-year longer transition period than the Commission's proposal, represented by point 47 on the issue scale. Finally, the Commission's proposal, supported by the Netherlands, the rest of the member states and EP, is represented by position 100. The final outcome was 47.

The second issue, on the exceptions to the phasing out of the inefficient ballast types, has five alternative positions. The reference point, zero, was supported by the magnetic ballast-producers, with the exception of Spain, which supported the next point 30, together with the Commission and a large group of member states. Denmark supported point 50, calling for more restrictions to the exceptions, emphasising the environmental importance of the directive. Point 80 was supported by the Dutch delegation. In line with their industry's interests in promoting efficient ballasts, they supported an even more restrictive set of exceptions to the phasing out of inefficient ballasts. Finally, the EP took the

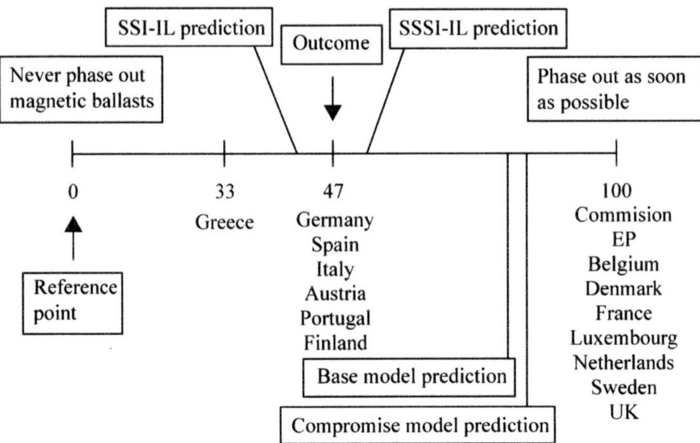

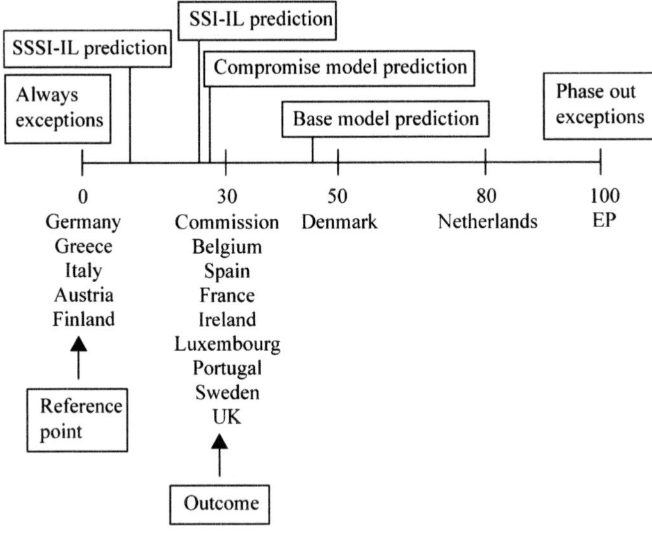

Figure 9.4. Illustration of model predictions on a Commission proposal for a Council directive on energy efficiency requirements for ballasts for fluorescent lighting

most extreme position, favouring a complete phasing out of exceptions, represented by position 100. The EP wanted to send the industry a stronger signal than the Commission. The final outcome was 30. These positions are depicted in Figure 9.4.

It is worth pointing out that in both issues the Netherlands, as an electric ballast producer, only had something to gain, while for Finland and other magnetic ballast producers the proposal raised the prospect of costs. The main debates were dominated by the ballast-producing countries and Greece, which attached relatively high levels of salience to the issues. For countries in which ballast production did not take place, the salience was very low; they simply didn't care.

Predictions of the base model, compromise model and the issues line models (SSI-IL and SSSI-IL)

On issue 1 the issues line models give good predictions: the SSI-IL model 43.0 and the SSSI-IL model 52.3. These predictions are almost equally far from the outcome (47), but are on opposite sides of the outcome. The base and compromise models do not predict as accurately. The base and compromise models predict 79.2 and 82.9, respectively.

With respect to issue 2, the SSSI-IL model does not predict as well: its forecast is 10.9 compared to the actual outcome of 30. The SSI-IL model comes closer to the outcome with its prediction of 22.5. The best prediction appears to be the compromise model prediction of 26.8, while the base model ends up further away at 46.4.

To the same extent, the base model tends to overestimate the policy shift from the reference point when there is a considerable number of actors supporting a policy that is not acceptable to a blocking minority of actors. In both issues in the illustration, Germany, Italy, Greece, Austria and Finland form, together with some other countries, such a minority, but there is a powerful group of actors at position 100 on issue 1 and at 30 and above on issue 2. In the second issue, the position of the EP gives weight to position 100. In the compromise model the salience of the issue influences the predictions. On issue 1, which is relatively more salient to the countries at position 100, incorporating salience into the prediction shifts it in the wrong direction. On issue 2, which is relatively more salient to the group of countries at the reference point, salience offsets the overestimation of the base model and leads to a rather accurate prediction.

The SSI-IL model has a tendency to give conservative predictions on the issues, as in our illustration, as it gives weight to the blocking minority, which in this proposal has a common modified position on the issues line. The degree of conservatism of the model increases if a blocking minority has a position at the reference point on one of the issues.[11] At the issue level in this example, the SSI-IL model gives predictions that are biased towards the reference point compared to the actual outcome. When we take salience into account it does not improve the accuracy of our predictions. In the second issue, it makes the predictions even more conservative, since the issue is more salient to the blocking minority at the reference point position.

In sum, the illustration serves as an example in which the SSI-IL and SSSI-IL models work better than the base and compromise models at the proposal level. The average error of the former is 6.3 and 12.2. For the base and compromise models the average errors are 24.3 and 19.6 respectively. This, and the fact that base and compromise models give rather poor predictions, especially on issue 1, suggests that the issues of this proposal were linked. The issues line models predict most accurately if this is the case. Interestingly, the issue level salience does not seem to have had the expected role in the final decision: the blocking minority at the reference point, that attached a higher level of salience to issue 2, made a compromise in favour of the group of countries that attached a lower level of salience, at position 30. On issue 1, the group of countries and the EP at position 100, which attached a higher level of salience to this issue, made a compromise in favour of the blocking minority at position 47, which attached a lower level of salience to the issue.

9.5 RESULTS

Of the 113 issues included in our analysis, there are four issues on which the base model prediction is perfect, and its largest error is 76.9. With respect to the compromise model the best prediction has an error of 0.15 while the largest error is 79.12. On just over 50 per cent of the issues examined, both the base and compromise models have prediction errors of less than 20. On less than 10 per cent of the issues, the prediction errors of these models are greater than 50. Hence, in general, both models seem to work quite well. However, the base model seems to predict a bit better. For details see Table 9.1.

Compared to the base and compromise models, the distribution of prediction errors of the SSI-IL and SSSI-IL models are more skewed towards the largest errors. The prediction errors of these models on

[11] The reader can check this by projecting one point of the x-axis, e.g. in two-dimensional space on to a line, and compare that to a projection of some other point that is right above the point on the x-axis to the same line.

Table 9.1. *Number of issues in 10 error categories in base, compromise, SSI-IL and SSSI-IL models*

Prediction error	Base model		Compromise model		SSI-IL		SSSI-IL	
	Number of issues (n=113)	Cumulative (per cent)	Number of issues (n=113)	Cumulative (per cent)	Number of issues (n=113)	Cumulative (per cent)	Number of issues (n=113)	Cumulative (per cent)
$0 \leq x \leq 10$	40	35.4	38	33.6	31	27.4	32	28.3
$10 < x \leq 20$	21	54.0	20	51.3	13	38.9	13	39.8
$20 < x \leq 30$	17	77.9	19	68.1	14	53.3	13	51.3
$30 < x \leq 40$	16	83.2	16	82.3	13	62.8	11	61.1
$40 < x \leq 50$	5	87.6	3	85.0	13	74.3	14	73.4
$50 < x \leq 60$	3	90.3	7	91.2	8	81.4	8	80.5
$60 < x \leq 70$	5	94.7	3	93.8	10	90.3	9	89.4
$70 < x \leq 80$	6	100	7	100	2	92.9	2	91.1
$80 < x \leq 90$	0	100	0	100	1	93.8	2	92.9
$90 < x \leq 100$	0	100	0	100	8	100	8	100

Table 9.2. *Average absolute error across issues*

Model	All issues ($n = 113$)	CNS QMV ($n = 38$)	CNS unan. ($n = 19$)	COD QMV ($n = 45$)	COD unan. ($n = 11$)
Base model	23.43	24.22	14.73	27.74	18.06
Compromise model	24.34	24.81	18.00	27.40	21.19
SSI-IL	34.15	31.90	32.66	36.94	33.05
SSSI-IL	34.07	31.89	31.89	36.98	33.43

about one-tenth of the issues belong to the highest categories of prediction errors: larger than the largest errors of the base and compromise models. The SSI-IL model does predict 15 issues perfectly, which is 11 more than the base model is able to do. All these 15 issues are, however, cases where the *status quo* prevails. It seems that the larger average prediction error is due to the fact that SSI-IL and SSSI-IL models tend to give rather conservative predictions.

Across the 113 issues, the average absolute errors of the models vary between 23.43 and 34.15, as can be seen from Table 9.2. The best model is the base model. As the models are not specific to any legislative procedure, this aspect should not have an impact. It was therefore not to be expected that significant differences would exist among the error averages between groups of issues subject to different legislative procedures: consultation—co-decision, or, qualified majority voting—unanimity voting. These categories are reported in Table 9.2. Comparing the error averages reveals that there is a pattern. The base and compromise models predict issues decided on by unanimity considerably better than those subject to QMV. This does not seem to be the case for the SSI-IL and SSSI-IL models. A possible cause of this variation could be the differences in the number of cases between the QMV and unanimity issues. The worst category across all the models is COD+QMV.

The division of the issues into different policy areas should have even less impact on the model predictions than the division into different legislative procedures. In Table 9.3, the issues are divided into three categories. For the SSI-IL and SSSI-IL models, there are virtually no differences in the average prediction errors on issues in the areas of agriculture, internal market and other policy areas. There are differences in the average errors of the base and compromise models among these three categories.

Table 9.3. *Average absolute error across issues*

Model	Agriculture ($n = 27$)	Internal market ($n = 29$)	Other policy areas ($n = 57$)
Base model	25.73	29.35	19.33
Compromise model	27.03	29.62	20.39
SSI-IL	33.54	33.81	34.61
SSIS-IL	33.86	33.89	34.26

Table 9.4. *Average absolute error across issues*

Model	Dichotomous ($n = 20$)	Rank order ($n = 83$)	Scale ($n = 10$)
Base model	40.38	20.24	16.01
Compromise model	39.50	21.76	15.52
SSI-IL	40.98	32.99	30.13
SSSI-IL	41.06	32.90	29.76

In Table 9.4, an interesting division is made between different types of issues. The policy positions on the issues could be on a real scale, a rank ordered scale (most of the issues are rank ordered), or on a dichotomous issue space, where only two policy points exist. Due to the properties of the models, it could be expected that the models would perform similarly on rank ordered and scale issues. A dichotomous issue space, by contrast, could affect the predicted outcome negatively. The results in Table 9.4 give support to the suspicion that all of the four model variants have almost exactly the same average errors. The scale issues are predicted the best by all models, and compared to the dichotomous cases the difference is rather huge. Notably, the rank ordered issues are predicted very well, especially by the base and compromise models, and the differences between rank and scale issues is not large.

As noted above, the SSI-IL and SSSI-IL models tend to give conservative predictions at the issue level. Therefore, it might be interesting to investigate how the policy shift, i.e. the distance between the reference point and the outcome, affects the prediction errors of the models. Let us start by taking two Commission proposals as examples. The first one is the proposal for a Council regulation COM(1999)384 on the 'Jurisdiction and recognition of judgements in civil and commercial matters'. The proposal was decided using consultation procedure and unanimity voting rule in the Council. The proposal had two controversial issues. In the first issue the reference point and the outcome are both 60. There is a large majority behind point 60 (12 out of 17 voters including the Commission and Parliament), while five Member States took other initial positions (20, 30, 40, 50 and 75). On this issue, both base and compromise models predict the outcome almost perfectly, and have errors of 5.3 and 3.5 respectively. On the second issue, the reference point and the outcome are both at 50. A majority of the member states are behind position 50, but other positions are taken as well (0, 25 and 100). Also on this issue, the base model predicts the outcome well, with only a small error of 3.1, while the compromise model error is a greater at 13.7.

The second proposal is the proposal for a Council directive COM (1999)188 'On the marketing of forest reproductive material'. The proposal was decided using the consultation procedure and QMV rule in the Council. This proposal raised three issues. The second issue is not applicable since no reference point is contained in the data. Regarding the first issue, the SSI-IL and SSSI-IL models predict the outcome almost perfectly, while the predictions have large errors on the third issue. A common feature of the first and the third issues is that the issue spaces are dichotomous. Moreover, in both cases there is also nearly a unanimous support for the outcome point. At first sight, it is rather surprising that the model succeeds perfectly in one issue and fails badly in the other.

While based on the above, it does not appear to be straightforward to analyse the effect of voter positions on the model performance, it is possible that the models could be sensitive to the location of the reference points. The difference between the above two issues is that the reference points are located at the opposite extremes with respect to the outcome point. On issue 1, where the SSI-IL and SSSI-IL models' predictions are very good, the reference point is the outcome point. Thus the absolute difference between the reference point and the outcome is 0. On issue 3 there is again almost unanimous support for the reference point 0. However, the outcome point is the other extreme, 100, i.e. the absolute distance between the reference point and the outcome is 100.

Table 9.5 shows the average prediction errors for different groups of the 113 issues. The left column represents the grouping criteria, which are the absolute distances between the reference points and the outcomes. The number of issues in each category is shown in the next column. The last two columns represent the SSI-IL and SSSI-IL prediction error averages within the categories. The table reveals that when the distance

Table 9.5. *The SSI and SSSI model absolute errors across seven groups of issues*

Absolute difference between the reference point and outcome	Number of issues	Base model average errors	Compromise model average errors	SSI-IL average errors	SSSI-IL average errors
=100	15	32.85	30.36	67.54	67.91
<100	98	21.99	23.42	29.04	28.89
<90	91	21.70	23.17	26.83	26.63
<70	71	23.43	25.70	22.46	22.15
<50	46	28.18	30.13	12.78	12.31
<30	32	32.55	35.10	11.19	9.93
<10	24	38.27	38.40	10.74	9.62

between the reference point and the outcome is 100, the models predict rather badly, as expected, if we compare this to cases where the distance is less than 100. Looking down the column to a distance of less than 10, reveals something quite unexpected: the closer the reference point is to the outcome, the more poorly the base and compromise models predict. We would have expected just the opposite.

Table 9.5 confirms that the SSI-IL and SSSI-IL models are not able to capture large policy shifts accurately. This is due to the conservative nature of these models' predictions. This feature is more visible if there is a blocking minority of actors located at the reference point position.

The reasoning behind the grouping in Table 9.5 is, of course, just like forecasting yesterday's weather, since in order to predict an outcome well, we would need to know the outcome before it even exists. Thus, the model cannot be improved upon on the basis of this analysis. However, this analysis is instructive since it shows that the SSI-IL and SSSI-IL models are sensitive to the location of the reference point.

9.6 CONCLUSIONS

In this chapter, we introduced two models that combined cooperative and non-cooperative modelling. In these models we assumed that either the base or the compromise model determines a restricted policy space. This restricted policy space, the issues line, was assumed to go through the reference point and the base or compromise model prediction. The issues line was also assumed to work as a binding constraint when the actors play a procedural uni-dimensional spatial voting game in the second stage, according to the formal rules of the game. This means that each actor's ideal point was mapped from its original positions to the closest location on the issues line—the modified ideal point. The models stem from the idea that when a proposal consists of several issues, these issues are somehow put together, and that the way in which this is done forms a binding *a priori* compromise.[12] The models in this chapter are, thus, primarily designed to predict at the proposal level.

We also compared the predictions of two different two-stage models to the base and compromise models. It turned out that the latter gave on average more accurate predictions of the outcomes than our models, irrespective of the procedure or policy domain. It thus seems that postulating a formal game that is conditional on an *a priori* compromise does not lead to predictive power. The main reason for this is that a spatial voting game on the issues line has a tendency to make conservative predictions of the outcome. This is especially true on dichotomous issues, and on the issues where there is a blocking minority of actors with positions close to the reference point on at least one issue of a proposal. The voting game of the second stage, which considers all issues of a proposal together, may thus artificially increase the *status quo* bias. The model predicts small policy shifts from the reference point more accurately than large ones, even more accurately than do the base and compromise models. The base and compromise model predictions are more accurate when policy changes are larger, whereas the opposite holds for the SSI-IL and SSSI-IL models. There seems to be an in-built *status quo* bias in the SSI-IL and SSSI-IL models, and they are not able to predict considerable policy changes. The base and compromise model predictions always differ from the reference point if there is at least one player with a policy position that differs from the reference point and a salience greater than zero.

The average absolute error of both two-stage models is 34 points on a scale of 0 to 100. If we filter out maximal errors (100), the average error falls to 29 points. The highest errors are in dichotomous issues. There are no substantial differences in errors in different policy domains. If we compare different procedures, the model performs better in the

[12] In single issue proposals, SSI-IL model predictions correspond with procedural model predictions in consultation procedure (see Chapter 3). In co-decision procedure, this is not the case even in single issue proposals due to different modelling of the procedure.

consultation procedure than in the co-decision procedure. This may be due to the fact that the role of the Commission is over-emphasised when the base model is used to determine the compromise line, and because it is implicitly assumed that the EP and Council pivot cannot renegotiate it in the Conciliation Committee. Moreover, the Nash bargaining solution in the Conciliation Committee game between the Council pivot and the EP, which forms the base for the model predictions in co-decision procedure, makes the predictions even more conservative, since the solution is skewed towards the position of the actor that is closer to the reference point on the issues line.

The findings of this chapter suggest that detailed modelling of the voting procedure does not contribute to the predictive power of the model, but makes it perform less accurately. This may be partly due to our models' attempts to deal with all issues in one proposal simultaneously, which might in some cases rule out possible logrolling over the issues.

It is worth noting that the base and compromise model predictions also make use of data on preferences and salience but in an indirect way. Players' capability to shape events is based on their average power, which makes all issues in the data set dependent. Salience and spatial voting add issue and procedure specific elements, which seem to make the predictions worse. This provides some evidence of issues' dependence and is in line with earlier findings, for example that a simple power index model explains member states' budget receipts from the EU budget very well.[13]

In sum, it seems that the informal models like the base or compromise model are able to predict the outcomes more accurately than a model in which the formal procedure is taken into account. This is not, however, generally true. As the prediction errors in Table 9.5 above demonstrate, formal procedures can be seen as fallback options if unanimity cannot be reached.

In general, there are several other ways to combine the informal and formal parts of a decision-making game. Despite the not so promising results of this chapter, we feel that future research should be carried out using models that mix elements of non-cooperative and cooperative games.

[13] For details see Baldwin *et al* (2000; 2001) and Kauppi and Widgrén (2004). See, however, Pajala and Widgrén (2004), which shows significant average differences between the empirical Banzhaf index predictions based on actors' ideal policy positions and convex coalitions and the issue outcomes in the data set examined here.

10

Evaluating political decision-making models

CHRISTOPHER H. ACHEN

10.1 HOW WELL DO THE MODELS FORECAST?

Stocks have reached what looks like a permanently high plateau.

Irving Fisher, prominent professor of mathematical economics at Yale University, 17 October 1929

The previous chapters in this book have elaborated many different models of political decision-making in the European Union. To make their forecasts, some of these models focus on the incentives created by EU legal regulations or decision-making rules. Other models emphasise the power of bargaining in political decision-making. Still others start from logrolling, coalitions, or the spatial theory of voting.

The aim of this book is to set out all these models of EU decision-making, and then to evaluate how well the models predict actual decisions. Most of the discussion is quantitative. Yet in important respects, we mean to integrate prior case studies, formal theory, and statistical methods. For example, each of the modelling approaches represented in this book builds on one or more central aspects of political life known

I am grateful to the Center for the Study of Democratic Processes, Princeton University, and the Department of Political Science, University of Michigan, who provided released time from teaching for this research. A research fund at the University of Michigan donated by Norma Shapiro supported the overseas trips so important to international collaboration, and I thank her for her help. I also thank the authors of the other chapters in this book plus Simon Hug, John Jackson, and Andy Moravcsik for many constructive comments and suggestions. Marcel Van Assen, Larry Bartels, and the graduate students in Politics 583 at Princeton in Spring Term 2004 also gave helpful additions and criticisms, as did seminar participants at the University of Michigan, National Chengchi University of Taiwan, and Rutgers University. Robert Thomson and Jacob Dijkstra skilfully carried out the calculations and produced the tables. Remaining errors are my own.

from dozens of skilful case studies of political decisions. All competent model-building depends on careful qualitative research in which explanatory factors are identified and tentative empirical generalisations are formulated. No model is worthwhile if, like some formal theorising, it applies to nothing in particular. Case studies have generated most of the interesting hypotheses in political science. They are the essential foundation for most model building.

Moreover, case studies play a crucial role in evaluating theory. Indeed, the entire dataset used in this book consists of short case studies, which are then coded for quantitative analysis. Nearly all the chapters discuss one or more of these cases and demonstrate that the models under discussion succeed in explaining some aspects of the outcome. Failures are also discussed, with the aim of improving future theory. Thus for theory testing and criticism, too, we treat case studies as indispensable.

Yet case studies alone, like formal theories alone, have limitations. By their nature, case studies derive their conclusions from short periods of political history, often filled with intense conflict among vivid personalities. Analysts struggle to separate suggestive patterns from irrelevant distracting details. Even if they are successful in doing so, the findings, however insightful, are of unknown generality.

For all these reasons, even the best case study findings achieve greater precision and theoretical fecundity when they can be accounted for, at least in part, by a formal model (Achen and Snidal 1989). In fact, purely at the theoretical level, formulating models with precise predictions has sharpened our understanding of the empirical generalisations deriving from case studies and strengthened our conceptual grasp of EU decision-making, as previous chapters in this book have demonstrated. The exactitude of the models' formulations enables researchers to pinpoint our explanatory weaknesses and improve our knowledge in ways that were wholly unmatched and unforeseen in the days of purely verbal treatments of political decision-making. In turn, this knowledge feeds back into case study analyses, sharpening their interpretations and adding power to their inferences. Thus the empirical accuracy of historical study and the theoretical precision of formal models are neither grand opposing explanatory frameworks nor minor differences of technique. Instead, both are part of an integrated social science research methodology that adds to our comprehension of both theory and individual cases.

Lastly, statistical methods, too, are needed. For case studies plus theoretical sophistication alone do not suffice: predictive accuracy across multiple cases matters, too. The interplay between models and case studies is not meant merely to summarise interesting history or to play out intriguing concepts, but rather to capture the precise workings of some central aspects of reality. Hence we need to know how well a model tracks the details of new political decisions, not just those it was constructed to explain.

Models reproduce only part of reality, and so all models sometimes fail. Yet some fail less than others. With a plethora of models in hand, then, we need comparative model evaluation. Here statistical methodology enters.

Thus having developed a range of models in previous chapters, each of them drawing on prior case studies, we arrive at the statistical evaluation of the models. How good are these models? How much of reality do they capture? How well do they perform relative to very simple forecasting rules that require much less theory? Answers to these questions are obviously important for formal theorising about the EU.

We believe, however, that the findings of this book are just as important for the case study tradition. Quantitative and qualitative methods relate to each in the manner of optical and radio telescopes: sometimes they see the same things differently, and sometimes one sees what is invisible to the other. But their conclusions are mutually beneficial and reinforcing, making their joint value much higher than their individual parts. In the same way, we hope that the results of our comparative model evaluations will inspire not only formal theorists, but also case study specialists and statistical empiricists, to build on our work. The best broad-gauge understandings of the EU will emerge from that dialogue.

10.2 FORECASTS AND BASELINES

No theory copes with all the peculiarities of politics. Proposal COM/2000/604 in our dataset, for example, contained three issues dealing with sugar quotas and storage subsidies, with two of the issues dichotomous (yes/no). On these two, the Commission was opposed by nearly everyone else, and some of the other actors felt strongly. Thus most of the models in this book foresee very probable defeat for the Commission.

In fact, however, the Commission got its way on both issues. Finland received an exemption from one clause; Italy, Portugal, and Spain were excused from another. These sidepayments quieted several of the Commission's opponents, but they are not 'issues' in the usual sense and so are not part of the dataset. Moreover, some unusual aspects of the decisions meant that the Commission could impose its will if the member states failed to agree. Thus the standard Shapley Shubik Index (SSI) values fail to represent the Commission's real power in this particular case. In short, the opponents were much less concerned than they appear to be in our codings, and the Commission was far more weighty.

The result is a substantial prediction error for most of the models. The culprits are the unavoidable limitations of event coding and the daunting complexity of the political world. Some errors of this kind are inevitable. Models and theories are meant to give insight into what usually happens. They are not meant to replace detailed descriptions of individual cases.

This example raises a central issue in model evaluation. Suppose that on a 100-point scale, we can predict decision outcomes on average to within 20 points. Is that good or bad forecasting? Is a 20-point average error a brilliant success, given the complications of political life, or is it a routine accomplishment that should surprise no one? Implicitly, the question asks whether an average error of 20 points is better or worse than a naive or atheoretical forecast. Thus formal political models need a baseline against which to compare their predictive accuracy.

Experience with baselines is commonplace in other disciplines where prediction is important. Meteorology is a particularly instructive example. During most of the twentieth century, meteorologists possessed impressive mathematical theories of how weather patterns occurred. Nevertheless, with the data they had available, their forecasts were not very good. Forecasts were often compared against a simple 'persistence' baseline: 'The weather tomorrow will be like the weather today'. Another common baseline was 'climatological': 'The weather tomorrow will be like the usual weather at this time of year'. Only in recent decades, with the advent of weather satellites and other improvements in data-gathering, plus more powerful computing, have meteorologists been able to outperform baseline models, at least in short-term forecasts covering the next few days (Murphy and Winkler 1984).

Economists have faced similar forecasting difficulties, and they, too, have paid attention to proper baselines. Beginning in the 1960s, ever more complex models of national macro-economies were constructed, sometimes involving many dozens of equations. These models were estimated with historical data, then used to forecast. Forecasting accuracy was often rather poor. Eventually, good baseline models were constructed using atheoretical time series statistical techniques. The baseline models were vector autoregressions—essentially an econometric version of the persistence model. ('The economy next quarter will be like the economy has been lately.') The baseline models often outperformed their more sophisticated theoretical counterparts (Granger and Newbold 1986: 287–94).

The science of evaluating forecasts has learned much from experience with meteorological and macroeconomic models. In some instances, their baselines can be borrowed without modification. For example, in budget studies, last year's budget plus inflation is an excellent baseline for assessing budget forecasting models. In the quieter areas of politics, where essentially the same decisions are repeated annually on a more or less routine basis, finding a good baseline is relatively easy.

Unfortunately for most studies of political decisions, however, borrowing a baseline from meteorology or economics is impossible. Neither the climatological nor persistence analogues work well in politics generally, since public decisions come along steadily in political life, but they virtually never repeat themselves in the same form or with the same meaning. When a new public problem enters the political arena, as they frequently do in the dataset used in this book, a prediction that 'the EU will do the same thing that it did last year', or that 'the EU will do what it always does', is meaningless. For political baselines, analysts must turn elsewhere.

10.3 DOWNSIAN AND RELATED BASELINES

Baselines for political predictions must take into account the specific features of the issue at hand. The most prominent feature of any political issue is the set of policy preferences held by the key political actors. The task for any political model is to use those preferences, along with the intensities that the actors bring to the issue, to predict what will happen within a given institutional structure. A good baseline model would generate predictions of that kind, using only the simplest, most transparent logic.

The most popular choice for a baseline prediction is the Downsian model (Hotelling 1929; popularised by Downs 1957). Choices are assumed to be made by round-robin majority rule, whereby each alternative is matched against every other alternative, and the one that defeats all the others is the winner. Alternatives are assumed to be confined to a single dimension. That is, each of the alternatives must be positioned from left to right on an ideological scale, and all voters must agree on their locations. Voters themselves must occupy a position on the same scale, and when given a vote, they must select the alternative closest to themselves on the dimension. Then, as is well known, round-robin majority rule voting always produces a single winner, and that winner is the preference of the median voter.[1] This model is so simple and so well-known that in many empirical applications to decision-making under majority rule, the Downsian predictions are simply assumed to be correct. Often, no other possibilities are even considered.

The Downsian model also applies to decision-making under weighted majority voting. If some voters have more than one vote, then the preferences of the *weighted* median voter are determinative under majority rule. The logic is virtually identical to that of the unweighted case. The Downsian analysis applies to these and other situations in which the decision is made by all actors jointly and simultaneously, using some version of majority rule.

More complex decision-making structures do not have the simple form that the Downsian logic requires, for example, those in which a qualified majority or unanimity is required (such as in the Council of Ministers); in which some actors may have agenda control (like the EU Commission); in which different subgroups of actors may vote separately (as when a parliament has an upper and lower house); or in which bargaining may be used to settle some issues (as when conference committees must reconcile dissimilar decisions by two different voting bodies). In such cases, the median voter's preference is often not the equilibrium solution, and game-theoretic solution concepts such as subgame perfection are used to generate the predicted outcome of the extensive form game. Then the median or weighted median has only an informal justification, as an approximation, perhaps rather crude and inaccurate, to the outcome of the voting game (Krehbiel 1998: 232).

In a similar way, the mean of all the actors' positions has a rough-and-ready interpretation as an approximation to complex decision-making procedures. Caplin and Nalebuff (1988; 1991) showed that if a voting rule is 64 per cent majority rule (or more), and if certain additional requirements on the distribution of voter opinions are met, then the mean cannot be defeated when paired against any other alternative. In general, many alternatives will be undefeated; the Caplin-Nalebuff result is that the mean will be among them.

Since the Council of Ministers has always used a weighted voting rule requiring more than two-thirds majorities, the 64 per cent result has

[1] This statement assumes an odd number of voters, so that there is only one median voter, but with obvious modifications the statement holds for an even number of voters as well.

some appeal for forecasting EU decisions, at least as one forecast among others. The difficulty, though, is that the EU does not use a simple supra-majority rule to make decisions because the Council does not act alone. In the presence of agenda control, multiple decision-making bodies acting sequentially, and all the other complexities of EU decision-making, the 64 per cent rule has no direct logical application to EU decisions. It may function adequately as an approximation for some purposes, but its theoretical relevance is questionable. Like the median, the mean has only an informal justification.

In summary, for the forecasting of governmental decisions, the median and the mean behave like the atheoretical baselines used in meteorology and macroeconomics. That is, they do not embody the theory appropriate to the outcomes being predicted. Moreover, a brief look at the outcomes in the data set used for this book will demonstrate that both the median and the mean are far from perfect predictors. In that respect, too, they parallel the meteorological and econometric baselines. However, the median and mean do incorporate a substantive intuition that is known to apply to other, simpler cases of political decision-making. In that sense, they are logical starting points for our analysis of predictive success. A fair test of a model is that it does better than very simple baselines which are known not to be theoretically correct.

For this chapter, a variety of other baselines were also tried. For example, three weighted medians (with capabilities, saliences, and the product of capabilities and saliences as weights, respectively) were examined, but they proved slightly less successful on average than the simple unweighted median, and so they were dropped.[2] Similarly, the actor mid-range (the point equidistant from the two most extreme actor positions) proved to be about as accurate as the median and not as good as the mean. Since it has less theoretical justification than either of them, it, too, was dropped. For the purposes of this book, therefore, the baseline models we evaluate are the unweighted median and the mean, each of them computed across all actors, with the Commission and the European Parliament each treated as a single actor. With these two baselines used as the standard of comparison, the models of this book may be evaluated for their forecasting power.

[2] Weighted means are also represented in the book, though not as baseline models: the base model and the compromise model forecasts, both discussed in Chapter 4, are just weighted means, with capabilities and the product of capabilities and saliences as their respective weights.

10.4 MEASURES OF MODEL SUCCESS

The topic of model evaluation and comparison has generated a vast literature in statistics. (A classic discussion in econometrics is Gaver and Geisel 1974.) Governments, too, pay attention to political decision-making models and conduct their own evaluations. The American Central Intelligence Agency once became quite enthusiastic about Bueno de Mesquita's challenge model, which is set out in Chapter 5 (Feder 1987).

Yet all such assessments are riven by disputes. In its simplest form, the debate centres around this question: given a series of models, and given a data set to which all the models apply, which model fits best? Deep conceptual puzzles surround the topic, beginning with questions about the meaning of the word 'best'. Best for what? No general agreement has emerged.

Within particular statistical traditions, the issue of model comparison can sometimes be formulated clearly and sharply. Among Bayesians, for example, the best model is simply the one that has the largest subjective probability, given the data. (A recent brief review is Robert 2001: Chapter 7.) Computational challenges and intellectual difficulties arise in executing this programme, particularly in defining the initial state of ignorance from which the data are meant to elevate us. Nevertheless, the goal is clear, the fundamental conceptual apparatus is agreed on, and practical conclusions are often unaffected by the details of implementation. In many respects, Bayesian analysis would be the most attractive way to proceed, and it would allow us to make statements such as, 'the mean has a 15 per cent chance of being the best model for this dataset, while the median has only a two per cent probability'. Thus the predictive prowess of models could be ranked, and the chance of ranking errors would be made explicit. See Raftery (1995) for a simple Bayesian model evaluation procedure that has received attention in the social sciences, and Bartels (1997) for a substantively sophisticated Bayesian evaluation of competing statistical models arising in political science.

For our purposes, however, the difficulty with all this literature, Bayesian and non-Bayesian, is that the models in this book are deterministic. That is, they lack the probability forecasts that are the starting point for statistical model comparisons. A deterministic model may forecast an outcome of 60, while the actual result is 75. Is this 'close'? The answer to that question depends on how likely the outcome 75 is under the model, but no such answer is available. The prediction is simply 60, *tout court*.

In that sense, deterministic models in the social sciences are always scientifically incomplete. None of the standard model evaluation procedures can get underway.

Now of course, it is always possible to impose a stochastic structure on a deterministic model. Typically, an additive error term is appended, so that the model becomes incorporated into a statistical specification:

$$\text{outcome} = \text{model forecast} + \text{error} \tag{10.1}$$

Then, by adding some assumptions about the form of the errors, a likelihood function can be generated. Normal (Gaussian) errors are often assumed.

The challenges of this approach are twofold. First, the error structure is not part of the original model. It is tacked on by another analyst. The new statistical assumptions must be consistent with the original structure if the model is not to be penalised for inappropriate additions made by someone else.

Equally important, the choice of the error structure must respect the form of the data. For example, in the data set used in this book, many of the decisions were dichotomous in character (yes/no). If we code yes = 100 and no = 0, then what does a forecast of 70 mean? Should we round it to 100, so that the forecast is 'yes' with probability 100 per cent? Or does 70 mean that 'yes' will occur with probability 70 per cent? Or is the prediction 100 with some allowance for measurement error in the data, so that the actual forecast is, perhaps, 85 per cent chance of 'yes'? (See Chapter 4, Appendix 3.)

Each of these choices could be defended, and statistical analysis could be undertaken to choose among them. For now, however, we have resisted the temptation to impose an elaborate and debatable statistical structure on the models. In consequence, we do not give a full Bayesian comparative analysis of the models. Instead, we adopt a more flexible quantitative approach, evaluating the models on several different statistical criteria.

In the absence of a statistical specification for each forecasting model, the problem of choosing a criterion for model evaluation is analogous to the problem of choosing a voting rule. Think of the forecasting models as the set of candidates standing for election. Treat the individual EU issues as the voters, with each issue counting equally. Each outcome corresponds to that issue's most preferred point. Then using the issues to select models near the outcomes is exactly parallel to having individual voters select the candidates near their most-preferred points. In each case, one needs a voting procedure.

Arrow's Theorem (Arrow 1951 [1963]) tells us that no voting rule will satisfy all ethical criteria. In parallel, no evaluation criterion will meet all our demands. Nevertheless, the analogy of voting rules suggests that we should look for evaluation rules that resemble sensible voting rules. For example, we could adopt a utilitarian voting rule, in which the sum of individual losses from the candidate choice is minimised. Or we could use the 'method of majority decision' (round-robin majority rule), in which each candidate is matched against every other candidate one at a time, and the candidate who defeats all other candidates by simple majority rule is declared best. We could also try less familiar rules such as approval voting (Brams and Fishburn 1983), in which each voter selects all candidates acceptable to him or her, and the candidate who has the most 'approval votes' is declared best.

The following sections translate these and other voting rules to the context of model evaluation. This latitudinarian style lets us compare models without imposing arbitrary statistical assumptions, and it brings insights of its own. Best of all, it turns out that the ranking of models is little affected by choice of voting rule.[3]

10.5 THE ISSUE OF FREE PARAMETERS

One additional area of concern needs to be addressed before the model evaluations are presented. The models in this book all operate without conventional 'free parameters', unknown constants that can be adjusted to improve their fit. On closer inspection, however, most of the models have made use of something equivalent. Thus, for example, we have measured power in three different ways—two versions of the Shapley Shubik Index and one set of expert opinions. When the second version of the Shapley Shubik values worked best, that became the definition of 'power'. Models that require power measures, such as the compromise model (and models like the exchange model, the coalition model, and the issue line model, which make use of the compromise model in their

[3] In addition, as mentioned in Chapter 2, the data seem free of systematic distortions that might distort the model rankings. For example, when we examine just those issues whose expert respondents were affiliated with the permanent representatives of the member states, the accuracy of the models does not differ significantly from those issues whose experts had a different affiliation. Thus national biases in the data themselves are not worrisome, and we can proceed to the evaluations.

calculations) thus have in effect a free parameter available to improve their fit to the outcomes.

Some models have additional 'degrees of freedom' as well. As discussed in Chapter 5, the exchange model can be run for one or more rounds. The number of rounds is a free parameter, and that parameter was chosen in combination with the power measure to maximise the fit. This gives the exchange model a total of two free parameters.

The procedural models discussed in Chapters 3 and 8 thus are at a disadvantage, since they make no use of power measures. However, the disadvantages are not all one–sided. Most of the procedural models make no forecast at all on two dozen or more of the 162 issues, so that their errors are based on a different sample from that used by the other models. In effect, they are free to choose the issues they will forecast—a substantial benefit. For example, if the compromise model were allowed to drop the 30 cases in which no bargaining agreement was reached, its average prediction error would drop from 22.9 to 20.1, making it an easy and substantial victor over all the other models in this book—so long as they were forced to predict the full 162 cases (see Chapter 4). In effect, picking one's cases for prediction is a free parameter, too. In this respect, the procedural models are advantaged.

All these considerations make the model error comparisons inexact. It is not clear how severely additional free parameters should be penalised, nor whether models with missing predictions should be downgraded, and if so, by how much. Moreover, should we credit most of the procedural models for their parsimony in ignoring the intensities of the actors, or discount them because they do not have to cope with the measurement errors in the saliency measures? Rather than attempting to adjudicate all these deep problems of model evaluation, we simply present the average forecast errors for those issues that a given model is able to forecast. And in the interests of scientific honesty, each chapter has presented the results of alternate choices. For example, Chapter 4 sets out how well the compromise model performs under different measures of power, and Chapter 5 does the same for the exchange model, assessing the impact of both the power measure and the number of rounds the model was run. Thus the reader is free to compare not only the findings of this chapter, which gives the fit of the best models, but also the performance of alternate versions of each model. In general, these comparisons show that the real differences in forecasting power occur *across* models, not *within* them. That is, different versions of the same model have very similar predictive power. Hence the model evaluations of this chapter are sensible.

10.6 MEAN ABSOLUTE ERROR PER ISSUE: THE MAE

We now take up the model evaluations themselves. The first measure is the simplest, easiest to understand, and perhaps the best overall—the mean absolute error (MAE). The reader has already encountered it in previous chapters. The MAE is just the average size of the forecasting mistake. Choosing models for smallest average error corresponds to a utilititarian voting rule. That is, maximising total satisfaction of the citizens is the same as maximising average satisfaction, and that in turn is the same as minimising average loss. Utilitarian ideas have a long history in ethics and economics, and their analogues for model evaluation are a natural starting point. Minimising average loss for citizens corresponds to minimising the average forecasting error for models.

Thus for outcomes y_i $(i = 1, \ldots, n)$, and a model M with corresponding forecasts $\hat{y}_i$, we define the MAE as:

$$\mathrm{MAE}_M = \sum_{i=1}^{n} |y_i - \hat{y}_i|/n \qquad (10.2)$$

This measure has the advantage of answering a simple question: how far wrong is the model, on average? Of course, to make the measure sensible, all issues must be scaled to the same range. In this book, that range is taken to be 0 to 100. Thus an MAE of 30 means, for example, that on average across all issues, the difference between the model prediction and the actual outcome is 30 points. Note that the unit of analysis for the MAE is the issue. All issues are counted equally, regardless of whether they occurred singly in a proposal or as part of a package of several issues included in a single proposal.

In Table 10.1, we show the mean absolute error (MAE) for eleven models from this book, plus the two baseline models (the median and the mean). The table shows only the MAEs for the best model from each of the previous chapters. (The MAE values for less successful models appear in the chapters where they were introduced.) The challenge model, which played a prominent role in Bueno de Mesquita and Stokman (1994) and was by some measures the most successful model in that book, is also included in Table 10.1, as is the state-centric realist model, patterned after Mearsheimer (1994–95), which has received considerable attention in the literature.[4]

[4] For purposes of comparability, the version of the challenge model assessed here is the same as that used in Bueno de Mesquita and Stokman (1994). Modifications to

Table 10.1. *Mean absolute error (MAE) of models by legislative procedure* (n *in brackets if lower than maximum)*

Model	CNS QMV (max $n = 55$)	CNS unan. (max $n = 39$)	COD QMV (max $n = 56$)	COD unan. (max $n = 12$)	Total (max $n = 162$)
Baseline models					
Median voter (unweighted)	30.62	21.03	30.64	31.75	28.40
Mean voter	24.28	18.82	26.18	18.78	23.21
Substantive models					
Compromise model—SSI-2 (Van den Bos)	23.31	17.33	27.28	19.24	22.94
Exchange model (Arregui/Stokman/Thomson)	26.16	18.67	26.29	19.26	23.89
Coalition model (Boekhoorn/Van Deemen/Hosli)	25.38	18.94	29.52	17.62	24.69
Realism model (adapted from Mearsheimer)	26.79	17.33	28.04	20.75	24.50
Expected utility model (Bueno de Mesquita)	30.11	23.90	29.82	23.60	28.03
Procedural model (Steunenberg/Selck)	34.49 (38)	29.31 (19)	26.38 (42)	33.54 (8)	30.32 (107)
Domestic constraints model (Bailer/Schneider)	27.08	19.27	30.04	20.81	25.76
Procedural exchange model (König/Proksch)	30.87 (38)	28.79 (19)	29.09 (45)	32.91 (11)	30.01 (113)
Tsebelis model (König/Proksch)	30.21 (38)	28.79 (19)	32.84 (45)	32.91 (11)	31.28 (113)
Coleman model (König/Proksch)	34.26 (38)	20.89 (19)	36.49 (45)	30.18 (11)	32.50 (113)
Issue line model (Widgrén/Pajala)	31.89 (38)	31.89 (19)	36.98 (45)	33.43 (11)	34.07 (113)

The right-hand column of Table 10.1 conveys an important message: *most of the models considered in this book are not as good at predicting outcomes as either the median or mean baseline models.* In fact, the simple mean is a very strong predictor of outcomes in this data set, and no other model is substantially better. Only the compromise model (Chapter 4), the exchange model (Chapter 5), the coalition model (Chapter 7), the state-centric realism model (Chapter 4), and the domestic constraints model (Chapter 6) are approximately as good as the mean, perhaps because each of them either makes substantial use of means and weighted means in their predictions or else uses the Nash bargaining model, which has much the same effect. By contrast, the theoretically powerful procedural models do much less well as a group.

The models break up into four categories of predictive success. The first category includes the compromise model, the mean, and the exchange model. This triumvirate is the most successful, with the compromise model finishing very slightly ahead, but not in a statistically reliable way. All three models 'split the difference' among the actors' preferences in a bargaining or exchange style.

The second group contains models very close in predictive power to the compromise model, the mean, and the exchange model. In fact, their statistical performance cannot be reliably distinguished from the top group. This set of models includes the coalition model, the state-centric realism model, and the domestic constraints model.[5] Each of these models is based on bargaining, exchange, and/or coalition formation. All of them use either the compromise model and/or the Nash bargaining solution at some stage of their calculations. Like the mean, compromise, and exchange models, none of these takes explicit account of the details of the EU decision rules or legal procedures (apart from the list of winning coalitions specified by the various treaties establishing the EU).

The third category of predictive success has two members—the median and the challenge model due to Bueno de Mesquita. These two models perform distinctly less well than the best six models. (In difference of means tests, these two models lose to all the models in group one

the challenge model that may have been made since the first book was published are not included. This model and the exchange model are not in the academic public domain; they are proprietary.

[5] Difference of means tests (paired observations) for these data show that two models must have MAE values that differ by about 3.5 or 4 to be statistically significant at the conventional .05 level. (The precise difference needed varies slightly from one model pair to another.)

at least at the .20 level, and most of the differences are significant at .05.) This second group of models share an emphasis on the median rather than the mean as a predictive tool. They also ignore the details of the legal procedures.

The fourth and final category of models, the least successful, do drastically less well than the models in the first category, with mean errors as much as 50 per cent larger and very significant difference of means tests. They also do somewhat less well than the models in the second group.[6] This fourth group of models includes, for example, all the procedural models based on EU decision-making rules (Chapter 3). The Tsebelis model falls into this highly unsuccessful category, as do other, non-procedural models such as Coleman's. Like the models in the third category, the models in this fourth group generally make no use of mean or weighted mean forecasts in their calculations.

In summary, means are better than medians, and both are better than extensive form games.

Table 10.1 also presents MAE values under four different European Union voting procedures—consultation with qualified majority in the Council, consultation under unanimity, co-decision with qualified majority, and co-decision with unanimity. Broadly speaking, the pattern of model success is similar across these procedures, with the same models doing well each time. However, as close inspection of the table will show, there are intriguing unexpected successes and failures scattered here and there. For example, the generally unimpressive Coleman model predicts in only half the cases of consultation under unanimity, but when it does so, it is very successful. Whether this and other deviations from average success represent genuine theoretical information, the ease of predicting particular subsets of issues, or just random variation due to small numbers of cases, awaits further research.

Table 10.2 presents the same average forecast errors, this time organised by issue area. For agriculture and 'other' policy areas, the general pattern holds, with the same models doing well and poorly as in the overall rankings. However, for nearly all the models, the internal market

[6] The worst models in this third group are statistically distinguishable at the .05 level from all the models in group two, and the Tsebelis model is nearly so. The other procedural models (from Chapters 3 and 8) differ from group two only at approximately the .25 level, which of course is not a reliable difference. However, if we add the consideration that all the procedural models fail to forecast in nearly one third of the cases, it seems fair to place them below the first two groups in overall predictive power.

Table 10.2. *Mean absolute error (MAE) of models by policy area (*n *in brackets if lower than maximum)*

Model	Internal market (max n = 34)	Agriculture (max n = 40)	Other areas (max n = 88)
Baseline models			
Median voter (unweighted)	39.60	33.29	21.85
Mean voter	28.16	26.44	19.84
Substantive models			
Compromise model—SSI-2 (Van den Bos)	31.28	26.61	18.05
Exchange model (Arregui/Stokman/Thomson)	28.72	29.85	19.32
Coalition model (Boekhoorn/ Van Deemen/Hosli)	33.30	28.45	19.65
Realism model (adapted from Mearsheimer)	27.47	29.67	20.99
Expected utility model (Bueno de Mesquita)	33.80	30.07	24.88
Procedural model (Steunenberg/Selck) (Steunenberg/Selck)	36.86 (28)	37.46 (27)	23.08 (52)
Domestic constraints model (Bailer/Schneider)	33.44	27.90	21.82
Procedural exchange model (König/Proksch)	31.90 (29)	29.07 (27)	29.49 (57)
Tsebelis model (König/Proksch)	35.21 (29)	30.67 (27)	29.58 (57)
Coleman model (König/ Proksch)	46.72 (29)	36.22 (27)	23.51 (57)
Issue line model (Widgrén/ Pajala)	33.89 (29)	33.86 (27)	34.26 (57)

issues seem more difficult to predict than the other two issue categories, and their prediction errors rise proportionately. Two exceptions are the exchange model, which does very well on internal market issues, and the state-centric realism model, which finishes first in that issue area. Is the internal market the true realm of state power in the EU, while agriculture is not? Doubts about that claim would be buttressed by noting that the internal market contains only 33 issues and that the prediction errors have large variances, meaning that chance plays a substantial role in these comparisons.[7] Thus additional detailed investigation, both statistical and historical, will be required to uncover whether the empirical differences in the various models' success across policy categories are theoretically informative.

Table 10.3 again displays the MAE values, this time categorised by the measurement level of the issue outcome. Dichotomous outcomes have the largest prediction errors, ranked outcomes are next, and interval scales have the smallest errors, as would be expected from their levels of measurement. However, with some allowance for sampling error, the pattern of errors seems quite similar across the scale types, with the same models doing relatively well and badly on each of them.

There are two important exceptions to the generalisation that scale type does not affect the relative performance of the models. The first occurs in comparing the mean versus the median. The mean outperforms the median except on dichotomous issues, where the median's advantage is substantial. Similarly, the exchange model, which is an average performer otherwise, scores a brilliant success on the dichotomous items, where it is easily the best model. By contrast, two other very successful models struggle with the dichotomous items. The compromise model performs only modestly well, and the mean finishes well below its usual rank, beaten by eight other models.

Further investigation (not shown) demonstrates that the exchange model achieves its advantage on the dichotomous items primarily by doing well on multi-issue proposals.[8] The cross-issue trades emphasised by the exchange model probably affect dichotomous items the most, since these items have no intermediate positions. Vote exchanges and trades move dichotomous outcomes a long way on our scales, and the exchange model seems to take the best account of that.

One must remember, however, that large forecasting errors are particularly common on dichotomous items: one forecast of 30 when the outcome is 100 adds by itself more than two points to the MAE. Two or

[7] In addition to the usual caveats, it is worth remembering that a t-test comparing a model's best performance to its average performance exaggerates the statistical significance of the difference. By picking the best performance to compare, the researcher has capitalised on chance in a way that violates the assumptions underlying the test. Put another way, we would *expect* to see some substantial statistical differences in model performance across issue types just by chance, even if all were due to random noise.

[8] In particular, since the exchange model and the compromise model make identical forecasts on single-issue items, the exchange model's advantage over the compromise model on dichotomous items is *entirely* due to multi-issue proposals.

Table 10.3. *Mean absolute error (MAE) of models by issue type (*n *in brackets if lower than maximum)*

Model	Dichotomous (max $n = 33$)	Ranked (max $n = 109$)	Scale (max $n = 20$)
Baseline models			
Median voter (unweighted)	30.30	29.42	19.70
Mean voter	35.21	21.14	14.75
Substantive models			
Compromise model—SSI-2 (Van den Bos)	33.05	21.02	16.73
Exchange model (Arregui// Thomson)	26.17	23.28	23.44
Coalition model (Boekhoorn/ Van Deemen/Hosli)	32.69	23.14	19.92
Realism model (adapted from Mearsheimer)	33.13	23.27	16.92
Expected utility model (Bueno de Mesquita)	34.25	27.02	23.30
Procedural model (Steunenberg/Selck)	48.55 (19)	26.19 (78)	27.86 (10)
Domestic constraints model (Bailer/Schneider)	31.37	25.30	19.03
Procedural exchange model (König/Proksch)	40.00 (20)	27.93 (83)	27.30 (10)
Tsebelis model (König/Proksch)	35.00 (20)	30.87 (83)	27.30 (10)
Coleman model (König/Proksch)	40.00 (20)	31.33 (83)	27.30 (10)
Issue line model (Widgrén/Pajala)	41.07 (20)	32.90 (83)	29.76 (10)

three substantial prediction errors occurring by chance among 33 dichotomous forecasts can easily change a model's average error by five points or even more, enough to turn one of the best models into one of the worst. Thus as with all the other statistical evaluations, in the absence of additional detailed case studies of the dichotomous issues and careful statistical analysis, interpretive caution is warranted.

10.7 MEAN EUCLIDEAN ERROR PER PROPOSAL: THE MEE

The second measure of closeness differs from the MAE in two ways. First, to take account of the fact that EU proposals often contain several issues considered jointly, we make the unit of prediction the proposal rather than the issue. Second, we adopt a measure of closeness designed for a multi-issue prediction space, namely the Euclidean distance from the prediction to the outcome. The squared Euclidean distance is divided by the number of issues within the proposal to give the average squared distance per issue, and a square root is taken.[9] This is the notion of root mean squared error, computed in this case within each proposal. Finally, these square roots are averaged across proposals, with all proposals counted equally.

This measure treats all the issues as if they were continuous scales, when in fact many are discrete and even dichotomous. However, treating discrete and ordinal data as continuous has long been statistically defensible as a good approximation to far more complex calculations, and we have adopted that approach here (Abelson and Tukey 1959). Similarly, embedding the non-continuous issues in Euclidean space and treating the resulting 'distances' as continuous is intended to be merely heuristic.

As a voting rule, the MEE makes the proposals the voters, not the issues. It also treats losses as essentially quadratic rather than linear. Thus it corresponds, perhaps, to a 'functional representation' voting rule, in which groups, not people, are the voters. The groups, not necessarily all the same size, are then weighted equally in a utilitarian calculation. Thus again this criterion has less appeal than the MAE's straightforward utilitarian perspective, but it does provide an alternate perspective emphasising proposals rather than issues as fundamental.

To spell out this definition, suppose that there are m proposals altogether, each with n_j ($j = 1, \ldots, m$) issues included in it. Thus the total number of issues is, as before, $n = \sum n_j$. Denote the ith issue in the jth proposal by y_{ij} ($i = 1, \ldots, n_j$). Then we define the mean Euclidean error (MEE) for model M as follows:

$$\mathrm{MEE}_M = (1/m)\sum_{j=1}^{m}\left[\sum_{i=1}^{n_j}((y_i - \hat{y}^i)^2/n_j)\right]^{.5} \qquad (10.3)$$

With this definition, the MEE is a straightforward extension of root mean squared error (RMSE), familiar from engineering and economics applications. Here the RMSE is computed across issues within each

[9] Note that without the division by the number of issues in each proposal, those proposals with large numbers of issues would dominate the average, violating the goal of this measure, which is to average over proposals rather than over issues.

Table 10.4. *Mean euclidean error (MEE) by legislative procedure (*n *in brackets if lower than maximum)*

Model	CNS QMV (max $n = 22$)	CNS unan. (max $n = 18$)	COD QMV (max $n = 21$)	COD unan. (max $n = 5$)	Total (max $n = 66$)
Baseline models					
Median voter (unweighted)	32.62	25.59	32.03	33.96	30.62
Mean voter	25.65	20.87	27.22	21.65	24.54
Substantive models					
Compromise model–SSI-2 (Van den Bos)	25.69	19.98	29.96	21.87	25.20
Exchange model (Arregui/Stokman/Thomson)	25.72	20.66	29.04	22.24	25.13
Coalition model (Boekhoorn/Van Deemen/Hosli)	27.92	20.43	33.74	20.85	27.19
Realism model (adapted from Mearsheimer)	28.49	19.98	29.24	23.89	26.06
Expected utility model (Bueno de Mesquita)	35.06	27.93	32.59	27.39	31.75
Procedural model (Steunenberg/Selck)	37.19	32.25 (15)	27.32 (19)	36.32 (4)	32.77 (60)
Domestic constraints model (Bailer/Schneider)	30.94	23.51	32.38	25.23	28.94
Procedural exchange model (König/Proksch)	29.44 (22)	29.64 (15)	27.67 (20)	24.32	28.51 (62)
Tsebelis model (König/Proksch)	28.92 (22)	29.64 (15)	30.42 (20)	24.32	29.21 (62)
Coleman model (König/Proksch)	29.31 (22)	21.21 (15)	27.49 (20)	22.87	26.24 (62)
Issue line model (Widgrén/Pajala)	37.27 (22)	35.77 (15)	35.97 (20)	37.26	36.49 (62)

proposal, in accordance with the standard definition of Euclidean distance. Then the RMSE is averaged across proposals, with all proposals weighted equally, to give the MEE.

Table 10.4 displays the MEE values for each model. We regard this table primarily as a check on the previous tables, which used absolute values and averaged over issues. Happily, Table 10.4 shows that Euclidean distances and averages over proposals do not affect the fundamental ranking of the models. To be sure, there are mild differences here from the previous tables due to the altered definitions. But again the mean, the exchange model, and the compromise model perform best, again with no statistically reliable differences among them. (This time the mean is a bit better than the other two, which are essentially tied.) The coalition, state-centric realism, and Coleman models are the next best performers, close enough that with a larger sample, any of them might prove to be the best performer. The other models are all less successful, as before.

10.8 CORRELATIONS SIMPLISTIC AND SENSIBLE

The third definition of closeness used in this chapter is 'goodness of fit'. For this purpose, we set out two different correlation measures. The first is the simple Pearson correlation coefficient between each model's predictions and the outcomes. The Pearson r has the advantage of familiarity and simplicity. Moreover, with every model judged by the same actual outcomes, the correlations generated by different models may be sensibly compared.[10]

It is important to remember, however, that Pearson correlations do not actually measure 'closeness' in the usual sense. They do not capture how well predictions fit the outcomes. Instead, they are measures of how well *a linear transformation of the predictions* would fit the outcomes. For example, suppose that the actual policy outcomes from three issues are 0, 50, and 100. A first model predicts 0, 50, and 99. A second model predicts 25, 26, and 27. Obviously the first model is vastly better, in the sense of being nearer the outcomes. However, by the Pearson correlation criterion, the second model is the better model, since it correlates perfectly ($r = 1.0$) with the outcomes, while the first model does not.

The problem here is that the Pearson correlation allows 25, 26, and 27 to be transformed linearly before they are compared to the outcome. By subtracting 25 from each of them, then multiplying by 50, they turn into 0, 50, and 100, so their fit is perfect. But this result is a considerable distortion of the usual meaning of predictive accuracy. Thus the correlation coefficient can be quite misleading in this context. It also has no meaningful interpretation as an analogue to a voting rule. For measuring predictive power, it is the least satisfactory measure among those we use.

[10] Comparing correlations across *different* samples is much harder, if not impossible, as good statistical texts remind readers.

Table 10.5. *Pearson correlation between models and observed outcome*

Model	Correlation
Baseline models	
Median voter (unweighted)	.315
Mean voter	.451
Substantive models	
Compromise model—SSI-2 (Van den Bos)	.470
Exchange model (Arregui/Stokman/Thomson)	.490
Coalition model (Boekhoorn/Van Deemen/Hosli)	.444
Realism model (adapted from Mearsheimer)	.410
Expected utility model (Bueno de Mesquita)	.353
Procedural model (Steunenberg/Selck)	.238 (n = 107)
Domestic constraints model (Bailer/Schneider)	.383
Procedural exchange model (König/Proksch)	.342 (n = 113)
Tsebelis model (Koenig/Proksch)	.309 (n = 113)
Coleman model (Koenig/Proksch)	.275 (n = 113)
Issue line model (Widgrén/Pajala)	.257 (n = 113)

Nevertheless, the examination of correlations can be helpful in comparing forecasts. A particular model may be predicting systematically low or high or within too small a range, but if the *pattern* of its forecasts has a linear relationship to outcomes, that information may be exploitable in subsequent model-building.

Table 10.5 displays the Pearson correlations for each model. The exchange model is slightly the best by this criterion, primarily due to its advantage on the dichotomous items with their wide range of outcomes. The compromise model and the mean are close behind, and the coalition and state-centric realism models once more finish in the fourth and fifth positions, while the other models have lower values. Again, as is well known, correlations are particularly noisy measures, so that the precise order of finish has no special importance.[11] As with all the other tables in this chapter, the only sure conclusion is that the top half-dozen models perform better as a group on this criterion than those nearer the bottom. However, these rankings have all the limitations of Pearson correlation coefficients, and we regard them primarily as indirect clues for building better models rather than as true forecasting evaluations.

[11] This is particularly true in the present case, with non-normally distributed data and thus an unknown sampling distribution for the correlations.

A more sensible and useful correlation may be defined. To see how, recall that the conventional R^2 in regression analysis gives the 'percentage of the total variance accounted for' by the model. In that case, 'total variance' is the variance in the dependent variable, i.e. the squared error remaining after the mean of the dependent variable alone has been used to forecast outcomes. The usual R^2 uses a regression model to compute how much of the remaining error can be accounted for with a linear transformation of the explanatory variables in the model.

To define a new correlation coefficient, we need a starting point similar to the mean of the dependent variable. However, the mean will not work here. The decision outcomes analysed in this book are recorded on 0-100 scales, each of which has no natural left-to-right orientation. Flipping some of them left to right would not change their meaning, though it would change the mean of the dependent variable. Thus computing their mean makes little sense. Moreover, we do not wish to allow linear transformations of the forecasts. Hence we need to proceed differently in constructing a correlation coefficient.

First, we choose a value in the observations that is invariant under a left-to-right transformation. For that purpose, we select the midpoint 50 on all our issue scales. Obviously, flipping the scale left to right leaves this value unchanged. Thus the starting prediction, the analogue of the mean in the regression case, is just the midpoint of the scale on each issue.

Next, models are evaluated for their ability to improve on the forecast of 50. We will call this forecast the midrange model. The average squared error of the outcomes around this 'middle prediction' gives us a 'total variance to be explained'.[12] Then, finally, we define a 'pseudo-R^2' for a given model as the model's percentage reduction in mean squared errors compared to the midrange model. No transformation of the model forecasts is allowed: the actual forecasts are used in their original form.

The pseudo-R^2 is defined formally as follows. Call the actual outcomes y_i ($i = 1, \ldots, n$), and let the predicted values from the midrange model be denoted by $\hat{y}_{MM}$. Then the sum of squared errors for the midrange model is $SS_{MM} = \sum_{i=1^n} (y_i - \hat{y}_{MM})^2$. The sum of squared errors for any other model M is denoted by SS_M and is defined in parallel fashion. Then the pseudo-R^2 for model M is defined as:

$$R^2_{\text{pseudo}} = 1 - \frac{SS_M}{SS_{MM}} \tag{10.4}$$

[12] Of course, this quantity is not a variance, hence the quotation marks.

Table 10.6. *Pseudo R^2 (as defined in the text)*

Model	Pseudo R^2
Baseline models	
Midrange model (comparison model)	0.0
Median voter	−0.43
Mean voter	0.16
Substantive models	
Compromise model SSI-2 (Van den Bos)	0.18
Exchange model (Arregui/Stokman/Thomson)	0.15
Coalition model (Boekhoorn/Van Deemen/Hosli)	0.10
Realism model (adapted from Mearsheimer)	0.07
Expected utility model (Bueno de Mesquita)	−0.30
Procedural model (Steunenberg/Selck)	−0.04
Domestic constraints model (Bailer/Schneider)	−0.22
Procedural exchange model (König/Proksch)	−0.59
Tsebelis model (König/Proksch)	−0.62
Coleman model (König/Proksch)	−0.59
Issue line model (Widgrén/Pajala)	−0.54

Thus starting from the midrange model, the pseudo-R^2 gives the additional fractional reduction in explained sum of squares achieved by a given model. Note that, unlike the usual R^2, the pseudo-R^2 can take on negative values if a model performs worse than the midrange model.[13]

In addition to its advantages over the Pearson correlation coefficient, the advantage of the pseudo-R^2 compared to simple MAE or MEE measures is that it takes account of the level of measurement. For example, dichotomous measures convey less statistical information and thus are more difficult to predict than interval-level measures, so that larger errors on the dichotomous items are likely for *all* models. Expressing the squared errors for each model as a percentage of the squared errors for the midrange model is one way to adjust for the differences in scale type.

The pseudo-R^2 values of the best models from previous chapters are given in Table 10.6. As a glance at the table will show, only a few models did as well or better than the midrange model. The compromise model, the mean, and the exchange model have pseudo-R^2 values of just under .2,

[13] The pseudo-R^2 also has an interpretation as an (unweighted) utilitarian rule that uses quadratic losses as its utility measure.

with the compromise model performing slightly better than the other two. The coalition and state-centric realism models are fourth and fifth best, with pseudo-correlation values of about .1. All the other models in this study perform less well than the midrange model, and therefore they have negative pseudo-R^2 values. That is, they perform less well than a model that simply predicts the value 50 all the time.[14]

Again, not too much should be made of the exact order of finish in Table 10.6. The point is rather that we arrive at the same relative ranking of models by this criterion as by previous measures: the top five models do better than those further down the list. Nor is this finding a surprise. The main point of the pseudo-R^2 measure was to adjust for scale types. But Table 10.3 showed that the ranking of models is very little affected by the scale of measurement. Models that did well on the interval-scale issues generally also did well on the ranked and dichotomous issues, and those that did poorly on one type of measurement did poorly on the others as well. Hence the adjustment for scale type has only small marginal effects.

10.9 PAIRWISE COMPARISONS OF MODELS

The next measure of model performance is comparative. We match each model pairwise against every other model. For each pair, we determine the proportion of issues on which the first model is closer to the actual outcome than the second model. That is, we compute the proportion of issues on which the first model is a better forecast. This fraction may then be evaluated statistically by the sign test, and statistically significant differences between models can be distinguished from those that are more likely to be due to chance.

Regarded as a voting rule, this criterion for model evaluation corresponds to the method of majority decision, sometimes called round-robin majority rule. Under that procedure, as noted above, all candidates are matched against each other pairwise. The candidate, if any, who defeats all the others in one-on-one contests by majority rule is declared elected. For model evaluation, it is the issues that have 'votes'. They determine

[14] Other pseudo-R^2 definitions might be proposed. For example, instead of averaging over issues, we might wish to average over proposals, using the MEE values from Table 10.4. The new pseudo-R^2 would then be defined as in Equation 10.3, with each model's MEE replacing the SS values. A glance at Table 10.4 will demonstrate that the same models do well and poorly under this definition as in the other comparisons of this chapter.

whether there is a model that in pairwise competion defeats all the other models. A winning model must enter every one-on-one competition against all the other models and defeat them in the sense of being closer to the actual outcomes on a majority of issues. Using this ancient voting procedure has an obvious appeal as a criterion for model evaluation.

The central advantage of this measure is that, like majority rule and unlike utilitarian rules, it makes use only of ordinal information on each issue.[15] It asks: which of these two models was closer in predicting this decision? Essentially, the measure just counts which model won each issue, and then computes a winning percentage. Thus this measure is relatively robust and quite conservative in its assumptions. Its weakness, of course, is that it counts a close win the same as a big victory, and thus loses some information relative to the MAE and MEE. But used in conjunction with other measures, it brings its own strength, which is very limited dependence on the type of scale used for each issue.

Tables 10.7 computes the pairwise winning percentages among the models, where a 'win' is a prediction closer to the outcome than the other model being compared. Statistical significance is computed for each pair using the sign test.

Again the ranking of the models is very similar to that of the other tables. The compromise model is the only one with a winning percentage above 50 per cent against every other model. However, it just barely defeats the mean and coalition models, and has success rates of approximately 55-60 per cent against the others. Thus the compromise model wins, but not in a landslide.

The other models fall into a near-rank order in the comparisons. Thus the mean loses only to the compromise model and defeats everyone else, the coalition model loses only to the compromise model and the mean, state-centric realism and the exchange model are next best, down to the issue line model, which loses to everyone.[16] Thus the comparisons form almost a (stochastically) transitive scale, with only a few close reversals

[15] This is not quite true. If the two model forecasts fall on opposite sides of the outcome, the spacing of ordinal items on the underlying scale matters in determining which forecast is 'closer'. However, it is certainly true that the sign test is much less dependent on interval-level assumptions than our other measures of model accuracy.

[16] The exchange model's highly focused success on the dichotomous items, combined with its average performance on other scales, means that it will do less well on these paired comparisons, which average across all issues, than it does on hit rates, which reward great success on a minority of items.

Table 10.7. *Proportion of times row was closer to outcome than column (number of comparisons in brackets)*[a]

	Med.	Mean	Comp.	Exch.	Coal.	Real.	Exp.ut	Proc.	Dom.c.	Proc.ex	Tsebe.	Colem.	IssueL.
Med.	–												
Mean	0.57[b] (157)	–											
Comp.	0.57[b] (155)	0.51 (162)	–										
Exch.	0.52 (153)	0.44 (162)	0.42[b] (137)										
Coal.	0.55 (150)	0.48 (162)	0.47 (161)	0.52 (160)	–								
Real.	0.49 (148)	0.40[c] (162)	0.41[c] (135)	0.51 (144)	0.45 (161)	–							
Exp.ut	0.51 (117)	0.43[b] (162)	0.42[b] (154)	0.46 (154)	0.45 (158)	0.43 (148)	–						
Proc.	0.45 (71)	0.41[b] (107)	0.44 (105)	0.46 (105)	0.47 (100)	0.48 (101)	0.51 (84)	–					
Dom.c.	0.52 (141)	0.45 (162)	0.43[b] (160)	0.49 (161)	0.49 (158)	0.51 (158)	0.53 (150)	0.57 (100)	–				
Proc.ex	0.42 (69)	0.46 (113)	0.46 (111)	0.45 (111)	0.43 (106)	0.47 (109)	0.47 (96)	0.48 (58)	0.44 (109)	–			
Tsebe.	0.41 (73)	0.43 (113)	0.42 (111)	0.44 (111)	0.42 (106)	0.44 (109)	0.46 (97)	0.47 (58)	0.42 (109)	0.53 (15)	–		
Colem.	0.30[c] (37)	0.38[c] (112)	0.39[c] (111)	0.41[b] (111)	0.38[c] (106)	0.42 (105)	0.36[c] (75)	0.41 (68)	0.34[c] (102)	0.46 (65)	0.43 (69)	–	
Issue l.	0.34[c] (92)	0.36[c] (113)	0.38[c] (111)	0.41[b] (111)	0.41[b] (108)	0.40[c] (111)	0.42 (106)	0.38[b] (74)	0.39[c] (108)	0.38[b] (71)	0.39[b] (71)	0.44 (91)	–

Notes: [a]Comparisons aren't made when either one of the models made no prediction, or the models tied in closeness.
[b]$p \leq 0.10$
[c]$p \leq 0.05$

in the middle. Again, the implied ranking is essentially the same as in all the previous tables. Obviously, however, each successful model's margin of victories is small and subject to substantial randomness. The significance tests again show that the same three groups of models—best, middle, and worst—obtain here, although the lines between them are indistinct and the precise rank order cannot be determined.

10.10 HIT RATES

We now take up the 'hit rate', that is, the percentage of time that a model forecast, rounded to the nearest possible answer, was correct. For example, on dichotomous issues (scored either 0 or 100), a hit was scored if the model prediction fell on the correct side of 50. A similar procedure was used for the ranked scales. On interval scales, a hit was scored if a model came within ten points of the actual outcome.

This criterion for model evaluation corresponds to an approval voting rule, in which voters are allowed to select as many candidates as they approve of, giving one vote to each. The winner is then the candidate with the most votes. In the same way, in counting hits, each issue "approves" a model if its forecast is near the outcome. Issues can approve as many models as they like, giving a hit to each one. The model with the most hits is the best model under this criterion.

Obviously this measure, like the corresponding voting rule, is a rather special criterion lacking the long–standing appeal and history of utilitarian or majority rule procedures. Nevertheless, we include it here because it may detect a model that behaves like the proverbial little girl: when she was good, she was very, very good, but when she was bad, she was horrid. That is, the hit-rate measure favours models that are sometimes very, very good at prediction, even if they are bad, or even horrid, at other times. Despite their errors, models with occasional dramatic successes can be quite informative for the next round of model building.

Table 10.8 gives the 'hit rates' for each of the models. Approximately the same overall ordering of the models holds once again. Now the mean finishes first, with the exchange model, the compromise model, the state-centric realism model, and the coalition model all very close behind. Of course, none of the differences among these five models are statistically significant, or even close to significance. Thus, once again, no special meaning attaches to the detailed order of finish.

As it did on the pseudo-correlation measure, the domestic constraints model falls out of the first group and into the second category, since it

Table 10.8. *Hits per model by scale type (*n *in brackets if lower than maximum)*[a]

Model	Dichotomous (max $n = 33$)	Ordered ranking (max $n = 109$)	Scale (max $n = 20$)	Percent hits (max $n = 162$)
Baseline models				
Median voter (unweighted)	24	23	10	35
Mean voter	24	49	11	52
Substantive models				
Compromise model—SSI-2 (Van den Bos)	20	50	10	49
Exchange model (Arregui/Stokman/Thomson)	29	46	6	50
Coalition model (Boekhoorn/Van Deemen/Hosli)	21	47	8	47
Realism model (adapted from Mearsheimer)	22	46	9	48
Expected utility model (Bueno de Mesquita)	22	30	8	37
Procedural model (Steunenberg/Selck)	10 (19)	26 (78)	4 (10)	37 (107)
Domestic constraints model (Bailer/Schneider)	23	32	10	40
Procedural exchange model (König/Proksch)	12 (20)	31 (83)	4 (10)	42 (113)
Tsebelis model (König/Proksch)	13 (20)	29 (83)	4 (10)	41 (113)
Coleman model (König/Proksch)	12 (20)	15 (83)	4 (10)	27 (113)
Issue line model (Widgrén/Pajala)	13 (20)	21 (83)	3 (10)	33 (113)

Note: [a]For dichotomous and ordinal items, a hit was recorded if the model prediction was closer to the actual outcome than to any other possible outcome. The absolute error of the forecast was less than 10 points on the 100-point scale.

performs only a little better than the expected utility model and the median. Interestingly, too, by this measure the procedural models rise up to the second tier of models. In fact, they all out-perform the median. Is this a hint that procedural models sometimes get the outcome very nearly exactly right, but other times miss badly? Does that happen because strict legal procedures control some decisions, while bargaining dominates others? If so, there is more than one statistical 'regime' in EU decision-making, and procedural models would be expected to do fairly well on 'hits' and not very well on mean absolute forecast errors, just as they do in the decisions analysed in this book. Detailed statistical and case study analysis would be needed to answer these questions, but the effort seems worthwhile.

10.11 WHICH MODELS ARE BEST?

The five measures discussed thus far—the MAE, the MEE, the pseudo-correlation, the pairwise win percentages, and the hit rates—comprise the model evaluations undertaken in this chapter. We make no overarching claims for any of them. Each of them would make excellent sense statistically if certain distributional assumptions held for all the issues (for example, normal distributions for the MEE), but no such assumptions can apply to the variety of issues and levels of measurement present in the data. Instead, we adopt these five measures because each has substantial intuitive content. Their meanings are clear and familiar, as are their limitations. Thus our approach to model evaluation is heuristic rather than rigorous. Happily, it turned out that the conclusions of our analysis did not depend on the choice of evaluation measure that we employed.

In summary, all our model comparisons come to essentially the same result. The compromise model, the mean, and the exchange model perform somewhat better in our comparisons than their nearest competitors, with typical absolute errors of about 23 points on a 100-point scale. They also have predictions closer to actual outcomes in head-to-head competition with other models, along with higher 'hit rates'. These three models, closely related in their theoretical workings, monopolised the top three positions on nearly every overall test we performed.

Forced to choose a first-place model, one might say that the compromise model wins narrowly. It comes in first on three of the five relevant measures (the MAE, the pseudo-correlation, and the pairwise comparisons). Two of these victories occur on important criteria analogous to the utilitarian and majority-rule voting procedures (MAE and pairwise comparisons).[17]

[17] In the original plan of this book, the compromise model was to serve as a baseline to demonstrate the additional predictive power of other models. No theoretical development of the model was planned because no need for it was foreseen. When the compromise model unexpectedly performed as well as it did, however, the

The mean finishes second. It captures two top prizes analogous to weighted utilitarian and approval voting analogues (the MEE and the hit rate), and is second on the other three measures. The exchange model is third. In the model evaluations, it finishes second twice, third twice, and fourth once, yet always close to the top, and it wins the (less relevant) Pearson correlation. However, these differences are all small, statistically unreliable, and not independent of each other, meaning that the outcome among the three top models is best described as a virtual tie.

The coalition and state-centric realism models also predict well, and the domestic constraints model frequently does so—a difference in predictive power from the top three models that is occasionally statistically significant but not uniformly so. The median and Challenge models typically finish next best in our tests. All the other models generate more dramatic errors, and they also fail to predict on many of the issues. They are statistically clearly inferior to the best models.

As with the top three models, the evaluations of lower-ranked models do not change if Euclidean errors on multiple issues are used in place of absolute errors on single issues, nor are they altered if we average by EU proposal rather than by issues. Correlational measures, bilateral competitive tests, and point prediction 'hit rates' generated only small differences in model evaluations, none of them statistically reliable. By and large, too, the rankings are the same in different issue arenas and for different levels of measurement.

Thus we have some confidence that the overall rankings of the models reflect genuine differences in predictive power. In particular, the top five or six models virtually always rank best under any plausible measure of predictive success, with the compromise model, the mean, and the exchange model almost always taking the top three positions. That is the central finding of the model comparisons.

The remaining topic, then, is the theoretical inference to be drawn from these comparisons. We also take up the question of how our findings should influence future theorising.

10.12 CONCLUSIONS

Formal mathematical models in political science have become less abstract and more detailed in their description of institutions. Increasingly,

surprised author of this chapter turned his hand to developing the argument for the compromise model set out in Chapter 4.

they can be used to predict both quantitative outcomes in laboratory experiments and qualitative features of political life (Morton 1999). Some formal models, such as those discussed in this book, go further and generate precise predictions of actual political events, such as decisions by policy-makers.

The comparative statistical study of such models stems from Bueno de Mesquita and Stokman (1994). The present work has followed in their footsteps and attempts to advance the subject by exploring a variety of additional models and evaluating them for predictive accuracy with a much larger data set. What do these model evaluations teach us about our current theories? Five central conclusions seem to arise.

First, social scientists are very far from predicting political decisions accurately. Even our best models have average errors exceeding 20 points on a 100-point scale. To see how modest that level of predictive success is, suppose that outcomes occurred randomly and uniformly across the 100 points of the scale. Suppose further that we forecast a random point on the scale, also distributed uniformly and independently of the actual outcome. Such forecasts are obviously completely useless, and they correlate exactly zero with the outcomes. Thus they form a useful lower bound for comparison of prediction errors.

A little calculation shows that the mean forecast error (MAE) for this useless random model would be 33.3. Alas, most of the theoretically sophisticated procedural models discussed in this book, based on extensive form games, are performing only slightly better than that, with MAEs of 30 or more. Even our best models cut that error rate only by a third, to about 23. Clearly, on any absolute scale of predictive accuracy, we have far to go. Our models differ from reality far more than they differ from each other. For example, the forecasts from the compromise model and the exchange model correlate with each other at .87, but each correlates less than .5 with the actual outcomes.

Nor is that finding solely a judgement on formal models. Neither case studies nor statistical modelling have pointed the way to better predictions. In EU studies as in political science as a whole, we are far from having the conceptual tools of any methodological type that we need to forecast political decision-making well.

Second, as a group, the procedural models based entirely on the legal rules of EU decision-making do not perform well on average. However EU decision-making is carried out, it does not seem to be well described solely by the formal rules. Informal norms and procedures appear to play a more central role. Seen in this light, the prominent debate between

Tsebelis (1994) and Crombez (1996) over the proper extensive form for modelling the EU emerges as a rather minor concern. The forecasting weaknesses of extensive form games stem from deeper problems.

Third, the state-centric realism proposed by Mearsheimer (1994–95) also proves inadequate. This approach, in which national interests determine the behaviour of international institutions, does not fare badly in our statistical tests, but it is consistently outperformed by similar models that incorporate the postulates of liberalism. In particular, assuming that international organs such as the European Parliament and the Commission play an independent role beyond state interests leads to better forecasts.

Fourth, the disagreement (or reversion) point does not seem to play the central role in decision-making that extensive form games imply that it should. Consider, for example, those issues on which the decision outcome was far from the disagreement point. (Often the disagreement point is the *status quo*, so that outcomes far from the disagreement point result in a large change from current policy.) These are issues in which the disagreement point was weak. It was overcome in some way and did not constrain the decision-makers to locate nearby. In Table 10.9, decisions of that kind are treated as predictors of model errors. More precisely, the size of the outcome change from the disagreement point (denoted 'change') is correlated with each model's predictive errors.

Table 10.9 shows that the procedural models, many of which make crucial use of the disagreement point in predicting errors, tend to make larger errors when the disagreement point is weak in influence. That is, they put too much weight on it.[18] By contrast, the other models ignore the disagreement point, they do better overall, and their prediction errors do not generally grow worse when the decision outcome represents a large change from the disagreement outcome. More detailed investigation will be necessary to fully validate this claim about the over-emphasis on reversion points in the procedural modelling tradition, but Table 10.9 provides some evidence that coalitions and bargaining somehow down-weight the leverage that reversion points logically seem to have in our most powerful theoretical models.

[18] The domestic constraints model also employs the disagreement point in its calculations, but only as part of a Nash bargaining solution. That is, it uses the disagreement point to establish bargaining weights, but it does not employ an extensive form game that treats disagreement points as a crucial factor in actors' thinking about their decisions. Perhaps for that reason, the errors of the domestic constraints model are negligibly correlated with the variable change.

Table 10.9. *Pearson correlation of model errors with variable change [Number of observations in brackets]*

Model	Change[a] (max n = 129)
Baseline models	
Median voter (unweighted)	.065 (105)
Mean voter	.027 (105)
Substantive models	
Compromise model—SSI-2 (Van den Bos)	−.076 (105)
Exchange model (Arregui/Stokman/Thomson)	.001 (105)
Coalition model (Boekhoorn/Van Deemen/Hosli)	−.230[b] (105)
Realism model (adapted from Mearsheimer)	.076 (105)
Expected utility model (Bueno de Mesquita)	−.207[b](105)
Procedural model (Steunenberg/Selck)	.094 (88)
Domestic constraints model (Bailer/Schneider)	.107 (105)
Procedural exchange model (König/Proksch)	.327[c] (93)
Tsebelis model (König/Proksch)	.422[c] (93)
Coleman model (König/Proksch)	−.206[b] (93)
Issue line model (Widgrén/Pajala)	.630[c] (93)

Notes: [a]The variable change is defined as the absolute difference between the observed outcome and the disagreement point. Correlations were computed only for ordered ranked and scale issues. Negative correlation means that the model performs better at more extreme outcomes; a positive correlation means the reverse.
[b]significant at 5 per cent.
[c]significant at 10 per cent.

Fifth and perhaps most important, the models that are most successful all compute some sort of mean among actor preferences, weighted or unweighted. In these models, EU decision-making is treated as if extreme positions are accommodated rather than being ignored, even when ignoring them would still allow the other actors to get their way. Moreover, there is some evidence from the compromise, exchange, and coalition models that power and salience also matter. That is, powerful and intense actors are conciliated, even when they might legally be ignored. By bargaining and/or exchange, actors may give up certain goals they care less about in exchange for other goals they value more.

The conclusion that bargaining and compromise are central to EU decision-making will come as no surprise to political practitioners and participant observers. The case study literature has repeatedly emphasised the role of compromise and the striving for unanimity in EU decision-making. States are disinclined to follow the letter of their legal rights if doing so makes an enemy. Bargaining matters more than the official decision-making rules.[19]

In the data analysed in this book, too, the outcomes often show clear tradeoffs across issues, with states that care less about particular topics deferring to more intense states, while the less intense states in turn get their way on other issues of greater concern to them. But such tradeoffs do not occur in most procedural models, which typically analyse issues one decision at a time. By its nature, then, a single-issue analysis of the sort used by many conventional procedural models will struggle to capture the cross-issue trades that political actors make. Put another way, procedural models usually ignore intensity differences across different decisions simply because they look myopically at each decision on its own. The result is that they may be beaten in predictive accuracy, as they are in this book, by less theoretically sophisticated models that take those intensities into account. The inference would seem to be that good forecasting requires that bargaining and intensity be part of the model.

It is important not to misread the evaluations in this chapter. It would be quite wrong to infer that procedural models should be discarded in favour of very simple models like the mean and the compromise model, or any of the other top-performing models of this book such as the exchange and coalition models. None of these successful models takes real account of the ways in which institutional forms and legal structures create actors' strategy spaces. Only procedural models do that, and in so doing, they have taught us too much to throw them away.

The lesson instead is that procedural models need theoretical extension. They need to take into account not just the formal rules, but also the informal processes that make up so much of what politicians do. Creating theoretical structures adequate to that challenge will not be easy. But combining bargaining and vote-trading theory on the one hand with the procedural framework on the other, and doing so in the theoretically coherent and defensible manner that is the hallmark of modern game theory—that, surely, is the future of forecasting political decisions.

[19] Andy Moravcsik has suggested to us that those issues suitable for bargaining may be more likely to become EU proposals and thus more likely to be included in our data set. But if so, this selection mechanism would bias the sample against the intractable, not against issues suited to other decision mechanisms. It is hard to see why issues suited to procedural decision-making would be excluded from EU proposals, for example.

11

Evidence with *insight: what models contribute to EU research*

GERALD SCHNEIDER, BERNARD STEUNENBERG AND MIKA WIDGRÉN

11.1 INTRODUCTION

The Treaties of Maastrict, Amsterdam, and Nice are milestones of European integration. In each case, the negotiation and ratification processes attracted widespread media and popular attention. More recently, the Treaty Establishing a Constitution for Europe also drew sustained interest from broad sectors of European society until it failed ratification in several member states during 2005. Academics are drawn to stirring events just as the press and public are, and thus many political scientists have written engagingly about the 'grand bargains' embodied in the successive EU treaties (e.g. Moravcsik 1998).

Day to day, however, the business of the EU does not make front-page headlines. Like any government, the EU spends most of its time deciding routine matters, such as the wording of health warnings on tobacco products or the funding of student exchanges in Europe. Indeed, both tobacco label and student exchange decisions appear in the data set used in this book. The EU's own organs decide these issues—the Commission, the Council of Ministers, and the European Parliament (EP). Mid-level civil servants and ordinary Members of the European Parliament (MEPs) may play critical roles. Prime ministers and chancellors, who loom so large in the grand bargains, do not.

In this volume, we have directed our energies toward the explanation of everyday EU decisions. We make no apology for doing so. Although some legislative acts are merely technical correctives or minor bureaucratic rule-making, the great majority of the decisions examined here

We would like to thank Christopher Achen, Frans Stokman, Daniela M. Bailer-Jones, Antoaneta Dimitrova, the reviewers and editors of this book for their helpful comments and suggestions. The title is a paraphrase of Singer (1969).

affect the lives of many Europeans. The daily multiplication of such decisions, cumulating over many years, has altered Europe dramatically and irrevocably, in ways visible to the entire world.

Thus understanding the quotidian political battles of the EU is not of minor concern. To the contrary, the relentless march of daily decision-making has at least as much importance and deserves every bit as much attention as the sporadic grand bargains that dot recent European history. Both are critical to understanding why the EU has had the impact it has had, and why it is among the world's most effective supranational political organisations. But only the grand bargains have enjoyed extensive discussion. Hence the focus of this book: how can we explain everyday decisions in the European Union?

The approach we have taken derives from rational choice theory, simply because the recent upsurge in game-theoretic models of EU decision-making has added so dramatically to our understanding. Yet the accomplishments of the past few years have been primarily conceptual: we learned a great deal about the internal coherence of our ideas and about the logical implications of our explanations. Contradictions in our previous informal explanations were discovered, and our attention was directed to seemingly minor aspects of EU policy-making that turned out to have large, previously unnoticed theoretical consequences. However, until the publication of this volume and an accompanying special issue of *European Union Politics,* we did not know nearly as much about how these competing approaches fare in explaining and predicting a broad set of decision outcomes. The dual purpose of this volume, therefore, has been to set out the wide variety of existing rational choice models, and then to explore how well they predict actual EU legislative outcomes.

The models in this volume fall into three main sets. The first group, the *procedural models*, emphasise the decision-making rules and formal procedures that constrain the actors. The sequence of moves by the various actors within those rules is taken to be the crucial element of EU decision-making. These models use the formal legislative rules in order to describe the game form, that is the definition of players, their decision-making rights and the sequence in which they can make their choices. Of course, some aspects of EU decision-making are not formalised and thus are subject to alternate interpretations. Is the Commission a gatekeeper, in the sense that it can ignore requests by the Council and EP to initiate legislative proposals? Does the Council or Parliament move first in drafting a compromise proposal under the co-decision procedure? Scholars disagree. Most models developed in this approach therefore combine the formal rules with an interpretation of the informal norms, as Chapter 3 demonstrated. The procedural models then use the Nash equilibrium or its refinements for identifying and predicting outcomes.

The second set of models in this book stress the informal bargaining and negotiations that occur before the formal decision-making takes place. We label this category *bargaining models*. The proponents of this theoretical tradition do not assume the institutional setting away. They maintain that formal rules and procedures create settings for informal negotiations, as well as fallback options when negotiations fail. The legal rules determine which actors are included in the negotiation process and how much weight is given to their positions, but they are not the actual decision mechanism themselves. Bargaining is the central decision-making process, not voting.

The bargaining models in the present volume assume that only actors with formal voting power matter. National and cross-national interest groups may have shaped the positions adopted by the member states, for example, but that activity is prior to the starting point of the data set under study. Thus the bargaining models in this book generally assume that the weights of actors in the informal negotiations primarily depend on their formal voting power. Hence they take the Shapley Shubik Index (SSI) as a good estimate of these weights. Some of the bargaining models in this book assume that the grand coalition of all actors forms. Others investigate bilateral deals between actors, which have positive or negative externalities for other actors, and still others investigate non-cooperative bargaining solutions. The cooperative solutions base their predictions on the Nash bargaining solution.

The third group of models attempts to combine a partial characterisation of an extensive form bargaining game with the procedural voting game played according to legal rules. We call these *mixed models*. These approaches presume that pre-play agreements can be interpreted as a first step in the decision-making process. A compromise, for instance, might amount to an exchange of votes or to an agreement on the relative importance of different conflictual issues in one legislative proposal. However, formal rules and procedures determine the solution of remaining controversies. For the latter, non-cooperative equilibrium concepts are normally applied, but within the restricted set of feasible outcomes of the pre-play negotiations.

Most of the models presented here have been developed in other contexts. The procedural models, for instance, have been employed mainly to explain how rules structure legislative interactions within the

US Congress. Cooperative bargaining models enjoy a rich intellectual heritage starting with the seminal contributions of Edgeworth and Nash. Bargaining models have been used extensively for political forecasting and strategic intervention (Bueno de Mesquita 2002; Stokman *et al* 2000). In this book, the models have been adapted to the context of the European Union. Each model and the mechanisms behind its predictions are illustrated with case studies which help validate the assumptions, but also show where potential weaknesses lie.

The last and perhaps most important feature of this volume is that the different models are tested empirically against baseline models and against each other. This collaborative research effort is to our knowledge the largest attempt ever undertaken to empirically evaluate competing decision-making models. Until now, due to the absence of a common data set that could be used to assess the predictive power of alternative models, it has been impossible to compare different explanations of EU policy-making (Gabel *et al* 2002). Critics could always attribute the failures of their favourite models to the differences in case selection strategies. By contrast, our research design focuses all models on a common data set. This research strategy is relatively new to legislative studies, and combined with the size of the decision sample, it provides a unique opportunity to assess closely the empirical validity of different explanatory models.

In the remainder of this chapter, we will summarise which models predict best and discuss why the performance of the models differs. Then, because the theoretical and empirical findings presented in this book open avenues to improving both the models and the strategies for testing them, we will conclude by attempting to foresee what future research on this topic might accomplish.

11.2 THE MAIN FINDINGS AND THEIR IMPLICATIONS

The theoretical debate on European integration has long focused on unwieldy questions with either unknowable or obvious answers: what is the true nature of regional collaboration? Among regional collaborations, is the European Union *sui generis* or can it be compared to other political entities? Questions of this kind are definitional or at best descriptive; they are not researchable in any deeper sense.

Since the 1990s, however, we have witnessed an increasing number of studies that present testable hypotheses. The neo-institutionalist approach has been particularly instrumental in moving the field towards 'normal science' (Aspinwall and Schneider 2000; Dowding 2000). The theoretical and empirical research reported in this volume aims to push these discussions one step further.

The first area in which this book attempts a contribution is the procedural theory of legislative choice. While examinations of the choices made by the European Parliament or other EU institutions were largely behaviouralist until the mid-1990s, the simultaneous publication of two examinations of the cooperation procedure gave impetus to the rigorous formal study of legislative rules (Steunenberg 1994a; Tsebelis 1994). As noted above, one disturbing aspect of these studies has been the frequent disagreement among researchers about the 'game' institutional actors are supposed to be playing. The first dispute focused on the question of whether or not the institutional changes of the 1980s empowered the European Parliament.

A second debate arose in the 1990s when the European Union introduced the co-decision procedure. Tsebelis (1997) claimed that this constitutional change weakened rather than strengthened the legislature, while Crombez (2001) and Steunenberg (1997; 2002a) attributed more power to the Parliament. These divergent theoretical claims can now be confronted with empirical results. As indicated by Steunenberg and Selck in Chapter 3, Parliament appears, next to the Council, to be a strong and important legislative actor under the co-decision procedure. By making the initial proposal to the intergovernmental body, Parliament in their view has a first-move advantage, which forms the starting point for further negotiations. This suggests that Parliament may not have lost its 'conditional agenda-setting power', as Tsebelis claimed it had. On the contrary, it can engage in direct negotiations with the Council, a power it did not have under the cooperation procedure. This result, which is supported by other empirical work (Kasack 2004; König and Pöter 2001; Selck and Steunenberg 2004), may indicate that the current co-decision procedure has indeed strengthened Parliament's power.

The second contribution of this volume to legislative analysis lies in bargaining interpretations of EU policy-making. As a broad conclusion, the empirical analyses in Chapter 10 suggest that bargaining models perform better than procedural models, and that among the models that incorporate bargaining, pure bargaining models based on cooperative game theory do better than those that mix procedural and bargaining aspects. Put another way, at this stage of our understanding, pure bargaining models predict best as a class, while pure legalist models perform worst. The more mixed models include procedural aspects, the worse they do.

This set of findings is supported by parallel studies, where other game theory concepts interpretable as bargaining outcomes also performed quite well in explaining outcomes of EU decision-making. In a study on EU budget allocations, Baldwin *et al* (2001) find that a straightforward cooperative solution concept like the Shapley Shubik Index explains receipts far more accurately than does the income level of a country or the share of agriculture in its GDP, which are the two main ingredients of budget transfers. More recently, Kauppi and Widgrén (2004) reached the same conclusion using a considerably enlarged data set on EU budget receipts between 1976 and 2001. The Shapley Shubik Index was not, however, able to capture all variation in budget transfers. The explanatory power of this cooperative solution improved considerably when *a priori* coalitions among member states were allowed. Surprisingly, the best performing coalition structures were relatively stable over time, consisting of the same member states. This confirms our own finding that cooperative models need to take the detailed structure of actors' preferences into account and to use the Shapley Shubik values as important influences on the outcome rather than as final predictions. That is what the models in this book do.

Another implication of the bargaining perspective follows as well. If the final vote is less important than the haggling taking place before it, we should question the relevance and reliability of the numerous studies that try to uncover the issue dimensions in the Council of Ministers or the European Parliament using data on roll call voting (Matilla and Lane 2001; Carruba *et al* 2004). Valuable as those studies have been, they may be improved by further work that takes voting positions as strategic choices rather than the original raw preferences, as bargaining theory suggests.

Why is the bargaining perspective more successful in predicting outcomes than other models? Part of the reason is that unanimity appears to be a strong norm in EU legislation, even when qualified majority voting (QMV) is allowed. EU personnel believe that consensus is the right decision mode. This suggests that legal characteristics of the decision-making procedure, such as the voting rule or the order in which political actors may propose legislation or cast their vote, shape the final outcomes less dramatically than procedural models imagine.

Procedural models probably suffer most from their implicit assumption that day-to-day decision-making consists of thousands of unrelated single-shot events, so that political actors ought to maximise their self-interest on every one. However, even when the rules permit it, exploiting the weak is not regarded as being an appropriate way of making decisions. Unilateral aggressive moves, however 'rational' from the single-play perspective of most procedural models, may lead in practice to unfavourable responses by other players, which both endanger the proper functioning of the institution and damage the potential exploiter as well. This perspective helps explain why, among the various models discussed in this volume, those using the procedural variation in legal contexts to predict outcomes frequently misfire. As our collective research effort indicates, adopting EU legislation by unanimity, whenever possible, is a shared norm no matter what the legal context, and that norm seems to overpower the legal rules.

In addition, the alignments of EU actors are often highly case specific. A single dimension statistically accounts for only one third of the variance of all actor positions (Thomson *et al* 2004; Zimmer *et al* 2005). In policy areas without stable patterns of coalition formation, actors can be confident that every other actor will need their help at some future date. Thus the concessions they make to actors who have high interests in the issues currently being discussed will be compensated in future situations when their own interests matter more. Such reciprocal, non-negotiated exchanges are highly important in generating unanimously supported solutions, even when a qualified majority is legally able to impose its will (Stokman 2004; 2005). All these conditions strongly facilitate the universally inclusive, compromise mode of decision-making that predicts outcomes best.

Under these conditions, and assuming that actors have quadratic loss functions on the issue continua (implying risk aversion), Achen showed in Chapter 4 that the average of the policy positions, weighted by the product of each actor's power and salience, is a first-order approximation of the cooperative Nash bargain solution. It is this solution, denoted the compromise model, that gives the best predictions of all models. This model implies that powerful actors who attach most salience to the issues receive the largest concessions from the other negotiators. However, all actors are conciliated to some degree even if they could legally be ignored.

Another variation of the bargaining model stresses the importance of positional exchanges. The position exchange model investigates whether explicitly negotiated bilateral deals between actors, involving issue linkages, can improve upon the predictive accuracy of the Nash bargaining solution. Such bilateral deals can contribute to consensus-building when the resulting shifts in the outcomes have positive externalities for the other actors, i.e., when the outcomes shift in the direction of the preferred positions of third actors, not involved in the exchanges. When the decision outcomes move away from the preferred positions of actors not directly involved in the exchange, negative externalities are created. When this is the case, such bilateral deals are likely to hinder consensus-building.

The distribution of positions and saliencies on the controversial issues within the 66 European Commission proposals studied here is such that the negative externalities of the bilateral exchanges predicted by the position exchange model are about twice as high as the positive externalities. This shows that purely bilateral exchanges in these proposals tend *not* to contribute to consensus-building. Arregui, Stokman and Thomson (Chaper 5) see this as the most important reason why the exchange model did not improve upon the accuracy of the compromise model, whereas it did so in a test with a smaller data set (Bueno de Mesquita and Stokman 1994) and in other applications.

If common interests and reciprocal exchanges between permanently changing coalitions indeed prevail, then negotiation strategies backed by power dominance or implicit threats will be uncommon in EU decision-making. Hence we would expect the non-cooperative bargaining model developed by Bueno de Mesquita (the challenge model presented in Chapter 5 of this book) to predict only modestly well. Indeed, in our study the challenge model performs only a bit better than the procedural models and much less well than the compromise and exchange models.

This finding differs from that of Bueno de Mesquita and Stokman (1994), who examined a small data set on decision-making in the Council of Ministers. In that study, Bueno de Mesquita's model performed as well or even a bit better than the compromise and exchange models, though the differences were not statistically significant. It now appears from our larger sample that, if our data set is indicative, the challenge model was favoured by statistical good fortune in the earlier, smaller trial.

These findings do not imply that Bueno de Mesquita's threat mechanisms are unimportant. On the contrary, consensus on the prevailing common interests will not survive long if it cannot be connected with a sanctioning mechanism that ensures the enforcement of compromises. Formal rules provide safeguards to actors in case fundamental problems arise or some actors misbehave. However, regular use of implicit threats probably does not account for much EU decision-making. The more often member states or other EU actors have to resort to threats, the more fragile the consensus norm will become. In a private relationship, referring a conflict to the court to enforce a contract usually results in the ending of that relationship. Similarly, frequent use of the letter of the law decision by decision is likely to undermine the perception of common interests (Stokman 2004; 2005). It is this gap between daily life in the EU and the assumptions of Bueno de Mesquita's model that may account for the relative lack of success of his model in our data.

If self-interested exploitation of procedural rules undermines the consensus norm, and if unanimous decisions are desirable, partial agreements supported by majorities only will be avoided. This perspective helps explain why a Nash bargaining solution or compromise model applied solely within minimal winning coalitions encounters prediction errors. Thus in the model presented in Chapter 7, minimal winning coalitions are evaluated against each other on the basis of the amount of conflict expected within them. Conflict is assumed to depend either on the spread of the initial positions of the actors within the coalition, or on how evenly losses are distributed among the actors in the coalition. The less conflictual coalitions form, and the compromise model determines payoffs within them. The model is intuitively appealing and its predictive performance places it among the better models, but nonetheless it predicts less well on average than the compromise model, which uses the same payoff formula but applies it to the grand coalition involving all actors.

Two other mixed models also appeared in this book. The *procedural exchange model*, presented in Chapter 8, assumes that actors first exchange power resources, giving extra weight to issues that are of high interest to them at the expense of issues in which they are less interested. Subsequently, decisions are taken according to the relevant procedural rule, taking into account the redistribution of actors' power during the prior exchange process. The second such model, the *conditional procedural model* presented in Chapter 9, assumes that complexity increases quickly with the number of controversial issues in a Commission proposal. The model therefore assumes that all controversial issues are first reduced to one overall dimension of conflict. Subsequently, the relevant procedural rule is applied to determine the outcome on that integrated dimension. Both these models generate predictions with a high average error.

11.3 THE LIMITS OF PREDICTIVE POWER AND THE NEED FOR ADDITIONAL DATA

During the past few years, discussion of the linkage between theoretical and empirical work has intensified in political science (e.g. Morton 1999), economics (e.g. Stigum 1990), and sociology (e.g. Opp 1990), and this debate has already led to discussion on the appropriate tools to test models (e.g. Signorino 1999; Clarke 2003). Sophistication about testing is important. For example, the different chapters in this volume show that naïve models such as the mean of actor preferences often do better than those with a solid theoretical foundation. The game-theoretical work on the European Union, it should be pointed out, is not alone in this regard. If prediction is the only yardstick for the evaluation of a social-scientific explanation, 'role playing', for instance, may produce more accurate forecasts than sophisticated theoretical models (De Gooijer 2002; Erev *et al* 2002).

Ad hoc predictions and 'rules of thumb' have limited explanatory value. Meteorologists are not satisfied theoretically by 'the weather of tomorrow will be like the weather of today', even though that statement has a high likelihood of forecasting correctly. Similarly, the median and the mean might predict EU decisions reasonably well, but they give no insight into the underlying causal mechanisms. *Why* did the decision end up in the middle of actor preferences? Only theoretically informed models that model individual human choices—micro-foundations—can answer that question. Prediction and explanation are not the same thing.

To paraphrase Singer (1969), we need evidence *with* insight. Neglecting one aspect at the expense of another leads to either anaemic 'model platonism' (Albert 1965) or to barefoot empiricism[1] (see also Morgan and Morrison 1999). As Achen noted in Chapter 10, however, the challenge in studying the EU is that at present, our insightful models do only modestly well with the evidence, while those that track the data, like the mean, median, and even the compromise model, provide only limited insight into the causal processes. Thus much remains to be done.

To do better in future, more attention will need to be paid to measurement issues. There is a subtle reciprocal relationship between collection of the data needed for modelling and construction of models to fit those

[1] Philosophers of science disagree over the place of models in the scientific process. For a recent discussion see Bailer-Jones (2003).

data. A fascinating case study by Van den Bogaard (1999) details how choices about model specification and data usage were intertwined in setting up the Tinbergen model in the 1930s, which became the central modelling device of the Dutch Central Planning Bureau 20 years later. She writes that this influential macro econometric model 'was used as an aid in decisions concerning measurement and was itself used as a reason to develop the measurement system' (Van den Bogaard 1999: 308–309).

Similarly, we need to address both the implications of the empirical results for the theoretical models and the implications of the way in which we measured crucial concepts for the performance of the models. Some models in this book required data that were difficult to collect because the expert practitioners used as informants could not easily recognise the concepts at issue. A task for future research is whether the data collection procedures or those models need to be rethought.

Another critical measurement problem is the construct validity of the variables we measured. This technical term stands for the extent to which key factors are measured adequately. The research team collectively considered various options for measurement and data collection, aiming at the best data attainable within budget constraints (see Chapter 2 for a more detailed discussion). Inevitably, tradeoffs were made. Data sets are imperfect, and this one is no exception. For example, we asked the expert observers to assign interval scale scores to ordinal data, even when we suspected that other policy options unknown to us were probably discussed by the actors involved but omitted from our ordinal rankings. Some members of the group were concerned that applying quadratic loss computations to the resulting ordinal and dichotomous measures, including multi-dimensional versions of those versions, as we did in Chapter 10, might have worse consequences than just the usual minor difficulties of any approximation. They felt that doing so might violate the basic assumptions of the spatial theory of voting (Enelow and Hinich 1984; Hinich and Munger 1997), or might inappropriately distort the rankings of model performance. They preferred other preference measures developed within the social choice literature, but not yet applied to the context of European Union decision-making.[2] Other members of the group disagreed.

[2] See, for instance, Holler's (1994) extension of a model proposed by Steunenberg (1994b) on regulatory policy-making, and Van Hees and Steunenberg's (2000) model of how courts rule.

To flag such issues, authors of some chapters have appropriately pointed out these and other possible weakness of the data set, which should be taken into account in further research, as Bueno de Mesquita (2004) discusses in detail. In particular, it would be very helpful to estimate accurately the full number of options that were available to the stakeholders. To do so, future researchers will undoubtedly supplement the interview material with the protocols from the Council and other decision-making bodies.

Finally, we note that we analysed 'successful' decisions in this study. The error reported in the different chapters concerns the difference between the outcome predicted by some models and the actual outcome. Only cases for which a final proposal was made are included. This means that the empirical analysis does not account for the withdrawal of a proposal by the Commission, or cases that were not decided within the timeframe used for the data collection. The main finding of consensual decision-making among the member states in the Council and between the Council, Commission and Parliament may have been affected by this choice. Further analysis of the cases of non-decision-making, in which the Commission withdraws a proposal or the member states postpone further discussion, may help in understanding the conditions under which consensual decision-making in the Union is effective.

11.4 THEORETICAL ISSUES FOR FUTURE RESEARCH

What are the ways ahead for theory development? The findings presented in this volume show some ways to improve future EU research based on the experiences and findings from the current project.

First, we assumed that the Commission and the Parliament can be represented as unitary actors.[3] We all know that the Commission consists of different Commissioners who are responsible for distinctive EU policies and bring their own ideology and commitments to the cabinet meetings in Brussels. Yet a strong norm of unanimity operates within the Commission. Parliament, too, consists of different national and

[3] In fact, we asked our experts whether different actors within these supranational institutions played a role. Our experts, however, always believed that the Council of Ministers needs to be disaggregated, but not the Commission and the Parliament. One could easily accuse our contributions to be biased in favour of the member states. We believe, however, rather that most of the current research underestimates the importance of the Council and concentrates on actors that have often only a marginal influence on the decision-making processes.

party groups, yet they do not act cohesively on all legislative proposals. Moreover, the parliamentary discussions are channelled through the standing committees and their individual rapporteurs, another source of diversity. Further research is needed to analyse the aggregation of these preferences into the 'official' or group preference, and to determine how consequential our unitary actor assumption is for model predictions.

This view of EU policy-making has implications for the analysis of legislative decision-making. The preparatory process, during which working groups of representatives from the different national ministries and permanent representations are active, might thus be much more important for the final result than the more formalised legislative negotiations on which some of the models in this volume focus. The work of these diplomatic 'sherpas' often leads to proposals that are passed without further discussion within the Council (see Beyers and Dierickx 1997). At what level—the working group, committee of permanent representatives (COREPER), or ministerial—are the early-stage controversies resolved?

The growing importance of the Parliament as a co-legislator has also led to the development of informal structures to accommodate them early on. Starting with the conciliation committee meetings, in which the Council and Parliament formally negotiate on controversial issues, the Commission has initiated informal meetings with representatives from the Council and Parliament to discuss their points of view. As Farrell and Héritier (2003: 588) describe, these 'trialogues' have become a normal practice, allowing officials to clarify and modify proposals.

We anticipate that different negotiation mechanisms may be at work in these different settings, with more member state influence in the early stages and more interplay between the Council and the European Parliament at the end. A comparison of four member states shows that the role of private interests and the agenda-setting ministries is particularly important, for example, while parliamentary actors are only rarely able to influence these domestic pre-negotiations (Schneider and Baltz 2005).

This view of EU policy-making is closer to that of the 'mixed models' in this volume, which combine a single preliminary round of negotiation or position exchanges with a subsequent procedural voting stage. However, in reality, there may be several preliminary rounds among different sets of actors, and there is no guarantee that the same norms and procedures apply to all. Further work will be needed to match the models more closely to the political facts.

In this enterprise, the data set used in this book should help improve the realism of future models. For example, Garrett and Tsebelis (2001a) suggest modelling the conciliation committee negotiations between the Council and Parliament under co-decision as a bargaining game. In contrast, Napel and Widgrén (2004b) consider the internal decision-making rules in the Council and the European Parliament as a part of the bargaining model. This is done by assuming that bargaining in the conciliation committee is a two-person game between the pivotal players of the Council and Parliament. When the Nash bargaining solution is used as a solution concept in the model, the results suggest that QMV gives the Council a substantial bargaining advantage over the Parliament in the co-decision procedure. If unanimity is the norm in the Council, then Parliament is even more disadvantaged. Our data set makes possible straightforward empirical investigation of this theoretical result.

11.5 THEORETICAL TOOLS FOR FUTURE RESEARCH ON EU POLITICS

In this study, the research teams focused on some mainstream rational choice models that have been developed for explaining EU politics. Other alternatives are of potential relevance to the study of legislative decision-making in the Union. One route is to analyse legislative decision-making under the assumptions of incomplete information, in which the Council members as well as the relevant groups within Parliament adapt their positions during the decision-making process to the yet unknown preferences of others. The experience gained in related situations with models of incomplete information is encouraging. Some studies are available, for instance, on how the Commission adapts to information problems (Broscheid and Coen 2003), on the selection of Commissioners and how they affect policy (Crombez 2002), and on the usage of threats in the deliberations of the European Council (Schneider and Cederman 1994).

Although most legislative bargaining models have relied on cooperative game theory, there are some tools in non-cooperative game theory that could be exploited. One important recent contribution has been the *n*-actor models that Baron and Ferejohn (1989) and Merlo and Wilson (1995) have developed, and that are briefly discussed in the contribution by Bailer and Schneider. These models have also been applied to the question of government formation. It is possible to use these models to study coalition formation in a dynamic setting.

The results of our study indicate that common interests and shared norms play a large role in the EU decision-making process. From a game-theoretic view, equilibria of that kind are customarily derived from dynamic models in which actors have an extended past and future in common. In the EU as in the models, reciprocal, non-negotiated exchanges create expectations among the actors that present concessions will be rewarded in the future, when their own interests are particularly at stake. Future models should explicitly incorporate the conditions under which norms are enforceable, and should adapt their predictions according to the condition that is applicable (Stokman 2004; 2005).

Another possible way forward is to add complexity to the goals actors pursue in the political process. Some rational choice models assume that actors aim not only at self-interested gain, but that hedonic and normative goals are also important (Lindenberg 2001). Normative goals in particular provide a way to avoid the complications of dynamic game theory and still explain why the unanimity norm seems so prevalent. According to March and Olsen (1989) relevant political actors sometimes refrain from exploiting their strategic advantage due to a 'logic of appropriateness'. Instead, they follow certain rules that prescribe the behaviour expected of them. These rules might very well yield predictions about outcomes that are located between the various points of view of the actors, somewhere in the 'centre' or the 'middle' of the political spectrum, as the cooperative bargaining models do. It is in such a context that Jacques Chirac could break the opposition of Cyprus against the December 2004 settlement regarding the beginning of talks with Turkey by saying: 'This is not the way we do business in the EU, *mon cher* Tassos'.[4] The potential of such models has hardly been touched upon in EU research.[5]

Similarly, evolutionary game theory, which builds upon psychological theories of human behaviour and learning, may help limit the assumptions of excessive human rationality in current models (Weibull 1995; Fudenberg and Levine 1998). Models with limitedly rational actors could highlight why decision-makers in the Council of Ministers often use cultural affiliation when they decide on where they obtain information (Beyers and Dierickx 1997). On the empirical side, future comparative evaluations of models could explore whether cultural factors or

[4] Information obtained from Dutch diplomats, as reported in the weekly *Elsevier* of 22 January 2005, p 23.

[5] A partial exception is Kollman's (2003) computational model of the rotating presidency of the Council of Ministers.

coalitional considerations affect the bargaining processes within the European Union.

11.6 THE FUTURE OF THE EUROPEAN UNION

This study indicates that the preferences of the member states still have considerable impact on the outcomes of legislative decision-making. At the same time, we have also found that knowing the member states' preferences alone is not enough. Forecasts improve when the Commission and Parliament are taken into account. A strictly defined intergovernmental perspective is therefore no longer helpful for understanding the day-to-day decision-making in the EU. The preferences of the Commission and Parliament matter. The daily decision-making in the Union can therefore be characterised as a mixture of intergovernmental and supranational bargaining.

These findings raise hope for the Union's long-term legitimacy. The strong emphasis on consensual decision-making and the involvement of Parliament indicate that outcomes reflect centrist European opinions. Admittedly, national positions and parliamentary preferences may not be identical to popular views. Nevertheless, the effective involvement of Parliament in the decision-making process strengthens the procedural legitimacy of the Union. In this respect, Europe is on the right track.

The substantive or 'social' legitimacy (Weiler 1999: 80), that is, the general acceptance of the system of collective decision-making, is a different matter. The low turnout at European Parliament elections is revealing. Various proposals have been made to improve the Union's legitimacy, including more than transparent decision-making procedures, the avoidance of informal meetings in which compromises are made, and greater involvement by Parliament. Some of us in the research project believe these changes would be effective, while others are sceptical. What we are agreed on is that the Union needs greater acceptance of its decisions by the people of Europe.

The findings in this volume also bear on the enlargement process and the now-stalled European Constitution. The member states had great difficulty changing some of the procedural rules in the Treaty of Nice (2001) and in the recent negotiations over the European Constitution draft (2004). One of the main lessons of this project has been the importance of informal bargaining and compromise seeking. Applied to an EU of 25 or 27 members, the widely stated fear of paralysis is obvious if those members hold rather heterogeneous views and are not willing to compromise. Previous analyses indicate that the shape of future preference profiles of the various member states, including the new ones, is crucial in determining whether this happens (König and Bräuninger 2000; Steunenberg 2001; 2002b). For building the grand coalitions that promote consensus and accommodation of minorities, they argued that flexible and changing coalitions over time are important and that rigid factions must be avoided.

The EU enlargement from 15 to 25 member states increases the number of bilateral contacts from 105 to 300, which will make round-robin consultations more difficult and grand coalitions more unwieldy. However, it is well to remember that previous enlargements with countries such as Spain and Portugal did not lead to substantial problems. Incidental blockades have always existed, including the British vetoes on all legislative proposals during the 'mad cow' crisis and the temporary attempt to exclude Austria from EU policy-making following the 'Haider' election. Furthermore, analyses of the Nice reform package, which was intended to prepare the Union for the 2004 enlargement, show that this package made the introduction of changes in existing EU policy more difficult and, in addition, preserves the power positions of the larger member states after enlargement (Steunenberg 2002b). Although the 2004 enlargement of the Union has put substantial stress on the Union's abilities to bring together different views, as Zimmer *et al* (2005) show, the member states recognised this and planned for it. The now defunct European Constitution, for example, proposed only marginal changes in the formal decision-making rules, in an effort to maintain the stability of day-to-day decision procedures.

The larger worry is not the formal rules but the informal norms. Common understandings are harder to enforce as groups grow in size. The erosion of shared norms in a larger Union may affect the Union's decision-making capability as enlargement proceeds. Only further analysis of the interdependency between the formal rules and the informal, day-to-day decision-making practices can confirm whether current fears concerning enlargement will materialise. The approaches developed in this book provide a starting point for this kind of analysis, and our findings point toward issues that need to be taken into account.

11.7 CONCLUSION

Will formal models of policy-making like those in this book ultimately become reliable aids to policy-makers? We do not share the pessimism of

Rubinstein (2000: 74–75) who attributes no predictive power to game theory: 'I am not convinced that Game Theory is more valuable than a detective novel, a romantic poem, or a game of chess' in improving the strategic capabilities of practitioners. In particular, he points to the artificiality of some concepts, like mixed strategies, and notes that the usage of mathematical symbols 'creates an illusion of preciseness which does not have any basis in reality'. To the contrary, we all believe that our models can enlighten political debates, even when, as now, they have achieved only modest levels of predictive success.

Translating between the academic world and the policy world is never easy, however. Complicated models require explanation in plain language, with their limitations and imprecisions conveyed clearly to non-specialists. Commercial opinion surveys have made much progress in this regard, and the best of them include in their reports information on their sample size, margin of error, and the response rates. Similarly, many evaluation associations impose a set of standards on their members who do practical research. We have tried to meet those standards throughout this book and particularly in Chapter 10, where our forecasting successes and limitations are described in detail.

The present volume has shown that a critical dialogue between different modelling traditions applied to a single data set forces researchers to make their modelling choices transparent, as honest science requires. It also makes the models vulnerable to empirical findings, a critical step in intellectual progress. Then, when models reach a certain stage of maturity and empirical success, reporting the results of such dialogues to policy-makers in accessible form seems to us part of the scholarly mission.

In short, we feel that this book itself proposes a model beyond those included in the individual chapters—a working model for collaborative social scientific research that aims at addressing issues of broad social interest and concern. In this project, we have engaged in a 'double dialogue' in which different theoretical claims encountered each other while each model faced a common data set. This kind of work is not easy, it is not cheap, and it imposes substantial administrative and managerial burdens on its practitioners. But when it is possible, both science and policy benefit. We are glad we did it.

But of course, the present book is just a beginning. We are confident that subsequent double dialogues will build on our findings, correct our errors, and continue to improve our common understanding of EU decision-making.

Appendix I

Selection of Commission proposals

Chapter 2 describes the criteria used to select the Commission proposals included in our study. They had to be subject to either the co-decision or consultation procedures, be pending in the years 1999 and/or 2000, and be to some extent controversial.

With regard to 14 of the 26 co-decision proposals, a change to the legislative procedure nevertheless did occur. The significance of this change is open to debate. Proposals subject to the co-decision procedure were included in the selection, even if they had been introduced as co-decision proposals before the Amsterdam Treaty came into effect, and were decided upon afterwards. Such proposals underwent a procedural change, since the co-decision procedure was amended by the Amsterdam Treaty. In particular, the previous (Maastricht) version of the co-decision procedure allowed the Council to reaffirm its common position in the face of protracted disagreement between the Council and the European Parliament (EP). The proposal was then adopted in accordance with the Council's common position unless an absolute majority of all Members of European Parliament (MEPs) voted to reject it. The Treaty of Amsterdam removed what some have interpreted as the Council's ability to make a 'take it or leave it' offer to the EP. In the new version of the co-decision procedure, the Council and the EP have to reach an agreement if the legislation is to pass. While some have attributed great importance to this change, others see it as a formalisation of what had been standard practice in previous years (see debates in and following Crombez, Steunenberg and Corbett 2000). All 14 of the 26 co-decision proposals introduced prior to the entry into force of the Amsterdam Treaty were decided on after that treaty came into effect. This meant that in decision-making leading to the final decision on those proposals, the EP had all the rights conferred to it according to the Amsterdam Treaty.

Concerning the time period, most of the Commission proposals under scrutiny were introduced between October 1997 and December 2000 (only seven of the 66 proposals were introduced before this period). Almost all the Commission proposals were decided on between May 1999 and February 2002. One exception concerns a proposal that was decided on in March 1998 (CNS/1996/160, Council Regulation (EC) No 850/98 of 30 March 1998 for the conservation of fishery resources through technical measures for the protection of juveniles of marine organisms). Initially, we had included a later, but related Commission proposal in the selection. When we approached an expert on the EU's fishing policy, he recommended we select this piece of parental legislation instead, since, in his view, this was more important politically.

66 COMMISSION PROPOSALS WITH FINAL DECISION OUTCOMES

Agriculture (14 Commission proposals, 40 issues)

Reference	Name	No. issues
CNS/1998/092 COM(1998)135	Council Directive 1999/74/EC of 19 July 1999 laying down minimum standards for the protection of laying hens	6
CNS/1998/109 COM(1998)158/3	Council Regulation (EC) No 1254/1999 of 17 May 1999 on the common organisation of the market in beef and veal	2
CNS/1998/110 COM(1998)158/4	Council Regulation (EC) No 1255/1999 of 17 May 1999 on the common organisation of the market in milk and milk products	2
COD/1998/323 COM(1998)623	Regulation (EC) No 999/2001 of the European Parliament and of the Council of 22 May 2001 laying down rules for the prevention, control and eradication of certain transmissible spongiform encephalopathies	3

Agriculture (14 Commission proposals, 40 issues) (continued)

Reference	Name	No. issues
CNS/1999/072 COM(1999)130	Council Regulation (EC) No 1308/ 1999 of 15 June 1999 amending Regulation (EC) No 2377/90 laying down a Community procedure for the establishment of maximum residue limits of veterinary medicinal products in foodstuffs of animal origin	3
CNS/1999/092 COM(1999)188	Council Directive 1999/105/EC of 22 December 1999 on the marketing of forest reproductive material	3
CNS/1999/202 COM(1999)492	Council Regulation (EC) No 1051/ 2001 of 22 May 2001 on production aid for cotton	2
COD/1999/204 COM(1999)487	Regulation (EC) No 1760/2000 of the European Parliament and of the Council of 17 July 2000 establishing a system for the identification and registration of bovine animals and regarding the labelling of beef and beef products and repealing Council Regulation (EC) No 820/97	4
COD/1999/217 COM(1999)456	Directive amending Directive 64/ 432/EEC: health problems affecting intra-Community trade in bovine animals and swine	1
CNS/1999/235 COM(1999)582	Council Regulation (EC) No 216/ 2001 of 29 January 2001 amending Regulation (EEC) No 404/93 on the common organisation of the market in bananas	2
CNS/1999/236 COM(1999)576	Council Regulation (EC) No 1672/ 2000 of 27 July 2000 amending Regulation (EC) No 1251/1999 establishing a support system for producers of certain arable crops, to include flax and hemp grown for fibre	2

(continued)

Agriculture (14 Commission proposals, 40 issues) (continued)

Reference	Name	No. issues
CNS/1999/246 COM(1999)608	Council Regulation (EC) No 1670/2000 of 20 July 2000 amending Regulation (EC) No 1255/1999 on the common organisation of the market in milk and milk products	2
CNS/2000/250 COM(2000)604	Council Regulation (EC) No 1260/2001 of 19 June 2001 on the common organisation of the markets in the sugar sector	3
CNS/2000/358 COM(2000)855	Council Regulation (EC) No 1513/2001 of 23 July 2001 amending Regulations No 136/66/EEC and (EC) No 1638/98 as regards the extension of the period of validity of the aid scheme and the quality strategy for olive oil	5

Internal market (13 Commission proposals, 34 issues)

Reference	Name	No. issues
COD/1995/341 COM(1995)655	Proposal for a 13th European Parliament and Council Directive on company law concerning takeover bids	3[1]
COD/1996/085 COM(1996)097	Directive 2001/84/EC of the European Parliament and of the Council of 27 September 2001 on the resale right for the benefit of the author of an original work of art	4
COD/1996/112 COM(1995)722/1	Directive 2000/36/EC of the European Parliament and of the Council of 23 June 2000 relating to cocoa and chocolate products intended for human consumption	4
CNS/1996/114 COM(1995)722/3	Council Directive 2001/110/EC of 20 December 2001 relating to honey	3
CNS/1996/115 COM(1995)722/4	Council Directive 2001/112/EC of 20 December 2001 relating to fruit juices and certain similar products intended for human consumption	2

Internal market (13 Commission proposals, 34 issues) (continued)

Reference	Name	No. issues
COD/1996/161 COM(1995)520	Directive 1999/44/EC of the European Parliament and of the Council of 25 May 1999 on certain aspects of the sale of consumer goods and associated guarantees	2
COD/1997/264 COM(1997)510	Directive 2000/26/EC of the European Parliament and of the Council of 16 May 2000 on the approximation of the laws of the member states relating to insurance against civil liability in respect of the use of motor vehicles and amending Council Directives 73/239/EEC and 88/357/EEC (fourth motor insurance Directive)	1
COD/1997/359 COM(1997)628	Directive 2001/29/EC of the European Parliament and of the Council of 22 May 2001 on the harmonisation of certain aspects of copyright and related rights in the information society	3
COD/1998/134 COM(1998)226	Regulation (EC) No 2700/2000 of the European Parliament and of the Council of 16 November 2000 amending Council Regulation (EEC) No 2913/92 establishing the Community Customs Code	4
COD/1998/191 COM(1998)297	Directive 1999/93/EC of the European Parliament and of the Council of 13 December 1999 on a Community framework for electronic signatures	3
COD/1998/240 COM(1998)450	Regulation (EC) No 141/2000 of the European Parliament and of the Council of 16 December 1999 on orphan medicinal products	1
COD/1998/325 COM(1998)586	Directive 2000/31/EC of the European Parliament and of the Council of 8 June 2000 on certain legal aspects of information society services, in particular electronic commerce, in the Internal Market ('Directive on electronic commerce')	3

(continued)

Internal market (13 Commission proposals, 34 issues) (continued)

Reference	Name	No. issues
COD/1999/158 COM(1999)329	Directive 2001/5/EC of the European Parliament and of the Council of 12 February 2001 amending Directive 95/2/EC on food additives other than colours and sweeteners	1

[1] This proposal was rejected by the European Parliament. The decision outcomes on these three issues therefore correspond with the reference point. There was also a fourth issue described by the experts. It was, however, not possible to define a reference point on this fourth issue due to the presence of fundamentally different legislative regimes in the different member states. Therefore, this issue cannot be included in the testing of the accuracy of the models' forecasts.

Fisheries (7 Commission proposals, 13 issues)

Reference	Name	No. issues
CNS/1996/160 COM(1996)296	Council Regulation (EC) No 850/98 of 30 March 1998 for the conservation of fishery resources through technical measures for the protection of juveniles of marine organisms	1
CNS/1998/347 COM(1998)728	Council Regulation (EC) No 2792/1999 of 17 December 1999 laying down the detailed rules and arrangements regarding Community structural assistance in the fisheries sector	2
CNS/1999/047 COM(1999)055	Council Regulation (EC) No 104/2000 of 17 December 1999 on the common organisation of the markets in fishery and aquaculture products	3
CNS/1999/050 COM(1999)070	Council Regulation (EC) No 1447/1999 of 24 June 1999 establishing a list of types of behaviour which seriously infringe the rules of the common fisheries policy	1
CNS/1999/138 COM(1999)345	Council Regulation (EC) No 2791/1999 of 16 December 1999 laying down certain control measures applicable in the area covered by the Convention on future multilateral cooperation in the north-east Atlantic fisheries	2
CNS/1999/163 COM(1999)382	Council Regulation (EC) No 657/2000 of 27 March 2000 on closer dialogue with the fishing sector and groups affected by the common fisheries policy	2

Fisheries (7 Commission proposals, 13 issues) (continued)

Reference	Name	No. issues
CNS/1999/255 COM(1999)636	Council Regulation (EC) No 1298/2000 of 8 June 2000 amending for the fifth time Regulation (EC) No 850/98 for the conservation of fishery resources through technical measures for the protection of juveniles of marine organisms	2

ECOFIN (6 Commission proposals, 10 issues)

Reference	Name	No. issues
CNS/1998/189 COM(1998)320	Council Directive 1999/81/EC of 29 July 1999 amending Directive 92/79/EEC on the approximation of taxes on cigarettes, Directive 92/80/EEC on the approximation of taxes on manufactured tobacco other than cigarettes and Directive 95/59/EC on taxes other than turnover taxes which affect the consumption of manufactured tobacco	2
COD/1998/252 COM(1998)461	Directive 2000/46/EC of the European Parliament and of the Council of 18 September 2000 on the taking up, pursuit of and prudential supervision of the business of electronic money institutions	2
CNS/1998/331 COM(1998)693	Council Directive 1999/49/EC of 25 May 1999 amending, with regard to the level of the standard rate, Directive 77/388/EEC on the common system of value added tax	2
CNS/1999/056 COM(1999)062	Council Directive 1999/85/EC of 22 October 1999 amending Directive 77/388/EEC as regards the possibility of applying on an experiment basis a reduced VAT rate on labour-intensive services	1
CNS/1999/151 COM(1999)364	Council Regulation (EC) No 2040/2000 of 26 September 2000 on budgetary discipline	1
CNS/2000/223 COM(2000)537	Council Directive 2001/41/EC of 19 January 2001 amending the sixth Directive (77/388/EEC) on the common system of value added tax, with regard to the length of time during which the minimum standard rate is to be applied	2

Appendix I

Justice and Home Affairs (5 Commission proposals, 15 issues)

Reference	Name	No. issues
CNS/1999/116 COM(1999)260	Council Regulation (EC) No 2725/2000 of 11 December 2000 concerning the establishment of "Eurodac" for the comparison of fingerprints for the effective application of the Dublin Convention	1
CNS/1999/154 COM(1999)348	Council Regulation (EC) No 44/2001 of 22 December 2000 on jurisdiction and the recognition and enforcement of judgments in civil and commercial matters	2
CNS/1999/274 COM(1999)686	2000/596/EC Council Decision of 28 September 2000 establishing a European Refugee Fund	3
CNS/2000/030 COM(2000)027	Council Regulation (EC) No 539/2001 of 15 March 2001 listing the third countries whose nationals must be in possession of visas when crossing the external borders and those whose nationals are exempt from that requirement	6
CNS/2000/127 COM(2000)303	Council Directive 2001/55/EC of 20 July 2001 on minimum standards for giving temporary protection in the event of a mass influx of displaced persons and on measures promoting a balance of efforts between member states in receiving such persons and bearing the consequences thereof	3

General Affairs (6 Commission proposals, 14 issues)

Reference	Name	No. issues
CNS/1998/299 COM(1998)600/1	Council Regulation (EC) No 764/2000 of 10 April 2000 regarding the implementation of measures to intensify the EC-Turkey customs union	2
COD/1998/300 COM(1998)600/2	Regulation (EC) No 257/2001 of the European Parliament and of the Council of 22 January 2001 regarding the implementation of measures to promote economic and social development in Turkey	3

General Affairs (6 Commission proposals, 14 issues) (continued)

Reference	Name	No. issues
CNS/1998/354 COM(1998)768	1999/847/EC Council Decision of 9 December 1999 establishing a Community action programme in the field of civil protection	2
CNS/1999/132 COM(1999)312	Council Regulation (EC) No 2454/1999 of 15 November 1999 amending Regulation (EC) No 1628/96 relating to aid for Bosnia and Herzegovina, Croatia, the Federal Republic of Yugoslavia and the former Yugoslav Republic of Macedonia, in particular by the setting up of a European Agency for Reconstruction	1
CNS/1999/214 COM(1999)494	Council Regulation (EC) No 2698/2000 of 27 November 2000 amending Regulation (EC) No 1488/96 on financial and technical measures to accompany (MEDA) the reform of economic and social structures in the framework of the Euro-Mediterranean partnership	2
COD/2000/032 COM(2000)030	Regulation (EC) No 1049/2001 of the European Parliament and of the Council of 30 May 2001 regarding public access to European Parliament, Council and Commission documents	4

Other Sectoral Councils (15 Commission proposals, 36 issues)

Reference	Name	No. issues
	Culture	
CNS/1999/066 COM(1999)111	1999/784/EC Council Decision of 22 November 1999 concerning Community participation in the European Audiovisual Observatory	1
COD/1999/275 COM(1999)658/1	Decision No 163/2001/EC of the European Parliament and of the Council of 19 January 2001 on the implementation of a training programme for professionals in the European audiovisual programme industry (MEDIA-Training) (2001–2005)	1

(continued)

Other Sectoral Councils (15 Commission proposals, 36 issues) (continued)

Reference	Name	No. issues
CNS/1999/276 COM(1999)658/2	2000/821/EC Council Decision of 20 December 2000 on the implementation of a programme to encourage the development, distribution and promotion of European audiovisual works (MEDIA Plus — Development, Distribution and Promotion) (2001–2005)	5
	Development	
COD/2000/062 COM(2000)111/1	Regulation (EC) No 1724/2001 of the European Parliament and of the Council of 23 July 2001 concerning action against anti-personnel landmines in developing countries	3
CNS/2000/062B COM(2000)111/2	Council Regulation (EC) No 1725/2001 of 23 July 2001 concerning action against anti-personnel landmines in third countries other than developing countries	1
	Employment	
CNS/1999/192 COM(1999)440	2000/98/EC Council Decision of 24 January 2000 establishing the Employment Committee	2
CNS/1999/225 COM(1999)565	Council Directive 2000/78/EC of 27 November 2000 establishing a general framework for equal treatment in employment and occupation	2
	Energy	
COD/1999/127 COM(1999)296	Directive 2000/55/EC of the European Parliament and of the Council of 18 September 2000 on energy efficiency requirements for ballasts for fluorescent lighting	2
	Health	
COD/1999/244 COM(1999)594	Directive 2001/37/EC of the European Parliament and of the Council of 5 June 2001 on the approximation of the laws, regulations and administrative provisions of the member states concerning the manufacture, presentation and sale of tobacco products	5
	Industry	
CNS/1998/288 COM(1998)546	Proposal for a Council Regulation (EC) amending Regulation no 17: First Regulation implementing Articles 85 and 86 of the Treaty	3

Other Sectoral Councils (15 Commission proposals, 36 issues) (continued)

Reference	Name	No. issues
	Social Affairs	
COD/1998/195 COM(1998)329	Decision No 253/2000/EC of the European Parliament and of the Council of 24 January 2000 establishing the second phase of the Community action programme in the field of education *Socrates*	3
	Transport	
COD/1999/083 COM(1999)158	Directive 2000/61/EC of the European Parliament and of the Council of 10 October 2000 amending Council Directive 94/55/EC on the approximation of the laws of the member states with regard to the transport of dangerous goods by road	1
COD/1999/252 COM(1999)617	Directive 2001/16/EC of the European Parliament and of the Council of 19 March 2001 on the interoperability of the trans-European conventional rail system	3
COD/2000/060 COM(2000)137	Directive 2002/7/EC of the European Parliament and of the Council of 18 February 2002 amending Council Directive 96/53/EC laying down for certain road vehicles circulating within the Community the maximum authorised dimensions in national and international traffic and the maximum authorised weights in international traffic	2
COD/2000/067 COM(2000)142	Regulation (EC) No 417/2002 of the European Parliament and of the Council of 18 February 2002 on the accelerated phasing-in of double hull or equivalent design requirements for single hull oil tankers and repealing Council Regulation (EC) No 2978/94	2

Appendix I

Four proposals on which data on issues, positions and levels of salience were collected, but final outcomes were not included in the data set: either pending or last stage of data collection incomplete (4 Commission proposals, 11 issues)

Reference	Legislative act.	No. issues
	Internal Market	
COD/1999/238 COM(1999)577	Proposal for a Directive of the European Parliament and the Council amending for the 22nd time Directive 76/769/EEC on the approximation of the laws, regulations and administrative provisions of the member states relating to restrictions on the marketing and use of certain dangerous substances and preparations (phthalates) and amending Council Directive 88/378/EEC on the approximation of the laws of the member states concerning the safety of toys	3
	ECOFIN	
CNS/1998/087 COM(1998)067	Proposal for a Council Directive on a common system of taxation applicable to interest and royalty payments made between associated companies of different member states	2
CNS/1998/193 COM(1998)295	Proposal for a Council Directive to ensure a minimum of effective taxation of savings income in the form of interest payments within the Community	3
	Telecommunications	
COD/2000/184 COM(2000)393	Proposal for a Directive of the European Parliament and the Council on a common regulatory framework for electronic communications networks and services	3

Appendix II

Comparison of expert judgements with each other and with information from Council documentation

ROBERT THOMSON

Obtaining information from policy area experts was essential in this research project given that decision-making in the European Union, and particularly in the Council, is often a secretive and specialised affair. Documentation on Council decision-making on politically sensitive dossiers has, until very recently, not been available. Many experts we interviewed spoke of an unwritten rule, according to which information on other member states' positions in the Council should not be divulged. Still, many were willing to provide this information, given the scientific nature of our inquiry, and under the condition that they would be thanked not by name, but by institutional affiliation. We obtained Council documents on the discussions on some of the Commission proposals included in our selection, and these provided fascinating information that supplements, rather than substitutes the information provided by experts. Policy discussions in the Council, particularly at working group level, are often of a technical nature. This makes it difficult and often impossible to distinguish between peripheral technical matters and political issues that form the most important elements of the debate. Consultations with experts are essential to making such distinctions, and to drawing our attention to the links between apparently separate points that are in fact parts of the same issue. Furthermore, content analysis of documentation does not offer acceptable operationalisations of some of the concepts contained in our models: for instance, the level of importance actors attach to the issues being discussed.

This makes interviews with key informants essential to obtaining the information required to apply and test our models. This appendix provides a comparison of expert judgements on two Commission proposals with information obtained from Council documentation. It also contains an illustration of two sets of expert judgements on the same Commission proposal, and how a selection was made between these two sets of estimates. The information from experts and Council documentation is shown to be largely consistent. The comparison reveals that when specifying the issues, experts focus on what were considered to be the main issues; they discarded many points of contention that were of concern to only few actors and that were raised infrequently. The differences found point clearly to the conclusion that documentation provides an inadequate source of information for the analyses. It is often the case that the Council documentation refers to policy alternatives actors were *willing* to accept once the discussions were well under way, rather than the alternatives they initially favoured.

The Commission proposal on the sale and manufacturing of tobacco products and the proposal on resale rights for artists are examined. We obtained Council documentation on the Council meetings on the proposals referred to; these were mostly meetings at working group level, but also committee of permanent representatives (COREPER) and ministerial meetings. These documents provide details of the points raised during the discussions on each article of the proposals, including the names of the actors who voiced reservations on particular points and the nature of these reservations. Each of the following two sections begins by summarising the information provided by the experts. The issues specified by the experts are then compared with those found in the documents. Finally, the extent to which the experts' judgements on actors' favoured decision outcomes match the views the actors expressed during the Council meetings is examined. Section AII.3 contains a comparison between two sets of expert judgements.

AII.1 THE DIRECTIVE ON THE MANUFACTURING AND SALE OF TOBACCO PRODUCTS: COMPARING EXPERT JUDGEMENTS AND COUNCIL DOCUMENTATION

Chapter 2 referred to the tobacco directive (COD/1999/244) to illustrate the way in which issues are conceptualised, and how experts were asked to describe actors' most favoured policy alternatives and the levels of importance they attached to different issues. Two issues were described in chapter two:

- The first issue concerned the question of whether the maximum permitted yield levels (of tar, carbon monoxide and nicotine) should also apply to products manufactured in the EU, but intended for export to third countries. Germany, Greece, Spain, Luxembourg and Austria were said to be against the application of these yield levels to exported cigarettes, while the other actors were for.

- The second issue referred to the size and strength of the health warning on tobacco products. Germany, Luxembourg and Austria were said to favour the continuation of the current EU legislation on this point, which stipulated certain warnings and that these warnings cover 4–8 per cent of the packaging. The EP preferred the largest and strongest warnings.

In addition to these two issues, another three were also specified:

- The third issue concerned the question of what arrangements should be made for the disclosure of information on the ingredients contained in tobacco products. All actors were in favour of moving away from the current situation where there is limited disclosure, and where this is left primarily to the tobacco industry itself. All agreed on the need to move toward a common list of permitted ingredients, as is currently the case in Belgium and France. There were, however, differences among the actors on whether this list should be drawn up immediately or left until a later date.
- The fourth issue concerned the nature of the committee that would write a report on the basis of which the directive could be amended in the light of new scientific evidence. The Commission proposed that it would draw up this report itself (Article 10). Most of the actors supported this arrangement, although Germany, Spain, France, Ireland and the UK would have preferred that an independent scientific committee be established. This was said to be an inter-institutional disagreement, since the member states would have to be consulted more in connection with the establishment of a scientific committee.
- The fifth and final issue was about the question of whether product descriptions, such as the terms 'light' and 'mild', should be banned, since they have the connotation that these products are less harmful. Some actors wanted to ban the term 'light' only, others wanted to ban both terms, while some wanted to ban both terms and other terms that might also have positive connotations.

The outcome of the decision-making was a victory for the health lobby. After a short transition period, EU rules on maximum yield levels apply to tobacco products for export, and those who pursue this old-fashioned pastime are today subjected to disconcerting health warnings. But is this dossier as much of a success story for our data collection procedures? Were the same issues found to be prominent in the discussions in the examination of the relevant documents? Were there other issues not mentioned by the experts? To what extent do the preferences of the actors, as identified by the experts, accord with the views they expressed in the meetings?

Each of the 28 Council documents we obtained on the discussions relating to this proposal was examined to identify the points of concern raised by the actors. A note was taken of every time two or more actors expressed different views on a particular point. This was facilitated by the way in which the discussions proceeded according to the documentary records. During the working group meetings, each article of the proposed legislation was examined line by line, whereby each delegation had the opportunity to express reservations on certain provisions, and others could respond to these statements. The 28 documents refer to eight Council meetings in which this dossier was discussed: five meetings at working group level and three at COREPER level. Some of the 28 documents were not notes on the meetings, but accompanying papers.

The examination of the documents yielded a total of 31 'points of contention' between the actors. The first point identified concerns the object of the directive, stated in Article 1. The Commission's proposal stated that one of the objectives is 'the approximation of the laws . . . concerning the tar yields of *cigarettes*' (emphasis added). During the meeting of the Working Group on Health Questions on 12 and 13 January 2000, the Dutch delegation requested that the various yield levels also apply to rolling tobacco, which is consumed in relatively large quantities in the Netherlands. The Commission responded by stating that internationally recognised measurement methods existed only for manufactured cigarettes, and that this request could not be incorporated. At the next working group meeting, on 22 February 2000, the Dutch delegation, supported by Germany, Denmark and Belgium, asked that the future presentation of proposals on the subject of rolling tobacco be explicitly provided for in the legislation, as new measurement methods were developed. The French delegation believed it premature to refer to rolled cigarettes as long as there was no internationally recognised measurement method. The Commission representative present at the meeting stated he was willing to consider an explicit reference. The reference to rolled tobacco was indeed included in the text and no further mention was made of this point. This point was coded as one on which six actors took a total of three different initial positions. The initial positions of the

Commission and France were for no mention of rolling tobacco, the Netherlands' initial position was for the yield levels to apply, and the initial position of Belgium, Germany and Denmark was for an explicit reference to future legislation in this area. This particular point does not relate to any of the issues specified by the experts.

All five of the issues specified by the experts were covered by some of the 31 points of contention found in the documents. When comparing the points identified in the documents and the issues specified by the experts, it becomes clear that the experts were able to incorporate several points into single issues. Eight of the 31 points can be related directly to the five issues specified by the experts (Table AII.1). For example, the second issue, on the size and strength of the health warning, relates to two points found in the documents: one on the size of the warnings, and one on the content of the warnings. The third issue, on the disclosure of product information, also relates to two points: one on whether there should be an immediate move toward a common list, and a second on the timetable for the work in preparation for this list. Without detailed knowledge of the subject matter, it is unclear how such points should be integrated into single issue continua. The comparison indicates that experts can be helpful in this regard.

The experts also succeeded in distinguishing the main issues involved in the decision-making from the peripheral points of contention. This becomes evident when a comparison is made between the eight points that do relate to the issues specified by the experts with the 23 that do not (see Table AII.1). The points that do relate to the experts' issue specification are those on which more actors took positions. The points not included in the issue specification are generally peripheral in the sense that few actors took positions on them. Moreover, the points of contention included in the issue specification were generally disagreements that were more enduring than those that were not included; they were raised in a larger number of (generally consecutive) meetings. Finally, while more than half of the points covered by the experts in their issue specification were discussed at COREPER level, the vast majority of points that were not covered by the experts were resolved at working group level, more often than not in a single meeting. A more qualitative examination of the points identified in the documents confirms that the experts' issue specification includes the most important elements. Of the points of contention that do not relate to the experts' issues, the most likely candidates for inclusion are perhaps the points that were not included in the specification despite being discussed in COREPER. One of these

Table AII.1. *Points of contention raised by the proposed tobacco directive*[a]

Related to experts' issues?	Number of points of contention identified in documents	Actors with positions on point of contention. Average (range)	Number of Council meetings at which point was raised. Average (range)	Number of points of contention discussed in COREPER (rest at working group level)
Related	8	7.9 (4-17)	3.0 (1-6)	5 of 8
Unrelated	23	4.8 (2-9)	1.7 (1-4)	4 of 23

Note: [a]A comparison of points of contention identified in Council documentation with experts' issue specification. NB: Points discussed in COREPER were of course also discussed at working group level.

Table AII.2. *Match between first positions found in documents and most favoured positions identified by expert concerning the tobacco proposal (COD/1999/244)*

Total number of actor positions in documents that relate to experts' issue specification	Total number of actor positions that can be compared to expert judgements on 'most favoured positions'	Matches	Differences
63	53	48	5

includes the derogation clause for Greece. Although a derogation was included in the original proposal, the Greek delegation requested at a COREPER meeting that this be extended to cover not only tar yields, but also nicotine and carbon monoxide yields. Only three other actors were concerned enough about this point to state a position on it. One is not left with the impression that anything particularly vital has been excluded from the analyses in the experts' issue specification.

The actors' expressed positions (according to the documents) on the eight points relating to the issues specified by the experts were compared with the actors' most favoured alternatives (according to the experts). Three observations are relevant in this regard. First, the positions expressed by the actors on the points of contention correspond to a large extent with the expert's judgements on the actors' most favoured decision outcomes. To the extent that these differ, this at least partly reflects the distinction between actors' most favoured positions and the views they expressed in the meetings. There are 63 positions expressed (in the documents) relating to the issues specified by the expert's (see Table AII.2). Of 10 of these 63, it cannot be said whether they confirm or refute the expert's estimates. For example, four of these 63 refer to member states' proposals for particular formulations of the wording of the health warning. It was unclear whether these placed the actors to the left or right of the experts' second issue continuum about the size and strength of the health warning. Of the remaining 53 points, 48 (91 per cent) correspond to the placement of the actors by the expert. For example, on the first issue, about whether the rules should apply to cigarettes manufactured in the EU but intended for export, both the documents and the expert indicated that Germany, Greece, Spain, Luxembourg and Austria were initially against this, while the other 12 actors were in favour. At least two of the five differences that were found between the documents and the expert judgements relate to the difference between stated positions in the meetings and the actors' 'most favoured' positions. For example, with regard to the second issue, about the size and strength of the health warning, the expert estimated that Luxembourg's most favoured outcome was a continuation of the *status quo* (4–8 per cent of the package as stipulated by the then existing directive 89/622/EEC). However, during the working group meeting of 22 February 2000, this delegation proposed a label of 15–20 per cent: still lower than the 25 per cent proposed by the Commission. Although different, Luxembourg's proposal does necessarily contradict the expert's judgement on the decision outcome favoured most by this member state delegation.

Second, the expert judgements provide a more complete picture of the most favoured positions of the actors on the specified issues than do the Council documents; in general fewer actor positions are reported in the documents than reported by the experts. The Council documents are in fact summaries of the meetings, rather than transcripts of what was said. They usually do not report the positions of all the actors on each point of contention. As shown in Table AII.1, on the eight points of contention that relate to the five issues specified by the experts, an average of 7.9 actors took positions. By contrast, the expert judgements specified the most favoured positions of on average 16.6 actors on the five issues. Experts are able to draw on their experience of all that was said during the Council meetings, rather than just the summaries given in the documentation. Further, they are able to base their judgements on their knowledge of the interests of the actors involved, not only what they did or did not say in the meetings.

The third observation is that the documentation confirms that actors' positions tend to be grouped together, rather than spread evenly or otherwise along a scale of alternatives. For example, with regard to the first issue, on whether the rules should apply to exported cigarettes, only two positions were favoured most by the actors: the rules should either apply or not apply. It was only during the course of the negotiations that other, intermediate alternatives were formulated: that exported cigarettes should conform to legislation in the importing country, or that there should be a transition period. This is confirmed by the documentation. On the eight points of contention from the documents that relate to the experts' issues, the actors took either two or three different positions (on average 2.4). Similarly, on the five issues identified by the experts, the actors favoured between two and four different alternatives (on average

2.8). The slightly higher number of positions defined on the experts' issues is attributable to the fact that several contentious points identified in the documents were incorporated into a single issue continuum.

AII.2 THE DIRECTIVE ON RESALE RIGHTS FOR ARTISTS: A COMPARISON OF EXPERT JUDGEMENTS AND COUNCIL DOCUMENTATION

In March 1996, the Commission approved a proposal for a directive on resale rights for artists (COD/1996/085, OJ C 1996/178/16). The directive's aim was to introduce harmonised legal arrangements governing the resale right for artists. The proposal was contested due to the fact that there was no uniform legal arrangement for resale rights in the international art market outside the EU. The fear among member states that have large art markets was that the introduction of such a right would cause the market to relocate to New York and Geneva. Essentially, the UK, Ireland, the Netherlands, Luxembourg and Austria, supported to some extent by the Nordic countries, expressed these concerns. The leader of the opposition to the directive was the United Kingdom, the home of Christies and Sothebys, which hosts 70 per cent of the EU's art market. In terms of their preferences, the UK and these other member states were far from the other states, the Commission and the EP.

Four issues were said to form the main elements of the discussion, two of which are depicted in Figure AII.1:

- The first issue concerns the threshold above which the resale right should apply. Should the resale right apply to relatively inexpensive works of art, or should it be restricted to expensive ones only? The policy alternatives preferred by the actors ranged from €500, supported by the EP in its first reading, to €5,000 or more, supported by the UK among others.
- The second issue concerns the date of transposition of the directive. Here, the policy alternatives favoured by the actors range from the preference of the Commission, for a period of 18 months after entry into force, to that of the UK and some other member states, for a period of 20 to 25 years for those countries that did not at that time have a resale right.
- The third issue (not depicted) concerns the degressivity of the system of payments: in particular, the question of what percentage of the sale price the artist should receive for very expensive art works.

Issue 1: What should be the threshold above which the resale right should apply?

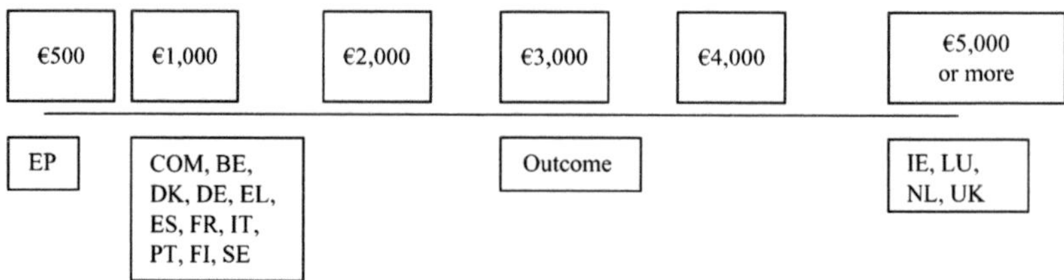

Issue 2: What should be the maximum period of time after entry into force for transposition of the directive?

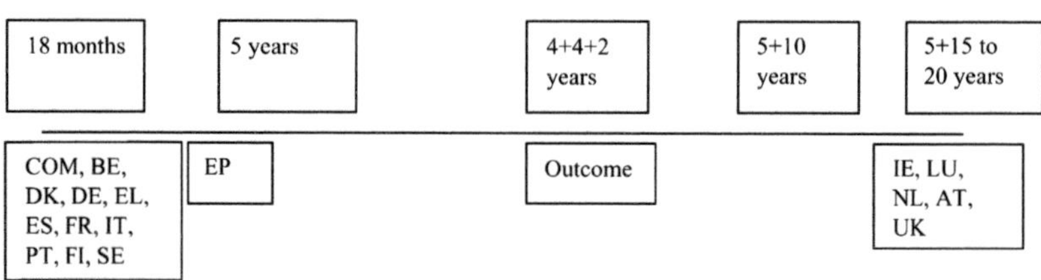

Figure AII.1. First two issues in the resale rights for artists proposal (COD/1996/085)

- Finally, the fourth issue was about whether or not there should be a cap, or maximum, on the amount received by artists, and if so, how high this figure should be.

A total of 34 Council documents on the resale rights proposal were obtained and examined. These relate to 13 Council meetings in which this dossier was discussed (eight working group meetings, one COREPER meeting and four ministerial-level meetings, including the meeting in which the common position was formally adopted). The documents cover the period 7 June 1996, when the Council working group held its first meeting on this dossier, to 23 January 2001, when the Council reviewed the EP's second reading and concluded that the conciliation committee had to be convened.

A comparison of the points of contention identified in the documents with the issues specified by the experts leads to similar conclusions as the tobacco products proposal (see Table AII.3). All four of the issues described by the experts were found to be prominent elements of the decision-making documented. As in the previous case, the documents also referred to many detailed points of contention not included in the experts' issue specification. A comparison of the points of contention that do relate to the experts' issues with those that do not reveals the

Table AII.3. *Points of contention raised by the proposed resale rights for artists directive*[a]

Related to experts' issues?	Number of points of contention referred to in documents	Actors with position on point of contention. Average (range)	Number of Council meetings at which point was raised. Average (range)	Discussed in working groups only	Discussed in COREPER (but not by ministers)	Discussed by ministers
Related	5	12.6 (6-17)	6.4 (4-9)	0 of 5	0 of 5	5 of 5
Unrelated	19	9.6 (2-17)	2.9 (1-6)	9 of 19	10 of 19	0 of 19

Note: [a]A comparison of points of contention referred to in Council documentation with experts' issue specification. NB: Points discussed at higher Council levels were also discussed at lower Council levels.

Table AII.4. *Match between first positions found in documents and most favoured positions identified by expert concerning the resale rights proposal (COD/1996/085)*

Total number of actor positions in documents that relate to experts' issue specification	Total number of actor positions that can be compared to expert judgements on 'most favoured positions'	Matches	Differences
63	57	18	39

types of points experts considered to be issues. Compared to the points that were excluded from the experts' descriptions, those that were included were of concern to more of the member states, took longer to resolve, and were discussed at higher levels of the Council's hierarchy. A point of contention that was rather prominent, but did not feature in the experts' issue specification, concerned the question of whether there was any need at all for a directive in this area. The UK was the most prominent actor in questioning the need for EU action in this area. While the experts did state that this was an aspect of the discussions, we decided to incorporate opposition to the directive into the positions taken on the substantive issues it raised. For example, the position that the right should apply only to very expensive works of art, that there should be a low maximum on the amount paid, and that transposition should be delayed for as long as possible. Compared to the tobacco directive, these issues were more difficult to resolve; it took more meetings at higher levels of the Council. The UK delegation in particular dug its heels in on the resale rights directive. There was no evidence of such opposition in the tobacco case discussed above.

The documentation on the resale rights proposal illustrates clearly why documentation is an inadequate source of information for our purposes. We require information on 'the policy alternative *initially* favoured by each stakeholder *after the introduction of the proposal before the Council formulated its common position*' (wording of questionnaire). By contrast, the Council documents frequently indicate the policy alternatives many actors were willing to accept some time into the discussions.

Consider, for example, the issue of the threshold above which the resale right should apply. After the introduction of the proposal in 1996, the first working group meeting at which this issue was raised was in May 1997. The UK stated that the €1,000 proposed by the Commission was much too low, and argued that there was no need for any European legislation for sales of less than €50,000. It was argued that such sales primarily take place within national art markets and that European legislation was therefore unwarranted (Council document 8424/97). The Commission defended its proposal for €1,000. By December 1998, the UK was joined by Luxembourg, the Netherlands and Ireland in calling for a much higher threshold. It was not until the end of the German presidency in June 1999, that a compromise proposal was made for a threshold of €2,500. This proposal received the support of many actors in the Council, six of whom had not stated a position earlier: at least not one reported in the documents. Expressing support in response to a presidency proposal can hardly be considered an indication of the position favoured at the outset of the discussions.

Similar differences were found between the most favoured decision outcomes indicated by the experts, and the first positions found in the documents on the issue concerning the timing of the transposition. The experts indicated that the outcome favoured by the Commission and most member states was for the directive to be transposed into national law within 18 months after coming into effect. This is common practice for directives. Indeed, the Commission's proposals did not contain any special provisions in this regard, indicating that it would have favoured following common practice in this case. The issue was not raised until January 1999 (Council document 5336/99), when the delegations from the UK, the Netherlands, Luxembourg and Ireland called for a longer transposition period of two years for most member states, and an additional five years for member states that did not yet apply the resale right. Although not registered as a formal position in the Council documentation, one of our experts, who was from one of these delegations, indicated that this is the position they initially took. In response to the demand for a long transposition period, the German presidency proposed that the directive be transposed not later than four years after adoption (Council document 8851/99). This proposal was extended to five years, and received the support of seven Council members, none of whom had previously expressed a position. Again, this support does not indicate the alternative they favoured.

AII.3 THE DECISION ON THE EUROPEAN REFUGEE FUND: A COMPARISON OF TWO SETS OF EXPERT JUDGEMENTS

The decision creating the European Refugee Fund was proposed by the Commission on 14 December 1999, and adopted by the Council on 28

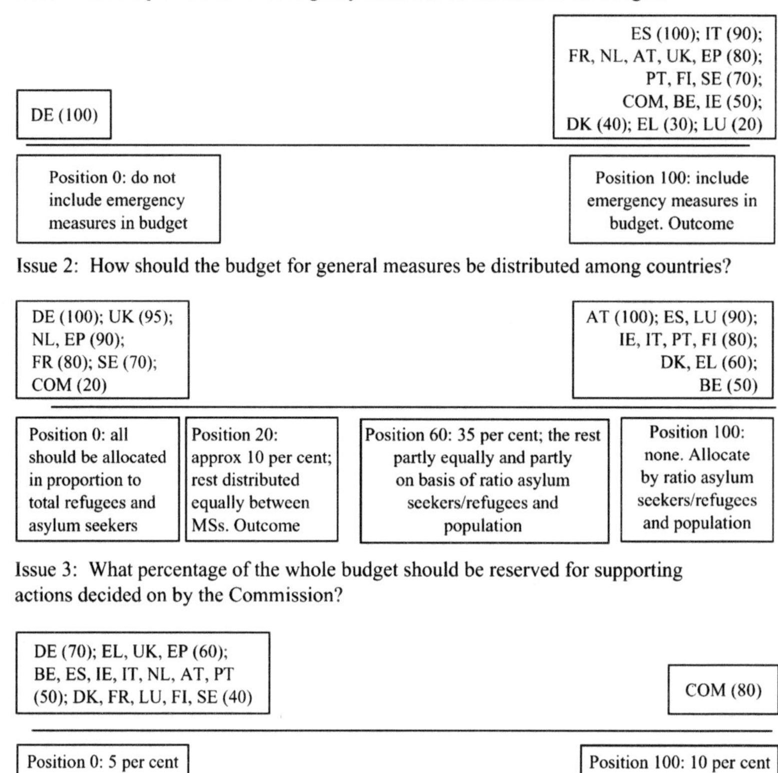

Figure AII.2. Estimates from expert A on the decision on the European Refugee Fund

September 2000 (CNS/1999/274; OJ L 252/12). The European Refugee Fund reserves a total of €216 million over a period of five years to support measures in the member states to receive and accommodate refugees and displaced persons. The preamble to the legislative text indicates that this includes measures to 'grant appropriate reception conditions to refugees and displaced persons, including fair and effective asylum procedures' and 'actions by member states intended to promote their (refugees and displaced persons) social and economic integration'. The decision also notes that the 'preparation of a common policy on asylum. . . is a constituent part of the European Union's objective of creating an area of freedom, security and justice'. Despite these noble aims, our interviews with close observers of the decision-making on this dossier revealed controversy over the distribution of funds to be allocated within the

Issue 1: Should provisions for emergency measures be included in the budget?

Issue 2: How should the budget for general measures be distributed among countries?

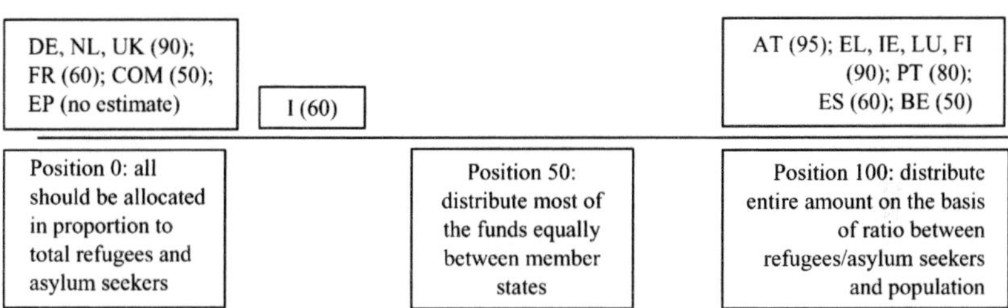

Figure AII.3. Estimates from expert B on the decision on the European Refugee Fund

programme. Five experts were interviewed while this decision-making process was underway. Most of these did not result in complete data sets, but in qualitative background information. This was partly due to the sensitive nature of the discussion. Two data sets were obtained independently from different experts. These are presented below to illustrate the types of differences encountered between different sets of estimates and how we selected one for inclusion in our analyses.

The first set of estimates are those included in the analyses. Three issues are specified in this first set of estimates.

- The first issue concerns the question of whether or not there should be a provision allowing resources from the European Refugee Fund to be allocated for emergency measures, in the event of a sudden mass influx of displaced persons.
- The second issue concerns the question of the percentage of the total budget that should be allocated according to the numbers of refugees and asylum seekers each member state has. The remainder of the budget would be allocated more equally between member states.

- The third issue concerns the percentage of the budget that should be appropriated for 'Community action', as distinct from actions by member states. The main difference between Community actions and actions by member states is that the Commission decides on the allocation of funds to projects that fall under Community actions.

Both experts (we refer to the experts as A, whose estimates were included in the analyses, and expert B) agreed that these three issues were the main issues and, moreover, that the first two issues could be described as the main controversial elements of the discussions. Although expert B agreed with A that the third (Community action) issue should be included in the specification, she was not able to provide information on the positions taken by the member states.

The first issue, on whether or not a provision should be included that made possible the financing of emergency measures, was described in exactly the same way by the two experts. Both characterised this as a dichotomous issue, whereby no compromise alternative was mentioned. This is a plausible description of the issue, since, almost by definition, it is not possible to specify the size of a budget for an unexpected mass influx of refugees.

In addition, both experts indicated that only the German delegation objected to the Commission's proposal to include such a provision. The reasoning behind this objection was that Germany had taken in the largest number of refugees in the previous years. Any reduction in the budget allocated on the basis of the numbers of refugees would therefore reduce the funds available for German projects. The German delegation was of the opinion that provisions for emergency measures should be made via a separate act, and that money for emergency measures should not be taken from the funds available for existing refugees and asylum seekers. According to both experts, this was a very important issue for the German delegation. Indeed, both indicated that the German delegation would have been willing to block the passing of the decision if it did not receive a concession on this point. Accordingly, they allocated a maximum salience of 100 for the Commission on this issue. In the event, the decision on the Refugee Fund did include a provision that allows emergency measures to be financed. However, the German delegation received a concession on a related issue in another dossier also included in our data set: Council directive 2001/55/EC of 20 July 2001 on minimum standards for giving temporary protection in the event of a mass influx of displaced persons.

Both experts indicated that of the group in favour of including a provision for emergency measures in the decision, the Spanish delegation attached the highest level of salience to the issue; expert A gave Spain a salience score of 100 while expert B gave it a score of 90. They both reported that Spain expected to benefit from the inclusion of such a provision, since it is the destination of many persons who are suddenly displaced, for example from North Africa.

The second issue, on the distribution of funds from the 'general measures' part of the budget (as opposed to the 'Community actions' part of the budget), was defined in a similar way by the two experts. At one end of the issue continuum (position 0) they placed the Commission's most favoured position, that the entire budget should be allocated in proportion to the numbers of refugees and asylum seekers in each member state. At the other end point (position 100), they located the alternative that the budget should be allocated according to the ratio of refugees/asylum seekers and the total population of each member state. The intermediate positions on the scale differ somewhat. Expert A defined position 60 on the scale in some detail: the policy alternative that 35 per cent of the budget should be allocated on the basis of the number of asylum seekers and refugees; the rest being allocated by a mixture of equal distribution (32.5 per cent) and on the basis of the ratio of asylum seekers/refugees and population sizes (32.5 per cent). By contrast, expert B provided a more general description of an intermediate point on the scale. She defined position 50 as the alternative that the allocation should be partly based on total numbers of refugees and asylum seekers and partly on the basis of the ratio. Expert A was able to provide a specific estimate of the location of the decision outcome, while expert B could only indicate that it was somewhere to the left of the issue scale.

There is a large amount of agreement between the two experts on the location of the actors' most favoured positions on this issue. The differences pertain to the estimates of the positions of Denmark, Sweden and Italy. Regarding the positions of Denmark and Sweden, expert B was not able to provide an estimate, while expert A stated that they did have positions. It is important to note that expert B indicated she did not know what their positions were, rather than that they were completely indifferent. Expert A provided a different estimate for the location of Italy. We checked this discrepancy with a third expert who placed the Italian delegation on position 100, as did expert A. Note also the similarities in the pattern of salience scores attributed to the actors by the experts. Expert A estimated that the second issue was as important to the German delegation as the first issue, while expert A gave only a slightly lower salience score to Germany on the second issue. According to both experts, Austria had a particular interest in attempting to secure a system of allocation based on the ratio of asylum seekers/refugees to the population size; Austria was said to have attached the highest level of salience to this issue of the member states on position 100.

As mentioned above, expert B noted the third issue as a point of contention worth including in our issue specification, but was unsure as to the positions of the actors on this issue. Expert A, by contrast, indicated that the actor alignment was very simple, with the member states on one position and the Commission on the other. This raised the concern that perhaps expert A's account of the decision situation was insufficiently nuanced. Therefore, the positions and salience estimates were checked with other experts who confirmed that this simple actor alignment was accurate.

AII.4 CONCLUSIONS

The above-mentioned examples show that the positions registered in the Council documents do not necessarily refer to the policy alternatives the actors initially favoured most. A quantitative comparison of the positions found in the documents with the experts' judgements on actors' favoured positions in the discussions on the resale rights directive shows there are more differences than similarities (Table AII.4). Far from discrediting the use of expert judgements, this exercise reveals that they are indispensable. The initial positions found in the Council documents frequently pertain to the alternatives actors were willing to accept in response to more extreme demands by other actors, or to proposals by the Council presidency. Such information is certainly useful for some analyses, particularly those that focus on the shifts in actors' positions over time. However, for the purposes of our analyses, these documents do not provide appropriate indicators.

The comparison of two sets of expert judgements on the European Refugee Fund decision illustrated the differences found between different sets of judgements. Although close observers may differ in their views on complex decision situations, there is a substantial amount of agreement on the issues that were at stake and the interests of the actors in those issues. Of course, differences are inevitable regarding the precise specification of the issues and the absolute values of some of the estimates. These differences can be evaluated by comparing the level of detail contained in the estimates and the supporting argumentation. On the basis of such an evaluation, it is almost always possible to make an informed judgement on which set of estimates should be included in the analysis. This is a quite different process from blindly comparing estimates from different experts to produce a measure of reliability, or from combining different judgements to produce composite indicators. The approach adopted in the present study is more concerned with the quality of the argumentation experts use to support their numerical estimates. This ensures that, given the limitations of the expert data we draw on, the models are tested on the best available data on the decision situations selected.

References

Abelson, R. P. and Tukey, J. W. 1959. 'Efficient conversion of non-metric information into metric information', *Proceedings of the Social Statistics Section of the American Sociological Association*, 226–230. Reprinted in Tufte, E. R. 1970. *The Quantitative Analysis of Social Problems*. Reading, Massachusetts: Addison-Wesley, pp. 407–417

Achen, C. H. 1999. 'Measurement puzzles in decision-making models', Paper presented at a meeting on decision-making in the European Union, Enschede, the Netherlands

Achen, C. H. and Snidal, D. 1989. 'Rational deterrence theory and comparative case studies', *World Politics* 41: 143–169

Agence Europe 2000. 'Common definition of honey is subject of policy agreement (with opposition from Spain)', *Europe Daily Bulletins* No. 7726, 27 May 2000

Albert, H. 1965 'Modell-Platonismus. Der neoklassische Stil des ökonomischen Denkens in kritischer Beleuchtung', in Topitsch, E. (ed.) *Logik der Sozialwissenschaften*. Köln/Berlin, Kiepenheuer and Witsch, pp. 406–434

Alesina, A. and Rosenthal, H. 1995. *Partisan Politics, Divided Government, and the Economy*. Cambridge: Cambridge University Press

Almond, G. A. 1988. 'The return to the state', *American Political Science Review* 82: 853–874

Arregui, J., Stokman, F. N. and Thomson, R. 2004. 'Bargaining in the European Union and shifts in actors' policy positions', *European Union Politics* 5: 47–72

Arrow, K. 1951 [1963]. *Social Choice and Individual Values* [1963 2nd ed.]. New York: John Wiley

Aspinwall, M. D. and Schneider, G. 2000. 'Same table, separate menu. The institutionalist turn in political science and the study of European integration', *European Journal of Political Research* 38: 1–36

Axelrod, R. 1970. *Conflict of Interest: A Theory of Divergent Goals with Applications to Politics*. Markham: Chicago

1997. *The Complexity of Cooperation: Agent-based Models of Competition and Collaboration*. Princeton University Press: Princeton

Bailer, S. 2004. 'Bargaining success in the European Union: the impact of exogenous and endogenous power resources', *European Union Politics* 5: 99–124

Bailer, S. and Schneider, G. 2002. 'Macht und Einfluss in EU-Verhandlungen: das Integrationsdilemma Deutschlands in vergleichender Perspektive', in Hegmann, H. and Neumärker, B. (eds.) *Die Europäische Union aus Politökonomischer Perspektive*. Marburg: Metropolis, pp. 177–203

Bailer-Jones, D. 2003. 'When scientific models represent', *International Studies in the Philosophy of Science* 17: 59–74

Baldwin, R., Berglöf, E., Giavazzi, F. and Widgrén, M. 2000. 'The EU reforms for tomorrow's Europe', Centre for Economic Policy Research Discussion Paper 2623

Baldwin, R., Berglöf, E., Giavazzi, F. and Widgrén, M. 2001. 'Nice try – should the Treaty of Nice be ratified, monitoring European integration 11', London, Centre for Economic Policy Research

Baldwin, R. and Widgrén, M. 2004a. 'Winners and losers under various dual majority schemes' in Wiberg, M. (ed.) *Reasoned Choices – Essays in Honor of Academy Professor Hannu Nurmi on the Occasion of his 60th Birthday.* The Finnish Political Science Asssociation

Baldwin, R. and Widgrén, M. 2004b. 'Council voting in the Constitutional Treaty: devil in the details', Centre for European Policy Research Policy Brief 53

Banfield, E. C. 1961. *Political Influence*. Glencoe, Illinois: Free Press.

Banzhaf, J. F. 1965. 'Weighted voting doesn't work', *Rutgers Law Review* 19: 317–43

Baron, D. P. 1991. 'Majoritarian incentives, pork barrel programs, and procedural control', *American Journal of Political Science* 35: 57–90

Baron, D. P. and Ferejohn, J. A. 1989. 'Bargaining in legislatures', *American Political Science Review* 83: 1181–1206

Barr, J. and Passarelli, F. 2004. 'Who has the power in the EU?' Dartmouth College and Bocconi University, working paper

Bartels, L. M. 1997. 'Specification uncertainty and model averaging', *American Journal of Political Science* 41: 641–674

Bentley, A. F. 1967 [1908]. *The Process of Government*. Cambridge, Massachusetts: Harvard University Press

Bergman, T. 1997. 'National parliaments and EU affairs committees – notes on empirical variation and competing explanations', *Journal of European Public Policy* 4: 272–87

Berveling, J. 1994. *Het Stempel op de Besluitvorming. Macht, Invloed en Besluitvormig op Twee Amsterdamse Beleidsterreinen*. Amsterdam: Thesis Publishers

Beyers, J. and Dierickx, G. 1997. 'Nationality and European negotiations. The working groups of the Council of Ministers', *European Journal of International Relations* 4: 435–471

Binmore, K. 1987a. 'Nash bargaining theory', in Binmore, K. and Dasgupta, P. (eds.) *The Economics of Bargaining*. Oxford: Basil Blackwell, pp. 27–46

1987b. 'Perfect equilibria in bargaining models', in Binmore, K. and Dasgupta, P. (eds.) *The Economics of Bargaining*. Oxford: Basil Blackwell, pp. 77–105

Binmore, K. 1998. *Game Theory and the Social Contract II. Just Playing.* Cambridge: MIT Press

Black, D. 1958. *Theories of Committees and Elections.* Cambridge: Cambridge University Press

Bouwen, R. 1993. 'Organizational innovation as a social construction: managing meaning in multiple realities', in Lindenberg, S. and Schreuder, H. (eds.) *Interdisciplinary Perspectives on Organization Studies.* Oxford: Pergamon Press, pp. 133–149

Brams, S. J. 1975. *Game Theory and Politics.* New York: Free Press

Brams, S. J. and Affuso, P. 1985. 'New paradoxes of voting power on the EC Council of Ministers', *Electoral Studies* 4: 135–139

Brams, S. J. and Fishburn, P. C. 1983. *Approval Voting.* Boston: Birkhauser

Bräuninger, T., Cornelius, T., König, T. and Schuster, T. 2001. 'The dynamics of European integration. A constitutional analysis of the Amsterdam intergovernmental conference', in Schneider, G. and Aspinwall, M. D. (eds.) *The Rules of Integration. Institutionalist Approaches to the Study of Europe.* Manchester: Manchester University Press, pp. 46–68

Broscheid, A. and Coen, D. 2003. 'Insider and outsider lobbying of the European Commission', *European Union Politics* 4: 165–190

Bryce, J. 1893. *The American Commonwealth*, 2 vols. New York: Macmillan

Bueno de Mesquita, B. 1994. 'Political forecasting: an expected utility model', in Bueno de Mesquita, B. and Stokman, F. N. (eds.) 1994. *European Community Decision Making: Models, Applications and Comparisons.* New Haven: Yale University Press, pp. 71–104

2000. *Principles of International Politics. People's Power, Preferences and Perceptions.* Washington: CQ Press

2002. *Predicting Politics.* Columbus: The Ohio State University Press

2004. 'Decision making models, rigor and new puzzles', *European Union Politics* 5: 125–138

Bueno de Mesquita, B., Newman, D. and Rabushka, A. 1985. *Forecasting Political Events: The Future of Hong Kong.* New Haven: Yale University Press

Bueno de Mesquita, B. and Stokman F. N. (eds.) 1994. *European Community Decision Making: Models, Applications and Comparisons.* New Haven: Yale University Press

Butler, C. K. 2004. 'Compromise and the two-level game. Modeling compromise at the international table', *Conflict Management and Peace Science* 21: 159–77

Cameron, D. R. 1992. 'The 1992 initiative: causes and consequences', in Sbragia, A. M. (ed.) *Euro-Politics: Institutions and Policymaking in the 'New' European Community.* Washington D.C.: The Brookings Institution, pp. 23–74

Caplin, A. and Nalebuff, B. 1988. 'On 64%-majority rule', *Econometrica* 56: 787–814

1991. 'Aggregation and social choice: a mean voter theorem', *Econometrica* 59: 1–23

Carruba, C. J., Gabel, M., Murrah, L., Clough, R., Montegomery, E. and Schambach, R. 2004. 'Off the record: unrecorded legislative votes, selection bias, and roll-call vote analysis', unpublished manuscript

Carrubba, C. J. and Volden, C. 2000. 'Coalitional politics and logrolling in legislative institutions', *American Journal of Political Science* 44: 255–271

Chong, D. 1991. *Collective Action and the Civil Rights Movement*. Chicago: University of Chicago Press

Clarke, K. A. 2003. 'Nonparametric model discrimination in international relations', *Journal of Conflict Resolution* 47: 72–93

Coleman, J. S. 1966a. 'The possibility of a social welfare function', *American Economic Review* 56: 1105–1122

1966b. 'Foundations for a theory of collective decisions', *American Journal of Sociology* 71: 615–627

1971. 'Foundations for a theory of social action', *American Journal of Sociology* 76: 615–627

1990. *Foundations of Social Theory*. Cambridge, MA: The Belknap Press of Harvard University.

Corbett, R. 2000. 'Academic modelling of the codecision procedure: a practitioner's puzzled reaction', *European Union Politics* 1: 373–8

2001. 'A response to a reply to a reaction (I hope someone is still interested!)', *European Union Politics* 2: 361–4

Council of the European Communities 1990. *The Council of the European Community*. Luxembourg: Office of Official Publications of the European Communities

Council of the European Union 2000. 'A-item note: vertical directives on foodstuffs: proposal for a Council directive relating to honey, political agreement', *COREPER Document 8701/00*, 24 May 2000

Crombez, C. 1996. 'Legislative procedures in the European Community', *British Journal of Political Science* 26: 199–288

1997. 'The co-decision procedure in the European Union', *Legislative Studies Quarterly* 22: 97–119

2000a. 'Institutional reform and co-decision in the European Union', *Constitutional Political Economy* 11: 41–57

2000b. 'Co-decision: 'towards a bicameral European Union', *European Union Politics* 1: 363–8

2000c. 'Spatial models of logrolling in the European Union', *European Journal of Political Economy* 16: 707–37

2001. 'The Treaty of Amsterdam and the co-decision procedure', in Schneider, G. and Aspinwall, M. D. (eds.) *The Rules of Integration. Institutionalist Approaches to the Study of Europe*. Manchester: Manchester University Press, pp. 101–122

2002. 'Information, lobbying and the legislative process in the European Union', *European Union Politics* 3: 7–32

2003. 'The democratic deficit in the European Union', *European Union Politics* 4: 101–20

Crombez, C., Steunenberg B. and Corbett, R. 2000. 'Understanding the EU legislative process: political scientists' and practitioners' perspectives', *European Union Politics* 1: 365–85

Dai, X. 2002. 'Political regimes and international trade: the democratic difference revisited', *American Political Science Review* 96: 159–65

Davis, O., De Groot, M. and Hinich, M. 1972. 'Social preference orderings and majority rule', *Econometrica* 40: 147–157

De Gooijer, J. G. 2002. 'Introduction to forecasting decisions in conflict situations', *International Journal of Forecasting* 1: 319–320

De Swaan, A. 1973. *Coalition Theories and Cabinet Formation*. Elsevier Scientific Publishing Company: Amsterdam

De Vries, M. 1999. *Governing with your Closest Neighbour: An Assessment of Spatial Coalition Formation Theories*. Ph.D Thesis. University of Nijmegen

de Zwaan, J. W. 1995. *The Permanent Representatives Committee: its Role in European Union Decision-making*. Amsterdam, New York: Elsevier

Dimitrova, A. and Steunenberg, B. 2001. 'The search for convergence of national policies in the European Union: an impossible quest?' *European Union Politics*. 1: 201–226

Dinan, D. 1999. *Ever Closer Union. An Introduction to European Integration*. Boulder/London: Lynne Rienner

Dobbins, M., Drüner, D. and Schneider, G. 2004. 'Kopenhagener Konsequenzen: Gesetzgebung in der EU vor und nach der Erweiterung', *Zeitschrift für Parlamentsfragen* 35: 51–68

Dowding, K. 2000. 'Institutionalist research on the European Union', *European Union Politics* 1: 125–144

2002. 'Rational choice and institutional change: an overview of current theories', in Steunenberg, B. (ed.) *Widening the European Union: The Politics of Institutional Reform and Change*. London: Routledge, pp. 21–38

Downs, A. 1957. *An Economic Theory of Democracy*. New York: Harper and Row

Edwards, G. 1996. 'National sovereignty vs. integration? The Council of Ministers', in Richardson, J. (ed.) *European Union: Power and Policy-making*. London: Routledge, pp. 127–147

Elster, J. and Roemer, J. E. 1991. *Interpersonal Comparisons of Well–being*. Cambridge: Cambridge University Press

Enelow, J. M. and Hinich, M. 1984. *The Spatial Theory of Voting: An Introduction*. Cambridge: Cambridge University Press

Erev, I., Roth, A. E., Slonim, R. L. and Barron, G. 2002. 'Predictive value and the usefulness of game theoretic models', *International Journal of Forecasting* 18: 359–368

European Commission 1996. 'Proposal for a Council directive relating to honey', *Official Journal* C 231, 9 August 1996, 10

2001. *General Report on the Activities of the European Union, 2000*. Luxembourg: Office for Official Publications of the European Communities

Evans, P. B. 1993. 'Building an integrative approach to international and domestic politics: reflections and projections', in Evans, P. B., Jacobson, H. K. and Putnam, R. D. (eds.) *Double-edged Diplomacy: International Bargaining and Domestic Politics*. Berkeley: University of California Press, pp. 397–430

Evans, P. B., Jacobson, H. K. and Putnam, R. O. (eds.) 1993. *Double-edged Diplomacy: International Bargaining and Domestic Politics*. Berkeley: University of California Press

Farrell, H. and Héritier A. 2003. 'Formal and informal institutions under codecision: continuous constitution-building in Europe', *Governance* 16: 577–600

2004. 'Interorganizational negotiation and intraorganizational power in shared decision-making: early agreements under codecision and their impact on the European Parliament and Council', *Comparative Political Studies* 37: 1184–1212

Fearon, J. D. 1994. 'Domestic political audiences and the escalation of international disputes', *American Political Science Review* 90: 715–735

Feder, S. A. 1987. 'FACTIONS and Policon: new ways to analyze politics', *Studies in Intelligence* 31: 41–57. Originally classified 'Secret.' Reprinted in Bradford Westerfield, H. 1995. *Inside CIA's Private World*. New Haven: Yale University Press, pp. 274–292

Feld, L., Kirchgässner, G. and Weck-Hannemann, H. 2002. 'Enlargement and the European budget: budgetary decision making and fiscal constraints', in Steunenberg, B. (ed.) *Widening the European Union: The Politics of Institutional Reform and Change*. London: Routledge, pp. 144–162

Felsenthal, D. and Machover M. 1998. *The Measurement of Voting Power. Theory and Practice, Problems and Paradoxes*. Cheltenham: Edward Elgar

2001a. 'Myths and meanings of voting power', *Journal of Theoretical Politics* 13: 81–87

2001b. 'The Treaty of Nice and qualified majority voting', *Social Choice and Welfare* 18: 431–464

Franzese, R. J. Jr. 1999. 'Partially independent central banks, politically responsive governments, and inflation', *American Journal of Political Science* 43: 681–706

Friedkin, N. E. and Johnsen, E. C. 1990. 'Social influence and opinion', *Journal of Mathematical Sociology* 15: 193–205

1997. 'Social positions in influence networks', *Social Networks* 19: 209–222

Friedkin, N. E. and Johnsen, C. 1999. 'Social influence networks and opinion change', *Advances in Group Processes* 16: 1–29

Friedman, J. W. 1990. *Game Theory with Applications to Economics*. New York: Oxford University Press

Fudenberg, D. and Levine, D. K. 1998. *The Theory of Learning in Games*. Cambridge: MIT Press

Gabel, M., Hix, S. and Schneider, G. 2002. 'Who is afraid of cumulative research? Improving data on EU politics', *European Union Politics* 3: 481–500

Garrett, G. 1995. 'From the Luxembourg compromise to codecision: decision making in the European Union', *Electoral Studies* 50: 289–308

Garrett, G. and Tsebelis, G. 1996. 'An institutional critique of intergovernmentalism', *International Organization* 50: 269–299

1997. 'More on the codecision endgame', *Journal of Legislative Studies* 3: 139–143

1999a. 'Why resist the temptation to apply power indices to the EU?', *Journal of Theoretical Politics* 11: 291–308

1999b. 'More reasons to resist the temptation to apply power indices to the EU', *Journal of Theoretical Politics* 11: 331–338

2001a. 'Understanding better the EU legislative process', *European Union Politics* 2: 353–361

2001b. 'Even more reasons to resist the temptation to apply power indices to the EU', *Journal of Theoretical Politics* 13: 99–105

Gaver, K. M. and Geisel, M. S. 1974. 'Discriminating among alternative models: Bayesian and non–Bayesian approaches', in Zarembka, P. (ed.) *Frontiers in Econometrics*. New York: Academic, pp. 49–77

Gilligan, T. and Krehbiel, K. 1995. 'The gains from exchange hypothesis of legislative organization', in Shepsle, K. A. and Weingast, B. R. (eds.) *Positive Theories of Congressional Institutions*. Ann Arbor: University of Michigan Press

Grafstein, R. 1992. *Institutional Realism*. New Haven: Yale University Press

Granger, C. W. J. and Newbold, P. 1986. *Forecasting Economic Time Series*, 2nd ed. Orlando, Florida: Academic

Greenberg, J. 1979. 'Consistent majority rule over compact sets of alternatives', *Econometrica* 47: 627–36

Gul, F. 1989. 'Bargaining foundations of Shapley value', *Econometrica* 57: 81–95

Haas, E. B. 1958. *The Uniting of Europe*. Stanford: Stanford University Press

1975. *The Obsolescence of Regional Integration Theory*. Berkeley: Institute of International Studies

Hall, P. and Taylor R. 1996. 'Political science and the three new institutionalisms', *Political Studies* 44: 936–957

Hammond, T. H. and Miller G. J. 1987. 'The core of the constitution', *American Political Science Review* 81: 1155–174

Hammond, T. H. and Prins, B. C. 1999. 'The impact of domestic institutions on international negotiations: a taxonomy of results from a complete-information spatial model', paper presented at the Annual Meeting of the American Political Science Association, Atlanta, Georgia, 2–5 September 1999

Harsanyi, J. C. 1963. 'A simplified bargaining model for the n-person cooperative game', *International Economic Review* 4: 194–220

1977. *Rational Behavior and Bargaining Equilibrium in Games and Social Situations*. Cambridge: Cambridge University Press

Hart, S. and Mas-Colell, A. 1996. 'Bargaining and value', *Econometrica* 64: 357–380

Hayes-Renshaw, F. 2001. 'The Council and enlargement: a challenge or an opportunity?', *Journal of International Relations and Development* 4: 9–12

Hayes-Renshaw, F. and Wallace, H. 1995. 'Executive power in the European Union: the functions and limits of the Council of Ministers', *Journal of European Public Policy* 2: 559–582

1997. *The Council of Ministers*. Basingstoke: Macmillan Press

Herstein, I. N. and Milnor, J. 1953. 'An axiomatic approach to measurable utility', *Econometrica* 21: 291–297

Hinich, M. J. and Munger, M. C. 1994. *Ideology and the Theory of Political Choice*. Ann Arbor: University of Michigan Press

Hinich, M. and Munger, M. C. 1997. *Analytical Politics*. Cambridge: Cambridge University Press

Hix, S. 1998. 'The study of the European Union II: the 'New Governance' agenda and its rival', *Journal of European Public Policy* 5: 38–65

1999. *The Political System of the European Union*. London: Macmillan

Hix, S. and Lord, C. 1997. *Political Parties in the European Union*. New York: St. Martin's Press

Hoffmann, S. 1966. 'Obstinate or obsolete? The face of the nation State and the case of Western Europe', *Daedalus*, 95: 892–908

Holler, M. J. 1994. 'Comment', in Herder-Dorneich, P., Schenk, K. E. and Schmidtchen D. (eds.) *Neue Politische Ökonomie der Reguliering, Dereguliering and Privatisierung (Jahrbuch für Neue Politische Ökonomie, Volume 13)*. Tübingen: Mohr, pp. 66–71

Holler, M. J. and Widgrén, M. 1999. 'Why power indices for assessing EU decision-making', *Journal of Theoretical Politics* 11: 321–330

Hosli, M. O. 1993. 'Admission of European Free Trade Association states to the European Community: effects of voting power in the European Community Council of Ministers', *International Organization* 47: 629–643

1995. 'The balance between small and large: effects of a double-majority system on voting power in the European Union', *International Studies Quarterly* 39: 351–370

2000. 'Smaller states and the new voting weights in the Council', working paper. Clingendael Institute of International Relations: The Hague

Hosli, M. O. and Machover, M. 2004. 'The Nice Treaty and voting rules in the Council: a reply to Moberg (2002)', *Journal of Common Market Studies* 42: 497–521

Hosli, M. O. and Van Deemen, A. 2002. 'Effects of enlargement on efficiency and coalition formation in the Council of the European Union', in Hosli, M. O., Van Deemen, A. and Widgrén, M. (eds.) *Institutional Challenges in the European Union*. London: Routledge

Hosli, M. O. and Wolffenbuttel, R. F. 2001. 'Estimating the vote distribution in the Council of the European Union', *Journal of International Relations and Development* 4: 38–54

Hotelling, H. 1929. 'Stability in competition', *Economic Journal* 39: 41–57

Huber, J. and Inglehart, R. 1995. 'Expert interpretations of party space and party locations in 42 societies', *Party Politics* 1: 73–111

Hubschmid, C. and Moser, P. 1997. 'The cooperation procedure in the EU: why was the European Parliament influential in the decision on car emission standards', *Journal of Comman Market Studies* 35: 225–42

Hug, S. 2002. *Voices of Europe. Citizens, Referendums and European Integration*. Lanham: Rowman and Littlefield

Hug, S. and Christin, T. 2002. 'Referendums and citizen support for European integration', *Comparative Political Studies* 5: 586–618

Hug, S. and König, T. 2002. 'In view of ratification: governmental preferences and domestic constraints at the Amsterdam intergovernmental conference', *International Organization* 56: 447–476

Iida, K. 1993. 'When and how do domestic constraints matter? Two-level games with uncertainty', *Journal of Conflict Resolution* 37: 403–426

Johnson, H. and Broder, D. 1996. *The System*. Boston: Little Brown

Kalai, E. and Smorodinsky, M. 1975. 'Other solutions to Nash's bargaining problem', *Econometrica* 43: 513–518

Kasack, C. 2004. 'The legislative impact of the European Parliament under the revised co-decision procedure. Environmental, public health and consumer protection policies', *European Union Politics* 5: 241–260

Kauppi, H. and Widgrén, M. 2004. 'What determines EU decision-making: needs, power or both?', *Economic Policy* 39, 221–266

Keeney, R. L. and Raiffa, H. 1993. *Decisions with Multiple Objectives*. Cambridge: Cambridge University Press

Kirman, A. and Widgrén, M. 1995. 'European economic decision-making policy: Progress or paralysis?', *Economic Policy* 21: 421–460

Knoke, D., Pappi, F. U. and Broadbent, J. 1996. *Comparing Policy Networks: Labor Politics in the US, Germany, and Japan, Cambridge Studies in Comparative Politics*. Cambridge: Cambridge University Press

Kollman, K. 2003. 'The rotating presidency of the European Union as a search for good policies', *European Union Politics* 4: 51–74

König, T. 1992. *Entscheidungen im Politiknetzwerkβ: Der Einflua von Organisationen auf die Arbeits- und Sozialrechtliche Gesetzgebung in den 80er Jahren*. Wiesbaden: Deutscher Universitäts-Verlag

1997. *Europa auf dem Weg zum Mehrebenensystem. Gründe und konsequenzen nationaler und parlamentarischer Integration*. Opladen: Westdeutscher Verlag

König T. and Bräuninger, T. 1998. 'The inclusiveness of European decision rules', *Journal of Theoretical Politics* 10: 125–141

2000. 'Governing the enlarged European Union: accession scenarios and institutional reform', *Central European Political Science Review* 1: 42–62

König, T. and Hug, S. 2000. 'Ratifying Maastricht, parliamentary votes on international treaties and theoretical solution concepts', *European Union Politics* 1: 89–122

König, T. and Pöter, M. 2001. 'Examining the EU legislative process: the relative importance of agenda and veto power', *European Union Politics* 2: 329–351

Krehbiel, K. 1988. 'Spatial models of legislative choice', *Legislative Studies Quarterly* 13: 259–319

1991. *Information and Legislative Organization*. Ann Arbor: University of Michigan Press

1998. *Pivotal Politics*. Chicago: University of Chicago Press

Kreppel, A. 1999. 'The European Parliament's influence over EU policy outcomes', *Journal of Common Market Studies* 37: 521–538

Lane, J. E. and Ersson, S. 2000. *The New Institutional Politics. Performance and Outcomes*. London and New York: Routledge

LaPalombara, J. 1960. 'The utility and limitations of interest group theory in non-American field situations', *Journal of Politics* 22: 29–49

Laruelle, A. 1998. 'The EU decision making procedures: some insight from non-cooperative game theory', IRES Discussion Papers, 97/27

2002. 'The EU decision making procedures: some insight from non-cooperative game theory', in Hosli, M., Van Deemen, A. and Widgrén, M. (eds.)

Institutional Challenges in the European Union. London: Routledge, pp. 89–112

Laruelle, A. and Widgrén, M. 1998. 'Is the allocation of power among EU states fair?', *Public Choice* 94: 317–339

2001. 'Voting power in a sequence of cooperative games', in Holler, M. and Owen, G. (eds.) *Voting Power And Coalition Formation*. Dortrecht and Boston: Kluwer Academic Publishers

Laver, M. and Shepsle, K. 1996. *Making and Breaking Governments: Cabinets and Legislatures in Parliamentary Democracies*. New York: Cambridge University Press

Leech, D. 2002. 'Designing the voting system for the Council of Ministers of the European Union', *Public Choice* 113: 437–464

Leenders, R. Th. A. J. 1995. *Structure and Influence. Statistical Models for the Dynamics of Actor Attributes, Network Structure and their Interdependence*. Amsterdam: Thesis Publishers

2002. 'Modeling social influence through network autocorrelation: constructing the weight matrix', *Social Networks* 24: 21–48

Lewin, L. 1991. *Self-interest and Public Interest in Western Politics*. Oxford: Oxford University Press

Lewis, J. 2000. 'The methods of community in EU decision-making and administrative rivalry in the council's infrastructure', *Journal of European Public Policy* 7: 261–289

Lindberg, L. N. 1963. *The Political Dynamics of European Economic Integration*. Stanford: Stanford University Press

Lindblom, C. E. 1965. *The Intelligence of Democracy*. New York: Free Press

Lindenberg, S. 1997. 'Grounding groups in theory: functional, structural and cognitive interdependencies', *Advances in Group Processes* 14: 281–331

2001. 'Social rationality versus rational egoism', in Turner, J. H. (ed.) *Handbook of Social Theory*. New York: Kluwer Academic and Plenum Publishers

Lohmann, S. 1997. 'Linkage Politics', *Journal of Conflict Resolution* 41: 38–67

Lowndes, V. 2002. 'Institutionalism', in Marsh, D. and Stoker, G. (eds.) *Theory and Methods in Political Science*. Basingstoke: Palgrave Macmillan, pp. 90–108

Manley, J. F. 1970. *The Politics of Finance*. Boston: Little, Brown

2000. 'Free to trade: democracies, autocracies and international trade', *American Political Science Review* 94: 305–322

Mansfield, E. D., Milner, H. V. and Rosendorff, P. B. 2002. 'Replication, realism, and robustness: analyzing political regimes and international trade', *American Political Science Review* 96: 167–169

March, J. G. and Olsen J. P. 1984. 'The new institutionalism: organizational factors in political life', *American Political Science Review* 78: 734–749

March, J. and Olsen, J. 1989. *Rediscovering Institutions: the Organizational Basis of Politics*. New York: The Free Press

Marks, G., Hooghe, L. and Blank, K. 1996. 'European integration in the 1980s: state-centric vs. multi-level governance', *Journal of Common Market Studies* 34: 341–378

Marsden, P. V. and Friedkin, N. E. 1993. 'Network studies of social influence', *Sociological Methods and Research* 22: 127–151

Martin, L. 2000. *Democratic Commitments-Legislatures and International Cooperation*. Princeton: Princeton University Press

Mas-Colell, A., Whinston, M. D. and Green, J. R. 1995. *Microeconomic Theory*. Oxford: Oxford University Press

Mattila, M. and Lane, J. E. 2001. 'Why unanimity in the Council? A roll call analysis of Council voting', *European Union Politics* 2: 31–52

Mavrogordatos, G. 1984. 'The Greek party system: a case of limited but polarised pluralism', *West European Politics* 7: 156–169

McKelvey, R. D. 1976. 'Intransitivities in multidimensional voting models and some implications for agenda control', *Journal of Economic Theory* 12: 472–182

1979. 'General conditions for global intransitivities in formal voting models', *Econometrica* 47: 1085–1112

McKelvey, R. D., Ordeshook, P. and Winer, M. 1978. 'The competitive solution for N-person games without transferable utility: with an application for committee games', *American Political Science Review* 72: 599–615

Mearsheimer, J. J. 1994–95. 'The false promise of international institutions'. *International Security* 19: 5–49

Merlo, A. and Wilson, C. 1995. 'A stochastic model of sequential bargaining with complete information', *Econometrica* 63: 371–399

Milner, H. V. 1997. *Interests, Institutions, and Information*. Princeton: Princeton University Press

Milner, H. V. and Rosendorff, P. B. 1996. 'Trade negotiations, information and domestic politics', *Economics and Politics* 8: 145–89

1997. 'Democratic politics and international trade negotiations. Elections and divided government as constraints on trade liberalization', *Journal of Conflict Resolution* 41: 117–146

Mo, J. 1995. 'Domestic institutions and international bargaining: the role of agent veto in two-level games', *American Political Science Review* 89: 914–924

Moberg, A. 2002. 'The Nice Treaty and voting rules in the Council', *Journal of Common Market Studies* 40: 259–282

Mokken, R. J., Payne, D., Stokman, F. N. and Wasseur, F. W. 2000. 'Decision context and policy effectuation: EU structural reform in Ireland', *Irish Political Studies* 15: 39–61

Molm, L. 1996. *Coercive Power in Social Exchange*. Cambridge: Cambridge University Press

Moravcsik, A. 1993. 'Introduction: integration international and domestic theories of international bargaining', in Evans, P. B., Jacobson, H. K. and Putnam, R. D. (eds.) *Double-Edged Diplomacy*. Berkeley: University of California Press

1998. *The Choice for Europe*. Ithaca, NY: Cornell University Press

Morgan, M. S. and Morrison, M. (eds.) 1999. *Models as Mediators: Perspectives on Natural and Social Science*. Cambridge, Cambridge University Press

Morgenthau, H. 1948. *Politics Among Nations: The Struggle for Power and Peace*, New York: Knopf

Morrison, M. and Morgan, M. S. 1999. 'Models as mediating instruments', in Morgan, M. S. and Morrison, M. (eds.) *Models as Mediators: Perspectives on Natural and Social Science*, Cambridge, Cambridge University Press, pp. 10–37

Morton, R. B. 1999. *Methods and Models: A Guide to the Empirical Analysis of Formal Models in Political Science*. Cambridge: Cambridge University Press

Moser, P. 1996. 'The European Parliament as a conditional agenda setter: what are the conditions? A critique of Tsebelis (1994)', *American Political Science Review* 90: 834–838

1997a. 'A theory of the conditional influence of the European Parliament in the co-operation procedure', *Public Choice* 91: 333–350

1997b. 'The benefits of the conciliation procedure for the European Parliament: comment to George Tsebelis', *Aussenwirtschaft* 52: 57–62

Moser, P D., Schneider, G. and Kirchgässner, G. 2000. *Decision Rules in the European Union: a Rational Choice Perspective*. New York: St. Martin's Press

Moulin, H. 1988. *Axioms of Cooperative Decision Making*. Cambridge: Cambridge University Press

Murphy, A. H. and Winkler, R. L. 1984. 'Probability forecasting in meteorology', *Journal of the American Statistical Association* 79: 489–500

Muthoo, A. 1999. *Bargaining Theory With Applications*. Cambridge: Cambridge University Press

Myerson, R. B. 1991. *Game Theory*. Cambridge: Harvard University Press

Napel, S. and Widgrén, M. 2002a. 'Strategic power in EU decision making procedures', unpublished manuscript

2002b. 'Strategic power revisited', Munich: CESifo Working Paper No. 736

2004a. 'Power measurement as sensitivity analysis – a unified approach', *Journal of Theoretical Politics* 16: 517–538

2004b. 'The inter-institutional distribution of power in EU codecision', Munich: CESifo Working Paper No. 1347, *Social Choice and Welfare*, forthcoming

Nash, J. F. 1950. 'The bargaining problem', *Econometrica* 18: 155–162

1953. 'Two-person cooperative games', *Econometrica* 21: 128–140

Nicholson, M. 1989. *Formal Theories in International Relations*. Cambridge: Cambridge University Press

Noury, A. G. 2002. 'Ideology, nationality and Euro-Parliamentarians', *European Union Politics* 3: 33–58

Nugent, N. 1999. *The Government and Politics of the European Union*. Durham: Duke University Press

Opp, K. D. 1990. *Empirischer Theorienvergleich: Erklärungen sozialen Verhaltens in Problemsituationen*. Opladen: Westdeutscher Verlag

O'Reilly, C. A. 1983. 'The use of information in organizational decision making: a model and some propositions', *Research in Organizational Behaviour* 5: 103–139

Ostrom, E. 1986. 'An agenda for the study of institutions', *Public Choice* 48: 3–25

Owen, G. 1972. 'Multilinear extensions of games', *Management Science* 18: 64–79

Owen, G. 1995. *Game Theory.* 3rd edition. San Diego: Academic Press

Pahre, R. 1997. 'Endogenous domestic institutions in two-level games and parliamentary oversight of the European Union', *Journal of Conflict Resolution* 41: 147–174

2001. 'Divided government and international cooperation in Austria-Hungary, Sweden-Norway and the European Union', *European Union Politics* 2: 131–162

Pajala, A. 2002. *Expected Power and Success in Coalitions and Space: Empirical Voting Power in 17 European Parliaments and the Council of the EU.* Doctoral Dissertation. Turku: University of Turku

Pajala, A. and Widgrén, M. 2004. 'A priori vs. empirical power in the EU Council of Ministers', *European Union Politics* 5: 73–97

Pappi, F. U. and Henning, C. 1998. 'Policy networks, public policy-making and visualization – policy networks: more than a metaphor?' *Journal of Theoretical Politics* 10: 553–576

Payne, D. 1999. *Policy Making in the European Union. An Analysis of the Impact of the Reform of the Structural Funds in Ireland.* Amsterdam: Thesis Publishers

Peters, G. 1999. *Institutional Theory in Political Science: the 'New Institutionalism'.* London: Pinter

Peterson, J. and Bomberg, E. 1999. *Decision Making in the European Union.* London: Macmillan Press

Plott, C. R. 1967. 'A notion of equilibrium and its possibility under majority rule', *American Economic Review* 57: 787–806

1991. 'Will economics become an experimental science?' *Southern Economic Journal* 57: 901–920

Putnam, R. D. 1988. 'Diplomacy and domestic politics: the logic of two-level games', *International Organization* 42: 427–460

1993. 'Diplomacy and domestic politics: the logic of two-level games' in Putnam, R. D., Evans, P. and Jacobson, H. (eds.) *Double-Edged Diplomacy. International Bargaining and Domestic Politics.* Berkeley: University of California Press, pp. 431–468

Rabinowitz, G. and MacDonald, S. E. 1986. 'The power of the states in US presidential elections', *American Political Science Review* 80: 65–87

Raftery, A. E. 1995. 'Bayesian model selection in social research', *Sociological Methodology* 25: 111–163

Raiffa, H. 1953. 'Arbitration schemes for generalized two-person games', in Kuhn, H. W. and Tucker, A. (eds.) *Contribution to the Theory of Games II: Annals of Mathematics Studies.* Princeton: Princeton University Press, pp. 361–387

Raub, W. and Weesie, J. 1990. 'Reputation and efficiency in social interactions: an example of network effects', *American Journal of Sociology* 96: 626–654

Ray, J. L. and Russet, B. 1996. 'The future as arbiter of theoretical controversies: predictions, explanations and the end of the cold war', *British Journal of Political Sciences* 26: 441–470

Ray, J. L. and Singer, D. J. 1990. 'Measuring the concentration of power in the international system', in Singer, D. J. and Diehl, P. F. (eds.) *Measuring the Correlates of War.* Ann Arbor: University of Michigan Press

Richardson, J. (ed.) 1996. *European Union: Power and Policy-making.* London: Routledge

Riker, W. H. 1962. *The Theory of Political Coalitions.* New Haven: Yale University Press

1980. 'Implications from the disequilibrium of majority rule for the study of institutions', *American Political Science Review* 74: 432–446

Riker, W. H. and Brams, S. J. 1973. 'The paradox of vote trading', *American Political Science Review* 67: 1235–1247

Riley, J. 1988. *Liberal Utilitarianism.* Cambridge: Cambridge University Press

Robert, C. P. 2001. *The Bayesian Choice*, 2nd ed. New York: Springer

Rojer, M. 1999. 'Collective decision-making models applied to labour negotiations in the Netherlands: a comparison between a position exchange model and a conflict model', *Rationality and Society* 11: 207–235

Roth, A. E. 1979. *Axiomatic Models of Bargaining.* Berlin: Springer-Verlag

Rubinstein, A. 1982. 'Perfect equilibrium in a bargaining model', *Econometrica* 50: 97–109

2000. *Economics and Language.* Cambridge: Cambridge University Press

Schelling, T. C. 1960. *The Strategy of Conflict.* Cambridge: Harvard University Press

Schneider, G. 1994. 'Getting closer at different speeds: strategic interaction in widening European integration', in Allan, P. and Schmidt, C. (eds.) *Game Theory and International Relations.* Cheltenham: Edward Elgar

1995. 'Agenda-setting in European integration: the conflict between voters, governments and supranational institutions', in Laursen, F. (ed.) *The Political Economy of European Integration.* Maastricht: European Institute of Public Administration, pp. 31–61

Schneider G. and Aspinwall, M. D. (eds.) 2001. *The Rules of Integration. Institutionalist Approaches to the Study of Europe.* Manchester: Manchester University Press

Schneider, G. and Baltz, K. 2003. 'The power of specialization: how interest groups influence EU-legislation', *Rivista die Politica Economica* XCIII: 253–283

2005. 'Domesticated Eurocrats: bureaucratic discretion in the legislative pre-negotiations of the European Union', *Acta Politica*, forthcoming

Schneider, G. and Cederman, L. E. 1994. 'The change of tide in political cooperation: a limited information model of European integration', *International Organization* 48: 633–662

Schneider, G., Finke, D. and Bailer, S. 2004. *'Bargaining power: an evaluation of competing models'*, University of Konstanz, working paper

Schneider, G. and Weitsman, P. A. 1996. 'The punishment trap: integration referendums as popularity contests', *Comparative Political Studies* 28: 582–607

Schofield, N. 1978. 'Instability of simple dynamic games', *Review of Economic Studies* 45: 575–594

Scully, R. M. 1997a. 'The European Parliament and the co-decision procedure: a reassessment', *Journal of Legislative Studies* 3: 58–73

1997b. 'The European Parliament and co-decision: a rejoinder to Tsebelis and Garrett', *Journal of Legislative Studies* 3: 93–103

Selck, T. J. 2004. 'On the dimensionality of European Union legislative decision making', *Journal of Theoretical Politics* 16: 203–222

Selck, T. J. and Steunenberg, B. 2004. 'Between power and luck: the European Parliament in the EU legislative process', *European Union Politics* 5: 25–46

Shapley, L. S. 1953. 'A value for n-person cooperative games', in Kuhn, H. and Tucker, A. (eds.) *Contributions to the Theory of Games, vol II*. Princeton: Princeton University Press, pp. 343–459

1977. 'A comparison of power indices and a non-symmetric generalization', *RAND* Corporation, Paper P-5872

Shapley, L. S. and Shubik, M. 1954. 'A method for evaluating the distribution of power in a committee system', *American Political Science Review* 48: 787–792

Shepsle, K. A. 1979. 'Institutional arrangements and equilibrium in multidimensional voting models', *American Journal of Political Science* 32: 27–60

1989. 'Studying institutions: some lessons from the rational choice approach', *Journal of Theoretical Politics* 1: 131–147

Shepsle, K. A. and Weingast, B. R. 1981. 'Structure-induced equilibrium and legislative choice', *Public Choice* 37: 503–519

1984. 'Uncovered sets and sophisticated voting outcomes with implications for agenda institutions', *American Journal of Political Science* 28: 49–74

1987. 'Why are congressional committees powerful?' *American Political Science Review* 81: 935–45

1995. 'Positive theories of congressional institutions', in Shepsle, K. A. and Weingast, B. R. (eds.) *Positive Theories of Congressional Institutions*. Ann Arbor: University of Michigan Press, pp. 5–35

Sherrington, P. 1999. *The Council of Ministers: Political Authority in the European Union*. London and New York: Pinter

Shubik, M. 1982. *Game Theory in the Social Sciences*. Cambridge: MIT Press

Signorino, C. S. 1999. 'Estimation and strategic interaction in discrete choice models of international conflict', *American Political Science Review* 92: 279–297

Singer, D. J. 1969. 'The incomplete theorist: insight without evidence', in Rosenau, J. N. and Knorr, K. (eds.) *Contending Approaches to International Politics*. Princeton: Princeton University Press, pp. 63–86

Snidal, D. 1994. 'The politics of scope: endogenous actors, heterogeneity and institutions', *Journal of Theoretical Politics* 6: 449–472

Soetendorp, B. and Hosli, M. O. 2001. 'The hidden dynamics of EU Council decision making', *Acta Politica* 4, 252–287

Steunenberg, B. 1994a. 'Decision-making under different institutional arrangements: legislation by the European Community', *Journal of Theoretical and Institutional Economics* 150: 642–669

1994b. 'Regulatory policymaking in a parliamentary setting' in Herder-Dorneich, P. Schenk, K. E. and Schmidtchen, D. (eds.) *Neue Politische Ökonomie der Regulierung, Deregulierung and Privatisierung (Jahrbuch für Neue Politische Ökonomie, Volume 13)*. Tübingen: Mohr, pp. 36–57

1997. 'Codecision and its reform: a comparative analysis of decision making rules in the European Union', in Steunenberg, B. and Van Vught, F. A. (eds.) *Political Institutions and Public Policy: Perspectives on European Decision Making*. Dordrecht: Kluwer, pp. 205–229

2000a. 'Constitutional change in the European Union: parliament's impact on the reform of the codecision procedure', in Wagenaar, H. (ed.) *Government Institutions: Effects, Changes and Normative Foundations*. Dordrecht: Kluwer, pp. 89–108

2000b. 'Seeing what you want to see: the limits of current modelling on the European Union', *European Union Politics* 1: 368–373

2001. 'Enlargement and institutional reform in the European Union: separate or connected issues?' *Constitutional Political Economy* 12: 349–368

2002a. 'Playing different games: the European Parliament and the reform of codecision', in Steunenberg, B. and Thomassen, J. (eds.) *The European Parliament: Moving Toward Democracy in the EU*. Boulder: Rowman and Littlefield, pp. 163–83

2002b. 'An even wider Union: the effects of enlargement on EU decision-making', in Steunenberg, B. (ed.) *Widening the European Union: The Politics of Institutional Change and Reform*. London and New York: Routledge, pp. 97–118

Steunenberg, B. and Dimitrova, A. 1999. *Interests, Legitimacy, and Constitutional Choice: the Extension of the Codecision Procedure in Amsterdam*. Enschede: University of Twente. Mimeo

Steunenberg, B., Koboldt, C. and Schmidtchen, D. 1996. 'Policymaking, comitology, and the balance of power in the European Union', *International Review of Law and Economics* 16: 329–344

1997. 'Beyond comitology: a comparative analysis of implementation procedures with parliamentary involvement', *Aussenwirtschaft* 52: 87–112

Steunenberg, B., Schmidtchen, D. and Koboldt, C. 1999. 'Strategic power in the European Union: evaluating the distribution of power in policy games', *Journal of Theoretical Politics* 11: 339–366

Stigum, B. 1990. *Towards a Formal Science of Economics*. Cambridge: MIT Press

Stokman, F. N. 2004. '*What* binds us *when* with *whom*? Content and structure in social network analysis', extended version of keynote at the SUNBELT XXIV International Social Network Conference, Portorož (Slovenia), May 13 2004 (www.oprit.rug.nl/stokman/articles.htm)

2005. '*Was* verbindet uns *wann* mit *wem*? Inhalt und Struktur in der Analyse Sozialer Netzwerke', *Kölner Zeitschrift für Soziologie* (forthcoming)

Stokman, F. N. and Thomson, R. (eds.) 2004. 'Special issue: winners and losers in the European Union', *European Union Politics* 5: 1–138

Stokman, F. N., Van Assen, M., Jan der Knoop, J. and Van Oosten, R. 2000. 'Strategic decision making', *Advances in Group Processes* 17: 131–153

Stokman, F. N. and Van den Bos, J. M. M. 1992. 'A two–stage model of policy-making with an empirical test in the US energy-policy domain', in Moore G. and Allen Whitt, J. (eds.) *The Political Consequences of Social Networks*. Greenwich, Connecticut: JAI Press, pp. 219–253

Stokman, F. N. and Van Oosten, R. 1994. 'The exchange of voting positions: an object-oriented model of policy networks', in Bueno de Mesquita, B. and Stokman, F. N. (eds.) *European Community Decision Making: Models, Applications and Comparisons*. New Haven: Yale University Press, pp. 105–127

Stokman, F. N. and Zeggelink, E. P. H. 1996. 'Is politics power or policy oriented? A comparative analysis of dynamic access models in policy networks', *Journal of Mathematical Sociology* 21: 77–111

Stone Sweet, A. and Sandholtz, W. (eds.) 1998. *Supranational Governance: The Institutionalization of the European Union*. Oxford: Oxford University Press

Straffin, P. D. 1977. 'Homogeneity, independence and power indices', *Public Choice* 30: 107–118

1988. 'The Shapley-Shubik and Banzhaf power indices as probabilities', in Roth, A. (ed.) *The Shapley Value. Essays in Honor of Lloyd Shapley*. Cambridge: Cambridge University Press

Stratmann, T. 1997. 'Logrolling', in Mueller, D. C. (ed.) *Perspectives on Public Choice: A Handbook*. Cambridge: Cambridge University Press

Tallberg, J. 2003. 'The agenda-shaping powers of the EU Council presidency', *Journal of European Public Policy* 10: 1–19

Tarar, A. 2001. 'International bargaining with two-sided domestic constraints', *Journal of Conflict Resolution* 45: 320–340

Thomson, R., Boerefijn, J. and Stokman, F. N. 2004. 'Actor alignments in European Union decision-making'. *European Journal of Political Research* 43: 237–261

Thomson, R., Torenvlied, R. and Stokman, F. N. (eds.) 2003. 'Special issue: models of collective decision-making', *Rationality and Society* 15

Tollison, R. and T. Willet. 1979. 'An economic theory of mutually advantageous issue linkage in international organizations', *International Organization* 4: 425–449

Tsebelis, G. 1994. 'The power of the European Parliament as a conditional agenda setter', *American Political Science Review* 88: 128–42

1995. 'Will Maastricht reduce the 'democratic deficit'?' *APSA Comparative Politics* 6: 4–6

1996. 'More on the European Parliament as a conditional agenda setter: response to Moser', *American Political Science Review* 90: 839–844

1997. 'Maastricht and the democratic deficit', *Aussenwirtschaft* 52: 29–56

2002. *Veto Players: How Political Institutions Work*. Princeton: Princeton University Press

Tsebelis, G. and Garrett, G. 1996. 'Agenda setting power, power indices, and decision making in the European Union', *International Review of Law and Economics* 16: 345–361

1997a. 'Agenda setting, vetoes and the European Union's co-decision procedure', *Journal of Legislative Studies* 3: 74–92

1997b. 'Why power indices cannot explain decisionmaking in the European Union', in Schmidtchen, D. and Cooter, R. (eds.) *Constitutional Law and Economics of the European Union*. Cheltenham: Edward Elgar, pp. 11–31

2000. 'Legislative politics in the European Union', *European Union Politics* 1: 5–32

2001. 'The institutional foundations of intergovernmentalism and supranationalism in the European Union', *International Organization* 55: 357–390

Tsebelis, G., Jensen, C., Kalandrakis, A. and Kreppel, A. 2001 'Legislative procedures in the European Union: an empirical analysis', *British Journal of Political Science* 31: 373–399

Tsebelis, G. and Kalandrakis, A. 1999. 'The european parliament and environmental legislation: the case of chemicals', *European Journal of Political Research* 36: 119–154

Tsebelis, G. and Money, J. 1997. *Bicameralism*. Cambridge: Cambridge University Press

Tullock, G. 1959. 'Some problems of majority voting', *Journal of Political Economy* 67: 571–579

Van Assen, M. 2001. *Essays on Actor Models in Exchange Networks and Social Dilemmas*. Amsterdam: Thela Thesis

Van Assen, M., Stokman F. N. and Van Oosten, R. C. H. 2003. 'Conflict measures in cooperative position exchange models of collective decision-making', *Rationality and Society* 15: 64–84

Van Deemen, A. 1997. *Coalition Formation and Social Choice*, Amsterdam: Kluwer

Van Deemen, A. and Hosli, M. O. 1999. 'Conflict and cooperation in collective decision-making systems', working paper

Van den Bogaard, A. 1999. 'Past measurement and future prediction', in Morgan, M. S. and Morrison, M. (eds.) *Models as Mediators: Perspectives on Natural and Social Science*. Cambridge: Cambridge University Press, pp. 282–325

Van den Bos, J. M. M. 1991. *Dutch EC Policy Making. A Model-Guided Approach to Coordination and Negotiation*. Amsterdam: Thela Thesis

Van den Doel, J. and Van Velthoven, B. 1993. *Democracy and Welfare Economics*. Cambridge: Cambridge University Press

Van Hees, M. and Steunenberg, B. 2000. 'The choices judges make: court rulings, personal values, and legal constraints', *Journal of Theoretical Politics* 12: 299–317

Van Schendelen, R. 2002. *Machiavelli in Brussels: The Art of Lobbying the EU*. Amsterdam: Amsterdam University Press

Wagner, R. H. 2004. 'Bargaining and conflict resolution', in Maoz, Z., Mintz, A., Clifton Margan, T., Palmer, G. and Stoll, R. J. (eds.) *Multiple Paths to Knowledge in International Relations*. Lexington: Lexington Books, pp. 39–72

Wallace, W. 2000. 'Collective governance', in Wallace, H. and Wallace, W. (eds.) *Policy-Making in the European Union*. Oxford: Oxford University Press, pp. 523–542

Wallace, H. and Wallace, W. (eds.) 1996. *Policy-Making in the European Union*. Oxford: Oxford University Press

2000. *Policy-Making in the European Union* 4th edition. Oxford: Oxford University Press

Ward, H. 2002. 'Rational choice', in Marsh, D. and Stoker, G. (eds.) *Theory and Methods in Political Science*. Basingstoke: Palgrave Macmillan, pp. 65–89

Weibull, J. W. 1995. *Evolutionary Game Theory.* Cambridge: MIT Press

Weick, K. E. 1979. *The Social Psychology of Organizing*. Reading: Addison-Wesley

Weiler, J. H. H. 1999. *The Constitution of Europe. 'Do the New Clothes Have an Emperor?' and other essays on European Integration*. Cambridge: Cambridge University Press

Weingast, B. R. and Marshall, W. J. 1988. 'The industrial organization of congress; or, why legislatures, like firms, are not organized as markets', *Journal of Political Economy* 96: 132–163

Westlake, M. 1994. *A Modern Guide to the European Parliament*. London: Pinter

1995. *The Council of the European Union*. London: Catermill

Widgrén, M. 1994. 'Voting power in the EC and the consequences of two different enlargements', *European Economic Review* 38: 1153–1170

1995. 'Probabilistic voting power in the EU Council: the cases of trade policy and social regulation', *Scandinavian Journal of Economics* 97: 345–356

Wilson, W. 1885. *Congressional Government*. Boston: Houghton Mifflin

Zimmer, C., Schneider, G. and Dobbins, M. 2005. 'The contested Council: conflict dimensions of an intergovernmental EU institution', *Political Studies* 53: 403–422

Index

Index

Other books in the series *(continued from page ii)*

Jean Ensminger, *Making a Market: The Institutional Transformation of an African Society*

David Epstein and Sharyn O'Halloran, *Delegating Powers: A Transaction Cost Politics Approach to Policy Making under Separate Powers*

Kathryn Firmin-Sellers, *The Transformation of Property Rights in the Gold Coast: An Empirical Study Applying Rational Choice Theory*

Clark C. Gibson, *Politicians and Poachers: The Political Economy of Wildlife Policy in Africa*

Avner Greif, *Institutions and the Path to the Modern Economy: Lessons from Medieval Trade*

Stephen Haber, Armando Razo and Noel Maurer, *The Politics of Property Rights, Political Instability, Credible Commitments, and Economic Growth in Mexico, 1876–1929*

Stephan Haggard and Matthew D. McCubbins, eds., *Presidents, Parliaments, and Policy*

Ron Harris, *Industrializing English Law: Entrepreneurship and Business Organization, 1720–1844*

Anna L. Harvey, *Votes without Leverage: Women in American Electoral Politics, 1920–1970*

Murray J. Horn, *The Political Economy of Public Administration: Institutional Choice in the Public Sector*

John D. Huber, *Rationalizing Parliament: Legislative Institutions and Party Politics in France*

John E. Jackson, Jacek Klich, Krystyna Poznanska, *The Political Economy of Poland's Transition: New Firms and Reform Governments*

Jack Knight, *Institutions and Social Conflict*

Michael Laver and Kenneth A. Shepsle, eds., *Making and Breaking Governments: Cabinets and Legislatures in Parliamentary Democracies*

Margaret Levi, *Consent, Dissent, and Patriotism*

Brian Levy, Pablo T. Spiller, eds., *Regulations, Institutions, and Commitment: Comparative Studies of Telecommunications*

Leif Lewin, eds., *Ideology and Strategy: A Century of Swedish Politics*

Gary D. Libecap, *Contracting for Property Rights*

John B. Londregan, *Legislative Institutions and Ideology in Chile*

Arthur Lupia and Mathew D. McCubbins, *The Democratic Dilemma: Can Citizens Learn What They Need to Know?*

C. Mantzavinos, *Individuals, Institutions, and Markets*

Gary J. Miller, *Managerial Dilemmas: The Political Economy of Hierarchy*

Douglass C. North, *Institutions, Institutional Change and Economic Performance*

Elinor Ostrom, *Governing the Commons: The Evolution of Institutions for Collective Action*

Daniel N. Posner, *Institutions and Ethnic Politics in Africa*

J. Mark Ramseyer, *Odd Markets in Japanese History: Law and Economic Growth*

J. Mark Ramseyer and Frances McCall Rosenbluth, *The Politics of Oligarchy: Institutional Choice in Imperial Japan*

Jean-Laurent Rosenthal, *The Fruits of Revolution: Property Rights, Litigation and French Agriculture, 1700–1860*

Michael L. Ross, *Timber Booms and Institutional Breakdown in Southeast Asia*

Shanker Satyanath, *Globalization, Politics, and Financial Turmoil: Asia's Banking Crisis*

Norman Schofield, *Architects of Political Change: Constitutional Quandaries and Social Choice Theory*

Norman Schofield and Itai Sened, *Multiparty Democracy: Parties, Elections and Legislative Politics*

Alastair Smith, *Election Timing*

David Stasavage, *Public Debt and the Birth of the Democratic State: France and Great Britain 1688–1789*

Charles Haynes Stewart, *Budget Reform Politics: The Design of the Appropriations Process in the House of Representatives, 1865–1921*

George Tsebelis and Jeannette Money, *Bicameralism*

Nicolas Van de Walle, *African Economies and the Politics of Permanent Crisis, 1979–1999*

Georg Vanberg, *The Politics of Constitutional Review in Germany*

John Waterbury, *Exposed to Innumerable Delusions: Public Enterprise and State Power in Egypt, India, Mexico, and Turkey*

David L. Weimer, ed., *The Political Economy of Property Rights: Institutional Change and Credibility in the Reform of Centrally Planned Economies*